HARVARD

and the

UNABOMBER

HARVARD
and the
UNABOMBER

—The Education of—
an American Terrorist

★

BY ALSTON CHASE

W. W. NORTON & COMPANY   NEW YORK • LONDON

This book made use of the "Multiform Assessments of Personality Development Among Gifted College Men, 1941–1962" (made accessible in 1981, raw data files). These data were collected by H. Murray and are available through the archive of the Henry A. Murray Research Center of the Radcliffe Institute for Advanced Study, Harvard University, Cambridge, Massachusetts (producer and distributor). Prior to the author's access to the data, files of participants in the study whose identities were known to him were removed.

Portions of chapters 15 and 19 previously appeared in *The Atlantic Monthly*.

For information about permission to reproduce selections from this book, write to Permissions, W. W. Norton & Company, Inc., 500 Fifth Avenue, New York, NY 10110

Manufacturing by The Haddon Craftsmen, Inc.
Book design by Dana Sloan
Production manager: Amanda Morrison

Library of Congress Cataloging-in-Publication Data

Chase, Alston.
Harvard and the Unabomber : the education of an American terrorist /
by Alston Chase.—1st ed.
p. cm.
Includes bibliographical references and index.
ISBN 0-393-02002-9 (hardcover)
1. Kaczynski, Theodore John, 1942– 2. Serial murderers—United
States—Biography. 3. Serial murderers—United States—Psychology.
4. Bombers (Terrorists)—United States—Biography. 5. Bombers
(Terrorists)—United States—Psychology. I. Title.
HV6248.K235 C48 2003
364.15'23'0973—dc21

2002014205

W. W. Norton & Company, Inc.
500 Fifth Avenue, New York, N.Y. 10110
www.wwnorton.com

W. W. Norton & Company Ltd.
Castle House, 75/76 Wells Street, London W1T 3QT

1 2 3 4 5 6 7 8 9 0

TO THE MEMORY OF MY UNCLE
LT. COL. REED GRAVES
U.S. ARMY

Taken prisoner by the Japanese at Corregidor,
the Philippines, in June 1942

Locked into the hold of the "Hell Ship" Arisan Maru
with 1,800 other American POWs,
without food, water, or air, in October 1944

Perished when the Arisan Maru,
transporting its human cargo to slave labor camps in Japan
but carrying no identification as a prison ship,
was sunk by an American submarine in the South China Sea
on October 24, 1944

AND TO THE MEMORY OF HIS WIDOW, MY AUNT
LOUISE ALSTON GRAVES

who remained faithful to his memory
until her own death in 1994

with gratitude
for their
love, courage, and sacrifice

An "idealist," according to Eichmann's notions . . . was a man who *lived* for his idea . . . who was prepared to sacrifice for his idea everything and, especially, everybody.

—Hanna Arendt,
Eichmann in Jerusalem (1963)

One belief, more than any other is responsible for the slaughter of individuals on the altars of the great historical ideals—justice or progress or happiness of future generations, or the sacred mission or emancipation of a nation or race or class, or even liberty itself, which demands the sacrifice of individuals for the freedom of society. This is the belief that somewhere, in the past, or in the future, in divine revelation, or in the mind of an individual thinker, in the pronouncements of history or science, or in the simple heart of an uncorrupted good man, there is a final solution.

—Sir Isaiah Berlin,
Inaugural Lecture, Oxford University,
October 1958

Contents

PART ONE ■ The Unabomber: Crimes and Questions

PART TWO ■ The Education of a Serial Killer

Acknowledgments

THIS WAS A fascinating book to write. It was also a painful and difficult one to write. As a biography of a serial killer it was a story I never expected, or wanted, to tell. As a social history of post–World War II America, it was a story I had long hoped to recount. But in all respects it was not what I had expected.

As a former historian of higher education, I'd long wished to write a book about the 1960s. I wanted to show how that tumultuous decade transformed colleges and universities, and how these changes, in turn, affected the entire country. My working title was to be "How the 1960s changed America." But I failed to find a publisher and the book was never written.

Then in April 1996 Ted Kaczynski was arrested and charged with being the infamous "Unabomber." The media covered the story obsessively. Kaczynski, we learned, was a Harvard graduate and former University of California mathematics professor who gave up his teaching career in 1969 to live a hermetic life in Montana, where he launched a murderous campaign against "technological society." Most pundits concluded that the Unabomber was a "product of the 1960s." Kaczynski, they said, was transformed into the Unabomber while teaching at Berkeley during the most extreme period of that famously radical campus's history.

This thesis seemed plausible. And soon after Kaczynski's arrest, my friend and former editor, Richard Todd, called to tell me, "There's your 1960s book." Indeed, we both thought it would be.

I went to work almost immediately, before finding a publisher. For a time, I corresponded with Kaczynski himself. But as my research progressed I realized that the story would not be exclusively about the 1960s. Far more critical to Kaczynski's transformation into the Unabomber, I discovered, were not his years at Berkeley, but earlier years, from 1958 to 1962, while he attended Harvard. It was at Harvard that he first encountered the ideas he incorporated into his Unabomber philosophy, and it was there that he had his first unfortunate experiences with what he would later deride as "technological society."

Likewise, I found that the most transforming decade for America was not the 1960s, but the 1950s, and that the agents of this change were not campus radicals protesting the war in Vietnam (these young people were merely acting out a drama whose script had already been written), but federal efforts to fight the Cold War and the ensuing effects these had on college life and curricula during the earlier decade.

Thus began a long investigative odyssey; and ultimately, the creation of a book unlike anything I had expected. And I could not have taken a single step of this journey of discovery without the patient and generous help of many people.

Former FBI Unabom Task Force case agent James C. "Chris" Ronay, now retired, provided invaluable information and insight and was kind enough to review several chapters of the book manuscript. Many other active and retired FBI agents, including especially Don Sachtleben and Thomas Mohnal of the FBI Bomb Squad shared with me their uniquely qualified perspectives on the Unabomber investigation. Terry Brunner, former executive director of the Better Government Association of Chicago, and his colleague James Newcomb served as a critically important, *de facto* logistical support team during the Chicago phase of my researches.

My investigations at Harvard depended utterly on and benefited mightily from the aid and judgment of friends, family, and former colleagues. My oldest and dearest friends, Nicholas and Ruth Daniloff, put me up countless times at their Cambridge apartment, aiding my archival research as well. My former colleague Joseph P. Kalt, Ford professor of government at Harvard's Kennedy School, gave me vital research advice. My older son and daughter-in-law, David and Ellen Godolphin, and my brother and sister-in-law, Richard and Evi Chase, provided homes away from home in the Boston area during my research visits, and sustained this weary writer with their love, emotional support, and wonderful cooking.

My coverage of Kaczynski's trial in Sacramento and investigations of his crimes around the Bay area of California could hardly have been done without the hospitality of my friends Eva Auchinclos and Joe Mesics in San Francisco, and the very generous Sally Edwards, who let me stay at her house during the trial, while she was away.

In Montana, my younger son and daughter-in-law, Sidney and Margaret Godolphin, provided continuous love and support, and put me up when investigations took me to Lincoln and Helena.

Those who provided critical information, aided my bibliographical searches, contributed important documents, or patiently put up with my many questions are too numerous to mention. But I do want to give special thanks to professor Henry A. Murray's widow, Nina Murray, who graciously gave me permission to use material from her late husband's papers, kept at the Harvard University Archives.

I also want to thank Tom Nadeau, formerly with Sacramento's *Daily Recorder*, for the information he provided on Kaczynski's trial and appeal, and professor John Crosman of the University of Alaska, one of Kaczynski's former Harvard roommates, for allowing me to share with readers his account of Harvard undergraduate life during this period. Christopher Simpson, professor of communications at American University, provided bibliographical help on the portions of my book that pertain to Cold War social science and former Murray assistant and historian of psychology Eugene Taylor generously shared his knowledge both about Murray the man and Murray's place in the history of psychology. I am indebted to Dr. Diana Baumrind, professor of psychology at the University of California, Berkeley, for her insightful ethical critiques of deceptive psychological research.

I am also grateful to several archivists for their considerate and professional service, including especially Brian Sullivan and his colleagues at Harvard's Pusey Library, Darwin Stapleton of the Rockefeller Archive Center in Tarrytown, New York, and John Taylor and Gary Stern at the National Archives in College Park, Maryland.

Some individuals fall into the special category of providing not tangible help, but moral support and intellectual stimulation, without which I could not have written or completed the book. These include my former editor, Richard Todd, who suggested the project in the first place; my agent, Deborah Grosvenor, who believed in the book from its beginning and who has provided continuous support and advice all along the way; Michael Kelly and Cullen Murphy, editor and managing editor, respectively, of *The Atlantic*, whose faith in and first-rate editing of the magazine's publication of my Unabomber article provided invaluable support and editorial guidance; Starling Lawrence, my excellent and very professional editor, without whose advice, wisdom, judgment, and patience this book would never have been produced; my friend, writer and professor Toby Thompson, with whom I spent many hours discussing the story during long hikes and who, when I became discouraged, always lifted me up with his abounding confidence in me and the book; Steven Cahn, professor of philosophy at New York University, whose interest in my ideas and belief in my abilities over more than twenty years helped to give me the confidence I needed to tackle a project of this magnitude.

And there is no way I can thank enough those who, in addition to Chris Ronay, painstakingly reviewed the manuscript or portions thereof, checked for factual errors and helped improve the book in many ways, including social philosopher and Unabomber expert Scott Corey; Jonathan D. Moreno, professor of biomedical ethics at the University of Virginia; Daniel Guttman, attorney and former director of the Federal Advisory Committee on Human Radiation Experiments; Michael Mello, professor at Vermont Law School and former legal consultant to Ted Kaczynski; Eric Olson, psychologist and former student of Henry Murray's; and John Taliaferro, author, neighbor, and first-rate editor.

And how can I express the gratitude I feel toward my wife, Diana? After thirty-nine years of a very happy marriage, no words are adequate. Suffice to say, this book is as much hers as mine. She knows this without my saying it, just as she knows how grateful I am for her company, care, love, patience, courage, wisdom, and inspiration.

If readers, pundits, or history judge this to be a good book, Diana and these generous individuals deserve much of the credit. If it is deemed a flawed book, then I deserve all the criticism. For the opinions and facts adduced in it are mine alone, and do not necessarily reflect their views or those of anyone else.

Alston Chase
Paradise Valley, Montana
August 6, 2002

HARVARD

and the

UNABOMBER

1

The Crimson Killer

All Europe contributed to the making of Kurtz. His was a gifted creature. He was a universal genius. . . . No fool ever made a bargain for his soul with the devil.

> —JOSEPH CONRAD
> *Heart of Darkness*
> from Kaczynski's cabin library

LIKE MANY Harvard alumni, sometimes when I return to Cambridge I wander the campus, reminiscing about the old days and musing on how differently my life turned out from what I hoped and expected then.

And on a trip there recently I found myself on the north side of the campus, on Divinity Avenue. At the end of this dead-end street sits the Peabody Museum—a giant Victorian structure. When I was a young boy in 1943, my mother took me to view its spectacular exhibit of glass flowers. These left such a vivid impression that a decade later my recollection of them prompted me—then a senior in high school—to take the fateful step of applying to Harvard. And just around the corner, on Francis Avenue, was the former home of a kindly professor of philosophy, Raphael Demos, where as a freshman in 1953 I frequently came to tea.

But this time I had returned prompted not by nostalgia but curiosity. Number 7 Divinity Avenue is a modern, multistory office building today, housing the university's Department of Biochemistry and Molecular Biology, but in 1959, a homey-looking former family residence stood on the site. Known as the "Annex," or "Clinic," it served as a laboratory where staffers of the Department of Social Relations conducted research on human subjects.

From the fall of 1959 through the spring of 1962, Harvard researchers, led by the prominent psychologist Henry A. Murray, conducted an ethically questionable experiment there on twenty-two undergraduates. To preserve the anonymity of these student guinea pigs, experimenters referred to each by code name only. One, whom they dubbed "Lawful," was Theodore John Kaczynski, later the infamous Unabomber, who mailed or delivered sixteen package bombs over seventeen years, seriously injuring twenty-three people and killing three.

EARLIER IN THE WEEK, I had visited both the Harvard Archives and the university's Murray Research Center, named after the late Professor Murray himself, where I found that, among its other purposes, his experiment was intended to measure how people react under stress. Murray subjected his unwitting students to intensive interrogation— what Murray himself called "vehement, sweeping, and personally abusive" attacks, assaulting his subjects' egos and most cherished ideals and beliefs.

My quest was specific: to determine what effects, if any, the experiment may have had on Kaczynski. This was a subset of a larger question: What effects did Harvard have on Kaczynski? In 1998, as he faced trial for murder, Kaczynski was examined by Sally C. Johnson, a forensic psychiatrist, at the order of the court. In her evaluation, Johnson wrote that Kaczynski "has intertwined his two belief systems, that society is bad and he should rebel against it, and his intense anger at his family for his perceived injustices." The Unabomber was created when these two belief systems converged. And it was at Harvard, Johnson suggested, that they first surfaced and met:

> *During his college years he had fantasies of living a primitive life and fantasized himself as "an agitator, rousing mobs to frenzies of revolutionary violence." He claims that during that time he started to think about breaking away from normal society.*

It was at Harvard that Kaczynski first encountered the ideas about the evils of technology that would provide a justification for and a focus to an anger he had felt since junior high school. It was at Harvard that he began to develop these ideas into his ideology of revolution. It was at Harvard that Kaczynski began to have fantasies of revenge, began to dream of escaping into wilderness. And it was at Harvard that he fixed on dualistic ideas of good and evil, and on a mathematical cognitive style that led him to think he could find absolute truth through the application of his own reason.

Was, then, the Unabomber—"the most intellectual serial killer the nation has ever produced," as one criminologist has called him—created at Harvard?

Answering this would take me far beyond Harvard. And there would be surprises along the way. Kaczynski's college years, I discovered, were indeed a turning point in his life. But he is also a terrorist who killed for ideas. And the pattern of his thinking closely resembles that of other contemporary terrorists currently plaguing civilization. Understanding him therefore requires probing not merely his personal history and psychological health but also the source of these ideas. And the source would be more diffuse than merely Harvard. It would encompass the intellectual and social climates of the time in which he grew up, and especially, I would find, the Cold War's impact on American culture.

My search of Kaczynski's past would thus become an exploration of America's past as well. Through it would emerge not just a portrait of this Harvard-educated killer but of modern terrorism itself. And while Harvard would provide the key to some mysteries about Kaczynski, it was just a key—one, albeit important piece of a Kaczynski puzzle—which when put into a larger context would tell as much about the current worldwide rise of ideologically inspired violence as it does about him.

✧ ✧ ✧

I HAD A special interest in Kaczynski.

For many years, he and I had lived parallel lives to some degree. Both of us attended public high schools and then went on to Harvard, from which I graduated in 1957, he in 1962. At Harvard we took many of the same courses from the same professors. We were both graduate students and assistant professors in the 1960s. I studied at Oxford and received a Ph.D. in philosophy from Princeton before joining the faculty at Ohio State and later serving as chair of the Department of Philosophy at Macalester College, in Minnesota. Kaczynski earned a Ph.D. in mathematics at the University of Michigan in 1967, then joined the Berkeley Department of Mathematics as an instructor. At roughly the same time, we separately fled academe for the Montana wilderness.

In 1971, Kaczynski moved to Great Falls, Montana; that summer he began building a cabin near the town of Lincoln, eighty miles southwest of Great Falls, on a lot he and his brother David had bought. In 1972, my wife and I bought an old homestead fifty-five miles south of Great Falls. Three years later we gave up our teaching jobs to live in Montana full time. Our place had neither telephone nor electricity; it was ten miles from the nearest neighbor. In winter we were snowbound for months at a time.

In our desire to leave civilization, Kaczynski and I were not alone. Many others sought a similar escape. What, I wondered, had driven Kaczynski into the wilderness, and to murder? To what degree were his motives simply a more extreme form of the alienation that prompted so many of us to seek solace in the backwoods? Was his antitechnology philosophy sufficient to explain his flight and his crimes?

The last question especially piqued my curiosity. As a college professor I had specialized in the history of ideas, particularly as they pertained to science and education. For five years I had served as chair of the history and philosophy of science section of the Minnesota Academy of Sciences. I had written on the development of science for the National Academy of Sciences and Sigma-Xi, the Scientific Research Society. I had also written extensively on the history of curricular change at Harvard and many other universities. The "Unabomber Manifesto," in which Kaczynski expressed his antitechnology philosophy, embodied ideas with which I was familiar. And virtually all these ideas could be found in the lectures and reading that students encountered at Harvard and other liberal arts colleges during Kaczynski's undergraduate years. Were these ideas the source of the Unabomber philosophy? I wondered.

Many Americans think they already know the Unabomber story: That Kaczynski grew up in suburban Chicago, the son of second-generation Polish Americans; that he was a brilliant student in high school and entered Harvard in 1958, at sixteen, where he majored in mathematics, graduating in 1962; that he earned a Ph.D. at the University of Michigan in 1967; that he served as an assistant professor of mathematics at the University of California, Berkeley, for two years, then left abruptly in 1969; and that in 1971 he moved to Lincoln, Montana, where he built a cabin for himself in the wilderness and within a few years began making bombs.

Dubbed "the Unabomber" by the FBI because his early victims were associated with universities or airlines, Kaczynski conducted an increasingly lethal campaign of terrorism that began on May 26, 1978, when his first bomb slightly injured a Northwestern University public safety officer, Terry Marker. It ended on April 24, 1995, when a bomb he had mailed killed the president of the California Forestry Association, Gilbert Murray.

By 1995 his explosives had taken a leap in sophistication; and nearly simultaneously, he suddenly became loquacious, writing letters to newspapers, magazines, targets, and a victim. In September of that same year the *Washington Post*, in conjunction with the *New York Times*, published copies of the 35,000-word philosophical critique of technological civilization that Kaczynski, identifying himself only as "FC," entitled "Industrial Society and Its Future," and which the FBI called "the manifesto."

Recognizing the manifesto as Ted Kaczynski's writing, his brother David turned Kaczynski in to the FBI, which arrested him at his Montana cabin on April 3, 1996. Later that year Kaczynski was removed to California to stand trial for, among other crimes, two Unabomber murders committed in that state. On January 8, 1998, having failed to dissuade his attorneys from their intention of presenting an insanity defense, and having failed to persuade the presiding judge, Garland E. Burrell, Jr., to allow him to choose a new attorney, Kaczynski asked the court for permission to represent himself.

In response, Burrell ordered Sally Johnson to examine Kaczynski, to determine if he was competent to direct his own defense. Johnson offered a "provisional" diagnosis of paranoid schizophrenia, but she concluded that Kaczynski was nevertheless competent to represent himself. Burrell refused to allow it.

Kaczynski had wanted a show trial in which to feature his ideology of revolution. Instead, faced with the prospect of a humiliating inquisition in which his attorneys would portray him as insane and his philosophy as the ravings of a madman, Kaczynski capitulated: in exchange for the government's agreement not to seek the death penalty, he formally pleaded guilty to thirteen federal bombing offenses that killed three men and seriously injured two others, and additionally, according to the government's Sentencing Memorandum, "acknowledged responsibility" for all of the sixteen bombings from 1978 to 1995. On May 4, 1998, he was sentenced to life in prison without possibility of parole. Acting as his own counsel, Kaczynski then petitioned the Ninth Federal Circuit Court to grant him a new trial. When those judges turned him down, he appealed to the Supreme Court, which in March 2002 put a final end to his maneuvering by declining to hear his case.

As MANY of these facts are so widely known, nearly everyone has an opinion about Kaczynski. He has been alternatively characterized as a hermit, a nut, a genius, and an environmental martyr or apostate. And every one of these views is mistaken.

The majority of Americans believe that he is quite simply crazy—an unkempt hermit who for unknown reasons became a "paranoid schizophrenic." To the national media especially, Kaczynski is mentally ill, the Unabomber Manifesto a compendium of "delusional themes," and there is nothing more about him to interest us.

Some see these very same manifesto themes as signs not of insanity but philosophic genius. The environmental writer Kirkpatrick Sale averred in the *New York Times* that the Unabomber "is a rational man and his principal beliefs are, if hardly mainstream, entirely reasonable." UCLA professor James Q. Wilson noted in the *New York Times* that the manifesto "is subtle and carefully developed, lacking anything even faintly resembling the wild claims or irrational speculation that a lunatic might produce. . . . If it is the work of a madman, then the writings of many political philosophers—Jean Jacques Rousseau, Tom Paine, Karl Marx—are scarcely more sane."

To others, Kaczynski represents an ideology they love or hate. A few radical greens and anarchists perceive him as a "prisoner of war" whose only crime was trying to save the world. Most on the right view him as the embodiment of left-wing extremism who demonstrates with cruel clarity where the radical movement is taking us. The conservative columnist Tony Snow sees the Unabomber as a sort of evil, invisible twin brother of Al Gore—the Devil's Disciple of environmentalism. Sagebrush rebel Ron Arnold denounced Kaczynski as an "ecoterrorist," whose horrible acts showed how environmentalism inevitably leads to murder and anarchy. And apparently, everyone seems to believe that Kaczynski is "a product of the sixties."

Indeed, how one feels about Kaczynski is to many a litmus test that reveals one's attitude about that tumultuous decade. Those who believe it was a period of political extremism and cultural decline point to him and say, "This is where it led." Those who believe that decade represented the high tide of political idealism seem embarrassed by him, as though he is an ideological blood brother who went too far.

The *Boston Globe* suggested that Kaczynski's behavior may have been "rooted in the overheated passions of the '60s." *U.S. News & World Report* thought he had been influenced by Paul Goodman's *Growing Up Absurd*, "a 1960s indictment of 'the system' that includes a denunciation of the 'dominance' of science and its effect of alienating man from nature."

USA Today quoted the California state librarian Kevin Starr as saying that the "extreme radicalism" of Berkeley had "triggered" for Kaczynski "an absolute repudiation of his profession and his life." William J. Broad speculated in the *New York Times* that it was "Ted's fear that his students would become makers of atomic bombs that prompted him to quit Berkeley in 1969 after two years of teaching." Roger Lane, a professor at Haverford College and a consultant to the FBI, stated that Kaczynski "is a man whose reading had been done in the '60s. He was clearly educated in the '60s and stuck there." And in *Drawing Life: Surviving the Unabomber* (1997), David Gelernter—one of Kaczynski's victims—quoting the historian Paul Johnson, asserted that the Unabomber's ideological roots lay in the 1960s, "one of the most crucial decades in modern history, akin to the 1790s."

Once they had made up their minds about Kaczynski—whether deciding that he is insane, a profound philosopher, a misguided ideologue, or a representative of the sixties—many people lost interest in him. University scholars all too willing to devote seminars to such pop cultural dross as the Grateful Dead and *Star Trek* have virtually ignored the manifesto, producing, in the years since its appearance, so far as I can find just two articles on it. Conservatives went silent once they decided Kaczynski was just another radical environmentalist. Activist groups such as Earth First! seem embarrassed by someone who actually took their rhetoric of ecological "jihad" seriously. Mainstream environmentalists don't want to talk about him. Everyone, in short, just wants Kaczynski to disappear. It's apparently easier for them to dismiss him as insane than to take a closer look.

But these views miss the mark. Kaczynski is far more complex— more *interesting*—than they imply. Virtually everything people think they know about him and his crimes is false. His ideas derived from the 1950s, not the 1960s. His decision to retreat to the wilderness and launch his campaign of terrorism was made shortly after graduating from Harvard, not later, at Berkeley. He is neither revolutionary hero nor original philosopher nor genuine environmentalist. The manifesto is neither brilliant nor a symptom of mental illness. It is a compendium of philosophical and environmental clichés that expresses concerns shared by millions of Americans.

And his mental state is far more ambiguous. He is not the extreme loner he has been made out to be, nor is there any clear evidence that he is clinically insane. His unhappy childhood was not markedly different from the unhappy childhoods of many others. His social life in school and college was average. In almost every way, Kaczynski is average.

Why, then, did this strangely emblematic man turn to murder?

In his book *Bad Men Do What Good Men Dream*, the forensic psychiatrist Robert I. Simon observes that the difference between murderers and law-abiding citizens is merely a matter of degree. Ordinary people have the same fears and desires that killers do. The latter just give in to these desires and fears more easily. The "basic fallacy," he suggests, is

> *that destruction and violence reside only in the acts of bad men and women and not in the thoughts of good people. After 32 years of work as a treating and as a forensic psychiatrist, I am absolutely*

convinced that there is no great gulf between the mental life of the common criminal and that of the everyday, upright citizen. The dark side exists in all of us. . . . The basic difference between what are socially considered to be bad and good people is not one of kind, but one of degree, and of the ability of the bad to translate dark impulses into dark actions.

The case of Adolf Eichmann—that colorless bureaucrat responsible for the deaths of millions of Jews, whom every psychiatric report nevertheless diagnosed as sane and normal—demonstrates, Simon observes, how

great evil can be perpetrated by ordinary people, performing ordinary tasks and living ordinary lives. . . . Many among the Nazi executioners went home after a day of exterminating women, children, and old men, and resumed quite comfortable and normal lives in the bosoms of their families. They ate good food, listened to classical music, read a refined book, made love with their wives, coddled and embraced their children.

Kaczynski too came from an ordinary, working-class family, attended college, served as a professor, loves nature, and harbors widely shared concerns about the dangers of technology and destruction of wilderness. Yet he became a serial killer.

And as Simon implies, such a connection between averageness and violence is not unusual. If, as Hannah Arendt observed, Eichmann demonstrates "the banality of evil," then Kaczynski embodies the ordinariness of it. During the seventeen years of the Unabomber's bombing spree, 1978–95, America experienced more than 388,000 murders and over 22,000 bombings that killed an additional 386 people and injured 3,634 others. Forty million people were injured by criminals during the same period. "Every twenty-two seconds," Simon notes, "an American is beaten, stabbed, shot, robbed, raped, or killed." Terrorism—ideologically inspired violence such as plane hijackings and abortion clinic bombings—has become commonplace, claiming hundreds of innocents. So, too, are the all-too-familiar atrocities by high school students or company employees who run amok, murdering classmates and colleagues in revenge for perceived injustices.

✧ ✧ ✧

KACZYNSKI IS NOT even the first Harvard graduate to kill. Some of the most spectacular murders committed during the last 150 years were accomplished, or alleged to have been accomplished by those who wore Harvard crimson.

In 1850, a Harvard professor, John White Webster, killed his medical school colleague, Dr. George Parkman, because he owed Parkman money and couldn't pay it back. A janitor found parts of Parkman's body cemented behind a brick vault below Webster's laboratory. Investigators later found other body parts strewn around the lab.

In 1906, Harvard dropout Harry Kendall Thaw shot and killed America's most famous architect, Stanford White, at the rooftop garden restaurant of the old Madison Square Garden during the opening performance of *Mamzelle Champagne*, a musical review. Thaw had been incensed that before he married her, his wife had slept with White.

In 1977, according to prosecutors, former Harvard Kennedy School fellow Ira Einhorn bludgeoned his girlfriend Holly Maddux to death, striking her thirteen times with a hammer. Then, they said, he stuffed her body in a trunk which he kept in his closet. Detectives found Maddux's body, still in the trunk, eighteen months later. Einhorn, who fled the country and remained a fugitive for more than twenty years, was convicted of murder in absentia by a Philadelphia court in 1993. In July 2001, he was extradited from France and retried on the same charges. On October 17, 2002, he was convicted a second time.

On May 28, 1995, a twenty-year-old Harvard undergraduate, Sinedu Tadesse, an Ethiopian, murdered her roommate Tran Ho, a Vietnamese immigrant, because she was afraid Tran was rejecting her. Tadesse approached Tran as she slept, stabbing her forty-five times with a hunting knife she had purchased for the purpose.

These murders were motivated by money, jealousy, lust, and anger at rejection. And herein lies the difference: Kaczynski claimed to murder for an idea. Not coincidentally, he was also the first the media decided was crazy. Apparently they supposed sane Harvard men don't take ideas so seriously.

And indeed, like the serial killers Robert Simon discusses, Kaczynski stepped over a line that many reach but do not cross. He did so because in one respect he's not average. He is a profoundly alienated

intellectual—what the British writer Colin Wilson called an "Outsider."
This is why his mental state is so hard to classify. Outsiders do not fit
easily into either the category of the sane or the insane.

Wilson's philosophical blockbuster *The Outsider* appeared in 1956,
two years before Kaczynski matriculated at Harvard. Offering a portrait
of history's most disenchanted literary intellectuals, it became an
instant best-seller, universally hailed by critics and quickly translated
into over a dozen languages. Wilson became a celebrity, and *The Outsider* widely popular at Harvard and other campuses.

Wilson describes the Outsider as someone who is physically, emotionally, and intellectually outside society—an intensely solitary individual, who "sees deeper" and "who knows he is sick in a civilization that
doesn't know it is sick."

"Is he an Outsider because he's frustrated and neurotic?" Wilson
asks.

> *Or is he neurotic because of some deeper instinct that pushes him
> into solitude? . . . The Outsider's case against society is very clear.
> All men and women have these dangerous, unnameable impulses,
> yet they keep up a pretense, to themselves, to others; their respecta-
> bility, their philosophy, their religion, are all attempts to gloss over,
> to make look civilized and rational something that is savage, unor-
> ganized, irrational. He is an Outsider because he stands for Truth.*
>
> *The Outsider is a man who cannot live in the comfortable,
> insulated world of the bourgeois, accepting what he sees and
> touches as reality. He sees "too deep and too much" [quoting the
> Outsider hero of Henri Barbousse's novel L'Enfer] and what he
> sees is essentially chaos. . . . When he asserts his sense of anarchy
> in the face of the bourgeois' complacent acceptance, it is not simply
> the need to cock a snook at respectability that provokes him; it is a
> distressing sense that* truth must be told at all costs, *otherwise
> there can be no hope for an ultimate restoration of order. Even if
> there seems no room for hope, truth must be told. . . . The Outsider
> is a man who has awakened to chaos. [emphasis in the original]*

"To the objection that he is unhealthy or neurotic," Wilson continues, the Outsider replies by quoting H. G. Wells: "'In the country of the
blind, the one-eyed man is king.'" Many of the greatest writers, artists,

and thinkers of modern Western literature, or the fictional characters the novelists among them created, Wilson suggests, were Outsiders. He includes the British historian and science fiction writer H. G. Wells, the French philosopher Jean-Paul Sartre, the French novelist Albert Camus, German-language authors Hermann Hesse, Franz Kafka, and Thomas Mann, the German philosophers Friedrich Nietzsche, Arthur Schopenhauer, and Oswald Spengler, as well as such varied personalities as T. S. Eliot, Henry James, Ernest Hemingway, William Blake, T. E. Lawrence, Søren Kierkegaard, Vincent van Gogh, Nijinsky, and perhaps the most important Outsider of them all, the Russian novelist Fyodor Dostoyevsky.

Each of these explored or embodied a different dimension of what Wilson calls "Outsideriness."

Some explored the dimension of isolation: "I live alone, entirely alone; I never speak to anyone, never; I receive nothing, I give nothing" (Sartre's antihero in *Nausea*). "He had become so completely absorbed in himself, and isolated from his fellows that he dreaded meeting, not only his landlady, but anyone at all. He was crushed by poverty" (Dostoyevsky, *Crime and Punishment*).

Some examined the dimension of freedom: "And suddenly, Dostoevsky's beetle-man starts up, with his bad teeth and beady eyes, and shouts: 'To hell with your System. I demand the right to behave as I like, I demand the right to regard myself as *utterly unique*'" (Wilson describing a scene in Dostoyevsky's *Notes from Underground*). T. E. Lawrence is "the prophet of an idea . . . his power is the power of a man who can be *possessed by an idea*" (Wilson's italics). "I must create my own System or be enslaved by another man's" (Blake).

Some stressed asceticism and a vehement will: "'Today,' he muttered to himself. He understood that he was still weak but his intense spiritual concentration gave him strength and self-confidence" (Dostoyevsky's *Crime and Punishment*). "Extreme asceticism is not an essential of self-realization, for its purpose is only to test the will" (Wilson on Hermann Hesse).

Some just contemplated the dark at the bottom of the stairs: "Behind man lies the abyss, nothingness. The Outsider knows this," Wilson comments of Dostoyevsky's *Brothers Karamazov*. "It is his business to sink claws of iron into life, to grasp it tighter than the indifferent bourgeois, to build, to Will, in spite of the abyss."

And some explored the dimensions of murder: "You may have noticed that the most enthusiastic blood-letters have always been the most civilized of men. . . . The man's whole business is to prove that he is a man, not a cog-wheel" (Dostoyevsky, *Notes from Underground*). "I did not kill a human being, but a principle!" (*Crime and Punishment*). "Most men die like animals, not men" (Ernest Hemingway in "The Natural History of the Dead"). "For me to feel less lonely, all that remained to hope was that, on the day of my execution there should be a huge crowd of spectators, and that they should greet me with howls of execration" (The antihero, Meursault, in Camus's *The Stranger*, speaking on the eve of his execution for murder).

Like Colin Wilson's Outsider, Kaczynski lived in extreme isolation and poverty to escape a society he sees as sick. He believes he is the one-eyed man in the country of the blind. He is obsessed with freedom, and the need to possess a vehement will. And he killed for an idea. "Only revolution by outsiders," he wrote in the manifesto, "can save civilization."

It's Kaczynski's "Outsideriness" that makes a clinical diagnosis of his mental health so problematic. Since an Outsider is someone whose rational insights produce apparently irrational behavior, he doesn't fit the usual psychiatric categories. The therapeutic language of psychology has little application in the philosophic world of Outsiders. As Outsiders bridge the boundary between the two disciplines, neither can completely explain them. What a psychiatrist may identify as mental illness, a philosopher may see as a capacity to see "too deep and too much." While those who disagree with Outsiders may dub them insane, those who agree may say that they merely possess "intenser and deeper insight." That's why people cannot make up their minds about Kaczynski. Some apply a psychological measure and call him crazy; some invoke philosophical criteria and see him as a revolutionary.

"The madman," wrote G. K. Chesterton, "is the man who has lost everything except his reason." Thanks to the emphasis on Kaczynski's psychological state by his family, the media, and his attorneys, observers missed the other, more important key to understanding Kaczynski: his intellect. He is a mathematician who reads widely and knows several foreign languages. He's the alumnus of an elite university who had some unique and awful experiences there. Rather than being irrational, he takes ideas more seriously than most. He suffers from an *excess* of reason. Despite his averageness, Kaczynski possesses a greater than aver-age vulnerability to the power of ideas. He is an intellectual and a murderer. And the connection between these two lies at Harvard.

I FIRST HEARD of the Murray experiment from Kaczynski himself. We had begun corresponding in July 1998, two months after a federal court in Sacramento sentenced him to life in prison for the Unabomber crimes. Kaczynski, I quickly discovered, is an indefatigable correspondent. Sometimes his letters came so fast that it was difficult to answer one before the next arrived. They were written with great humor, intelligence, and care. And, I found, in his own way he was a charming correspondent. He has carried on a similarly voluminous correspondence with countless other people, often developing friendships through the mail.

At the same time, Kaczynski's letters revealed a darker side: an intellectual arrogance, an absolute certitude in his own conceptual and moral superiority. As a very bright man who had spent most of his life around people of lesser intelligence, he shows a condescending attitude toward others. His highly trained mathematical mind admits only to what philosophers call "two-valued logic": everything is either true or false. There are no gray areas. He alone, he seems to believe, never lied, never made a mistake. Kaczynski was also hypercritical and acutely sensitive to criticism. If someone said or wrote a falsehood, he assumed that person was lying. If someone disagreed with him, that person was not merely mistaken but had committed a logical howler.

In corresponding with Kaczynski, therefore, one was aware that he would catch the slightest misspelling and criticize even the most innocent inconsistencies. And while clearly anxious for real friendship, he was not above manipulating (probably unconsciously) others to serve his interests, and changing his opinions of them, from friend to foe back to friend again, for the slightest reasons.

Yet, Kaczynski is justifiably proud of his accurate memory. Based on my experience and that of others who knew him, it would appear that although he did not always tell the whole truth (sometimes omitting important details, if these omissions served his interests), he did for the most part tell nothing but the truth. Of his factual claims that I was able to check, most were verified.

And some of these factual claims concern the Harvard experiments. Tantalizingly, Kaczynski told me that the Murray Research Center had refused to reveal the study's psychological evaluations to his defense attorneys. His investigators reported that the center had told participating psychologists not to talk with his defense team. One, Kaczynski said, actually confessed to one of his defense team investigators that she feared divulging information could jeopardize her job.

Apparently, Kaczynski observed mysteriously, the Murray study's unsavory ethical dimensions had prompted its participants to adhere to the vow of "*omertà*, or the rule of silence."

After this intriguing start, Kaczynski told me little more about the Murray experiment than what I could find in the published literature. Murray's widow, Nina, could not provide answers to most of my questions. Many of the research assistants I interviewed seemed reluctant to criticize Murray. And Murray Center officials themselves turned out to be, as Kaczynski had reported, both suspicious and secretive. After considering my application, its research committee approved my request to view the records of this experiment, the so-called data sets, which referred to subjects by code name only. But because Kaczynski's alias was by then known to some journalists and his privacy could not be ensured, I was not permitted to view his records. And during the week that I worked there, staffers continued to watch me carefully—even eavesdropping when I made a call from a public phone next door.

After I first described the experiments on Kaczynski in an article for *The Atlantic* in June 2000, Harvard's efforts to preserve the secrecy intensified. In July, the Murray Center announced that Kaczynski's file would be "permanently removed." The Center's director, Annemetta Sorensen, told the *Harvard Crimson* that (in the newspaper's words), "There are no circumstances under which Kaczynski's file could be opened." During the same period, the editors of *The Atlantic* received letters from prominent research psychologists attacking the article.

At first, this response appeared paradoxical. Harvard, a prestigious university dedicated to the pursuit of truth and the free exchange of ideas, seemed determined to squelch both. Yet it is equally understandable that the psychological research community would want to protect Murray. After all, it was no accident that Harvard named a research center after him: as a founding father of modern personality theory, he occupies an almost godlike status among psychologists. His former assistants hold prestigious academic positions at major universities. And any criticism of him is taken as an attack on their profession.

Nevertheless, the university's and the psychological research establishment's circling of wagons seems a colossal overreaction. What is the source of their anxiety?

For the next two years, I continued to explore Professor Murray and his experiment—motivated not only by a desire to learn how they may have affected Kaczynski but also by curiosity as to why a prestigious university and a coterie of prominent scholars would be in such a froth about my quest. I interviewed scores of individuals who knew Murray, talked with investigators on Kaczynski's defense team, and pored over materials at the Library of Congress, the National Archives, Washington Federal Records Center, George Washington University's National Security Archive, and the Rockefeller Foundation Library.

Through this research, I learned why so many psychologists might have been alarmed by the *Atlantic* article: It pointed to the door of a closet that psychologists had kept locked for more than forty years. In this closet are many skeletons, some quite fresh. The fear is that I might open that door. And in this book I do.

"THERE'S A LITTLE bit of the Unabomber in most of us," Robert Wright wrote in *Time* magazine in 1995, referring to the manifesto. Kaczynski's life until he turned to crime was in many ways representative of his generation. The environment in which he grew up typified that of so many reared during the Cold War. He left academe for the wilderness in 1969, just as a national back-to-the-land movement was in progress. Indeed, even his alienation and willingness to use violence against a "system" of which he disapproves are not entirely unusual.

Rather, the only difference between Kaczynski and many others is that he is more extreme: more serious about ideas and more ready to use violence. By his long exposure to education and sensitivity to ideas, he is a bellwether dramatizing how schools and colleges nurture alienation, despair, and sometimes violence. As a product of an elite education, he is a kind of magnifying mirror, who reveals its flaws in bold relief.

And the nexus of his story lies at Harvard, not because this institution is "evil" but precisely because, like Kaczynski, it is an archetype. Just as

Kaczynski is the consummate philosophical Outsider, Harvard is the heart of America's intellectual life. It is the paradigmatic university, highlighting the virtues and flaws of this kind of institution. As a leader in higher education, its research and curricula are often the first to introduce ideas eventually embraced by colleges and universities elsewhere; and, as we shall see, it was the place where Kaczynski would first encounter the ideas he later incorporated into his manifesto. With a long tradition of doing research for the federal government, Harvard was a prominent player during the Cold War and a leading example of cooperation between the defense establishment and academe. And it was at Harvard that Kaczynski would for the first and last time come face to face with Professor Murray and the psychological research establishment.

The Unabomber story, therefore, is not just about Kaczynski but also concerns the times in which he lived, and ultimately the evils to which the intellect is heir. It's about how his affinity for learning and his twenty-three years as a student and professor helped to transform him into a murderous Outsider. It's about the dysfunctional high school environment which Kaczynski encountered that is still with us, that contributed to his alienation, and that today transforms young men like Kip Kinkel and the Columbine killers, Eric Harris and Dylan Klebold, into murderers.

It's about generations of Americans profoundly shaped by bleak visions engendered during the Cold War—a conflict that spanned almost forty-five years and created institutions that still shape our lives. It's about how the universities' cooperation with government in fighting this war and philosophical divisions within faculties combined to create a culture of despair that eventually spread throughout the educational system, changing those institutions and promoting patterns of violence that continue today. It's about Professor Murray's experiment, its purpose and its possible effects on Kaczynski.

Finally, it's a story about intelligence and violence and the dark heart of modern evil that lurks, not at the fringes of civilization but at its very center. Kaczynski is an intellectual and a murderer, and to understand him and his crimes we must understand the connections between these two facts.

PART ONE

THE UNABOMBER: CRIMES AND QUESTIONS

There are many criminal cases that remain unsolved, but here is one that went on for 18 years, in which the killer remained at large and continued his trade without apprehension. That takes an enormous amount of cunning.

—JAMES FOX,
　　dean of the College of Criminal Justice,
　　Northwestern University

If you say that everything—chaos, darkness, anathema—can be reduced to mathematical formulae—then man will go insane on purpose to have no judgement, and to behave as he likes.

—FYODOR DOSTOEVSKY,
　　Notes from Underground

2

A Man of Letters

The story of civilization is . . . the story of engineering. . . .
Civilization is a matter of power over the world and nature
and skill in exploiting this world. It has nothing to do with
kindness, honesty, or peacefulness.

> —L. Sprague De Camp,
> *The Ancient Engineers*
> from Kaczynski's cabin library

L ATE IN MARCH 1996, my younger son, Sidney Godolphin, was
sitting in his office on Helena's Last Chance Gulch when he
received a phone call from a man who identified himself as a
special agent of the Federal Bureau of Investigation. Did he manage
commercial real estate, the agent wanted to know, and did he have
office space available?

Yes on both counts, Sidney answered, wondering why the FBI
would need space when it already had an office just a block away in the
Arcade Building on Jackson Street. Sidney explained that he had a suite

available in the magnificent and historic Diamond Block, which his firm managed. And he'd be glad to show the agent the space.

When Sidney arrived at the Diamond Block, the first thing he noticed was the white Ford Bronco parked in front. This was soon after O. J. Simpson and Al Cowlings had been chased by police in a similar car and his first thought was, "No, there can't be a connection."

Rather than Simpson and Cowlings, four agents clambered out of the vehicle. They looked like stockbrokers on a fishing trip, but had better haircuts, Sidney thought. Their clothes came from L. L. Bean and Eddie Bauer. All carried beepers and wore fanny packs.

The agents signed a six-month lease. The next day, a convoy of Broncos and Ford Explorers arrived. The Diamond Block soon swarmed with federal officers in casually upscale recreational garb, each wearing the requisite fanny pack and carrying boxes of electronic equipment. Teams of technicians installed soundproofing, radios, and telephone lines. Soon, the building's roof boasted a "white stick" microwave antenna that could be seen throughout downtown Helena. More agents of the FBI, along with investigators from the Treasury Department and the U.S. Postal Inspection Service, began assembling in their new headquarters.

The Unabom Task Force had arrived.

Sixty miles north by road, in Lincoln, FBI special agent Don Sachtleben sat in the lounge at the 7-Up Lodge thinking, "Here we go again." Scores of times they had found what they thought was a good suspect, only to discover he had an iron-clad alibi. Sachtleben feared they were about to be disappointed yet again.

In fact, the FBI's pursuit of the man it dubbed the Unabomber was not so much a wild goose chase as a case of blind men trying to identify an elephant by each holding a leg. So many agents were involved (over 130 at one point), each assigned only one small task at a time (to interview a subject or track a fingerprint), that each knew only one small part of the puzzle. And the investigation had lasted so long that many originally assigned to it had retired, to be replaced by others unfamiliar with the early bombings, who developed different theories about the killer.

(Some of the agents who investigated the earliest bombings, for example, hypothesized that the killer was playing an elaborate game of "Dungeons and Dragons," and clung to this idea even after Kaczynski was caught.)

The FBI's highly efficient bomb squad took the lead in the investigation, focusing on the technical aspects of the killer's devices. Meanwhile, the agency employed a phalanx of psychological profilers, offering such widely divergent portraits of the killer that their cumulative effect was near-total confusion.

Few saw the big picture. Most investigators kept looking for psychological and physical associations: they explored hunches that the bomber knew his victims or lived near them; that he was personally angry at them for some imagined insult; that he was mad at the world because he had a physical handicap, or was homosexual. So they missed the major point: that Kaczynski's crimes not only had a psychological component but an intellectual one as well. As James Fox, dean of the College of Criminal Justice at Northeastern University and an expert on serial killers observed, Kaczynski was the most intelligent killer in modern history, and unlike every other serial murderer, he killed not for the enjoyment of it but to promote ideas.

"The Unabomber," Fox told the *Sacramento Bee*, "sees a loss of life as a necessary evil in his campaign against industrialized society. He found his niche—control, power and superiority—and was convinced what he knew, he knew better than anyone else. . . . He outsmarted the FBI for years."

Kaczynski was an omnivorous reader and prolific, albeit mostly unpublished, writer and correspondent, with synoptic interests. He wrote scholarly papers and short stories. He was fluent in Spanish and German, and had studied Finnish, Russian, French, Egyptian, and Chinese as well. His cabin shelves contained hundreds of books and scholarly papers as diverse as Herodotus' and Tacitus' *Histories*, Prescott's *History of the Conquest of Mexico*, treatises on relativity theory, Euell Gibbon's *Stalking the Wild Asparagus*, George Orwell's *1984*, James Fenimore Cooper's *Last of the Mohicans*, works on Greek mythology and the history of the German and Indo-European languages, as well as a wide range of classics by Conrad, Dostoevsky, Steinbeck, Dickens, Shakespeare, George Eliot, and many Spanish and German writers.

Kaczynski also kept the Lincoln town library staff busy ordering, on interlibrary loan, books so esoteric they couldn't even pronounce the titles. And he regularly visited Aunt Bonnie's Bookstore in Helena, exchanging books he'd read for others he hadn't.

While Kaczynski was deeply versed in etymology, psychology, and sociology, his deepest interests lay, to judge from his reading, in history and literature. These formed the warp and woof of his reality, a continuous thread running from the Trojan to the Cold War, from the invention of the wheel to genetic engineering. History and literature were complements, with no clear boundary between them. One learned as much about the ancient Greeks by reading Homer as Herodotus, as much about the end of the Middle Ages from Cervantes's *Don Quixote* as from the Harvard textbook found in his cabin, *The Middle Ages, 395–1500,* by Joseph R. Strayer and Dana Carleton Munro.

Or rather, one learned different but equally valuable things. History provides the big picture, literature the cameo. From history, we learn how Eli Whitney ignited the Industrial Revolution by inventing the cotton gin, and how this led to the growth of the cities and the creation of great fortunes but also to the spread of poverty and urban diseases. Writers such as Dickens, Dostoevsky, and Conrad introduce us to individuals touched by this "progress"—fictional characters like Oliver Twist, Beetle-Man (*Notes from Underground*), Raskolnikov (*Crime and Punishment*), and Winnie Verloc (Conrad's *The Secret Agent*).

History and literature therefore were complements, one a macrocosm, the other the microcosm, of human progress and its unintended side effects. And although one was supposedly "fact" and the other "fiction," only in their combination was the real truth revealed. Twined together, they tell one continuous story that runs from the advent of agriculture to the birth of cloning. And Kaczynski saw himself as a character in this story.

Somewhat paradoxically, he thought of himself as a scientist, embracing what philosophers call logical positivism—the theory that only empirically verifiable (i.e., scientifically testable) statements are meaningful. Further, he believed in positivism's parallel theory of ethics, sometimes called "emotivism," which holds that moral and spiritual judgments, being scientifically untestable, are mere "cognitively meaningless" expressions of emotion. To him, religious and ethical scruples are emotional attitudes produced by social conditioning and what he called "brainwashing." In building his bombs, Kaczynski followed the scientific method slavishly. He kept lab notebooks, written partly in Spanish, in which he carefully documented the design, construction, and deployment of 245 explosive devices. Like the Nazi doctors who performed sadistic tests on concentration camp victims, Kaczynski called each of his bombings of human targets an "experiment."

Kaczynski's killing, in short, was at once a literate and a scientific enterprise. As Donald Foster, professor of English literature at Vassar and specialist in literary forensics (identifying the authorship of documents based on their literary styles and word choices) would later put it after examining the Unabom documents for federal prosecutors in preparation for Kaczynski's trial, Kaczynski relied on his "literary pursuits" and "his evident use of fiction to help him make sense of his unhappy life."

Kaczynski's actions imitated not just any art but the literary classics. History and literature enhanced his capacity for cold-blooded murder because he thought they provided justification for it. He apparently imagined himself as a character in this great historic, literary, and continuing drama running from Machiavelli's *The Prince* to Ted R. Gurr's *Violence in America*, from Sidney Painter's *French Chivalry* to Victor Hugo's *Les Misérables*, from Lewis G. M. Thorpe's *Two Lives of Charlemagne* to Jacques Ellul's *The Technological Society*, from Dickens's *Tale of Two Cities* to Arthur Koestler's *Darkness and Noon*.

The printed word was his universe, and even his victims were characters in it. He chose them not through having known them or (for the most part) their institutions, but because of the *ideas* they represented. He read what they wrote, and located them through library reference works. For him, they assumed the ontological status of characters in a novel, or the abstractions of historians' imaginations.

And it would be the same academic habit of mind that made Kaczynski so hard to catch. He read books on criminology and the science of fingerprinting. He kept his notes in codes that an FBI cryptologist told me "no one, not even NASA computers, could have broken" had their searchers not found the key in his cabin. He was very careful. He wore gloves when building his bombs and still soaked each piece in soybean oil and salt water, to obliterate fingerprints. He took the covers off the batteries so investigators could not find the bar codes to determine where he bought them. He collected most of his materials from abandoned cars and junkyards rather than purchase them. Even the pipes for his bombs came from scrap.

When traveling to plant or mail his bombs or to search junkyards for scrap metal, Kaczynski wore elaborate disguises. He dyed his hair, changed eyeglasses frequently, put chewing gum under his lip or wax or Kleenex in a nostril to distort the shape of his face, used a variety of wigs and hats, and sometimes wore bulky coats or jackets under a raincoat to appear heavier than he was. He bought the stamps from vending machines and mailed them from drop boxes far from his Montana home so that they could not easily be traced back to him. He even planted false leads, once recording in his journal:

> *A while back I obtained two human hairs from the bathroom in the Missoula bus depot. I broke one of these hairs into two pieces, and I placed one piece between the layers of the electrical tape I used to wrap the wire joints inside the package (See Fig. 14).* The reason for this is to deceive the policemen, who will think that the hair belongs to whoever made the device.*

And Kaczynski played word games with his pursuers, placing literary, philosophical, and etymological hints that he arrogantly assumed they weren't sufficiently well read to catch. When government agents missed these clues, he laughed at their illiteracy and clumsy sleuthing.

Consider, for example, the word "wood": Early on, both the FBI and the media knew he was playing a game with it. They just didn't know what the game was. And, with the exception of one journalist, no one ever figured it out.

"Wood" was the leitmotif of the Unabomber campaign: The bombs came in wooden boxes. The third victim was named Percy Wood and lived in Lake Forest; the tenth lived in Ann Arbor; the fifteenth on Aspen Drive. The sixteenth, Gil Murray, had worked for the California Forestry Association, and the bomb that killed him had been sent from

---

*In his laboratory notebooks Kaczynski accompanied his text with elaborate and detailed drawings.

Oakland, California, and contained the address of a fictitious wood-working company, "Closet Dimensions." To mislead investigators, the bomber had given the name of a real Brigham Young University professor, Leroy Wood Bearnson, as the sender of the sixth bomb. During the bombing campaign, Jerry Roberts of the *San Francisco Chronicle* received a letter from the Unabomber, who signed himself "Isaac Wood" and listed his return address as "549 Wood Street, Woodlake, California." On June 24, 1993, the *New York Times* also received a letter from the Unabomber, who provided a Social Security number, 553-25-4394, as a means of identifying him in the future, should he choose to write the paper again. The number turned out to belong to an inmate of the California State Prison at Pelican Bay. The criminal sported a tattoo on his forearm that read, PURE WOOD.

Early on, some in the media concluded the Unabomber was an environmentalist, obsessed with preserving trees. But they should have done more research. As an expert in etymology, Kaczynski knew the history of English and Nordic languages. And he had put that knowledge to use. Only William Monahan, writing in July 1995 for the *New York Press*, got it right: the bomber was sending a message to his pursuers in Old English.

"The only constant and universal element in the Unabomber case for sixteen years," Monahan wrote, " . . . is wood. There is always wood involved in a 'Unabomb' bomb. That's how they know it's the Unabomber. Wood as a substance, in the components and casings and disguising of bombs; and wood as a key *semantical* element in the choice of targets." (Monahan's italics)

In Old English, Monahan noted, citing the *Oxford English Dictionary*, the word "wood" is used in "the sense of being out of one's mind, insane, lunatic." In Chaucer, "when people go *wood*, they generally do so because they've been tricked. They behave as though they were wood—like Curly going *wood* or *waxing wode wroth* before Larry gets the cheese. The word 'wood' is almost inevitable when someone is flummoxed, tricked by an intellectual superior."

Monahan explains that, as any college English major knows, "going wood" is a triple entendre, meaning being angry at having been tricked, being numb from trauma, and having an erection. "The Chaucerian 'wood' is an old joke, not esoteric, an English Department standard . . . almost anyone who reads Chaucer, gets the jokes."

And that was just part of the wordplay, Monahan suggested. For example, the package containing the bomb that killed Thomas J. Mosser of New Jersey listed a fictitious name, "H. C. Wickel," as the sender. In old English, the word "wicker" means wood. "H. C. Earwicker" is a ubiquitous character in James Joyce's *Finnegan's Wake*, who sometimes assumes the identity of the Norse god Woden. And "wicker" is missing an "ear"—just like another angry man, Vincent van Gogh.

"It's all words with this guy," Monahan concluded.

Investigators had been using an incomplete set of tools to catch their man. The FBI's technical work had been first rate, its psychological profiling largely worthless, and its literary sleuthing (until after publication of the manifesto) nonexistent. Would a philosophical detective have caught him sooner? Perhaps. Until the manifesto appeared, Kaczynski's ideas had remained largely unknown outside his family. But not entirely unknown. He shared his views with others through the mail—for example, with Jacques Ellul, author of *The Technological Society*, as well as, allegedly, with the editors of the *Earth First! Journal*. Within Luddite circles, he was a player.

In the long run, the principal effect of neglecting this intellectual component would be on public perceptions of Kaczynski himself. The investigators' oversight was the first of many steps that cumulatively created a false image of the Unabomber as an eccentric and loner rather than as a scholar and philosophical zealot—an image that would eventually be universally accepted. To a man with a hammer, everything looks like a nail. To federal agencies awash with psychologists, every criminal fits a predetermined personality profile. And in a therapeutic society such as ours, every kind of cruel or unusual behavior is seen as a symptom of mental illness. By relying so heavily on profiling as an investigative tool, federal officials would reduce their quarry to a psychological artifact. And the media would do likewise.

In March 1996, therefore, Special Agent Don Sachtleben had reason to be pessimistic. For seventeen years, the Unabomber had honed his bombmaking skills until he had become a true messenger of death. And despite its lavish efforts, the government seemed no closer to catching him. It had spent millions of dollars and employed scores of agents. It established a Unabom Task Force and chased down every lead, every suspect. Agents combed scrap metal junkyards and even—after determining that some of the bomb materials came from artificial limbs—visited plants where prosthetics were made, interviewing employees. Since 1993, they had offered a million-dollar reward for information leading to his capture and conviction. They established an information hot line. All for naught.

The psychological profilers repeatedly vacillated. At first, they described the killer as an obsessive-compulsive white male who held a string of menial jobs, moving frequently. Given his talent at constructing bombs, they theorized, he may have been a carpenter or machinist, and an extremely neat dresser. Later, they surmised he might be a college professor. After the manifesto appeared, authorities decided that the killer was in his forties, perhaps a college professor, probably in the social sciences, and an expert on the history of science. They ignored the 1993 portrait offered by prominent criminologist Robert O'Block that the bomber was probably a "logical thinker" who "hates social situ-ations" and who, although having "had a connection from the academic community," was now alienated from it. They paid little attention to the description provided by one of their own agents, Bill Tafoya of the San Francisco office, who argued that the Unabomber probably "had an advanced degree in a 'hard science,' such as engineering," and he proba-bly didn't live in the Bay area, but somewhere considerably more remote.

After an eyewitness claimed to have seen a man thought to be the Unabomber depositing a bomb in the parking lot of a computer sales company in Salt Lake City in 1987, the agency put together a composite sketch that was different again. The drawing depicted a man with a mustache, wearing what looked like Armani sunglasses and a hooded sweatshirt resembling what the Internet site MetroActive described as a "Boyz-in-the-hood hood." The caption described him as a white male in his late thirties, with reddish-blond hair. It was Kaczynski, wearing one of his disguises. So no one recognized him.

In 1993, following two bombs sent from Sacramento, authorities announced that the killer probably lived in Northern California. The FBI installed forty-five more agents in a new office in San Francisco. By then, suspecting that the killer might not be a single person but a revolutionary group, it began combing the Bay area in search of "leftists," concentrating attention on radical environmentalists.

And when, in 1993, more than fifty thousand people responded to the FBI's request to call its hot line ("1-800-701-BOMB") if they had clues, the agency had more than eight hundred suspects to investigate, even after culling the list.

None of the experts had suggested the bomber would be neither in his thirties or forties, nor an itinerant blue-collar worker or college professor, nor a historian of science, or a group, or even a hermit. Rather, on his arrest in 1996 he would prove to be a shy, fifty-four-year-old Harvard graduate and former college professor, living not in California but in Montana.

3

The Scientific Method

The question of value is an awkward subject which fits uneasily within our scholarly tradition of objective analysis.

—DEREK BOK,
Harvard President's Report, 1979

The fact that I was able to admit to myself that there was no logical justification for morality illustrates a very important trait of mine. . . . I have much less tendency to self-deception than most people.

—THEODORE J. KACZYNSKI,
Journal

FOR THE FBI, the hunt began on November 15, 1979, when the agency's top bomb expert, Special Agent James C. "Chris" Ronay, received a call from his boss, Stuart Case.

"Get to Dulles Airport right away," Case instructed. "A plane's about to land there with a bomb on board."

Ronay reached the tarmac just as airport security personnel were removing a large, smoking stainless-steel U.S. Mail container from the plane. Medics stood by, treating a dozen or so passengers for smoke inhalation.

American Airlines Flight 444 had been en route from Chicago O'Hare to Washington National when pilots heard a muffled *thump* and noticed the cabin pressure had begun to drop. Soon, smoke filled the body of the plane. They diverted to Dulles for an emergency landing.

Inside the container, Ronay found fragments of a meticulously constructed homemade bomb that had been mailed from Chicago. What struck him was how elaborately and carefully crafted it was—though made entirely from ordinary materials found in any hardware store. These included a cheap aneroid barometer altered to measure ambient pressure changes in the aircraft and altitude changes. The bomb was designed to explode when the plane reached over 2,000 feet in elevation. A second, redundant triggering system was fixed to ignite if the package were opened. A large juice can contained the main explosive charge of smokeless power and fireworks chemicals. The fusing system consisted of four "C" batteries wired to a modified barometer switch, all housed in a homemade wooden box. The postage on the box comprised several $1 "Eugene O'Neill" and "America's Light Fueled by Truth and Reason" stamps.

Ronay immediately asked Special Agent Thomas E. Barrett in the FBI's Chicago office to circulate queries to local law enforcement, asking whether they had encountered any similar bombs. They received an immediate response from Northwestern University campus security, in Evanston.

Six months earlier, on May 9, 1979, campus officials explained, a graduate student named John Harris had been injured by a similar bomb in a student meeting room of the university's Technological Institute in Evanston. Harris had noticed a "Phillies" Cigar box on a table between two study carrels. Curious, he opened it, triggering a loud explosion, which started a fire in the room. Harris, cut and burned slightly, was taken to the Evanston Hospital and released an hour later.

And this bomb wasn't their first, Northwestern authorities told Barrett. A year earlier, on May 25, 1978, a woman named Mary Gutierrez found a brown package in a parking lot adjacent to the Science and

Engineering Building at the University of Illinois Chicago Circle Campus. It was addressed to E. J. Smith, professor of rocket science at Rensselaer Polytechnic Institute in Troy, New York. The return address was given as Professor Buckley Crist, Jr., professor of computer science at Northwestern University's Technological Institute. Ten $1 "Eugene O'Neill" stamps had been put on the package. It was ready to mail.

Assuming the sender had intended to post the package, Gutierrez tried to shove it into the mailbox. But it wouldn't fit. As she lived near Evanston, she decided to return it to Crisp. The next day she called the professor, who sent a messenger to pick it up. Not recognizing the package, Crisp called campus security. When the officer, Terry Marker, started to unwrap it, the device exploded, injuring him slightly. The university notified the U.S. Bureau of Alcohol, Tobacco and Firearms (ATF). After cataloguing the bomb debris, bureau agents destroyed the evidence, filed a report, and forgot about it.

The three bombs, Ronay now saw, while differing in some respects nevertheless shared a family resemblance. The Crisp device employed a 1-inch diameter steel pipe about 9 inches long, sealed at the ends with wooden plugs and filled with smokeless powders and match heads. The American Airlines bomb did not use a pipe but a large (64-ounce) tin juice can filled with explosives, while the Harris bomb employed no metal container at all, but some sort of cardboard tube.

Yet the similarities were hard to miss: all came in carefully crafted wooden boxes, used smokeless powders as the main explosive charge, and were made out of ordinary household materials. The triggering systems revealed considerable imagination. Like the airline bomb, Harris's was fused with C-cell batteries, wired to improvised initiators made of hand-carved wooden dowels, each containing a pair of wires that ran into the explosive charge. Opening the package completed the electrical circuit, heating a thin bridge wire embedded in the matchheads, thus firing the matchheads, which in turn detonated the firecracker explosive. Crisp's employed a physical rather than electrical triggering mechanism: opening the box released rubber bands that drove a nail into the end of the pipe, igniting the matchheads, which in turn detonated the smokeless powders.

In short, despite some design differences, the craftsmanship, imagination, and design overlap of these three devices suggested the bureau was confronting a serial bomber. The FBI appointed Chris Ronay case agent for the investigation.

Odd, Ronay, thought; technically, these were primitive devices, yet exceptionally crafted. The boxes were beautifully made. Why the hand-carved wood initiators? Why were the pipe plugs homemade, when better, threaded caps could be found at any hardware store? What could possibly be the motive for these crimes?

And why the "Eugene O'Neill" stamps? They had been out of circulation for some time.

THE FBI suspected the O'Neill stamps were meaningful somehow, but was never able to determine their exact significance. Yet O'Neill was an appropriate and an ironic symbol for Kaczynski. Both he and the playwright identified with oppressed and outcast peoples. Both despised technology and materialism, and both idealized the simple life. But resemblances ended there. Kaczynski was a militant atheist who believed that violence was the only solution. O'Neill, a convert to Catholicism, saw America's worship of technology as a sign of its declining religious faith and believed that reviving this faith would be its only salvation.

O'Neill had experienced many disappointments before achieving success as a playwright. After dropping out of Princeton at the end of his freshman year, he had drifted from one menial job to another: working as a gold prospector in Honduras, at various odd jobs in Argentina and elsewhere, then for many years as a merchant seaman. Along the way he had come to identify with outcast and oppressed peoples, and had developed a thorough distaste for modern American materialism.

These themes appear in his plays. *The Hairy Ape* (1922) dramatizes technology's capacity to victimize and dehumanize. *The Great God Brown* (1925) ridicules the materialistic and spiritually empty life and reaffirms that the only salvation comes from the love of God. *Ah, Wilderness!* (1932), which O'Neill called a "Comedy of Recollection," sought to reincarnate the spirit of small-town America at the turn of the century.

But it was *Dynamo* (1928) that encapsulated O'Neill's belief that we have made technology our God and that it will eventually destroy us. Universally regarded as O'Neill's worst play, it was written, he later told a friend, when his first marriage was in trouble and "my brains were wooly with hatred."

Dynamo depicts the life and death of the teenager Reuben Light, the son of a didactic, overbearing minister, who revolts against his father's faith to embrace the religion of Electricity. Driven mad by the conflict between his lust for Ada, daughter of an atheistic hydroelectric plant superintendent, and his desire to attain a pure, idealistic oneness with the God, Electricity—or, as it gradually becomes transmuted for him, the "Mother-God Dynamo"—Reuben murders the girl and flings himself on the dynamo, electrocuting himself.

The play is not so much a screed against technology as a cautionary tale about what happens to those like Reuben who, seduced by "Lucifer, the God of Electricity," lose their religious faith. "There must be a center around which all this moves, mustn't there?" Reuben asks the superintendent's wife, May. "There is in everything else! And that center must be the Great Mother of Eternal Life, Electricity, and Dynamo is her Divine Image on earth. Her power houses are the new churches!" Reuben had become a true believer in technology. And soon he would be dead.

As a faithful disciple of the scientific method, Kaczynski never accepted the arguments of those who, like O'Neill, made pleas for the spiritual life. But this would not have stopped him from embracing the play's antitechnological message. For Kaczynski was a "cherry-picker": he took ideas he liked and left the rest. He regularly borrowed antitechnology arguments from literature while ignoring the spiritual messages most of these works contained. He had no interest in religious revival. He wanted revolution.

Kaczynski later recorded in his journal that he came back to the Chicago area in May 1978

> *mainly for one reason: so that I could more safely attempt to murder a scientist, businessman, or the like. . . . I took the bomb over to the U of Illinois Chicago Circle Campus, and surreptitiously dropped it between two parked cars in the lot near the Science and*

Technology Buildings. I hoped that a student—preferably one in a science and technology field—would pick it up and would either be a good citizen and take the package to a post office to be sent to Rensselaer, or would open the package himself and blow his hands off, or get killed. . . . I wish I had some assurance that I succeeded in killing or maiming someone.

As for the second bomb,

I had hoped that the victim would be blinded or have his hands blown off or be otherwise maimed. . . . At least I put him in the hospital, which is better than nothing. But not enough to satisfy me. Well, live and learn. No more match-head bombs. I wish I knew how to get hold of some dynamite.

And the third:

In some of my notes I mentioned a plan for revenge on society. Plan was to blow up airliner in flight. . . . Unfortunately plane not destroyed, bomb too weak.

WITH THESE BOMBS, Kaczynski had finally crossed the line. Ever since 1966, when he was a graduate student at the University of Michigan, he had repeatedly resolved to kill someone. But up to now, at the last moment he would shy away from taking the fateful step. Simultaneously, his plans to murder had coalesced around a philosophy. In an untitled 1971 essay presaging the manifesto, he warned that "continued scientific and technical progress will inevitably result in the extinction of individual liberty. . . .

"The power of society to control the individual person has recently been expanding very rapidly, and is expected to expand even more rapidly in the near future."

These techniques of control, Kaczynski enumerated, include "propaganda and image-making techniques"; a "growing emphasis among educators on 'guiding' the child's emotional development, coupled with

an increasingly scientific attitude toward education"; "operant conditioning" through such means as biofeedback, "'chemitrodes' inserted in
the brain"; and drugs, "genetic engineering," computers, and "surveillance devices."

"The principal effect of technology," the piece continued, "is to
increase the power of society collectively." This empowers social forces
that "are then able to use the machinery of society to impose their
choice universally. . . . The eventual result will be a world in which there
is only one system of values." It is imperative that this juggernaut be
stopped. This cannot be done by simply "propounding and popularizing
a certain libertarian philosophy" unless that philosophy "is accompanied
by a program of concrete action."

Kaczynski had decided by then on a "program of concrete action,"
but it would be many years before he screwed up the courage to launch
it. On Christmas Day, 1972, he wrote in his journal:

> About a year and a half ago I planned to murder a scientist—as a
> means of revenge against organized society in general and the tech-
> nological establishment in particular—unfortunately, I chickened
> out. I couldn't work up the nerve to do it.

Instead, in episodic fashion Kaczynski began to mimic the tactics of
radical environmentalists that they called "monkeywrenching"—sabotaging bulldozers, spiking trees, and stretching wires between trees,
with hopes of decapitating someone on a snowmobile.

Now, with the Crisp, Harris, and American Airlines bombs, he was
committed. There would be no turning back.

CHRIS RONAY didn't have to wait long before the bomber struck again.
The following June, in the posh Chicago suburb of Lake Forest, United
Airlines president Percy Wood received a letter from someone named
Enoch Fischer, promising to send Wood "a book that should be read by
all who make important decisions affecting the public welfare."

A few days later, on June 10, 1980—Wood's birthday—he received
a package posted from Chicago containing what seemed to be a copy of

Sloan Wilson's novel *Ice Brothers*. In fact, behind the title page the book had been hollowed out to contain a bomb. When Wood opened it, the device exploded, inflicting serious cuts to his face and upper left leg.

This bomb, Ronay noted, like its predecessors, was carefully— almost lovingly—put together, out of ordinary household materials. Inside the excavated book, the bomber had filled a section of galvanized pipe with smokeless powders, wired to a fusing system consisting of two D-cell batteries. Opening the cover completed an electrical circuit detonating the powder.

With *Ice Brothers* the bomber had sent a message, that he intended to "ice" his victim. And perhaps also he chose this book because, as Sloan Wilson suggested to me, being 517 pages long "it was big enough to contain a bomb." But, Wilson added, there was probably another reason. All his early novels had been angry works, and Kaczynski was angry. *Ice Brothers*, published in 1979, oozed disaffection.

> *If life was all that rotten, what was so bad about dying young? . . .*
> *The idea of fighting had a certain fascination—it was only the idea*
> *of losing that he didn't like, losing, being wounded and killed.*
> *Winning, he was convinced, would be marvelous, despite the fact*
> *that he would, almost without doubt, have to return to the same*
> *sort of dull job which would have been his lot if no war had res-*
> *cued him.*

By sending Wood *Ice Brothers*, Kaczynski made an indirect reference to Wilson's more famous work, *The Man in the Gray Flannel Suit* (1953). Like William H. Whyte, Jr.'s, 1956 nonfiction best-seller, *The Organization Man* (a copy of which the FBI would find in Kaczynski's cabin), *The Man in the Grey Flannel Suit* tells about the traps of middle-class life. The story of an ambitious young suburbanite, Tom Rath, who takes a job with a public relations firm because it pays well, only to discover he hates it, the novel treats themes that especially resonated with Kaczynski—how advertisers manipulate public opinion, and how modern life can become a prison.

Much to the consternation of the FBI, the literary mysteries mounted. First, "Eugene O'Neill" stamps; then *Ice Brothers*; then—also with the Percy Wood bomb—Ronay found a third: the letters "FC" stamped on a metal tag that Kaczynski had securely fastened inside the bomb, in a place its maker knew would survive the blast. No one knew what it meant.

After the Wood bombing, officials gave Ronay's investigation a name. Since the targets had been a university and two airlines, they dubbed it the Unabom Task Force—"Un" for universities, "a" for airlines, and "bom" for bomb.

The Wood bombing, like its predecessors, had disappointed Kaczynski, who shortly after mailing it found apparently more fulfilling mayhem in Montana by slashing tires and pouring sugar in the tanks of motorcycles belonging to loggers working near his cabin. This sabotage, he noted in his journal,

> *was particularly satisfying because it was an immediate and precisely directed response to the provocation. Contrast it with the revenge I attempted for the jet noise [that bothered him in Montana]. I long felt frustrated anger against the planes. After complicated preparation I succeeded in injuring the President of United Air Lines, but he was only one of a vast army of people who directly and indirectly are responsible for the jets. So the revenge was long delayed, vaguely directed and inadequate to the provocation. Thus it felt good to be able, for a change, to strike back immediately and directly.*

On October 8, 1981, the bomber struck again—this time in Salt Lake City. A University of Utah student leaving class in the Bennion Hall Business Building noticed a large package in the hall. As he started to pick it up, he saw a wooden stick drop partway out of the bottom. Fearing a bomb, he put it down immediately and called campus security. University authorities summoned the police bomb squad, which disarmed it in the women's bathroom down the hall.

Like the American Airlines bomb, this one made ingenious use of ordinary materials. Once again, smokeless powders had been packed inside a galvanized pipe sealed at both ends with carefully carved wooden plugs; two D-cell batteries were connected to an ordinary household "on/off" switch and then to a wooden dowel. The apparatus was attached to a can filled with gasoline.

The bomb had been designed so that when it was lifted, the dowel would drop through a hole in the bottom of the box, completing the electric circuit, igniting the matchheads and smokeless powders, which in turn would set off the gasoline, producing a kind of Molotov cocktail explosion. Once again, investigators found a metal plate stamped "FC."

> *My projects for revenge on the technological society, [Kaczynski complained later] are expensive . . . last fall I attempted a bombing and spent nearly three hundred bucks just for travel expenses, motel, clothing for disguise, etc., aside from cost of materials for bomb, and then the thing failed to explode. Damn, this was the firebomb found in the U. of Utah business school outside door of room containing some computer stuff.*

Meanwhile, Kaczynski continued his literary pursuits. He was particularly fond of the Uruguayan writer Horacio Quiroga—at least two of whose works he liked so much he translated into English. According to Vassar professor and federal prosecution consultant Donald Foster, one of these favorites that Kaczynski translated was "Juan Darien." The title character is a shy and studious boy, taunted by classmates for his rough hair and shyness. But actually, he's a tiger in human form. Teased beyond endurance, he renounces his humanity and takes revenge on a cat tamer, whom he carries into a canebrake and sets on fire, watching, with the other tigers, as the man is burnt to a crisp.

AFTER THE University of Utah incident, Ronay realized his quarry was not just a Chicago bomber. The FBI upgraded his investigation. Its scope would now be national.

As if to acknowledge this fact, the Unabomber widened his horizons further, sending increasingly sophisticated bombs to Tennessee, Berkeley, Washington State, and Michigan.

One arrived through the mail on May 5, 1982, at the Vanderbilt University office of a computer expert, Professor Patrick Fischer, with the return address of another computer expert, Brigham Young University professor Leroy Wood Bearnson. It had been posted from the BYU post office in Provo, Utah, with the familiar "Eugene O'Neill" stamps. But the bomber, having found Fischer's address in an out-of-date library reference work, had mistakenly sent it to Penn State University, where Fischer had worked before moving to Vanderbilt. Penn State forwarded it to Nashville, Tennessee.

Fischer was not present when the package arrived. His secretary, Janet Smith, opened it for him. The bomb blew up in her face, sending her to the hospital with severe burns and eye injuries. It contained the terrorist's "FC" signature.

Investigators continued to look for possible personal connections between the bomber and either Fischer or the places he had lived or worked. But this, Fischer thought, was a wild goose chase. There was nothing personal about this attack, he later told the *Washington Post*. The victims, he thought, were merely symbols in his campaign against technology.

> *Sent a bomb to a computer expert named Patrick Fischer. His secretary opened it. One newspaper said she was in hospital? In good condition? with arm and chest cuts. Other newspaper said bomb drove fragments of wood into her flesh. but no indication that she was permanently disabled. Frustrating that I can't seem to make lethal bomb.*

Two months later, on July 2, 1982, Diogenes Angelakos, director of the Electronics Research Laboratory at the University of California at Berkeley, found an odd-looking package with a lift-handle on its top sitting on the floor of Room 411 of the Cory Hall Mathematics Building. Thinking it had been left by a student, he lifted the handle. The explosion ripped into Angelakos's right hand, shredding his arm and burning him severely.

Like the University of Utah bomb, this device was a modified Molotov cocktail, designed to use gasoline to increase damage. Investigators found no "FC" plate, but they did find a note, which said: "Wu—It works! I told you it would.—RV." This reference to a Chinese dialect spoken by peoples who lived south of Shanghai would turn out to be another of many intentionally false clues. The bomber was toying with his pursuers.

> *I went to the U. of California Berkeley and placed in computer science building a bomb consisting of a pipebomb in gallon can of gasoline. According to newspaper, vice chairman of Computer Science dept picked it up. He was considered to be "out of danger of losing any fingers," but would need further surgery for bone and tendon damage in hand. Apparently pipe bomb went off but did not ignite gasoline. I don't understand it. Frustrated. Traveling expenses for raids such as the foregoing are very hard on my slender financial resources.*

There was an interval of almost three years. Then on May 15, 1985, John Hauser, a captain in the U.S. Air Force on special assignment as a computer engineering graduate student at Berkeley, walked into Room 264 of the Cory Hall Computer Science Building. On a table in the middle of the room, he noticed a black vinyl spiral binder sitting on top of a plastic file box. Thinking it might belong to another student, he picked up the binder to see if he could spot a name.

A flash of light blinded him. His right arm flew backward violently. Then *boom!* Hauser stared at the blood pouring from his arm. Several fingers were missing. His Air Force Academy ring had been blown off with such force that it left an intaglio imprint on the hard plaster wall. Splattered blood was everywhere. Fearing he might bleed to death, Hauser ran out into the hall. He encountered several graduate students who took one look at him and ran the other way in terror.

Coincidentally, it was the former Unabomber victim, Diogenes Angelakos, who saved Hauser. As a casualty of the earlier bomb, the older man knew what to do. He applied a tourniquet to stop the bleeding and called the hospital.

> *Success at last after many failures reported in these notes. Took me year and a half of intensive effort, largely neglecting other work to develop effective type bomb. . . . May 8 I planted a small bomb in the computer science Department at Berkeley. This is Experiment 83, apparatus number 2, in my notebooks.*

Berkeley bomb did very well for its size. It was sprung by air-force pilot, 26 yrs old, name Hauser. . . . He probably would have been killed if so positioned relative to bomb as to take the fragments in his body . . . witnesses said, "whole arm was exploded," "blood all over the place." One newspaper said arm was "mangled." Another said it was "shattered" and that he would never recover full use of arm and hand. Also there was damage to one eye . . . must admit I feel badly about having crippled this mans arm. It has been bothering me a good deal. This is embarrassing because while my feelings are partly from pity, I am sure they come largely from the training, propaganda, brainwashing we all get, conditioning us to be scared by the idea of doing certain things. It is shameful to be under the sway of this brainwashing. But do not get the idea that I regret what I did. Relief of frustrated anger outweighs uncomfortable conscience. I would do it all over again. So many failures with feeble ineffective bombs was driving me desperate with frustration. Have to get revenge for all the wild country being fucked up by the system. . . . Recently I camped in a paradise like glacial cirque. At evening, beautiful singing of birds was ruined by the obscene roar of jet planes. Then I laughed at the idea of having any compunction about crippling an airplane pilot.

Just a month after that, in June 1985, a package arrived at the Boeing Aircraft Company Fabrication Division in Auburn, Washington, which had been mailed from Oakland. Since it had not been addressed to a specific individual, it sat in the company's mailroom unopened. Eventually, an employee who began to open the package discovered it was a bomb. He called security, which disarmed it. No one was injured.

"Experiment number 82": outcome of Boeing bomb unknown.

IN HIS WIDELY READ critique of industrial society entitled *Where the Wasteland Ends* (1972), the countercultural guru Theodore Roszak warned readers of what he called "the reductionist assault . . . which degrades what it studies by depriving its subject of charm, autonomy, dignity, mystery." An example of this assault, Roszak suggested, is behavioral research that "claims to be nearer than ever to its long-sought goal of a fully engineered human psychology." Among those guilty of this hubris, wrote Roszak, was a psychologist whom he quoted at length:

> *"I believe," says Professor James V. McConnell of the University of Michigan, "that the day has come when we can combine sensory deprivation with drugs, hypnosis and astute manipulation of reward and punishment to gain absolute control over an individual's behavior. It should be possible then to achieve a very rapid and highly effective type of positive brainwashing that would allow us to make dramatic changes in a person's behavior and personality." Like many behaviorists, Professor McConnell has only the best of intentions at heart. His purpose is "to learn how to force people to love one another, to force them to want to behave properly." By which he means "psychological force." "Punishment," he insists, "must be used as precisely and as dispassionately as a surgeon's scalpel."*

Thirteen years later, on November 15, 1985, Professor McConnell was at his home overlooking the Huron River in Scio township, Michigan, when he received a package mailed from Salt Lake City. There was a letter inside the envelope that was glued to the outside of the package, purporting to be from Ralph C. Kloppenburg, and explaining that the parcel contained the manuscript of his doctoral dissertation. When McConnell's teaching assistant, Nick Suino, opened the box, an explosion ripped through the room, injuring both men.

The bomb had been hidden in a hollowed-out ream of paper. By reconstructing it after the blast, Ronay's team could see that, like its predecessors, it had been encased in a beautifully made, hand-carved wooden box. Again, the unnecessarily powerful battery fusing system. Again, the initials "FC" stamped at the end of pipe plugs. Again, the unique triggering mechanism. But the bomber was getting better at his craft, Ronay feared. The McConnell bomb would have done a lot of damage, had the pipe not split rather than fragmenting, as it should have.

Yet again, the $1 "Eugene O'Neill" stamps.

Experiment 100: Mid November 1985 I sent bomb in mail to James V. McConnell, behavior modification researcher at Univ. of Michigan. Only minor injuries to McConnell's assistant. Deflagrated, did not detonate. Must be either pipe was a little weak or loading density of explosive a shade too high at failure.

The devil, Ronay realized, was in the details. Although each bomb was made of pipe plugs and fusing systems powered by C- or D-cell batteries, each triggering mechanism was different, and showed a lot of imagination. But Ronay sensed that the craftsmanship was becoming increasingly and unnecessarily elaborate—redundancy in the fusing system, more electric power than necessary, metal and woodwork more precisely polished than necessary.

The Hauser bomb revealed the continuing evolution to ever more gratuitously painstaking construction. The pipe was not the ordinary galvanized kind found at any plumbing supply store, threaded at each end and capped with threaded plugs. Rather, it was made of super-hard stainless steel that could only be cut, Ronay suspected, with a power saw. And the plugs were custom-made of a similarly hard material, crafted with care. At each end of the pipe were precisely sized square holes that coincided exactly with similar-sized notches in the plugs. The plugs were kept in place by square dowels carved out of hard steel. It took an excellent craftsman with a strong power drill and grinder to do this kind of work.

More troubling, the bomber was learning how to seal the explosives more tightly, thereby amplifying potential damage. And he was concocting more potent explosives. With the Hauser bomb, he had for the first time used a mixture of aluminum powder and ammonium nitrate, producing a much bigger bang and signaling to Ronay that worse was to come.

MEANWHILE, the biggest literary clue of all remained a mystery: the letters "FC."

Ever since he was a boy, Kaczynski had identified closely with the Polish-born writer, Józef Teodor Konrad Korzeniowski, better known to English-speaking readers as Joseph Conrad. Kaczynski shared Conrad's first name, and reportedly used "J. Konrad" as an alias on occasion when taking trips to deposit or mail his bombs. As he grew older, he became passionately attached to Conrad's novels. And his favorite was *The Secret Agent*, which he urged his brother and mother to read and which he claims to have read himself a dozen times. And no wonder. For this novel about terrorist revolutionaries who declare war on science is practically a Unabomber instruction manual.

The Secret Agent is the story of Winnie Verloc, whom one critic described as "an inadequate human being surrounded by moral anarchy and spiritual decay." Winnie's husband, "a seller of shady wares," according to Conrad, spies for a foreign embassy. His shop is the meeting place for an anarchist group, "FP," or "Future of the Proletariat." Verloc is ordered by the First Secretary of the embassy, Vladimir, to blow up the famous Observatory in Greenwich. For "Science," Vladimir tells Verloc,

> is the sacrosanct fetish. All the damned professors are radicals at heart. Let them know that their great panjandrum has got to go, too. . . . The demonstration must be against learning—science. . . . The attack must have all the shocking senselessness of gratuitous blasphemy.

Dutifully, Verloc obtains a bomb from a mysterious terrorist known only as "the Professor"—a man obsessed with building "the perfect detonator"—and arranges for Winnie's half-witted brother, Stevie, to plant it. Unfortunately, Stevie botches the job and blows himself to bits. To avenge Stevie's death, Winnie murders her husband, then flees. Seeking to escape via the Channel steamer, she is robbed of everything she owns by the anarchist, Ossipon, and commits suicide by jumping overboard.

The Secret Agent is written with great irony and a strong moral tone, both of which Kaczynski seemingly missed. The theme is moral decay, not anarchism or the evils of science. Verloc and his co-conspirators are spiritually deficient people surrounded by corruption. To Conrad—who

ALSTON CHASE / 63

promises his readers to tell "Winnie Verloc's story to its anarchistic end of utter desolation, madness and despair"—terrorism, rather than being a solution to social ills, is a sign of sickness. And those who pursue it, like the Verlocs, are ultimately consumed by it.

As the Professor tells Ossipon, "You revolutionists . . . are the slaves of the social convention, which is afraid of you; slaves of it as much as the very police that stand up in the defence of that convention. Clearly you are, since you want to revolutionize it . . . the terrorist and the policeman both come from the same basket."

In a letter to *Penthouse* magazine publisher Bob Guccione on June 29, 1995, the bomber explained that "FC" stood for "Freedom Club." After Kaczynski's arrest investigators would learn that his fascination with *The Secret Agent* and the terrorist group "FP," depicted in the novel, had inspired him to use this signature. But in apparently seeking to imitate this fiction he had missed its message: that one who tries to topple technological society becomes a prisoner of it, and that his way would end in "utter desolation, madness and despair."

Instead, Kaczynski identified closely with the Professor, who, Conrad tells us, lived alone in a "cramped hermitage" suited to "the perfect anarchist," where he devoted himself to making "the perfect detonator."

4

The Perfect Detonator

"But what is it you want from us?" he exclaimed in a dead-ened voice. "What is it you are after yourself?"

"A perfect detonator," was the peremptory answer. . . . "I don't play; I work fourteen hours a day, and go hungry sometimes. My experiments cost money now and again, and then I must do without food for a day or two. . . . I've the grit to work alone, quite alone, absolutely alone. I've worked alone for years."

—JOSEPH CONRAD, *The Secret Agent* (1907)
from Kaczynski's cabin library

How shall I know when it is time to throw bombs? . . . when the very last wolves on this continent are trapped and caged for captive breeding (as the remaining Condors were, not so long ago), will it finally be time to throw bombs?

Or will it be too late?

—"Pajama,'"Bombthrowing: A Brief Treatise,"
Earth First! Wild Rockies Review (1993)

I T WOULD BE kind to call the pathetic collection of shops at 1537 Howe Avenue in Sacramento a "shopping center" or even a "strip mall." It looks more like a small, run-down motel squeezed between two gas stations, along one of those depressingly familiar stretches of commercial wasteland—featuring fast-food restaurants, discount stores, and car dealerships—that blight so much of suburban America. The mall's eight tiny shops seem to reflect more hopes and dreams than great commercial success. This is a place where marginal businesses struggle to survive.

Hugh Scrutton owned a small computer rental shop here, called Rentech. A mathematics graduate from Berkeley, Scrutton, thirty-eight, was a man of wide enthusiasms. He was, said his friend John Lawyer, "an inherent student of everything. . . . He really enjoyed life." An accomplished potter, he had made a kiln in his backyard. He traveled frequently. He loved to study foreign languages. He climbed mountains. And he was feeling especially good this day. Even though his business was failing and he was up to his ears in debt, he'd finally found the girl he wanted to marry.

At noon on December 11, 1985, Scrutton walked out the back door of the shop to the parking lot behind the building, telling his assistant Dick Knight he was on his way to an appointment. As he stepped outside, he noticed a block of wood on the ground close to the door, with nails protruding from each end. He stopped to pick it up.

A moment later, Knight heard a loud *pop* and then Scrutton crying out, "Oh my God! Help me!"

Knight ran out the back door to find Scrutton standing in his own blood. His right hand was missing and his heart half out of his chest. Then he collapsed. Nadia Bridson, owner of Nadia's Fashions next to Rentech, ran to Scrutton's side, then back inside the shop to call an ambulance, as Knight vainly administered CPR. It was too late. Scrutton was dead thirty minutes later.

The telltale signs were all there: the initials "FC," the homemade wooden box, D-cell batteries, lamp cord, wood, tape, nails, screws, the familiar explosive material and unique triggering system, lovingly and imaginatively constructed. But this device was far more sophisticated than its predecessors. The bomber was learning how to seal the pipes tightly, to amplify the explosive effect, by using three concentric layers of pipe, sealed at both ends by handmade hardened steel plugs.

> *Experiment 97: December 11, 1985, I planted a bomb disguised to look like a scrap of lumber behind Rentech computer store in Sacramento. According to the San Francisco Examiner, Dec. 20, the "operator" . . . was killed, blown to bits on December 12th. Excellent. Humane way to eliminate somebody. He probably never felt a thing. $25,000 reward offered. Rather flattering.*

Until the Scrutton killing, Ronay's task force had maintained a low profile. It kept secret the fact that it was investigating a serial bomber, reasoning that the less the public knew, the easier its job. But the Scrutton murder made such secrecy impossible. After the bombing, Sacramento's law enforcement authorities revealed the existence of the Unabomber to the media for the first time, putting the case into the national spotlight. They also reportedly told the press about the signature "FC," inspiring a succession of copycat bombers.

On February 20, 1987, Gary Wright, owner of a small Salt Lake City computer store named CAAMS, had just pulled into a parking spot behind his store when he noticed an apparent wooden chock with nails protruding, on the ground near the rear entrance. Like Scrutton, he reached to pick it up, and the object exploded. Later, FBI analysis would reveal that the Wright bomb was identical to the Scrutton device. It lifted Wright off his feet, filled his body with wood and metal shrapnel, severely damaged his face and mangled his left arm and hand, leaving them permanently numb. But it didn't kill him.

> *Experiment 121: The device was placed February 20th and worked the same day; it exploded and probably detonated but the results—as far as we could find out—did not do enough to satisfy us.*

And this time, the killer may have been seen. Just before Wright arrived at the parking lot, an employee in a nearby office saw a man through the blinds of her rear office window remove from a cloth bag what appeared to be two two-by-four pieces of wood nailed together, with other nails sticking out the sides. The man placed the object near the left rear wheel of her car. As she called a co-worker to the window to look, the man peered at her, then walked away through the parking lot, leaving the pieces of wood behind just as Wright showed up.

After the Wright bombing, more than six years would elapse without incident, puzzling investigators. Usually serial bombers accelerate their activities. This killer had seemed to enjoy taunting, even teasing, his pursuers. Why now was he so silent? Was it because he had been seen and was afraid of being caught?

Partly. But it was also because he had taken a sabbatical to pursue scientific research. Like the Professor in *The Secret Agent*, he was searching for "the perfect detonator." Frustrated at his inability to develop a dependably fatal bomb, Kaczynski, his frugal lifestyle sustained by a small annual stipend from his parents and income from the occasional odd job, went back to the drawing board, experimenting with different explosive mixtures, which he tested in the mountains behind his cabin.

He faced a twofold task: First, to concoct a far more powerful explosive than he had hitherto used, such as the famous "C-4" used by the military. Second, to find a detonator that would set it off.

Eventually, he found the right explosive recipe—a potent mix that could be molded into any shape. But this created another problem: it was not very volatile. Like C-4, which one can actually drop on the floor without suffering ill consequences, Kaczynski's new concoction couldn't be set off by the matchheads or smokeless powders he had used in previous bombs. For this purpose, professionals employed small explosive charges known as blasting caps as igniters. But Kaczynski didn't dare walk into a mining supply store and purchase one. He'd be arrested within a week. So he had to make his own.

Ultimately, he learned how, using junkyard materials and ordinary household ingredients. First, he melted scraps of aluminum into small blocks; he shaved these blocks with a rasp to create a fine, aluminum dust, then combined this with potassium chlorate. Second, he poured the mixture into a 6-inch-long, 3/8-inch-diameter copper tube, which he sealed at each end with metal plugs, secured by 1/8-inch pins. Third, he drilled a small hole in each plug and ran a thin copper wire through the holes down the middle of the pipe. And finally, he attached the copper wire to a triggering mechanism powered by 9-volt batteries. Switching the trigger turned on the current, which heated the wire, igniting the aluminum powder–potassium chlorate mix that had been packed around the wire and setting off an explosion sufficient to detonate the main explosive charge.

After testing his new design in remote areas of the backcountry behind his house, Kaczynski was ready to try it out in real-world situations.

TIBURON, IN Marin County, California, is the kind of laid-back Mediterranean bedroom community that most folks only dream of. Tucked near Sausalito across the bay from San Francisco, it looks like a stage set for the movie *The Serial*, in which folks worry about such things as Rolfing, Moonies, spouse-swapping, and primal scream therapy. But in June 1993, it signified something quite different to the Unabomber.

Dr. Charles J. Epstein lived there. Epstein, a world-renowned geneticist at the University of California San Francisco Medical Center, had been much in the news lately for having helped to discover the Trisomy 16 (Ts16) mouse—a rodent possessing genetic abnormalities associated with Down's syndrome. Epstein and his team had found that when they grafted brain tissue from Trisomy 16 into the brains of normal mice, these recipients developed symptoms of Alzheimer's disease. In another study, the researchers were able to reverse brain cell degeneration in Ts16 mice by using nerve growth factors.

In short, Epstein and his colleagues had made a major breakthrough in focusing research on the most productive ways to understand and treat Down's syndrome and Alzheimer's disease.

But the Unabomber was not pleased.

On Tuesday, June 22, 1993, Epstein left his office early, so that he could go home to work on a grant request he was preparing. On the way, he stopped at the Cove Shopping Center to pick up laundry and at the Strawberry Shopping Center for fish. When he arrived at Noche Vista Lane at 4:00 P.M., his house was empty. His wife was out of town at a conference. His daughter had left the mail on the kitchen table. In the pile was a package from Sacramento, postmarked June 18, with the return address of James Hill, Chemistry Department, California State University, Sacramento. The package felt like a cassette tape, but heavier.

As Epstein tore off the cover, he got a glimpse of a little wooden box. Then a bright blue flash and loud *boom!* filled the room, and he had, he said later, an "uh-oh" sensation. The blast drove him across the room and onto the floor. His right arm hurt terribly. He reached for the phone, which had been blown off the wall. But his fingers were useless. Desperate, he ran out the door and up the street until he encountered two gardeners working in a neighbor's yard. They called the police and an ambulance.

Not much was left of the Epstein bomb. While the usual batteries, wires, and wooden dowels were discovered amid the debris, no "FC" could be found.

Two days later, David Gelernter, associate professor of computer science at Yale University, just back from a vacation, walked into his office in the Computer Science Department. His secretary had stacked mail on his desk, and left a brown box on the chair beside it. The package had been posted from Sacramento, California, on June 18. It looked like a dissertation that someone had sent him to read, he thought. Picking it up, he noticed the package was unusually heavy and neatly wrapped. He was impressed with its neatness, he would tell investigators later. On top was a tab attached to what looked like a zipper.

Like Epstein, Gelernter had been much in the news. As a graduate student at the State University of New York at Stony Brook in the late 1970s, he had co-authored a highly successful software program called "Linda" that made it possible to link many small computers together to solve big problems. But he was no narrowly specialized cybernerd. Besides being devoted to music and art, he also wrote thoughtful books about the effects of computers on culture.

In his latest book, *Mirror Worlds: Or the Day Software Puts the Universe in a Shoebox . . . How It will Happen and What It will Mean,* which appeared in 1991, Gelernter couldn't seem to decide whether technology was a promise or a threat. Strangely ambivalent, the book was at once profound and naive, democratic and elitist, optimistic and pessimistic.

Its thesis was that someday soon computers will reflect all reality. People will be able to sit at their desks and receive a constant flow of information about what is happening at the moment, from traffic snarls to zoning board meetings. Then one could react to these events or participate in them as they're happening—all "without changing out of your pajamas," as Gelernter put it.

By making "the theoretically public actually public," Mirror Worlds, Gelernter said (ignoring how effectively governmental agencies control information made available on their Web sites), will allow America at last to become a fully open, participatory democracy. Yet after this egalitarian promise, he added a chillingly elitist warning: that Mirror Worlds will force us to embrace technology whether we like it or not, and that those who don't or can't will be left behind. And to Steve Courtney of the *Hartford Courant* the reporter who noted that Mirror Worlds seemed to entail placing a video monitor at every street corner, Gelernter backtracked, saying, "I'd have to say my vote is for less rather than more video."

Throughout, Gelernter's own feelings about this prospect seemed curiously equivocal. He confessed that "I'd be the last person to deny that mirror worlds are a frightening prospect." Yet he also seemed to suggest that, frightening or not, we ought to welcome it, because it's inevitable.

In an eerily waffling epilogue, Gelernter records a conversation between his two alter egos—Ed, who fears technology, and John, who welcomes it.

The consequences of technology, Ed warns, could be "serfdom . . . feudalism, actual or intellectual. . . . These things color your view of reality. They present the world to you. In a compelling way." So we are giving control of our own perception of reality to "the people who control these Mirror Worlds." We will become utterly dependent on them. Yet the machines will be too complex for ordinary people to understand. Society will be stratified between those who have mastered computers and those who have not. Status will be "based strictly on a person's fondness for playing games with machines."

But any average college student can understand computers, John replies. "If he can't learn *basic* science *and engineering*, what the hell is he doing in college? . . . *'Physics is beyond me'* is merely the polite, socially-approved way of saying *I'm too goddamned lazy. And you're too mush-brained to make me.* And this is precisely the *greatest thing* about Mirror Worlds. . . . They will *energize* people, once they're real. . . . Hey, wanna be a second class citizen No? Then turn on your brain and *learn*.

"The water level is rising," John continues. "Do people drown in droves or do they learn to swim?" People are *"going to have to understand the technology, not just use it blindly . . . and if they don't, that is a genuine disaster. . . . But. They will understand! They will learn . . . that's the best thing about Mirror Worlds: Ultimately they force people to learn how to swim. They force people to come to grips with technology."*

Finally Ed asks, "What if they don't learn and become intellectual serfs . . . to the Lords of the Mirror World Manor? . . . Doesn't it *concern* you, *at least a little?"* John replies, "Okay. It concerns me. At least a little" (Gelernter's italics passim).

It concerned Kaczynski.

When Gelernter pulled the tab on the brown box, he saw smoke escaping and heard a hissing sound, followed by pale gray smoke and—an instant later—a bright flash. He never heard the explosion. He remembered thinking, "Bombs must be going off all over the campus this morning."

Suddenly, he realized he couldn't see out of his right eye. Thinking that he had blood in his eye, he started for the bathroom down the hall to wash it off. Once there, he realized he was badly wounded and losing blood at a terrific rate. Bones were sticking out of his right hand at odd angles and his skin looked like parchment.

He clambered down the stairs five and a half stories to the ground level, spewing blood and somehow losing a shoe and his shirt in the process, then ran to the university health clinic, which was fortunately just across the street. By the time he reached the clinic, his blood pressure was zero. Personnel there rushed him via ambulance to the surgical intensive care unit of the Yale–New Haven Hospital. His chest and right leg had been gashed open, his lung was damaged, his left hand was broken and his right hand a mess—thumb and little finger gone, and the other digits badly mangled.

With these bombs Kaczynski's technology took a quantum leap forward. For the first time, FBI investigators found no physical evidence of a pipe or any other explosive containment device. Apparently, they surmised, the bomber had developed some sophisticated high-explosive material that did not require confinement. And from Kaczynski's perspective the important thing was that these "experiments" proved that the blasting cap worked. Now he knew he could mold even more potent explosives around the blasting cap to create a really big bang, one that would, indeed, kill.

> *Experiment Log, Experiment 225: I sent these devices during June 1993. They detonated as they should have. The effect of both of them was adequate but no more than adequate.*

ON JUNE 24, 1993, the *New York Times* received a letter from a sender claiming to be "an anarchist group calling ourselves FC." The letter, which had been mailed from the same location in Sacramento and on the same day as the Epstein and Gelernter bombs, called the paper's attention to the fact that its postmark preceded "a newsworthy event." The letter also revealed a barely legible notation, apparently left unintentionally by the sender, made by the imprint of a pencil on a sheet of paper that must have been lying on top of it. The message read: "Call Nathan R—Wed 7 pm."

Immediately, the FBI began combing the country for men named Nathan whose last name began with an "R." Of course, it was another Unabomber joke.

Nearly two years later, during the week of April 27, 1995, Gelernter himself received a letter from "FC."

"In the epilog of your book, *Mirror Worlds*," the letter writer said in part,

> *you tried to justify your research by claiming that the developments you describe are inevitable, and that any college person can learn enough about computers to compete in a computer-dominated world. Apparently, people without a college degree don't count. In any case, being informed about computers won't enable anyone to prevent invasion of privacy (through computers) genetic engineering (to which computers make an important contribution), environmental degradation through excessive economic growth (computers make an important contribution to economic growth), and so forth.*
>
> *. . . If the developments you describe are inevitable, they are*

not inevitable in the way that old age and bad weather are inevitable. They are inevitable only because techno-nerds like you make them inevitable. . . .

But we do not believe that progress and growth are inevitable.

IN NOVEMBER 1994, an environmental group calling itself the "Native Forest Network" held a meeting in Missoula, Montana, dubbed the "Second International Temperate Forest Conference." Its topic was "Focus on Multinationals." Up to five hundred people attended. Among the literature available at the convocation was a radical environmentalist publication, *Live Wild or Die!*, whose cover declared, "Hastening the downfall, hearkening the dawn."

This pamphlet also contained an "Eco-Fucker Hit List," which identified enemy number one as the Timber Association of California and gave readers the name and address of its communications officer, Roberta Anderson. Enemy number three was the Exxon Corporation— dubbed "Hexxon"—put there because of its culpability in the Prince William Sound oil spill. And a passing topic of discussion at the meeting was the charge, made in the June 21, 1993, issue of *Earth First! Journal*, that a public relations firm the magazine identified as "Burston-Marsteller" should share blame for the accident, for cleaning up the corporation's image afterward.

In fact, this information was inaccurate. Anderson had died several years previously. The association had changed its name to the California Forestry Association. There was no "t" in Burson, and this agency had never worked on the oil spill issue. But Kaczynski, who would later confess at his trial to have read the *Earth First! Journal* article, almost certainly saw the "Eco-Fucker Hit List," and may have even attended the conference, believed these false claims. And he would do something about it.

ON DECEMBER 10, 1994, at their home at 15 Aspen Drive in North Caldwell, New Jersey, Susan and Thomas Mosser, along with their two children—Kim, age thirteen, and Kelly, fifteen months—and Kim's friend Robin Sommese, who was visiting, had slept late. After lunch, they planned to pick out a Christmas tree.

Tom, an executive with Burson-Marsteller, had just come home from a business trip the day before. After fixing himself breakfast, he read a book to Kelly for a while, and played with her in her toy castle. Then, still in his bathrobe, he went to the foyer, where Susan had stacked the mail that had come in during his absence. He returned to the kitchen with a package that he put on the counter. Standing next to Susan and Kelly, he reached for a knife to open it. At that moment, Kelly scampered out of the room. Susan, wondering what she was up to, followed her daughter into the living room. The little girl told her mother she wanted to have a tea party.

A moment later, Susan recalled, "a thunderous noise resounded throughout the house. Stunned, I scooped Kelly up and put her near the front door. A white mist was pouring from the kitchen doorway. I raced through it to find out what happened."

The dust was subsiding by the time Susan got back to the kitchen. But she couldn't see Tom. As the mist settled to the floor, it gradually revealed her husband's body. He lay on his back, face blackened and stomach sliced open. Susan yelled at the children to get out of the house, dialed 911, picked up some towels and the baby's blanket, and returned to her husband.

"I knelt down," she recalled. "He was moaning very softly. I wasn't sure what I could touch or where I could touch. The fingers on his right hand were dangling just by skin. They had been cut through the bone."

"I did what I could, and I held his left hand. I told him help is coming, that he would be okay, and that I loved him."

After the police and ambulance arrived, Susan took her children to a neighbor, then waited outside the house. A fireman approached. "He's dead, isn't he?" she said to him. The fireman nodded his head. "I'm sorry," he said. "He didn't make it."

Susan then returned to the neighbor's house. Kim stood at the entrance. Seeing the fireman and the priest, her daughter knew something was wrong. Susan said her father had been hurt. "Fix him," she yelled.

"I told her he couldn't be fixed," Susan replied. "It was a bomb. He was dead."

Experiment 244: . . . The device in Experiment 244 was used in December 1994, and it gave a totally satisfactory result.

Chris Ronay retired three months before the Mosser killing, but his successor as laboratory case agent on the Unabom Task, Force Tom Mohnal, realized that "FC" had perfected his craft. The Epstein and Gelernter bombs revealed that he now knew how to make the perfect detonator. And the Mosser bomb demonstrated he could mix and shape very high explosives, thereby dispensing with pipes altogether. It was a unique construction: after mixing the explosive, the killer had flattened it into a kind of pancake, which he then rolled around a detonator, forming something like a hot dog in a bun. He then wrapped this with alternating layers of strapping tape and twine and covered the entire package in epoxy, producing a tight tube. Finally, he soaked the entire package in salt water and soybean oil to remove fingerprints.

The technology was impressive.

FOUR MONTHS after the Mosser murder, on April 24, 1995, the *New York Times* received a second letter from "FC."

"We blew up Thomas Mosser last December," the killer wrote in part, "because he was a Burston-Marsteller executive. Among other misdeeds," he continued,

> *Burston-Marsteller helped Exxon clean up its public image after the Exxon Valdez incident. But we attacked Burston-Marsteller less for its specific misdeeds than on general principles. Burston-Marsteller is about the biggest organization in the public relations field. This means that its business is the development of techniques for manipulating people's attitudes. It was for this more than for its actions in specific cases that we sent the bomb to an executive of this company. . . .*

Through our bombings we hope to promote social instability in industrial society, propagate anti-industrial ideas and give encouragement to those who hate the industrial system. . . .

Why do we announce our goals only now though we made our first bomb some seventeen years ago? Our early bombs were too ineffectual to attract much public attention or give encouragement to those who hate the system. . . .

So we went back to work, and after a long period of experimentation we developed a type of bomb that does not require a pipe, but is set off by a detonating cap that consists of a chlorate explosive packed into a piece of small diameter copper tubing. (The detonating cap is a miniature pipe bomb.) We used bombs of this type to blow up the genetic engineer Charles Epstein and the computer specialist David Gelernter.

Since we no longer have to confine the explosive in a pipe, we are now free of limitations on the size and shape of our bombs. We are pretty sure we know how to increase the power of our explosives and reduce the number of batteries needed to set them off. And, as we've just indicated, we think we now have more effective fragmentation material. So we expect to be able to pack deadly bombs into ever smaller, lighter and more harmless looking packages. On the other hand, we believe we will be able to make bombs much bigger than any we've made before. With a briefcase-full or a suitcase-full of explosives we should be able to blow out the walls of substantial buildings.

Clearly we are in a position to do a great deal of damage. And it doesn't appear that the FBI is going to catch us any time soon. The FBI is a joke.

The people who are pushing all this growth and progress garbage deserve to be severely punished. But our goal is less to punish them than to propagate ideas. Anyhow we are getting tired of making bombs. It's no fun having to spend all your evenings and weekends preparing dangerous mixtures, filing trigger mechanisms out of scraps of metal or searching the Sierras for a place isolated enough to test a bomb.

The mention of testing bombs in the Sierras sent law enforcement authorities scurrying on yet another wild goose chase. At the request of the FBI, forest rangers and sheriff's deputies combed the California countryside, sniffing the air in a search for smoke from incendiary devices. Kaczynski was surely delighted.

Further confusing for authorities was the fact that, with the Mosser bombing, the Unabomber's campaign seemed to have turned green. For the first time, he had explicitly targeted someone he saw as an enemy of the environment. Thanks to the similarities between the Unabomber's and the *Earth First! Journal*'s misspelling of "Burson," the agency inferred that the bomber had some ties to the group, and launched an intensive investigation of radical environmentalists.

After Kaczynski's arrest, the search of his cabin would prove that the FBI's hunch had been right. They found carbon copies of letters he had written to *Earth First!*, apparently seeking to enlist the organization as an ally. One was entitled "Suggestions for Earth First!ers from FC" (which Earth First! insists it never received), in which, correcting his earlier misspelling, Kaczynski admitted that "as for the Mosser bombing our attention was called to Burson-Marsteller by an article that appeared in *Earth First!, Litha*" (the magazine's way of describing the June 21, 1993, edition of that journal). He had also apparently written to *Earth First!*, *Live Wild or Die!*, and other radical environmental groups, offering secret codes for communicating and seeking meetings to discuss his "strategy for revolutionaries seeking to destroy the industrial system," including suggestions on "How to hit an Exxon Exec."

Unfortunately, authorities confined their search for these radicals to California, perhaps because they had long suspected, but had been unable to convict, two prominent Earth First! activists as bombers.

Back in May 1990, Earth First! leaders Judi Bari and Darryl Cherney had been driving down MacArthur Boulevard in Oakland, California, when their Subaru was nearly destroyed by a car bomb. Bari was critically injured and never fully recovered. Nevertheless, both the FBI and Alameda County police suspected that the two had built the bomb themselves, and that it had gone off accidentally while they were transporting it. They arrested the couple, but the charges were quickly dismissed for lack of evidence. Officials, however, continued to suspect that the two were guilty.

The Mosser bombing gave them an excuse to go after Cherney and Bari once again. They questioned them and their comrades closely, and combed the pot-growing environs of California's north coast, looking for suitably scruffy radicals (of which there were many).

But they never thought to look in Montana.

ON APRIL 24, 1995, Bob Taylor, staff biologist with the California Forestry Association in Sacramento, left his small office at the back of the building and walked out to the reception area to collect his mail. It was the noon hour. Michelle Goldsberry, the receptionist who normally sorted the mail, had gone to get an allergy shot. So Taylor, along with Jeannette Grimm, the controller, and Eleanor Anderson, the executive secretary, decided to sort it themselves.

When the association president, Gilbert Murray, walked in, Taylor called his attention to a small brown parcel, carefully fastened at each end with nylon strapping tape, that had been mistakenly addressed to Murray's predecessor, William Dennison, president of the California Forestry Association's antecedent, the Timber Association of California. The package had been sent from Oakland, hand-stamped with "Eugene O'Neill" and G-series "USA Old Glory" postal stamps. Taylor picked the package up and squeezed. It was heavy and hard and about the size and shape of a motorcycle battery.

"Maybe it's a bomb," Grimm joked. "Perhaps we should forward it to Bill."

"Let's open it first, to see what it is," Murray replied. "It could be association business, and belongs here."

Taylor cautioned Murray. The Oklahoma City bombing had occurred just five days earlier. They should be careful.

But Murray, forty-seven, a happy, outgoing man, didn't believe in conspiracy theories. A former marine, a Berkeley graduate, husband of a schoolteacher, and father of two boys, he loved nature. He had devoted his entire life to forestry, earning wide respect for his wise ecological approaches to land management that avoided both clear-cutting and herbicides. Why would he have enemies?

Murray started to open the package, then paused to ask Eleanor for scissors to cut the tough nylon packing tape. After snipping the tape, he lifted the package to his chest and began pulling the wrapper open with both hands. At that moment, the phone in the outer office rang, and Grimm went to answer it. Taylor, too, quickly left the room, joking, "I'm getting out of here before the bomb goes off."

About thirty seconds later, just as Taylor reached his desk, he heard a muffled *boom* and felt a strong pressure wave hit his face. He ran toward the reception area. Black smoke poured from the outer office. Both its doors were blown off their hinges and its suspended ceiling had collapsed, leaving a mound of tiles and insulation on the floor. The carpet had been incinerated. A huge fireball billowed through the raw opening that had once been a skylight. Furniture throughout the suite lay splintered. Shrapnel from the bomb had blasted like bullets through the thin partitions separating work areas, putting sledgehammer-sized dents in filing cabinets.

Outside the door where Murray had stood, Taylor found the women but no sign of their boss. Panicked, the biologist ran out the door and down the street to the fire station. All the trucks were out, the clerk told him.

Fire trucks and police began arriving just as Taylor returned. Murray was still missing. Then the police arrived. After evacuating the building and sifting through the rubble, they discovered why he had been so hard to find: He had literally been blown to bits.

"His face was ripped off; his arm was ripped off," the coroner said later. "There were parts of his body all over the room." Some pieces were so small, reportedly eleven body bags were needed to transport the remains.

In a covering letter to the *New York Times* sent on June 24, 1995, along with the manifesto, "FC" wrote: "We have no regret about the fact that our bomb blew up the wrong man, Gilbert Murray, instead of William Dennison, to whom it was addressed. Though Murray did not have Dennison's inflammatory style, he was pursuing the same goals, and he was probably pursuing them more effectively because of the very fact that he was not inflammatory."

The letter continued:

It was reported that the bomb that killed Gilbert Murray was a pipe bomb. It was not a pipe bomb but was set off by a homemade detonating cap. (The FBI's so-called experts should have been able to determine this quickly and easily, especially since we indicated in an unpublished part of our last letter to the NY Times—that the majority of our bombs are no longer pipe bombs.)

Indeed, "Experiment 245," as Kaczynski called it, wasn't a pipe bomb. Like "Experiment 244" that killed Mosser, the Murray bomb consisted of high explosive molded around a detonating cap.

Unlike Conrad's Professor, Kaczynski had actually found "the perfect detonator." And he was proud of it.

JUST AS KACZYNSKI's bombmaking emulated fiction, so, too, did his killing slavishly follow the "scientific method." He had transformed his victims into abstractions—mere "experiments"—that possessed neither flesh nor blood nor capacity for pain.

Indeed, his whole enterprise had become an abstraction. Kaczynski's reading of history augmented, for him, the importance and significance of his acts, while literature provided the role models. By murdering, he saw himself as a player in the next great revolution, one that would dismantle industrial civilization. He would exact revenge on behalf of all victims of the machine, from the forgotten people enslaved by the Pharaohs to build waterworks along the Nile to the Sioux mown down by Henry repeating rifles at Wounded Knee.

The books in his cabin library served as inspiration. He would avenge the Gallic king Vercingetorix, described in *Caesar and the Conquest of Gaul*, who lost the battle of Alesia in 52 B.C. to superior Roman engineering. He would strike back on behalf of the Aztec king Montezuma, whose culture, described by W. H. Prescott in the *History of the Conquest of Mexico* (1843), had been destroyed by Spaniards armed with gunpowder. He was Dostoevsky's Underground man, calling attention to alienated victims of "the system." He was Jean Valjean, the fugitive in Hugo's *Les Misérables*, pursued relentlessly by authorities for having committed a petty crime. He was Natty Bumppo in James Fenimore Cooper's *The Prairie*, lamenting, "How much has the beauty of the wilderness been deformed in two short lives!" He was Winston Smith fighting "Big Brother" in George Orwell's *1984*.

Kaczynski, in short, had become a cold-blooded killer not despite his intellect, but because of it. And when he occasionally began to feel sympathy for a victim (as he did momentarily for John Hauser), he would quickly catch himself. Sympathy had no place in research. Scientific method demanded that he suppress "subjective" feelings of compassion and focus on the "objective" results of his "experiments." Morality is unscientific, and twinges of conscience mere products of propaganda.

But intellect was only half the equation. Kaczynski was not merely acting out a philosophy; he was also very angry, not merely at an idea, but at *someone*. Only when these two streams—one intellectual, the other psychological—converged had he become a killer. His campaign against technological society incorporated this convergence. Anger provided the motivation, philosophy the rationale for murder.

Thus, the two streams ultimately became one. On October 2, 1990, Ted Kaczynski's father, Theodore Richard "Turk" Kaczynski, committed suicide. Around that time, according to Donald Foster, Kaczynski had a dream which impressed him so much he wrote a detailed account of it later. In it, Kaczynski is pursued by the "cult" of an evil personage known as "Lord Daddy Lombrosis."

The name is significant. Cesare Lombroso was a real person—a nineteenth-century Italian criminologist who believed in the inheritance of criminal traits and whose name appears briefly in *The Secret Agent*. In the novel, Conrad ridicules pseudoscience by depicting the gullible anarchist Ossipon as a Lombroso disciple.

According to Foster and to a parallel account that appeared in the *Washington Post*, Kaczynski describes his fierce encounter in the dream with three of Lord Daddy Lombrosis's henchmen, sent to enlist Ted's brother David in their "cult." But Kaczynski fights them off and kills them. Then Lombrosis himself appears, revealing, in Kaczynski's words, a "kindly, paternal, dignified expression on his face" and looking "like a man whom one could respect." So Kaczynski couldn't bring himself to kill Lord Daddy: "I felt awed by him and thought, 'This is God!' Yet in my heart I defied him." Lombrosis, he feared, sought to impose psychological dominance over him through "some sort of deception." While aware that Lombrosis was well intentioned, Kaczynski also realized that "the price that he demanded was *submission*"—that there can be no freedom for anyone until Lombrosis is overthrown. So Kaczynski stood in front of his brother, to shield him from Lord Daddy.

Rejected, Lombrosis starts to leave, but Kaczynski relents. For David's sake, he runs after Lombrosis and asks him to return:

> *I threw myself at his feet and cried, "No, don't leave my brother without hope, give him another chance!" and I started to say, "and me too," but I caught myself and said, "No! Not me! I will never give in!" . . . But the footprints just kept going off through the snow. And then I woke up with a terrible sense of fear and foreboding.*

Whom does Lombrosis represent? Foster suggests it is Turk. Kaczynski has denied this, suggesting the character symbolizes technological society. More likely, Lord Daddy embodies the convergence of the philosophical and the personal that Sally Johnson in her psychiatric report noted—of Kaczynski's concerns about society with his personal anger at someone. So this dream character embodies an abstract intellectual idea that simultaneously evokes a passionate, personal hatred.

Why is Kaczynski angry? At whom is his hatred directed? And what is the connection between this person or persons and the ideas that Kaczynski so despises?

Eventually, Kaczynski would provide clues. But no one would be listening.

5

The Face in
the Mirror

Without a revolutionary theory there can be no revolutionary movement.

—V. I. LENIN,
What Is to Be Done?

The nineteenth century dislike of Realism is the rage of
Caliban seeing his own face in a glass.

—OSCAR WILDE,
The Picture of Dorian Gray

B Y THE SUMMER of 1995, it was clear the Unabomber had a desperate urge for the world to take his ideas seriously. Since the Epstein and Gelernter bombings he had become a prolific correspondent, writing, under the alias of "FC," a dozen letters—to the *New York Times*, Gelernter, Nobel Prize–winning geneticists Richard Roberts and Phillip Sharp, the *San Francisco Examiner*, *Scientific American*, *Penthouse*, and the social psychologist Tom Tyler—claiming credit for bombings, making new threats, but above all, explaining his philosophy. And the last four letters contained an amazing enclosure.

In the last week of June 1995, the *New York Times*, the *Washington Post*, *Penthouse* magazine, and Tyler all received a 35,000-word document entitled "Industrial Society and Its Future, by FC," that the FBI quickly dubbed "the Unabomber manifesto."

In his covering letter to Tyler, the Unabomber expressed hope that his manuscript might stimulate a dialogue between himself and Tyler concerning social ills.

> *Do you think our analysis of PRESENT social problems is approximately correct? If not, why not? How would you answer our arguments?*
>
> *If you think we have identified some present social problems correctly, do you think anything can be done about them? Will they get better or worse with continued growth and progress?*

In his covering letter to the three publications, the Unabomber made an offer he hoped they couldn't refuse: Publish the manifesto, or someone would perish. To the *Times* and *Post* he promised, "If the enclosed manuscript is published reasonably soon and receives wide public exposure, we will permanently desist from terrorism. . . ." Realizing that publication in *Penthouse*, as a less "respectable" exposure for his ideas, wouldn't be as rewarding for his reputation as a thinker, the bomber made that magazine a less generous offer: "We promise to desist permanently from terrorism, except that we reserve the right to plant one (and only one) bomb intended to kill, after our manuscript has been published." In other words, the bomber believed that maintaining the "respectability" of his ideas was worth a human life. He gave all three publications three months to decide.

This set off a flurry of debate in the media over the ethics and wisdom of publishing, under duress, the works of a killer. The newspapers, fearing the precedent, were reluctant to accept this devil's bargain. But after Attorney General Janet Reno urged them to publish the manuscript with the hopes that someone might recognize its authorship, the newspapers reluctantly agreed. On the 19th of September, the *Wash-*

ington Post in collaboration with the *New York Times* published the entire essay as a special supplement. (*Penthouse* never did.)

The manifesto would turn out to be an extraordinary document. Since writing his 1971 essay, Kaczynski had added some intriguing twists, and fooled the entire country.

"The Industrial Revolution and its consequences," the manifesto begins, "have been a disaster for the human race." They have led to the growth of a technological system dependent on a massive social, economic, and political order, which suppresses individual freedom and destroys nature. "The system does not and cannot exist to satisfy human needs. Instead, it is human behavior that has to be modified to fit the needs of the system."

By forcing people to conform to the system rather than vice versa, technology creates a sick society hostile to human potential. It fosters rapid change that leads to the breakdown of local, human-scale communities. As it requires a high degree of social and economic organization, it encourages the growth of crowded and unlivable cities and of megastates, indifferent to the needs of citizens.

This evolution toward a civilization increasingly dominated by technology and the power structure serving it cannot be stopped. For the appeal of technology "is a more powerful social force than the aspiration for freedom," and "while technological progress AS A WHOLE continually narrows our sphere of freedom, each new technical advance CONSIDERED BY ITSELF appears to be desirable."

Hence, science and technology constitute "a mass power movement, and scientists gratify their need for power through identification with this mass movement." So "the technophiles are taking us all on an utterly reckless ride into the unknown."

Since human beings must conform to the machine, "our society tends to regard as a 'sickness' any mode of thought or behavior that is inconvenient for the system, and this is plausible because when an individual doesn't fit into the system it causes pain to the individual as well as problems for the system. Thus the manipulation of an individual to adjust him to the system is seen as a 'cure' for a 'sickness' and therefore as good."

This requirement has led to an entire social infrastructure dedicated to modifying behavior, which includes a plethora of law enforcement agencies with ever-expanding surveillance powers; an out-of-control regulatory system that is encouraging limitless multiplication of governmental regulations; an educational establishment that employs psychological science to promote conformism at the secondary level, while enforcing "political correctness" in colleges; ubiquitous "sex and violence" on television whose role is to offer people escape from the feelings of "stress, anxiety, frustration, dissatisfaction" that technological civilization brings into their lives, and a medical and psychological establishment that promotes the indiscriminate use of "anti-depressant drugs" as "a means of modifying an individual's internal state in such a way as to enable him to tolerate social conditions that he would otherwise find intolerable.

The mass media, in particular, "are mostly under the control of large organizations that are integrated into the system. To make an impression on society with words is therefore almost impossible for most individuals and small groups."

Hence, the economic, political, and educational establishments, by serving this power structure, are part of the problem, not the solution. Political ideologies are irrelevant. "Conservatives are fools: They whine about the decay of traditional values, yet they enthusiastically support technological progress and economic growth" that undermine these very values. "Leftists" are "over-socialized" victims of a technological system that requires conformism and preaches that it is "the duty of individuals to serve society and the duty of society is to serve individuals." They have been brainwashed to favor social planning, and remain hostile to individualism.

Consequently, "Industrial-technological society cannot be reformed." Rather, "it is likely that technology will eventually acquire something approaching complete control over human behavior." Possibly, society's most important decisions will come to be made by computers rather than humans. Then, our enslavement will be complete.

Since the system cannot be reformed, it must be destroyed. Indeed, at some time in the future the system will collapse on its own, when the weight of human suffering it creates becomes unbearable to too many. But the longer it persists, the more devastating will be the ultimate collapse. Hence, "revolutionaries" such as "FC," "by hastening the onset of the breakdown will be reducing the extent of the disaster. . . ."

"We have no illusions about the feasibility of creating a new, ideal form of society. Our goal is only to destroy the existing form of society." But this movement does have a positive goal as well. It is promoting "WILD nature," which is the opposite of technology. And while "eliminating industrial society" and promoting wild nature may have some "negative consequences . . . well, you can't eat your cake and have it too."

WITHIN HOURS after the *Post* had published the 56-page manifesto, several other newspapers followed suit. Time Warner put it on its Pathfinder, a free Internet site. By the end of the day, thousands of readers had downloaded the document. Soon, paperback editions appeared, becoming best-sellers.

Reaction was immediate. No other essay in recent times had elicited such a variety of responses. To many general readers, as well as a few in the mainstream press, the manifesto struck a sympathetic chord. "I've never seen the likes of this," observed Michael Rustigan, a criminologist specializing in serial killers. "Numbers of people . . . seem to identify in some way with him."

Writing for *Time* magazine, Robert Wright confessed that "We may not share his approach to airing a grievance, but the grievance itself feels familiar . . . we at times get the feeling that modern life isn't what we were designed for." Kirkpatrick Sale announced, in *The Nation*, that the manifesto's first sentence "is absolutely crucial for the American public to understand and ought to be on the forefront of the nation's political agenda." On the Internet—curiously, the medium of choice for radical anarchists—fan sites multiplied like computer viruses, the Church of Euthanasia Freedom Club, Unapack, the Unabomber Political Action Committee, alt.fan.unabomber, Chuck's Unabomb page, MetroActive, and Steve Hau's Rest Stop, among others. Some, such as the Unabomber Political Action Committee, sponsored him as a tongue-in-cheek presidential candidate, and suggested a bumper sticker that said: "Don't Blame Me—I Voted for the Unabomber."

A few university scholars praised the manifesto. University of Wisconsin professor David Lindberg noted that it was "extraordinarily well-written." Keith Benson, professor of medical history and ethics at the University of Washington, maintained that the manifesto was "certainly not the rantings of a crazy man . . . there is an element of truth to what he is talking about."

But while the manifesto did have a following among some ordinary folk, avowed anarchists, and writers and scholars, the vast majority of academicians and press pundits either condemned it or welcomed the opportunities it provided for tarring their political enemies. Jack Lesch, associate professor at the University of California at Berkeley, complained that the Unabomber's "vision of things is not scholarly." Catholic University classics professor William McCarthy dismissed it as "a long, tedious screed." Conservative commentators called attention to the resemblances between the manifesto and environmentalist rhetoric. Columnist Tony Snow noticed that "it sounds like Al Gore's book *Earth in the Balance.*"

For providing their enemies with such ammunition, most environmentalists abhorred the document. Betty Ball, a director of the Mendocino Environmental Center, complained that the similarities between the manifesto's message and that of the environmental movement "is turning the public off and alienating the public." Mainstream media and columnists of all political persuasions nonchalantly condemned the essay. The *Houston Chronicle* dubbed it a "diatribe"; *The* (Portland) *Oregonian* complained of its "obsessively repeated theme." Ellen Goodman called it "impenetrable." Maggie Scarf, writing in *The New Republic*, saw it as a sign of a "narcissistic personality disorder."

In short everyone had an opinion. And this is odd because, as the Newsbyte Network observed in October, "little of the attention is being focused on the ideas the bomber is trying to promote." Indeed as *The Oregonian* observed more succinctly (and with only slight exaggeration) at the time, apparently "nobody actually read it."

And soon, after the initial flurry of national attention died down, discussion of the manifesto's content disappeared entirely. The media continued to focus on whether the *Post* had been ethically justified in publishing it, but ignored the philosophy. College professors showed none of their usual penchant for analyzing pop cultural phenomena in excessive detail and passed on the manifesto—neither assigning it in classes nor writing about it themselves. Radical anarchists and Earth

First!ers, as well as moderate greens, embarrassed by the Una-bomber's apparent endorsement of their agenda to save "wild nature," simply wanted him to go away. Conservative libertarians, uncomfortable that the Unabomber had also endorsed their agenda of individual liberty, showed no desire to engage him in a philosophical discussion.

The manifesto was ignored, in sum, not because its ideas were so foreign, but because they were so familiar. Except for the call to violence, its message was ordinary and unoriginal. The concerns it evinced, about the effects of technology on culture and nature, are widely shared, especially among the country's most highly educated.

The manifesto was an academic—and popular—cliché, a mirror in which many people saw something about themselves they did not like. The Unabomber had committed murder to promote their very own ideas. And if these ideas can lead one person to kill, what did they say about the rest of us?

Tony Snow was therefore right that the Unabomber's ideas resembled Al Gore's. But he was right for the wrong reason. Not, as Snow would have it, because some special affinity existed between the two men, but because these ideas resembled virtually everyone else's opinions as well. For more than a generation, Americans had been gripped by fear of, or revulsion against, the very science and technology the Unabomber now warned about: genetic engineering; pollution, pesticides, and herbicides; brainwashing of children by educators and consumers by advertising; mind control, cars, SUVs, power plants and power lines, radioactive waste; big government, big business; computer threats to privacy; materialism, television, cities, suburbs, cell phones, ozone depletion, global warming; and many other aspects of modern life.

The manifesto, in short, embodied the conventional wisdom of the entire country. Its message was not just found in *Earth in the Balance*, but also in virtually every school and college textbook, every book on ecology or natural philosophy, every environmental best-seller for more than a generation. It was nothing less than the contemporary American creed.

Thus, *Rainforest*, a story for small children used in many preschools that eerily resembles Kaczynski's favorite tale, "Juan Darien," tells of a man on a bulldozer who destroys the rainforest and its animal life. Justice is done when the rains come and wash the bulldozer over a cliff, killing the man. A drawing shows the man falling to his death. "The Machine was washed away!" the book exclaims. "But the creatures of the rainforest were safe." A junior high school geography text, *Exploring a Changing World*, observes that China "has a lot to show the developing world about producing food. . . . They rely on human labor rather than expensive machines." A college text, *Environmental Science: Sustaining the Earth* by G. Tyler Miller, Jr., criticizes the Industrial Revolution as promoting overconsumption and a "throwaway worldview."

Where the manifesto observed that "only with the Industrial Revolution did the effect of human society on nature become really devastating," Barry Commoner's best-seller, *The Closing Circle* (1971), warned that "The chief reason for the environmental crisis that has engulfed the United States in recent years is the sweeping transformation of productive technology. . . ." Just as the manifesto prophesied that "the bigger the system grows the more disastrous the results of its breakdown will be," E. F. Schumacher's best-seller, *Small is Beautiful* (1973), lamented that "the modern world has been shaped by technology. It tumbles from crisis to crisis; on all sides there are prophecies of disaster and, indeed, visible signs of breakdown." As the manifesto declared that "people could be pushed only so far and no farther" by technology, Schumacher, too, drew the line in the sand, writing that "human nature revolts against inhuman technological, organizational, and political patterns, which it experiences as suffocating and debilitating."

Just as the manifesto warned of the increased use of "psychological techniques for controlling human behavior," so too, as we've seen, did Theodore Roszak warn of the same thing in *Where the Wasteland Ends*. Just as the manifesto lamented that "there are the methods of propaganda, for which the mass communication media provide effective vehicles," so Fritjof Capra's popular book *The Turning Point* (1982), observed that "advertising on television influences the content and form of all programs, including the 'news shows,' and uses the tremendous suggestive power of this medium . . . to shape people's imagery, distort their sense of reality, and determine their views, tastes, and behavior."

The manifesto complained of "the isolation of man from nature . . . and the break-down of natural small-scale communities such as the extended family, the village or the tribe." George Sessions and Bill Devall's *Deep Ecology: Living As If Nature Mattered*, which became the radical activists' bible, observed that "technological society not only alienates humans from the rest of Nature but also alienates humans from themselves and from each other."

The manifesto noted that "science and technology constitute a mass power movement." Kirkpatrick Sale's *Dwellers in the Land: The Bioregional Vision* declared that "the scientific worldview has become more encompassing and pervasive with each passing generation, each passing century and today it goes almost without challenge. . . . It is the source and sustenance of our economy. It is the latticework of our political system. . . . It has become, in short, our God."

The father of the Deep Ecology movement, Arne Naess, bemoaned in *Ecology, Community and Lifestyle* that "a global culture of a primarily techno-industrial nature is now encroaching upon all the world's milieux, desecrating living conditions for future generations." The manifesto noted that technology "will certainly subject human beings to greater indignities and inflict greater damage on the natural world."

And just as the manifesto suggested it was better to "build an icehouse or preserve food by drying or pickling than own a refrigerator," so Bill McKibben's best-seller, *The End of Nature*, recommended against "every family's owning a washer" and excoriated the "inertia of affluence." Kaczynski declared that "we . . . advocate a revolution against the industrial system. This revolution may or may not make use of violence." McKibben asked readers to consider "extreme solutions, [as] we live in an extreme time . . . if industrial civilization is ending nature, it is not utter silliness to talk about ending—or at least, transforming—industrial civilization."

If investigators, scholars, and the media had paid closer attention to the manifesto, however, they would have found it to be a far more equivocal document than they supposed, filled with clues whose solutions could have provided pointers about its author and his intentions.

The manifesto, for example, repeatedly warned of the dangers of science (declaring that "science marches on blindly, without regard to the real welfare of the human race" and that "technophiles are taking us all on an utterly reckless ride into the unknown"). Yet, as he made clear in his letters to the *Times* and others, Kaczynski carefully followed the scientific method. The manifesto warns of the threats posed by propaganda and behavior modification, and its author even bombed a leading behavioral psychologist (James McConnell), yet as social philosopher Scott Corey notes, the manifesto makes frequent use of behaviorist terminology. Just as this school of psychology focuses on observable determinants of behavior, such as rewards and punishment, goal formation, failure or success at achieving goals, so, too, the manifesto spoke of "deprivation with respect to the power process," "goals," "goal fulfilment," "non-attainment of goals," and "surrogate activities." It even defined its crucial concept of freedom behavioristically—"participation in the power process."

But a bigger clue was the manifesto's apparent debt to Jacques Ellul, the French Protestant philosopher and lay theologian whose book *The Technological Society* Kaczynski would later stress—to court psychiatrist Sally Johnson, to the Sacramento court, and in a letter to me— had been very important to him. In his critique of Johnson's report, he commented that "when I read the book . . . for the first time, I was delighted, because I thought, 'Here is someone who is saying what I have already been thinking.'" He had even corresponded with Ellul.

Indeed, the manifesto did seem to take several key points from *The Technological Society*: that "technology" represents a category of knowledge and not just machinery; that technological progress is irreversible; that the effects of innovation cannot be predicted; and that technology and the state are coeval and mutually dependent. But nowhere is Ellul cited in the manifesto. This may have been because Ellul had died by the time of its publication, and mention of him might have prompted the FBI to interview his heirs, thereby possibly turning up a letter from Kaczynski. But there is another possible reason: *The manifesto ignored—in fact, rejected—much of what Ellul wrote.* "Despite its debt to Ellul," as Corey put it, the manifesto's "program is in blunt defiance of his expressed beliefs."

Corey notes that Ellul's later works—*Autopsy of Revolution* (1971) and *The Ethics of Freedom* (1976)—retracted several key points the philosopher had written in *The Technological Society*. Even the earliest book explicitly rejected the idea that freedom could be achieved through political action, or through escape into wilderness. In his subsequent works, Ellul would warn that freedom and power are antitheses of one another (contravening the manifesto's definition of freedom as "participation in the power process"); that anarchists are hopeless utopians; that revolution will only lead to greater tyranny; and that the only significant revolution would be an intellectual and spiritual one, when people embrace reason and seek salvation through Jesus Christ.

In short, despite corresponding with Ellul, Kaczynski ignored virtually all that the French philosopher had written since 1964, particularly his pacifist and spiritual ideas. It would seem Kaczynski "imprinted" on early Ellul and ignored what followed. The later FBI search of Kaczynski's cabin would reveal that he did not even own a copy of *The Ethics of Freedom*. Kaczynski's faith in the efficacy of revolution had apparently remained unchanged despite, not because of, the later admonitions of Ellul.

KACZYNSKI'S COMMITMENT TO revolution also posed a problem for him in writing the manifesto: how to sway public opinion. And Ellul's ideas, even his later ones, were considered old-fashioned by 1995; they would not gain Kaczynski many converts. To make the manifesto a rallying cry for his war on technology, he needed to infuse it with more popular ideas.

For the manifesto was not just a philosophical treatise but also a political declaration. It was meant to attract and rally supporters, not merely offer a consistent exposition of ideas. It was opportunistic, intended to take advantage of the rare chance newspaper publication afforded for reaching a large audience. So the arguments it expressed included everything but the kitchen sink.

Thus, the manifesto's apparent resemblance to the conventional wisdom of contemporary America was no accident. In fact, it was entirely intentional. To capture a wide audience, it offered a veritable tossed salad of ideas. Like a literary supermarket from which readers could take what they wanted and leave the rest, it borrowed from or partially embodied the ideas of Aristotle, Jefferson, and Marx; social critics Lewis Mumford, Erich Fromm, Paul Goodman, and Eric Hoffer; economists Thorsten Veblen, E. F. Schumacher, and Leopold Kohr; philosophers Oswald Spengler, Arthur Schopenhauer, Friedrich Nietzsche, and

Hannah Arendt; cultural anthropologists Ruth Benedict and Margaret Mead; psychologists Sigmund Freud, Alfred Adler, and B. F. Skinner; sociologists Theodor W. Adorno and Talcott Parsons; and many, many other thinkers including, of course, Ellul.

Above all else, the manifesto was intended as a rallying cry for revolution. And the most coldly calculating part of this strategy was its apparently insincere embrace of environmentalism. Kaczynski had dressed his message in green not, it would seem, because he was a devoted environmentalist but because he thought it would make his treatise more popular. His mention of "wild nature" was, at best, an afterthought or a joke played on readers, but more probably a cynical attempt to win more supporters for his revolution.

Certainly, it's evident that Kaczynski did not care about ecology or the environment. His 1971 essay did not mention nature at all. His bombing campaign was more than sixteen years old before he targeted a victim (John Mosser) for supposedly environmental reasons. The manifesto, while making occasional passing references to environmental decline, never mentions ecology. Its first full discussion of "wild nature" does not appear until paragraph 183 of the 232-paragraph document, in the section entitled "Strategy" and clearly intended as a discussion of ways to recruit converts to his cause. "An ideology," he writes,

> in order to gain enthusiastic support, must have a positive ideal as well as a negative one; it must be FOR something as well as AGAINST something. The positive ideal that we propose is Nature. That is, WILD nature: those aspects of the functioning of the Earth and its living things that are independent of human management and free of human interference and control.

Later, FBI searchers would find an undated handwritten note in Kaczynski's cabin that confessed in part:

> I don't even believe in the cult of nature-worshipers or wilderness-worshipers (I am perfectly ready to litter in parts of the woods that are of no use to me—I often throw cans in logged-over areas or in places much frequented by people; I don't find wilderness particularly healthy physically; I don't hesitate to poach).

Scott Corey, one of the few scholars to analyze the manifesto thoroughly, calls it a "political compromise." The manifesto certainly put forward two incompatible theories: one philosophical, which Kaczynski probably believed; and the other environmental, which he knew would be popular.

The first—what appears to be Kaczynski's core philosophy—is a social theory. It is opposed to bigness—big government, big business, big science—because it supposed these destroy liberty. And technology, according to this view, not only makes bigness possible but also enhances the power of these institutions to destroy local cultures and limit human freedom. Pursuing cheap labor, multinational corporations move factories from one country to another, putting thousands out of work and destroying the economies of entire regions. Yet these corporations could not function without jet planes, computers, satellites, and telephones. Governments have become so huge, cumbersome, and impersonal that they have undermined their own democratic institutions. Yet they could not grow without the enormous power that big science gives them—through transportation, communications, and the capacity to make advanced weapons. Science and technology provide bureaucrats with the tools to control—through propaganda, the educational system, and surveillance—billions of people.

The solution, according to this first theory, is to replace bigness with smallness. Only solitary individuals or those in small, voluntary associations can enjoy freedom (defined by Kaczynski as "ability to participate in the power process"). Yet the only way to shrink institutions is to take away their tools of power, namely, technology. Technology serves the modern state and the state supports technology. The two rise or fall together. So the state cannot be overturned without destroying technology first.

The second theory, which Kaczynski may have proffered not because he believed it but for its popularity, is about nature: It supposes that at the beginning of time the world was perfect, and that it has been going downhill ever since. Therefore, it proposes to turn the clock back several millennia, to undo civilization and return the earth to its original state of nature. This view is sometimes called "Luddite," in reference to the incidents that took place in Nottingham, England, in 1811–16, when millworkers, angry at losing their jobs to machines and led by a masked man who called himself "General Ned Ludd," went on the rampage, destroying looms.

The first theory, in sum, Kaczynski seems to have truly believed; the second he apparently advocated merely for tactical reasons. The first concerns culture; the second, nature; the first, freedom; the second, preservation. The first is conservative, the second more liberal. The first wants government to shrink, allowing for local control by human-scale communities; the second wants it to grow (an implication of their agenda that neither Kaczynski nor many environmental activists seem to realize or care to admit), by annexing more national parks and National Forest wilderness. The first wants to redraw the map of the world into self-governing communities; the second wants to evict people entirely from much of the globe, returning the earth to wilderness. The first addresses issues of cultural survival for contemporary indigenous peoples; the second idealizes the Pleistocene aborigines who once roamed the planet, but not their modern descendants, contemporary natives, who are excoriated when they try to kill a seal or salmon.

And both ideas are very ancient.

In their landmark book, *Primitivism and Related Ideas in Antiquity*, the historians Arthur O. Lovejoy and George Boas identify two versions of what they call "primitivism" that have persisted in Western thought at least since the fifth century B.C.

The first, cultural primitivism, "is the discontent of the civilized with civilization, or with some conspicuous and characteristic feature of it. It is the belief of men living in a relatively highly evolved and complex cultural condition that a life far simpler and less sophisticated in some or in all respects is a more desirable life."

The second, chronological primitivism, in several of its iterations supposes "that the highest degree of excellence or happiness in man's life existed at the beginning of history." This is the notion embedded in the foundation myths of societies throughout history, such as the Garden of Eden of the Bible and the Golden Age, or Age of Cronus, in Greek mythology. Chronological primitivists therefore idealize aboriginal peoples, whom they suppose embody the innocence of mankind before the Fall, and they look back fondly to a time when people lived "close to nature."

Each kind of primitivism, Lovejoy and Boas explain, comes in various guises. Some chronological primitivists, for example, believe that while the world has been in decline since the beginning, this deterioration can be reversed, leading to restoration of a golden age. Cultural primitivists differ, depending on what it is about civilization they don't like: some reject the institution of marriage and advocate the "community of wives and children" or "sexual promiscuity, including incest." Others object to eating meat, supposing that in the "State of Nature," everyone had been a vegetarian. And some long to establish a preindustrial "state of nature," in which "the condition of human life . . . is most free from the intrusion of 'art,' i.e., in which none, or at most only the simplest and most rudimentary, of the practical arts are known."

The popularity of various primitivist ideas, these scholars explain, has waxed and waned throughout history. And at the time of their writing (1935), it was on the rise. "Since the beginning of the present century, Western man has become increasingly skeptical concerning the nineteenth century 'myth of progress,' increasingly troubled with misgivings about the value of the outcome of civilization thus far, and about the future to which it tends, and about himself as the author of it all."

And these concerns are very similar to the "doubts and apprehensions [that] found expression two millennia and more ago. In spite of the more complex and sophisticated general ideology of the contemporary exponents of these moods, there are striking parallels to be observed between certain of the [ancient] texts and some passages in, e.g., such writings as Freud's *Civilization and its Discontents* and Spengler's *Man and Technics*."

And striking parallels, too, between these ancient ideas and Kaczynski's manifesto. For its core philosophy—the one Kaczynski appears to believe sincerely—was a species of cultural primitivism. Following Lovejoy and Boas's definition, it expressed "discontent" with a "conspicuous aspect of civilization," namely, technology. And the document's second, or tactical, philosophy was an example of chronological primitivism. It advocated returning the earth to a state of nature.

After Lovejoy and Boas's book, cultural primitivism would become ascendant and remain so until the mid-1960s. Not just Freud and Spengler but countless contemporary writers, from the Harvard social philosopher Lewis Mumford to Ellul himself, warned that technological progress threatened the future of culture.

Many economists and ecologists prominent during this period carried this theme forward. One was Ellul. Another was E. F. Schumacher, whose *Small Is Beautiful* would be hailed as a seminal treatise on cultural revival. A third was Schumacher's close friend and colleague, the Austrian economist Leopold Kohr, whose book *The Breakdown of Nations* (1957) was among the first to preach the "ecology of scale."

In Great Britain in the 1960s, Kohr formed part of a small coterie of believers in "smallness" that included Schumacher, the Anglican priest John Papworth, and Edward Goldsmith, cousin of corporate raider Sir James Goldsmith. Meeting at Papworth's home, they founded what Papworth called the "Fourth World" movement, which rejected "the existing power structures . . . not because they are capitalist or Communist or fascist or whatever, but simply because they are too big." In 1971, Goldsmith started his own periodical, *The Ecologist*, and dedicated himself to protecting Third World peoples from the decimating effects of multinational commerce. And in 1973, Schumacher's *Small Is Beautiful* rocked the world.

To these people, the requirement that societies be small and diverse was merely the application to politics of the principle of biological diversity. Its corollary is that political mistakes have ecological consequences. The trend to bigness not only lowers living standards and destroys cultures, it is also the source of the world's environmental crisis. As institutions grow, they require more complex technologies to serve them, which in turn have devastating effects on the environment. History becomes a vicious circle, as each scientific advance produces a jump in population growth, leading to bigger political and economic units, still more massive technologies, further population growth, and greater social and ecological damage.

But as the modern environmental movement grew in the decades following publication of Rachel Carson's *Silent Spring* in 1962, national attention in America shifted from worry about culture to worry about nature. The small group of "Fourth Worlders" around Kohr and Schumacher got smaller still, as age and death reduced their numbers. American environmentalists in particular—both radicals and mainstreamers—became thoroughly Luddite, dedicated to the goals of chronological primitivism.

Groups such as the Sierra Club, Greenpeace, and the Wilderness Society grew into large, nationwide movements dedicated not to shrinking government but to enlarging it. By lobbying at the federal level, they sought to persuade Congress and successive administrations to purchase and manage more wilderness to "restore original ecosystems." By 1995, this campaign had been hugely successful. Restoring "pre-Columbian conditions" and "recreating the primitive scene" had become national policy, pursued by all federal land management agencies, including the U.S. Forest Service, the National Park Service, and the Bureau of Land Management.

As a would-be revolutionary, therefore, Kaczynski faced a problem. A small band of sexagenarians advocating a "Fourth World" philosophy of cultural primitivism conceived by a now-dead French theologian and led by a middle-aged Anglican priest would hardly serve as the core of hardened activists that the task at hand demanded. A real revolution had to be a mass movement. Fortunately, such a mass movement already existed. It was called environmentalism, which advocated chronological prmitivism. All Kaczynski had to do, therefore, was reach out to these people. First, by making contact with Earth First! and other radical green organizations, which he did. And second, by publishing a document that would appeal to as many environmentalists as possible. That meant he had to dress his ideas in the garb of chronological primitivism and advocate restoring "wild nature."

Of course, it is possible that Kaczynski put forward these two (chronological and cultural) theories not for tactical reasons but simply because he failed to note their incompatibility. But given his logical mind, this is unlikely. It is more probable that his proffering both theories was, indeed, tactical. And if so, then in having his manifesto published he had pulled off a colossal stunt. His previous deceptions, "Wu—It works! I told you it would.—RV," "Call Nathan R—Wed 7 pm," the word games with "wood" and package bomb addresses—may have momentarily confused the FBI. But now he had fooled the entire country, not just for a few weeks but for years! Everyone believed he was an environmentalist.

For a short while after the manifesto appeared, Kaczynski could enjoy his prank. He had fooled the country and gotten away with it. And he remained convinced he would never be caught. The FBI, as he told the *New York Times*, was "a joke." But ultimately, the joke would be on him. By promoting a philosophy as his own that had become conventional wisdom in the entire country, he did not win more adherents to his cause. Rather, he repelled most people because few wished to think that someone had committed murder on behalf of ideas that they cherished. And the very fact that his core philosophy (cultural primitivism) had remained substantially unchanged for decades would turn out to be the key leading to his capture.

6

Ah, Wilderness!

An American, insofar as he is new and different at all, is a
civilized man who has renewed himself in the wild.

—WALLACE STEGNER

No one does anything from a single motive.

—SAMUEL TAYLOR COLERIDGE,
Biographia Literaria

NORTHWEST OF HELENA, past the huge Sieben Ranch belonging
to the family of U.S. senator Max Baucus, up the winding road
toward the continental divide, over Fisher Pass, into the Lewis
and Clark National Forest, past Whiskey Gulch, and next to the Little
Blackfoot River lies Lincoln, Montana—the tiny town that sits along
U.S. Route 200 atop the continental divide, just below the Bob Marshall Wilderness.

In winter, the sun seldom shines in Lincoln. And when it is visible,
and the clouds that otherwise would be holding the warmth close to the

earth dissipate, the air gets so cold you can hear your boots squeak in the snow. Even then, the surrounding mountains block the light until late morning and bring darkness by midafternoon, while at midday, the big Douglas firs and ponderosa pine filter the light so it casts an eerie, twilight orange that locals call alpine glow.

Near the Stemple Pass road that parallels Poorman Creek, up a tiny tributary called Canyon Creek, not far from Butch Gehring's sawmill, it's darker still. There, tall trees cast perpetual shadows, creating a half-light phantasmagoria of shifting patterns along the stream bottom, where Kaczynski lived. The spot seems less to reflect the benign nature idealized in environmentalist imaginations than it does the foreboding forest of a medieval fairy tale: Until authorities removed it following his arrest in April 1996, Kaczynski's cabin stood here beneath the pines, like an obelisk memorializing some long-forgotten spirits. When I visited in the spring of 1997, an eight foot high chain link fence surrounded the building site, seemingly foretelling the fate that awaited the cabin's owner. Around the campfire next to it I could see a ring of blackened boulders, supporting a single, swordlike spit far too large for its intended purpose of skewering rabbits. Black plastic pipe that siphoned water from the creek snaked through the grass. The woven wire around what had been the vegetable garden lay badly trampled by night animals. The entrance to the spacious root cellar across the creek looked like an open sore on the ground.

SHORTLY AFTER the Civil War, Union veterans prospecting for gold found yellow ore in a gulch they named Abe Lincoln, establishing a town they called Springfield, in honor of the slain president's birthplace. Eventually, the community boasted two major placer mines and was renamed Lincoln.

When the mines played out, Lincoln became just another sleepy little rest stop on the highway between Great Falls and Missoula. Pine needles accumulated next to log buildings, where one could buy gas, maps, or hamburgers. The side streets remained gravel tracks leading to widely spaced cabins. At first glance, Lincoln seemed caught in a time warp—a place of 1930s tourist cabins and Mom-and-Pop diners where one could get honest-to-goodness milk shakes, made in a blender with real ice cream. And indeed, when Ted Kaczynski arrived in June 1971, Lincoln was still a place where folks from Great Falls stopped to get groceries on their way into the Bob Marshall, or to the Little Blackfoot River to cast flies at trout.

But although Lincoln still looks old-fashioned, it isn't any longer. Neither is it a modern resort or retirement community. And being on the major route between Great Falls and Missoula, it isn't even as isolated as it once was, or as it still seems to visitors from New York or Los Angeles.

In most regions of this sparsely populated state, everybody knows everybody. Inhabitants have some connection with ranching, have skin like leather, and wear Stetsons that look as though they've been used as truck seat cushions. Anyone encountered on the road with an unfamiliar face and not driving a three-quarter-ton four-wheel-drive pickup with a Winchester lever action 30–30 on a rack and a blue heeler herding dog riding in the bed is assumed lost.

But Lincoln, experiencing an influx of newcomers, no longer fitted this mold. It had become a community of strangers. Kaczynski's two closest neighbors had recently arrived from California. Two others maintained permanent residences elsewhere and visited Lincoln only occasionally.

Even before Robert Redford's movie A River Runs Through It appeared in 1992, western Montana had been discovered by the beautiful people. Upscale refugees from cities flocked to the mountains to catch trout, buy land, and build summer cabins. National magazines began describing it as "the last best place." And soon real estate prices were going through the roof.

This in turn attracted less affluent and equally opportunistic folk— blue-collar fortune hunters hoping to make a killing in real estate. The usual demographic forces that drove ranchers out of Aspen, ruined the fishing in Santa Fe, and spread ticky-tacky blight in Jackson, Wyoming, were now at work in Montana.

Towns like Bozeman, Livingston, and Big Timber, having already attracted movie stars, media moguls, and families with inherited wealth, took the brunt of this invasion. And because these places became chic ghettos for the super rich, they got the most attention.

But this immigration also affected less well known communities such as Lincoln, where blue-collar families arrived in increasing numbers searching for less expensive lots. Right behind them came the rednecked builders and real estate speculators, after quick bucks. And just down the road, Canyon Creek was becoming gentrified, as ranchers began selling parcels for million-dollar vacation homes to affluent bicoastal recreationists.

At the same time, the forests around Lincoln had been discovered by Earth First!ers, "Stumps Suck" activists, and other scruffy "back-to-the-landers," who built hippy shacks in mountain coulees, planted pot, and dreamed of Ecotopia.

Lincoln, in sum, had become a community without an identity. Even the few remaining old-timers had grown accustomed to seeing bearded, earth-toned hippies and soft-skinned strangers clad in Orvis fishing vests, morosely eyeing one another by the cash register at Garland's General Store. So it wasn't surprising that they didn't notice when, in mid-March 1996, six FBI agents from the agency's San Francisco office moseyed into town.

SPECIAL AGENTS Don Sachtleben, "Mad Max" Noel, and Jim Freeman ensconced themselves at the 7-Up Lodge, while their evidence response teammates Candice DeLong and John Gray set up in rooms at the Sportsmen's Motel. Freeman shared leadership of this little band with another agent from the San Francisco office, Terry Turchie. The two agreed to alternate their visits to Montana, so that one would be in Lincoln at all times. They made the 7-Up their headquarters and the Sportsmen's Lodge their observation post. Conveniently located on the corner of Highway 200 and Stemple Pass Road, the latter would provide the agents with a perfect view of anyone who drove or biked up or down Poorman Creek.

Yet, however hard they tried to be inconspicuous, these officials still looked like the urban yuppies they were. Dressed in spanking new Orvis Parkas and L.L. Bean boots, and driving the latest model SUVs, they stuck out like dudes at a cattle auction. DeLong complained of the cold and the bad restaurants. At times, they all seemed bored to tears.

As cover, Gray and DeLong, who were engaged, posed as a married couple researching a possible story for *National Geographic*. Sachtleben and Freeman pretended to be historians searching for old gold mines—something no sane person would be doing while several feet of snow still lay on the ground. Turchie and Noel described themselves as "sportsmen." But it was neither hunting nor fishing season.

Nevertheless, few Lincolnites noticed. They weren't even curious when these strangers rented a shack near Canyon Creek from Kaczynski's next-door neighbor, miner and logger Butch Gehring.

The object of the agents' attention was Kaczynski's cabin: a weathered frame structure with a single pipe chimney and no eaves, approximately ten by twelve feet in size. Possessing only one door that faced up Canyon Creek and away from the road and other cabins, it seemed to turn its back on the world.

From Gehring's shack on the bluff above Kaczynski's place, Noel and Sachtleben, using infrared binoculars and high-powered rifle sniper scopes and set up a twenty-four-hour watch. They hung listening microphones and motion detectors from trees in the forest; later they would bring in reconnaissance aircraft and enlist spy satellites to take hourly pictures of the ground below.

Throughout the last two weeks of March, Turchie, alternating with Freeman, worked with San Francisco prosecutors David Cleary and Steve Fraccero to prepare an affidavit for a search warrant for Kaczynski's place. Meanwhile, Lowell Bergman, a producer for CBS's *60 Minutes*, discovered that an arrest could be imminent. He called the FBI public affairs officer in Washington, D.C., George Grotz, who told him the news was premature and begged him to wait. Bergman agreed to hold off for a while, if he could be guaranteed an exclusive on the story should an arrest be made.

Given this incentive, the agents in Lincoln stepped up surveillance. But they didn't dare show themselves or arrest their quarry prematurely, before a search warrant was issued. If Kaczynski realized he was being observed, he would destroy evidence. Also, they knew their man had a deer-hunting license and was armed. If he was the person they sought, he might have booby-trapped his premises. Or, if he became aware of the surveillance, he might run into the wilderness, where he could elude pursuers indefinitely. In fact, however, the suspect seldom left his shack. Even with sniper scopes and satellite snapshots, all they saw was an extremely thin man occasionally emerging to fetch food from the root cellar.

On March 31, Turchie flew back to San Francisco to join in the celebration of his son's birthday, and Jim Freeman took his place in Lincoln. Two days later, April 2, the FBI learned that ABC and CNN News were also both onto the story, and CBS told FBI officials in Washington that it could no longer wait. Following further FBI entreaties, the network agreed to postpone coverage until the next day.

So Turchie snapped into action. By 9:30 A.M. on April 2 he had assembled a SWAT team of 150 agents from the San Francisco office, putting the first contingent on a Delta Airlines flight to Helena by noon. Then he, Cleary, and Fraccero lit the afterburners, working on the affidavit until, early in the evening, Turchie boarded a second Delta flight with the rest of the SWAT team, reaching Helena around midnight.

Immediately upon arriving in Helena, Turchie met with the assistant U.S. attorney there, the two completing the affidavit around 5:00 A.M. on April 3. They took it to Judge William Lovell at eight that morning, asking for permission to search Kaczynski's cabin for items that "would be utilized in the manufacture, construction, assembly, packaging, and mailing of . . . explosive devices," as well as typewriters, documents, and the books that had been cited in the manifesto. As soon as Lovell signed it, Turchie radioed the agents in Lincoln, telling them to move in and search the cabin.

IT WAS TED's younger brother, David, a social worker from Schenectady, New York, who broke the case.

In Greek mythology, Castor and Pollux were twin brothers who so loved each other that when Castor was killed in war, Pollux asked their father, the god Jupiter, to exchange his life for his brother's. According to one account, Jupiter was so touched that he partly consented, granting each brother life on alternate days, so that each spent one day under the Earth among the dead, and the next in the sky, among the gods. In another version, Jupiter honored their mutual love by allowing both brothers to live together among the stars, as Gemini, the Twins.

Ted and David were similarly devoted to each other, and shared certain ideals. Ted loved David so much, he could not bear to lose him, as a brother or as a philosophical acolyte; and when he did, he would not forgive the desertion. David loved Ted equally and admired his idealism, but ultimately, faced with a moral dilemma, turned his brother in. To do the right thing he not only had to put his brother's life at risk but also, apparently, compromise his own ideals. Now the two, like the Gemini Twins, are condemned to live alternate lives—the bad brother a living death in the bowels of a penitentiary, where he rots with anger; the good brother a celebrity among the stars, left to reflect on the Hobson's choice he had to make.

Despite their mutual affection, the brothers could not have been more dissimilar. Ted, more than seven years older and less athletic, thought of himself as the leader. He had more confidence in the truth of his own ideas and was more resolute in holding to them. He believed that his parents "valued" him more, because he was brighter. By contrast, David was more romantic, less sure of his intellectual powers and more willing to compromise. Whereas Ted sought to run from direct confrontations with others, David, gentler and more tactful than his older brother, used diplomacy to defuse conflicts.

Their habits of thinking—what psychologists would call their "cognitive styles"—differed, too. Ted had no patience for abstract philosophy or ethics. He claimed only to believe what was scientifically verifiable, and rejected everything else as pure emotion. He reports, for example, that when David "became a convert" to the highly abstract philosophy of the German philosopher Martin Heidegger, he was incensed. David, he felt, was falling for humbug simply because he found it subjectively attractive. "One could not assume," he claims he told David, "that a formulation had any other meaning than its emotive content simply because one felt subjectively that it had such meaning." Ted warned his brother that "the meanings of verbal formulations required study and analysis."

David, by contrast, believed Ted was overly rigid and dismissed his brother's "positivism" as outdated. But such replies merely infuriated his older brother. To Ted, David was weak, lacking initiative, energy, and persistence. He would become furious when his supposedly obedient disciple summoned up the courage to argue back. Then later, he would feel remorse for having treated his brother so cruelly. Over time, his feelings of guilt about this treatment of David grew.

For his part, David continued to admire his older brother for his brilliance and fierce determination. And there was much they shared. Both loved literature. Both liked to write. And both felt profoundly alienated from society and sought to escape from it.

In 1970, shortly after graduating from Columbia University with a degree in English literature, David moved to Great Falls to take a job with the Anaconda Copper Company, at its smelter. The following June, Ted came to visit. One weekend, the two drove to Lincoln, where they bought a small lot on Canyon Creek. Although not nearly as isolated as Ted would have liked, he decided to make it his home and immediately began to build a cabin.

In the fall of 1971, David enrolled at the College of Great Falls, to obtain his teacher's certificate. After earning the degree in the spring of 1973, David stayed in Montana some months, then left to teach at a school in Lisbon, Iowa, where his parents had once lived. Two years later, he gave up teaching and moved in with his parents, by then living in Lombard Illinois, where he devoted himself, without success, to creative writing. He then took a job at Foam Cutting Engineers near Lombard—the same plant where his father now worked—quitting this job, too, in 1978 to become a commuter bus driver.

In 1985, seeking a wilderness escape like his brother, David drove his old camper van to Alpine in the Christmas Mountains of West Texas, near Big Bend National Park, and purchased five acres of land. For a time, he lived in a hole he had dug in the ground, covered with a tarpaulin and corrugated sheets of roofing material held in place with heavy stones. Like Ted, his main transportation was an old bicycle. Eventually, David acquired thirty acres nearby, where he built a cabin, living there until 1989.

In those West Texas days, it was hard to distinguish between the philosophies of the two brothers. An Alpine neighbor and friend of David's, Melvin La Follette, later told *Time* magazine that "We both worried about the destruction of mankind from too much emphasis on technology."

Indeed, according to Ted, during the years David lived in Great Falls and Texas he was, if anything, even more disaffected than his older brother. David, he says, often complained about the excessive material-ism of our society and the need to revolt against it. In fact, Ted insists, David had been so alienated in those days that he would not have turned his brother in, but would have regarded him as a hero.

David, in sum, according to his friends as well as to Ted, had long shared his older brother's revolutionary ideas. He openly admired the "purity" of Ted's primitive lifestyle and for a while sought escape in wilderness himself. He fumed about "the system."

Whatever David's alienation may have been then, it did not last. In 1989, he abandoned his desert home and moved to Schenectady, New York, to join an old girlfriend, Linda Patrik, a philosophy professor at Union College. They were married in a Buddhist ceremony a year later.

By marrying Patrik, David had rejoined the middle class, which made Ted furious. Shortly after David's move, Ted wrote him a long let-ter, at the end of which he vented his anger at his brother for selling out. What most aggravated him, Ted claimed, was David's betrayal of their shared resolve not to capitulate to "the system."

In Ted's eyes, David had committed the ultimate sin: ideological disloyalty. Possessing a scientific mind, Ted believed all truths were like those in mathematics, either true or false. They gave no room for compromise or qualification. Since everyone knows the sum of two plus two is four, to say it is three signifies not merely an error but dis-honesty. Just so, it was equally obvious to Ted that industrial society was evil and compromise with it impossible. And, Ted was convinced, David knew this too. So by marrying Patrik and joining the system, Ted believed that David deliberately chose to live a lie, thereby proving his dishonesty.

David no longer behaved like an obedient pupil. Ted had lost what-ever emotional and intellectual control he may have thought he had over his younger brother. For this he blamed what he saw as David's weak-ness and Patrik's machinations.

Soon, David's doubts began. By the early 1990s he and Linda were already deeply concerned about Ted's growing alienation. And sometimes, Linda would voice her suspicions. "You've got a screwy brother," she'd say. "Maybe he's the Unabomber."

Following the Mosser and Murray bombings and the arrival of the manifesto at the offices of the *New York Times, Washington Post,* and *Penthouse,* the Unabomber was much in the news. By the summer of 1995, newspapers in Paris, where Linda was vacationing, also covered the story closely. As she read these accounts, her misgivings grew. And when David joined her in France later that summer, the two confronted the unthinkable: Was Ted the Unabomber?

Gradually, they saw connections: The Unabomber built his bombs of wood. Ted was adept at carpentry. Ted had always been fascinated with explosives and fireworks. They noticed the coincidence of the dates and locations of the bombings: Ted had lived in Chicago, Ann Arbor, Salt Lake City, and Berkeley. All the Unabomber's packages had been placed, or mailed to or from or near one of those locations. The first four placed the killer in Chicago, where Ted grew up. Several bombs were sent from, or placed in, Utah. One seriously injured a University of Michigan professor near Ann Arbor. Eight placed the killer near Berkeley.

Despite this circumstantial evidence, David sought reasons not to believe his brother was a killer. The bomber, he noted, traveled extensively, and Ted hated to travel. And then he noted something that especially reassured him. The first bomb had been deposited in the Engineering Building parking lot of the University of Chicago campus on May 25, 1978. But Ted, David was sure, was in Montana at the time. It seemed an ironclad alibi.

But doubts surfaced again in the fall. In October, after the couple had returned to Schenectady, Linda persuaded her husband to visit the local library, to read the manifesto. But the library's copy was missing, so instead they read excerpts on the Internet.

"After I read the first few pages," David recalled, "my jaw literally dropped." One sentence in particular jumped out at him: "It is obvious that modern leftist philosophers are not simply cool-headed logicians systematically analyzing the foundation of knowledge. They are deeply involved emotionally in their attack on truth and reality." Ted often used the phrase "cool-headed logicians" during philosophical discussions the brothers had carried on with each other over the years.

David was badly shaken. He felt "chills, I think . . . some anger," he later told the *New York Times*. "I was prepared to read the manifesto and be able to dismiss any possibility that it would be Ted, but it continued to sound enough like him that I was really upset that it could be him."

When David was eventually able to read the entire manifesto, his unease intensified. The entire document revealed an idiosyncratic style strangely resembling Ted's. One phrase in particular struck a chord: "You can't eat your cake and have it too." Normally, this saying is put the other way around—i.e., "You can't have your cake and eat it too." But Ted, he knew, always put "eat" before "have."

The " 'feel' and tone" of the manifesto seemed familiar. He and Ted had long argued whether art or science gave a truer picture of reality. Science was based on reason, Ted had insisted, whereas art merely expressed emotions. And emotions could not be trusted. By contrast, his own ideas, being based on a "rational ideal," justified any actions needed to support them.

David and Ted had disputed this issue for years, often by mail. The younger brother dug out Ted's old letters to him and began rereading them.

The first thing David noticed was that the manifesto and the letters contained the same curious word usage. In both, the spelling and choice of words was more English than American. In his letters, Ted spelled "analyze" the English way, "analyse." He wrote "willfully" as "wilfully," "license" as "licence," "installment" as "instalment," and "consisted in" instead of "consisted of." The same was true of the manifesto. And David found a letter that contained a sentence identical to one in the manifesto, even including the capitalization: "The radical environmentalists ALREADY hold an ideology that exalts nature and opposes technology."

The overlap was impossible to ignore. In a letter to David dated September 2, 1986, Ted referred to L. Sprague DeCamp's *The Ancient Engineers*. That book is one of only four mentioned in the manifesto. In another letter, dated August 21, 1981, Ted referred to Jacques Ellul's *Technological Society*. Tormented, David struggled with himself. Day by day, he recalled, he would "swing back and forth like a pendulum. One morning I would wake up and find some reason to believe that it had to be him, that the truth was looking in my eyes, and I had been in denial about it. I would wake up another morning and find a reason to believe that I had dreamed this up."

Finally, he decided the only way to resolve the issue was to visit Ted, and, by circumspect questioning, allay his own suspicions. So he wrote his brother, asking if he could visit. But Ted's reply, David claims, was not reassuring: "I get just choked with frustration at my inability to get our stinking family off my back once and for all, and 'stinking family' emphatically includes you. . . . I DON'T EVER WANT TO SEE YOU OR HEAR FROM YOU, OR ANY OTHER MEMBER OF OUR FAMILY, AGAIN."

David's vacillation continued. He and Linda pored over every shred of Ted's past in search of clues. Then a terrifying possibility hit them. Twice, he says, the Unabomber had struck shortly after the family had sent money to Ted, ostensibly to pay medical bills. Soon after David—by then a social worker in Schenectady, New York—had lent Ted $1,000 in December 1994, Thomas Mosser was killed by a mail bomb. And Murray was murdered in April 1995, less than three months after David had lent his brother another $2,000. Could the family have been unwittingly funding murder?

In late October, Linda Patrik turned to an old childhood chum, Susan Swanson, now a private investigator in Chicago. She and David gave Swanson a copy of the manifesto and five letters, to see if she thought they might have the same authorship. Swanson read everything she could on the Unabomber, then consulted Cliff Van Zandt, a former FBI analyst working as a private consultant in Virginia. Soon Van Zandt got back to her: there was a 60 to 80 percent chance of a match.

Was this probability sufficient to justify turning Ted in to the FBI? What if they were mistaken? A rash action could result in ruining Ted's life. Authorities might falsely accuse him, bringing ruinous publicity. Uncertain what to do, David continued to reread through the manifesto. Then something struck him: its emphasis on rationality and science resembled, almost word for word, what Ted had been saying to his brother for years.

Paragraph 17 of the manifesto especially struck a familiar chord:

Art forms that appeal to modern leftist intellectuals tend to focus on sordidness, defeat and despair, or else they take an orgiastic tone, throwing off rational control as if there were no hope of accomplishing anything through rational calculation and all that was left was to immerse oneself in the sensations of the moment.

Ted's positivism had given him away. Throughout their philosophical arguments, Ted had extolled the "rational ideal" and denigrated art. And here the author of the manifesto was expressing the same views, almost word for word. He could be the Unabomber, David decided.

David determined to approach the authorities, but carefully, through an intermediary, without disclosing Ted's identity until further proof was forthcoming. In January 1996, at Swanson's suggestion, David and Patrik contacted a former law school classmate of Swanson's, Anthony Bisceglie, an attorney in Washington, D.C. And early in February Bisceglie spoke with a friend in the FBI, Special Agent John Flynn, and turned over to him five of Ted's letters to David, with names and addresses all carefully redacted.

"Either this is a historic moment," Bisceglie told Flynn, "or the beginning of a wild-goose chase."

A delicate dance ensued. In mid-February, David and Bisceglie met face to face with authorities for the first time. The officials demanded to know who wrote the letters. But David and Bisceglie balked. They wanted assurances that the investigation would be conducted discreetly "and with the least intrusive measures," so that if Ted were innocent, he would not be harassed, provoked, or killed. They insisted that the Kaczynski family's identity be kept from the press and that the agency not approach the suspect's mother until they had notified David of their intention. And they sought assurances that during the investigation, authorities would not confront the suspect, "due to his fragile psychological state."

"The Subject," Bisceglie told the FBI, "has a heart condition, suffers from stress, is paranoid, and his reaction to any contact from a stranger could endanger his life. It could also endanger our client's [i.e., David's] life."

The cat was already out of the bag, however. Once the FBI knew David's identity, their team quickly realized the suspect must be David's older brother, Ted, and the agency began its surveillance in Lincoln. Then investigators insisted on interviewing David and Ted's mother,

Wanda. On March 14, as federal agents waited on the street around the corner from her house, David broke the news to his mother that Ted was a suspect in the Unabomber case.

"He was walking back and forth and the tears started raining down his face and I sort of sat there in shock," Wanda recalled. "I thought it, it, it couldn't be Ted. It, it, it just couldn't. It must be a mistake. And I said, I'm, I'm sure the investigation will rule him out."

A half hour later, the agents arrived at the door. They urged David and his mother to look for more examples of Ted's writing. In the attic, they came across a footlocker belonging to Ted. Inside, besides old letters, they found the 1971 essay. "In these pages," it began, "it is argued that continued scientific and technical progress will inevitably result in the extinction of individual liberty."

Later, Ted would vow never to forgive his brother for turning him in. David, he said, was "another Judas Iscariot." He had betrayed their shared ideals, selling out to an evil society bent on destroying the wilderness they both loved. And, predictably, Ted blamed Patrik most, without whose influence, he believed, David would never have turned him in. Perhaps he was right. For as Patrik told Ellen Becker and Tom Mcpheeters of the *Journal of Family Life* in 1998, "It was not David, the moral hero, making a moral decision, but we made a couple decision . . . . if I hadn't been in the picture, this drama (David's reporting Ted to the FBI), would not have taken place."

"Bad men do what good men dream." David may—or may not— have once wished to rebel against society, as Ted claimed. What matters is that he didn't do it. But if he had shared Ted's alienation, then his anguish was now twofold. To do the right thing, he had not only turned against the brother he loved but also, in Ted's eyes at least, abandoned ideals both had embraced. For his part, Ted had indeed done what his brother may have only dreamed. The mystery was not why he had done so, nor why David had not, but why both these Ivy League graduates had so rejected society in the first place.

On the morning of April 3, 1996, when Turchie radioed the agents in Lincoln to say the judge had approved the search warrant, Freeman had the SWAT team in place. Communicating through encrypted two-way radios, agents in "gulley suits" crawled up the creekbottom while others fanned out into the countryside surrounding Kaczynski's place. Meanwhile, Gray and DeLong hid in a cabin belonging to Kaczynski's next-door neighbor, Glenn Williams. And Sachtleben took up a position behind a nearby tree.

The plan was to lure Kaczynski out of his cabin before he could escape, set booby traps, or destroy evidence. When everyone was in place, the local Forest Service ranger, Jerry Burns, whom Kaczynski knew, approached the cabin on cue, along with Tom McDaniel of the Helena FBI office and "Mad Max" Noel. Knowing Kaczynski to be nervous about encroachments on his land, they argued loudly over the boundary as they stood outside.

At Kaczynski's door, Burns hollered, "Hey Ted, can you come out here and show us where it is?"

Kaczynski stuck his head out the door. "Sure," he said, "just let me go back in and get my jacket."

Before he could get back inside, Noel jumped him, quickly fastening handcuffs behind his back. The men led Kaczynski to the Williams place as the evidence response team, led by Satchtleben, swarmed into the suspect's cabin. Explosives ordnance specialists armed with X-ray guns searched for bombs, and others combed the ground around the cabin with metal detectors. Chemists looked for DNA samples.

At the Williams house, Noel seated Kaczynski in a chair at the head of a small pine table, while he and Paul Wilhelmus of the U.S. Postal Inspection Service sat beside him. DeLong built a fire in the woodstove.

Kaczynski's clothes, DeLong recalls, were "rotting off his body. . . . He smelled like warm dirt and was so filthy that even his long eyelashes were caked with soot—above the bluest eyes I have ever seen. He was missing a front tooth."

This was the face that, within a week, would grace the cover of virtually every national magazine, cementing for all time the public's impression of Kaczynski as a tattered hermit who never bathed. DeLong did not realize at the time that—as Sachtleben told me later—the searchers were simultaneously finding Kaczynski had perfectly presentable clothes, and even suits and ties, but that, like so many mountain men, while doing dirty jobs in winter he let dress and bathing slide.

And at the time of his arrest, Kaczynski was reportedly doing a dirty job. According to an FBI source, he was rasping aluminum blocks to make more aluminum powder for bombs. The dust was all over him.

At the Williams cabin, Kaczynski began to sweat and shiver. He asked if he was under arrest. They told him no, but that other agents were searching his cabin, and (thinking that the cabin may have been booby-trapped) they wanted to know if they faced any danger in doing so.

"Well," he replied, "this looks pretty serious, and they say if you're ever in serious trouble, you shouldn't talk without an attorney. So I think I'll wait until I have an attorney."

Kaczynski asked to see the search warrant. Then came whoops from his cabin.

INSIDE THE TINY dwelling, searchers encountered one surprise after another. Although crammed with Kaczynski's possessions—and in contrast to his appearance—the cabin was pin-neat. Everything had its place. A gun rack holding a deer rifle and .22-caliber "plinker" stood above the bed that also served as a couch. Snowshoes and animal hides hung on the inside of the door. A homemade chair sat in front of the woodstove. In one corner below a window stood the washbasin; in another, cross-country skis leaned against the wall; and in a third, Kaczynski's dress clothes hung on hooks. On one wall, floor-to-ceiling shelving held foodstuffs and books. Another row of shelves, containing more books, ran along the top of the other three walls.

The book collection could have served as a small college library—and indeed, much of it had come from Kaczynski's Harvard course syllabuses. There were works on Spanish, French, German, Latin, Chinese, Russian, Finnish, Egyptian, Indo-European etymology, and lost languages; books on Greek mythology, ancient history, Roman history, American history, European history, Spanish and Spanish American history, and Native American history; on the French and Russian revolutions, on Napoleon, Charlemagne, Hitler, Marxism, psychology, physics, nuclear energy, chemistry, electronics, mechanics, mathematics, and mysticism; concordances of the Bible, bird, mushroom, and

wildflower identification; fingerprinting, wilderness survival; rifle shooting; edible plants, a seed catalogue.

And there were many, many classics, including Mark Twain's *Life on
the Mississippi*; Steinbeck's *Of Mice and Men*; Orwell's *1984*; *The Pocket
Book of O. Henry Stories*; Hugo's *Les Misérables*; Ortega y Gasset's *Revolt
of the Masses* (in Spanish); William H. Whyte's *The Organization Man*;
Koestler's *Darkness at Noon*; and Cooper's *Last of the Mohicans* and
Deerslayer. There were novels by Joseph Conrad, including *Heart of
Darkness, Youth, Typhoon, The Nigger of the "Narcissus,"* and *The
Shadow-Line* as well as *The Secret Agent*; Somerset Maugham's *The
Razor's Edge*; Dostoevsky's, *The Brothers Karamazov*; Dickens's *Tale of
Two Cities, Hard Times*, and *David Copperfield*; Shakespeare's *Merchant
of Venice*; George Eliot's *Silus Marner*; Robert Louis Stevenson's *Trea-
sure Island*; Thomas Hardy's *Far from the Madding Crowd*; Rosemary
Sutcliff's *Tristan and Iseult*; and Walter Starkie's classic travelogue about
Gypsies in Hungary and Romania, *Raggle-Taggle* (1933).

Ellul's *Technological Society* and *Autopsy of a Revolution* were in the
collection. So was Paul Goodman's *Growing Up Absurd* and Ted Robert
Gurr's two-volume *Violence in America*. Most interesting, among the few
articles found among Kaczynski's possessions was a 1963 *American Sociologist* essay by Henry A. Murray entitled "Studies of Stressful Interpersonal Disputations," recounting experiments performed on twenty-two
members of the Harvard College class of 1962, including Kaczynski.

On the shelves next to these books and academic papers sat a veritable bomb factory that included, according to the FBI, "chemicals and
other materials . . . designed and intended for use in manufacturing a
destructive device, namely a bomb," ten three-ring binders containing
countless pages of "meticulous writings and sketches" of "plans for making bombs," three typewriters, a carbon copy of a draft of the manifesto,
and a personal journal—written partly in code, partly in Spanish, thousands of pages long and apparently maintained by the suspect since
1969. Finally, there was a piece of paper containing the false Social
Security number the Unabomber used to identify himself.

As the searchers continued their inventory, they found tableware, a
pillow and blanket, three mittens, two scarves, a container of salt, a
metal frying pan, a radio, waterproof matches, four measuring spoons, a
red hat, a straw hat, a flashlight, and a bottle of Trazadone antidepres-

sant. And they found notations in Kaczynski's handwriting, in which he outlined a carefully structured security classification system:

Class 1. *Hide carefully far from home.*
Class 2. *Hide carefully far from home, but can be destroyed at a pinch.*
Class 3. *Hide carefully, far from home, but can be burned at a pinch.*
Class 4. *Burn away from home.*
Class 5. *Burn in stove, eventually.*
Class 6. *Burn with glass jars.*
Class 7. *Destroy.*
Class 8. *Treat to make safe.*
Class 9. *Burn in stove, then dispose of remains.*
Class 10. *Dump in trash far from home.*
QQ   *Super Queer.*
Q   *Very Queer.*
R   *Moderately queer.*
S   *Slightly queer.*
B   *Burnable.*
NB   *Not Burnable.*

The evidence team also retrieved two sets of notebooks written mostly in Spanish, detailing Kaczynski's "experiments" and classified according to the above system. "Series I, #3, pp 261–262," for example, he designated as "queer 9," and "p 276–283" as "queer 10." And "almost all the rest of the notebook is queer 8." Similarly, some of Series II, #3, was designated as "queer 1 (embarrassing, not dangerous)"—apparently the least sensitive "queer" category—and another part as "queer 2 (but past statute of limitations)," while for "Series II, #4" he directed himself to "call this notebook queer 3. But very bad public relations."

Inside a green plastic bag in the neatly organized loft, the team discovered copies of the Harvard class of 1962 yearbooks; and lying in a corner was a Samsonite suitcase containing Kaczynski's master's and Ph.D. diplomas from the University of Michigan. Across the creek, other agents opened his root cellar, which contained sacks of potatoes, carrots, and other vegetables.

By the end of the afternoon, investigators had catalogued enough to book Kaczynski for "knowingly possessing [an unregistered] firearm—specifically components from which a destructive device such as a bomb can be readily assembled." Noel, accompanied by McDaniel, walked back to the Williams cabin, lifted Kaczynski to his feet, and said: "Ted Kaczynski, you are under arrest for the murder of three people."

Kaczynski didn't say a word, or even blink.

Now they had to hurry. The media had gotten wind of the arrest and around thirty reporters were already camped at Gehring's gate. Officials closed the Stemple Pass Road, creating a traffic snarl on this "wilderness" thoroughfare and greatly angering local residents as well as the sheriff, who knew nothing about the federal presence.

After dark, Noel and Turchie put Kaczynski in their white Ford Bronco and drove through the blockade past the waiting reporters. As photographers sought in vain to take the suspect's picture through the moving windshield, four journalism students from the University of Montana, stringing for the *New York Times*, pursued the fleeing federals in a Chevy Blazer. The SUVs careened in tandem at high speed over the dangerous mountain road, soft and muddy with snowmelt. When the officials reached the small Montana capital and unloaded their prisoner at the inconspicuous Arcade Building office, only the students were there. One took Kaczynski's picture as the ragged suspect entered the building, accompanied by the two law enforcement officers. That evening, the photo went out over the wire.

The media circus had begun.

7

Gridlock at Last Chance Gulch

Without the mass media there can be no propaganda.

—JACQUES ELLUL,
Propaganda
from Kaczynski's cabin library

T HE HANGING TREE is gone now, this instrument of early vigilantes having met the ax of one Reverend William Shippen, a Methodist minister, in 1876. But the events of early April 1996 demonstrated that Helena is still a wild and wooly town.

Shippen had not taken an ax to the tree out of any high-principled opposition to capital punishment, mind you. In fact, he was quite fond of the practice. Rather, as he explained to the angry mob that threatened to lynch him for "killing" the tree, it was purely an economic act: he needed the wood. But whatever his reason, local citizens sorely missed the tree. As Helena's only newspaper, the *Independent Record*, reported some decades later, "Even after nearly a half a century, they still grieved for its untimely conversion into firewood."

As soon as federal agents had taken Kaczynski into the FBI's Arcade Building office on Wednesday night, they sought to make their charge more presentable. Tom Corbett, the local deputy chief U.S. probation officer, lent a tweed jacket to Kaczynski and the arrest party sped to the county jail on Broadway Street, where the defendant spent the night. The next morning, still wearing the jacket, he was taken to the Federal Court House for arraignment, then back to jail, where wardens gave him a bath and a fresh orange prison jumpsuit. Then they called in the local barber, Dundee Worden, proprietor of Dundee's Barber Shop, to give him a haircut.

By now, journalists had arrived in force. And during the following weeks, television dishes, linked by thick electronic cables to nearby trailers, crammed into the available space at the Federal Building parking lot, while the print and electronic media took over the town. Journalists and photographers waited at the jail entrance or on the courthouse lawn or on the sidewalk in front of the Diamond Block and Arcade buildings. Cameras on tripods, tethered to the inevitable wiring, littered grass and pavement, while more restless reporters toured the town in rented cars, looking for targets of opportunity.

"This is the biggest thing that has ever happened around here in my whole life," the *Independent Record* quoted one resident as saying. And indeed it was. Helena is a small town of only 28,800 souls and suspects such as Kaczynski don't often visit.

"We're lacking in nationally ranked gunfighters," lamented a spokesman from the Montana Historical Society. Kaczynski, said another local historian, was the most famous prisoner since Isaac Gravelle was arrested for attempting to blow up a Northern Pacific Railroad train in 1903. The papers at the time described Gravelle as a "dynamiter, horse thief, burglar." He was shot and killed trying to escape from jail in 1904.

Now Helena could boast the famous felon it had always wanted. The town was on the map. Business boomed. When they weren't working, these representatives of the press were shopping. They swarmed into stores looking for cowboy boots, ten-gallon hats, and turquoise jewelry. And they clogged the streets in their rented cars.

For the first time in its history, Last Chance Gulch was experiencing gridlock.

This was Lincoln's fifteen minutes of fame, as well. Reporters checked into the motels just vacated by investigators and began interviewing everyone in sight. And while some inhabitants claimed they disliked the attention, many enjoyed it. Mom's Café put "Unaburgers" on its menu, and the 7-Up Lodge and Supper Club began selling Unabomber T-shirts.

"This was big for Lincoln," Jack Ward of AA Towing explained. "Before this, the biggest thing that ever happened in this town was the Firemen's Ball."

TED KACZYNSKI was accused of being the legendary Unabomber, a man willing to kill in order to warn the world that technological civilization threatened freedom and nature, that society was intolerant of anyone who did not fit within "the system," and that, to enforce conformity, authorities used sophisticated surveillance technology to spy on their citizenry and various strategies of behavior modification to control dissidents. Also among the manipulators, he had written, are the media, which promote misinformation and herd thinking. Now Kaczynski was caught in the very web he feared. Authorities had spied on him with virtually every surveillance device known. And soon journalists would, however inadvertently, use misinformation to create a stereotype.

By Thursday, April 4, hundreds of newspaper, magazine, and TV reporters around the country were on the trail of Kaczynski's past. Some sought his former acquaintances in the Carpenter Street, Chicago, neighborhood where he had lived until a teenager, and in the suburb of Evergreen Park, where he went to high school. Others located former classmates and professors who knew him at Harvard, the University of Michigan, and the University of California.

Desperate to report something, reporters poured into Lincoln and Helena, glomming onto anyone offering information. Those claiming familiarity with Kaczynski were invited to appear on national television.

Naturally, many said they knew him, whether they did or not. And to excuse their inability to say more, they cast him as "strange" or a "hermit."

Contrary to the impression the media gave in the weeks following the arrest, few journalists got close to Kaczynski's cabin because the Gehrings (whose property bordered Kaczynski's and who owned the only access road) and the FBI barred the way. Some tried to trespass but didn't succeed. The day after Kaczynski's arrest, three reporters tried wading up Canyon Creek through muck at night. But FBI infrared sensors spotted them and agents turned them back. On other occasions, reporters hiked up the back side of Baldy Mountain, then dropped over the top of the peak through the National Forest to approach the Kaczynski place. But they too were caught.

Unable to reach Kaczynski's cabin, many journalists settled on interviewing the Gehrings or other neighbors and various townsfolk, apparently chosen at random. But many of these people, like Gehring, worked in fields that Kaczynski abhorred, including construction, logging, mining, and real estate. Since he didn't approve of what they did, he had avoided them. Naturally, they thought this odd.

"He's a loner," they'd say.

"How well did you know him?" the reporter would ask.

"Didn't really know him," came the unvarying reply.

Few reporters suggested to their readers and viewers that Kaczynski might have shunned these people because they offended his values and that, for example, when Gehring told journalists that "Any conversation you had with Ted was short," this might reflect the fact that Kaczynski didn't like the man. In fact, Kaczynski, suffering from migraines and acutely sensitive to sounds, was driven to rage by the racket made by Gehring's sawmill and by what he called his neighbor's "irresponsible logging practices." He suspected Gehring was boring test holes in search of gold and he feared the logger used pesticides that might give him lymph cancer.

In this way, the media built a stereotype, and the stereotype soon became fixed: Kaczynski was an "eccentric" who lived in the "wilderness." The man smelled. He ate road-killed coyotes. He didn't have visitors, never went out, didn't own a watch, never had sex, and wasn't interested in money. He wouldn't drink coffee with the boys. He rode a bicycle in winter. And he didn't talk much. Not having seen the inside of his cabin, they described it as "a mess." Knowing nothing about his habit of saving his best clothes for trips and (like so many mountain men) bathing infrequently in winter, they called him a slob. Accustomed to paved streets and stop lights, these reporters from New York, Los Angeles, and Washington, D.C., described Kaczynski's cabin—four miles from town and just off the Stemple Pass Road—as "wilderness." Not bothering to tell readers that in Montana, Kaczynski's lifestyle was hardly unusual, they painted it as bizarre. He was a back-to-nature nut who had built his shack as an "exact replica" of the cabin Thoreau had constructed on Walden Pond in Massachusetts in 1845.

To *Time* magazine (April 15, 1996), Kaczynski was "the hermit on the hill" (even though his cabin lay in the Canyon Creek bottom) and "you could smell him coming." The *New York Times* (May 26, 1996) described him as "usually unwashed," *Newsweek* (April 15, 1996) as "pathologically reclusive."

In dubbing Kaczynski a hermit, the media confused misanthropy—dislike of people—with primitivism—antipathy toward civilization. One can abhor society, yet like company. Just so, Kaczynski sought to reject modern life, not avoid people. He was not unlike his brother David, as well as many others who sought the simple life. Anyone who has read a *Whole Earth Catalog* knows that the search for the primitive is a national movement, not a rare aberration. And anyone who ever attended the Earth First! gatherings known as "Round River Rendezvous" or spent time with the renegade enviro-radical group "Stumps Suck" knows that Kaczynski's scruffy image personified this movement.

Reportage at the time of Kaczynski's arrest had exhibited a feature of pack journalism: It was wide but shallow. Reporters followed each other's footsteps, interviewed the same people, and reached identical conclusions. And so, while the public was being overwhelmed with stories about Kaczynski, the man himself remained hidden from view.

Indeed, the media was building a caricature of both brothers. As for Ted, there was nothing strange about his lifestyle, nothing remote about where he lived, and nothing especially misanthropic about him. In a region generously populated with hippies, Earth First! activists, and myriad wilderness escapists, he fit right in. His cabin wasn't messy; he was quite capable of looking presentable.

By Montana standards, Ted's place, far from being "wilderness," bordered on suburban. Standing outside his door, one could hear traffic on the Stemple Pass Road. His neighbors were in businesses dedicated to reducing wilderness, not protecting it. Gehring harvested timber next door, and on many days one could hear his chain saw as it ground through trees near the cabin. Just a few hundred feet down the creek from Kaczynski stood a row of vacation cabins. One belonged to a builder, another to real estate agents.

And quite a few townsfolk liked Kaczynski. One was Teresa Garland, manager of Garland's Store. An attractive woman of about forty, she was one of the rare natives in town. Kaczynski, she told me, had once had a crush on her sister, Becky, president of the local chapter of Trout Unlimited. Kaczynski even wrote a long letter to Becky, in which he explained how he had been pushed so hard in academics by his parents that he had never had a normal life or learned how to feel at ease with women.

He felt at ease with Irene Preston, though. An elderly lady, Preston lives in a cluttered log cabin on the edge of Lincoln and also cherishes Kaczynski, remaining convinced he is innocent. She still gets letters from him. Preston is alone now, with her four cats. For years, she and her friend Kenneth Lee had a place just up the road from Kaczynski. They all became good friends. Kaczynski would invite them into his cabin, sharing his homemade beef jerky. Sometimes they played pinochle together. When Lee died in 1991, Preston moved into town, and only saw Kaczynski when he dropped by to give her some turnips or carrots from his garden. But once she moved, he wrote regularly. She showed me the letters. Invariably upbeat and humorous, they described his ongoing war with the "pesky rabbits" that were laying siege to his garden. He obviously liked Irene.

Even Chris Waits, a Kaczynski neighbor and local music teacher, despite also being a logger, said many good things about Kaczynski. Although complaining of the man's dislike of dogs and apparent aversion to his wife, Waits nonetheless enjoyed Kaczynski's company and their talk about history, gardening, survival techniques, hunting, and books they'd read.

The town library staff, too, adored Kaczynski. According to Sherri Wood, an ebullient, middle-aged individual, and her assistant, Mary Spurlin, Kaczynski is a "lovely man." Wood continued to correspond with him and would later learn that he was writing to many other women as well. ("There are women who are in love with him," she told the *Wall Street Journal*.)

"He was shy at first, but he gradually opened up," she explained. "Pretty soon, he got easy to talk to."

Kaczynski came to the library about once a month, Wood said, where they'd have long talks about books. He was always helpful. When the library needed remodeling in 1991, he worked with them to pack, move, and reshelve books. Later, he helped repaint the building. And when Wood's son, Danny, began having trouble in mathematics in school, Kaczynski tutored him. The two became fast friends. The boy even asked his mother if they could "adopt" Kaczynski.

But Kaczynski's friends for the most part kept a low profile. Some, not wanting to betray the relationship, refused to talk to the press altogether. Still, the portrait they paint is quite different from the media's cartoon image. While Kaczynski may have been quiet, shy, sometimes unkempt and socially awkward, he wasn't the filthy hermit he was made out to be.

The "hermit" image could have been quickly dispelled if good reporting had come to Lincoln. To be sure, some journalists did record the facts accurately. Richard Perez-Pena wrote in the *New York Times* on April 4, 1996, that Lincoln "has many seasonal residents and has attracted people as removed from the mainstream as back-to-the-land hippies and right-wing militias," so that "Kaczynski's reserve, self-sufficiency, long hair and beard drew little notice."

Kaczynski, reported Patrick Hoge in the *Sacramento Bee* on April 5, 1996,

> *attracted little attention during the twenty-five years he owned property here. To Main Street, the man police believe is the notorious Unabomber was just one of many unusual people living*

reclusive lives in the canyons and forests on Lincoln's fringe. "There's another 20 or 30 people living the same lifestyle that I can think of, and some of them look a lot more dangerous," said Virgil Roper, a retired El Dorado County sheriff's deputy. . . . Members of a group known as the "Sauerkraut Bunch" reportedly wear guns and knives into town, surrendering them to bartenders while they drink.

But while a few reporters such as Perez-Pena and Hoge sought to put Kaczynski's Lincoln lifestyle into perspective, most did not bother. Coming from big cities, they didn't notice Kaczynski's cabin wasn't wilderness. Few paid attention to testimony that did not fit the "loner" image.

The media ignored these facts because, rather than report the news, they sought to tell a story. And like all media fictions, there had to be a good guy and a bad guy. So they demonized Ted and deified David, ignoring facts that did not fit conveniently, such as David's own search for solitude in West Texas.

When they troubled to mention it at all, they described David's sojourn there as though it were a family vacation to Bar Harbor. *Time* magazine (April 15, 1996) would say only that David "occasionally retreated to his own isolated cabin in East Texas that he bought more than 10 years ago"—managing to make two factual errors in one sentence. And *Newsweek* (April 22, 1996) would point out that "while his brother studied wiring diagrams, David admired Gandhi and Thoreau. While his brother learned to hunt, David was a vegetarian. . . . David was quite sane."

David is, of course, a good man, and Ted an evil one. But the Unabomber crimes are about more than the relations between these two brothers. By packaging the story this way, the media trivialized it. Ignoring David's earlier alienation, they never asked what caused two Ivy League graduates to turn their backs on civilization. Portraying Ted Kaczynski as an unwashed hermit made him appear more pathetic than evil. It caused the public to forget the brilliance and brutality of his crimes, and the popularity of his manifesto philosophy. And it allowed people to overlook the possibility that the reasons he killed had little to do with bathing habits and wilderness lifestyles.

Everyone has a dark side, and as Carl Jung has said, until we recognize this fact and confront the dark side, we cannot control it. In some ways, Kaczynski embodies the dark side in all of us. By portraying him as a freak, by putting distance between "him" and "us," the media allowed America to deny its own dark side. It encouraged people to say, "He killed because he was weird," rather than ask, "Why did someone so like me commit murder?"

8

Kafka Comes to Sacramento

You may object that it is not a trial at all; you are quite
right, for it is only a trial if I recognize it as such.

> —FRANZ KAFKA,
> *The Trial*
> Kaczynski's Harvard reading

Protection, therefore, against the tyranny of the magistrate
is not enough: there needs protection also against the
tyranny of the prevailing opinion and feeling.

> —JOHN STUART MILL,
> *On Liberty*
> Kaczynski's Harvard reading

I N THE PREDAWN darkness of Monday, January 5, 1998, the Federal
Courthouse in Sacramento, California, looked like the set of an
outdoor Bayreuth production of Wagner's *Twilight of the Gods*.
Across the street, a block-long row of television spotlights, mounted on

wooden platforms beneath open-sided tents, cast a phosphorescent-green glow over the entire eight-story structure. Underneath the awnings, camera and sound technicians drank coffee, smoked cigarettes, and fiddled with equipment. At the courthouse entrance, a gaggle of reporters and photographers milled about impatiently in the rain, like a Greek chorus waiting for its cue.

The long-awaited drama—*United States* vs. *Theodore John Kaczynski*—was, we supposed, about to begin. As it turned out, it was about to end.

ALMOST UNNOTICED in this courthouse crowd were five other souls who had waited on the steps most of the night—who, indeed, had been there every night since jury selection began in October 1997: an unaffiliated Ph.D., a small-town newspaper reporter, and three aging ex-activists waiting for the five public passes to the trial, awarded on a first-come, first-served basis. This motley assortment represented the scores of others who took Kaczynski seriously but who were routinely turned away at the courthouse door. Following the trial in minute detail, they were more knowledgeable than most in the national media who walked past them up the steps without waiting, press passes in hand.

Without major media credentials, these five had no choice but to stand in line for public passes. Seeing themselves as ignored by the system, they recalled words from the manifesto—that "the mass media are mostly under the control of large organizations that are integrated into the system." All were intensely interested in the trial. Some, as Unabomber fans, viewed their hero as a victim of the system, too, fighting for disenfranchised Americans such as themselves.

Diagonally across the street from the courthouse, on the third floor of the Downtown Plaza Towers, an office building, in Suite 308 scores of journalists, phones cradled against one cheek, sat at long tables behind laptop computers and little signs that identified the newspapers and radio stations that sent them. Behind them, in private offices bordering the room, representatives of the bigger organizations such as the *New York Times*, Associated Press, and National Public Radio were hard at work in relative seclusion. In another room on the floor above, other reporters sat waiting to listen to trial proceedings over loudspeakers. On both floors, small groups of journalists could be found intensely discussing what should be the news angle that day. After reaching agreement, they returned to their phones and laptops to file the inevitably identical stories.

These were the precincts of a tightly knit guild, known as the Unabom Media Center, whose members represented mainstream press, radio, and television. Like circus performers, these itinerant scribes, rendezvousing to cover news stories wherever they broke—from Hurricane Hugo in South Carolina to the Oklahoma City bombing to O. J. Simpson's trial in Los Angeles—shared more with each other than with the public they served. They comprised a subculture with its own rules and values. And they liked to keep interlopers out.

Before jury selection for Kaczynski's trial began, the Clerk of the Court had delegated control of press passes to a consortium run by national and leading local (Sacramento) print and broadcast media. These news organizations, in turn, established the Unabom Media Center.

As the court had allotted so few public passes to the trial, this arrangement ensconced the national news media as gatekeepers, and these organizations limited attendance to themselves. Only "bona fide" journalists, the Media Center stipulated, could join. But the initiation fee was steep. Individuals had to pay $5,000 and take out liability insurance (another $1,500). Even this did not guarantee a seat at the trial, as all but a very few remained reserved for the large organizations. Rather, paying $6,500 only entitled independent or small-town journalists to participate in a lottery for the two unassigned press seats, and make use of a "listening room" which monitored the trial by audio.

As few ordinary citizens or small-town newspapers could afford such a steep initiation fee, the field was left to the media big boys, who soon reached a new conclusion about Kaczynski and his crimes. The man they had once hailed as a genius and then as a hermit, they now dubbed a nut.

AT 6:00 A.M. ON JANUARY 5, the courthouse doors opened and those with passes surged forward to form a line behind the metal detector leading

to the courtroom which opened at 8:00. Reporters took their stations in the Media Center listening room. The air was thick with anticipation.

Opening arguments had been scheduled for that day. The courtroom was soon packed with victims and scheduled witnesses. Professors Epstein and Gelernter were in attendance. So were David and Wanda Kaczynski, along with David Kaczynski's attorney, Tony Bisceglie. Kaczynski, wearing a brown sweater, his beard neatly trimmed, entered the courtroom accompanied by a guard.

But the arguments were never made. Instead, as soon as the judge, Garland E. Burrell, Jr., took his place on the bench, Kaczynski, still seated and speaking in a quiet, surprisingly high-pitched voice, addressed the court: "Your honor, before these proceedings begin I would like to revisit the issue of my relations with my attorneys. It's very important. I haven't stood up because I am under orders from the marshals not to stand up."

At this point everything stopped while Kaczynski conferred privately with Burrell, asking the judge for permission to fire his lawyers, since they insisted on basing his defense on the claim that he was mentally ill and he adamantly opposed this strategy. Instead, Kaczynski explained, he hoped the judge would allow him to replace these court-appointed attorneys with another attorney who would not invoke a "mental defect" defense.

After his conference with Kaczynski, the judge called a recess to discuss the request with prosecutors and the defense attorneys. Opening remarks, he assured everyone, would begin in the afternoon. But they did not. Nor would the trial resume later that week or the next.

What happened? The media would blame Kaczynski. The defendant, said the *Sacramento Bee*, had "derailed" the trial. Other commentators averred that he was "manipulating" the court system. The *New York Times* suggested that he had engaged in "a calculated disruption of the legal process."

But the media had things backward. Kaczynski didn't derail the trial. His own defense had. He wasn't manipulating the court system; he had been a victim of it. He was ambushed by the well-meaning but paternalistic machinations of his own family and defense team. And he had only just realized they had him trapped.

FOLLOWING KACZYNSKI'S arraignment in Helena, events had moved quickly. On June 18, 1996, a federal grand jury in Sacramento indicted him on ten counts related to the bombings of Scrutton, Epstein, Gelernter, and Murray. The same month, prosecutors in New Jersey prepared to try him there later, for Thomas Mosser's murder.

On June 23, Kaczynski was flown in a government jet to Mather Field, a former air force base, at Rancho Cordova near Sacramento. Wearing a bulletproof vest and surrounded by federal marshals, he was led into a black armored van with heavily tinted windows. Accompanied by a police motorcade of squad cars, motorcycles, and helicopters, he was sped to the downtown Sacramento jail at Sixth and I Streets. Two days later, he was driven the six blocks from the jail to the courthouse, for arraignment, where he pleaded not guilty.

Also, two days after Kaczynski's arrival in Sacramento, the court appointed Quin Denvir, a prominent Sacramento public defender, to represent him. And the next month (July 18, 1996), Denvir added Judy Clarke, a Spokane, Washington, attorney and noted death penalty defender, to his team. Shortly thereafter, they enlisted two other tacticians: Gary Sowards and Scharlette Holdman, well-known experts in plotting defense strategies based on the insanity plea in capital cases. Immediately this team faced a problem: The government search of Kaczynski's cabin had amassed an avalanche of evidence against their client.

At first, Denvir's team petitioned Burrell to throw out this evidence on the grounds that the search warrant had been legally flawed. But when in June 1997 the judge denied this petition, the defenders, having no other options left, filed with the court notice of their intent to pursue what is called in the law the "12.2(b)" or "mental defect" defense, which entailed calling mental health experts to the stand. They would admit that their client was the Unabomber, but seek to prove him not guilty because he suffered from a "diminished mental state." And if he was found guilty, the defense could cite diminished mental capacity as mitigating circumstances, to lessen the penalty.

To the defense, invoking this kind of insanity argument was made all the more urgent by Attorney General Janet Reno's May 15, 1997, announcement that the government intended to seek the death penalty for Kaczynski. Given the overwhelming evidence that Kaczynski's crimes had been carefully premeditated and committed without remorse, it was a virtual certainty that unless the defense could show Kaczynski suffered from a mental defect, he would not only be found guilty but be sentenced to death.

But this mental defect strategy also faced an obstacle: Kaczynski would object to it. As early as June 1997, Kaczynski maintains and the court record does not dispute, he wrote his attorneys, "I categorically refuse to use a mental status defense." He apparently wanted to purse a show trial and die a martyr to his ideas. Hiding behind a mental defect plea would undermine his efforts to convince the world to take his philosophy seriously.

Nevertheless, as Kaczynski later explained, "under pressure from the defense team," he reluctantly agreed to filing the 12.2(b) notice. He gave in, he says, because his attorneys claimed that filing their intention to submit this kind of defense was the only way the court would permit psychiatrists to testify to his sanity. As he told the appeals court, he was led to believe this stratagem was "only a legal device to enable a certain mental-health professional whom I know and like to tell the jury what kind of person I am." He says he was assured that the results of any psychiatric examination would be confidential—covered by attorney-client privilege—and would not be made public unless he wanted them to be.

Meanwhile, beginning in early 1997, David and Wanda Kaczynski, along with Linda Patrik and Tony Bisceglie, anxious to save Ted from the lethal injection needle, launched an intensive media blitz—which the *Washington Post* called "a campaign by the Kaczynski family to persuade prosecutors not to seek the death penalty"—to convince the public that Ted had suffered from mental illness since infancy. Eventually, they would give extensive interviews to virtually every major news medium— the *New York Times*, the *Washington Post*, CBS's *60 Minutes*, National Public Radio, public television, the Cable News Network, and the national newsweeklies—reiterating these claims. They conferred with Kaczynski's lawyers. They provided material on their brother and son for the psychologists who might offer expert testimony on his mental state.

Later, Kaczynski would complain that in seeking to save him from death, his brother and mother were hardly doing him a favor. David, he wrote in "Truth vs. Lies," "knows very well that . . . I would unhesitatingly choose death over incarceration."

Nevertheless, the family's campaign proved effective. Media and public opinion shifted. By the time jury selection began, nearly every pundit was attesting to Kaczynski's insanity. A *Washington Times* columnist referred to him as "a raving lunatic." Gerald Lefcourt, President of the National Association of Criminal Defense Lawyers, noted the defendant was "obviously disturbed." Donald Heller, a former federal prosecutor, offered that "This guy is not playing with a full deck."

As the family's media campaign continued, defense lawyers proceeded with their mental defect strategy, believing there was no other way to save their client.

But perhaps there was an alternative. Shortly after Kaczynski's arrest, J. Anthony Serra, a flamboyant San Francisco defense attorney, offered his services to Kaczynski, promising to fashion a defense based not on mental defect but on arguments from the manifesto. He would, he would later tell Kaczynski, use the "imperfect necessity" defense, suggesting the defendant had committed his crimes because he thought by doing so he would avert possibly more calamitous consequences. All Serra needed was to convince one juror that, having acted from such an idealistic motive, Kaczynski did not deserve the death penalty.

The defense team, however, saw such a strategy as bound to fail and therefore as nothing more than attorney-assisted suicide. This not only seemed unethical to them and a violation of the trial lawyer fraternity's unanimous opposition to capital punishment; it also flew in the face of their own expertise. Clarke and Sowards specialized in mental defect pleas. Holdman, a Ph.D. and not an attorney, was a well-known expert in "mitigation" in death penalty cases and, as she told me, was "always suspicious of conclusions by people who embrace free will." Therefore, presumably, for her no one was ever responsible for murder.

Circling the wagons, Kaczynski's attorneys reportedly refused to let Serra into the case and continued with the mental defect strategy. But they confronted yet another challenge: Making the best case for this required introducing expert psychological testimony, and Kaczynski would refuse to allow it. He had already made clear his resistance to being diagnosed as mentally ill, even before being moved to Sacramento. While still in the Helena jail, after two defense psychiatrists,

Ruben and Raquel Gur, had told him they believed he might be suffering from mental illness, Kaczynski broke off the interview, demanding that his attorneys fire them and not make their findings public.

Kaczynski's resistance to this strategy continued after he arrived in Sacramento. In October, according to his appeal brief and not disputed, he told Sowards, "I am bitterly opposed to the development of a science of the human mind."

To bypass this resistance, Clarke and Denvir invited Xavier F. Amador, a psychologist at Columbia University's College of Physicians and Surgeons, to evaluate Kaczynski's mental state without meeting with him but merely by examining his writings. And giving way to what Kaczynski later called "false promises and intense pressure" from the defense team, he agreed to meet with other mental health experts, including Karen Bronk Froming, a neuropsychologist at the University of California-San Francisco School of Medicine, because he thought that her examination would help establish that he was sane.

Kaczynski also reluctantly met with David Vernon Foster, a psychiatrist from nearby Auburn, California—"primarily," as Foster's report concedes, because Kaczynski believed Foster was there to "assist him in evaluating his health worries—such as his over sensitivity to sound, his sleep disturbance and his fear that his heart might burst from the anxiety of going through his trial." But when Foster brought up the subject of mental health, Kaczynski cut off the interview.

Quite predictably, these defense experts, like the Gurs, concluded that Kaczynski suffered from mental illness. Froming observed that Kaczynski exhibited a "predisposition to schizophrenia." Foster saw "a clear and consistent picture of schizophrenia, paranoid type." Amador described Kaczynski as "typical of the hundreds of patients with schizophrenia."

Raquel Gur believed Kaczynski met the diagnostic criteria for "Schizophrenia, Paranoid Type." Ruben Gur believed Kaczynski's symptoms were "not inconsistent" with this. Both based their provisional diagnosis, in part, on what they saw as Kaczynski's bizarre behavior, thought disorder, and "asociality," as well as the "imbalance" they detected between Kaczynski's high verbal intelligence and "impaired social functioning" (i.e., social awkwardness).

But other than the Gurs', little of this collective diagnosis rested on objective clinical data. Although tests alone suggested to Froming only that Kaczynski's answers were "consistent with" schizophrenia, she told *The New Yorker*'s William Finnegan that it was Kaczynski's writings—in particular, his "anti-technology" views—that cemented this conclusion for her. Foster, who met with Kaczynski a few times but never formally examined him, concluded that "Kaczynski's writings and life history provide a clear and consistent picture of schizophrenia, paranoid type," through his preoccupation with "delusional themes" and a lifestyle that evinced "social isolation" and "disorganized behavior." Kaczynski's classic symptoms, Amador declared, were his "neglect in his grooming," "withdrawal from social relations," and "delusional beliefs."

Most defense claims of mental illness, in short, rested on the diagnoses of experts whose judgments derived largely from their opinions of Kaczynski's philosophy and his personal habits—he was a recluse, a slob, a celibate—and from his refusal to admit that he was ill. Froming cited his "unawareness of his disease" as an indication of illness. Foster complained of the defendant's "symptom-based failure to cooperate fully with psychiatric evaluation." Amador said that the defendant suffered from "severe deficits in awareness of illness."

To cement the image in jurors' minds of their client's putatively insane lifestyle, Clarke and Denvir decided to enter his Montana cabin in evidence. After all, they reasoned, what could be more irrational than sleeping in a ten- by twelve-foot shack, heated only by a woodstove?

And so the cabin arrived at Mather Field on Friday, December 5, shrouded under a black tarpaulin on the back of a flatbed trailer, and accompanied by the usual caravan of reporters, cameramen, and curious onlookers.

"In our view," Quin Denvir said, "the cabin symbolizes what had happened to this Ph.D. Berkeley professor and how he had come to live."

"You really cannot understand this guy's life," he explained later, "unless you can get in that cabin. . . . This is not an idyllic, rustic cabin with a refrigerator and a wet bar."

Wet bars, apparently, are rational; woodstoves are not. Kaczynski's lifestyle, his ideas—even his denials of mental ill health—had been transformed into symptoms of mental illness.

Years earlier, in his journal, Kaczynski had anticipated such accusations.

I intend to start killing people. If I am successful at this, it is possible that, when I am caught (not alive, I fervently hope!) there will be some speculation in the news media as to my motives for killing. . . . If some speculation occurs, they are bound to make me out to be a sickie, and to ascribe to me motives of a sordid or "sick" type. Of course, the term "sick" in such a context represents a value judgment . . . the news media may have something to say about me when I am killed or caught. And they are bound to try to analyse my psychology and depict me as "sick." This powerful bias should be borne [in mind] in reading any attempts to analyse my psychology.

And he had been right. In truth, he was no more unkempt than many people on our streets. His cabin was less cluttered than the offices of many college professors—and far less chaotic than the settings of other, obviously sane people such as the computer guru Esther Dyson, whose New York office, according to *Vanity Fair*, contained larger heaps of debris than could have been thrown there by "tornadoes ripping down Fifth Avenue." The Montana wilds are filled with escapists like Kaczynski. Celibacy and primitivism are not diseases. Kaczynski wasn't a complete recluse. And his ideas were decidedly sane. He had published thousands of well-reasoned words explaining his motives precisely. On January 7, 1998, even Judge Burrell would remark that

I find him to be lucid, calm. He presents himself in an intelligent manner. In my opinion, he has a keen understanding of the issues. He has already seemed focused on the issues in his contact with me. His mannerisms and his eye contact have been appropriate. I know there's a conflict in the medical evidence as to whether his conduct, at least in the past, has been controlled by any or some mental ailment, but I've seen nothing during my contact with him that appears to be a manifestation of any such ailment. If anything is present, I cannot detect it.

Kaczynski saw himself as a revolutionary, seeking to topple "the system." He certainly was no less sane than many others who have killed for a cause, such as the Englishman involved in the "Gunpowder Plot," Guy Fawkes, who was executed for attempting to blow up the Houses of Parliament in 1605 as revenge for the persecution of Roman Catholics; or the abolitionist John Brown, put to death in the United States in 1859 for attempting to ignite an uprising against slavery by seizing the federal arsenal at Harpers Ferry, Virginia (since 1862, a part of West Virginia). The Unabomber's philosophy was more sane than the irate ramblings of Ramzi Yousef, convicted for his role in the 1993 World Trade Center bombing, and more sane than the ramshackle rationalizations of Oklahoma City bombers Timothy McVeigh and Terry Nichols. The latter were never seriously considered to be mentally ill. They were, nearly everyone seemed to agree, terrorists.

Kaczynski just wanted to be seen like them.

Not surprisingly, the mental health experts called by the prosecution didn't buy the defense mental defect arguments either. Phillip J. Resnick, professor of psychiatry at Case Western Reserve University School of Medicine, told me that Kaczynski's writings did not convince him that the defendant suffered from a mental disease. Park Elliott Dietz, another prominent psychiatrist called by the prosecution, expressed similar doubts, describing the manifesto as "eloquent."

In a report never made public, a third prosecution expert, Ohio neuropsychologist John T. Kenny, delivered a scathing critique of the Gurs and Froming examinations, observing that the data simply didn't support their conclusions that Kaczynski suffered from schizophrenia, much less paranoia.

When prosecution psychiatrists sought to examine Kaczynski themselves, however, Denvir and Clarke refused to allow it. Their client, they said, had a "pathological dread of examination by psychiatrists."

But Resnick and Dietz scoffed at this. It was the defense attorneys, they noted, not Kaczynski, who had refused to see them. If the defendant did not wish to be examined, he should be allowed to tell them so, face to face. "We have no credible evidence that Mr. Kaczynski has refused to meet with either Dr. Resnick or me," Dietz wrote the court.

We know only that counsel for Mr. Kaczynski have refused to allow us to determine whether Mr. Kaczynski will speak with us. . . . If Mr. Kaczynski suffered from a serious mental illness that would cause him to become uncommunicative in a face-to-face meeting with me, his lawyers would have let me meet with him. As long as counsel for Mr. Kaczynski block efforts to determine whether Mr. Kaczynski refuses to be examined, the most reasonable inference to be drawn from the record is that they are making a tactical decision on his behalf.

"It is my opinion," Resnick said, "that Mr. Kaczynski is not fearful of a psychiatric examination by government experts due to any mental illness." Rather, it may be that he "does not want to be unjustly labeled as mentally ill. He may have rationally concluded that if he were labeled mentally ill, his political anti-technology agenda would be denigrated."

Dietz concurred. Kaczynski, he wrote, "would probably welcome the opportunity to speak freely about his ideas, life, and crimes to someone who understood his true motives. His writings and his stance toward defense doctors lend support to the view that he dreaded defense doctors who seek to prove him mentally ill, but there is no reason to believe he would dread the opportunity to provide further evidence that he is not mentally ill."

Kaczynski claims not to have been made aware of the prosecution's request to have its mental-health experts examine him until nearly a month after his attorneys had refused to grant it.

In fact, he wasn't afraid of psychological examinations. On at least one occasion he had sought psychiatric help on his own. What he feared was an insanity diagnosis that would undermine public credibility of his ideas. And in all probability, prosecution psychiatrists would have provided precisely the imprimatur of mental health that he so anxiously sought.

COMPLICATING THE assessment of Kaczynski's mental condition were repercussions from an earlier episode in the defendant's life about which the media knew nothing and that Bisceglie described to me as his "bad experience at Harvard."

Indeed, even the defense team and the family knew next to nothing about his Harvard experience. They only knew that Kaczynski had participated in a three-year experiment at the university, conducted by Professor Henry Murray, during which he had been given a battery of psychological tests.

Anxious to disprove his family's claims that he had been mentally ill since childhood, Kaczynski asked his attorneys to obtain the results of these tests, which, he was convinced, would reveal that he had been normal at the time. "The assessment arrived at by the [Harvard] psychologists," Kaczynski explained later, "would be very useful in determining how people saw my personality."

But although the Murray Center at Harvard where these documents were kept gave Kaczynski's attorneys some raw data—his answers to test questions—it reportedly refused to provide the Murray team's analysis of that data.

Whatever the reason or extent of Harvard's reluctance to produce these analyses, Kaczynski's defense attorneys apparently didn't press very hard for them. They never subpoenaed the material. And they had a motive for not doing so: These Harvard evaluations might have undermined their case.

Rather than insist that Harvard turn over the Murray Center's own analyses of the tests, the defense team asked the Gurs and Froming to provide their own evaluation of answers Kaczynski had given on two of them—the Minnesota Multiphasic Personality Inventory and the Thematic Apperception Test (TAT). Predictably, they concluded that this data indicated Kaczynski had suffered from paranoid-type schizophrenia while at Harvard. After examining the same data, the prosecution's own expert, John Kenny, concluded the answers did not reveal mental illness at all.

As prosecution and defense experts argued over retrospective analyses of the Harvard data about whose purpose and circumstances they knew virtually nothing, the media, comprehending even less, jumped to the conclusion that if Kaczynski had received psychological evaluation as an undergraduate, he must have already shown signs of mental illness at the time. As ABC's Forrest Sawyer remarked during a *20/20* interview with David Kaczynski on May 4, 1998: "No one knows why, but at Harvard Kaczynski volunteered for psychological testing, and the results should have set off alarm bells, say doctors who recently reviewed them."

Thus, rumors about Kaczynski's Harvard experience served to cement the public perception that Kaczynski had been mentally ill since youth. Sawyer missed an opportunity to ask why the defendant's attorneys had not subpoenaed the Harvard analyses if they really believed these evaluations might have justified "alarm bells." Instead, the rumors were allowed to grow, while the media remained in the dark about the real significance of the Harvard data.

After the trial, Sawyer could have had his answer. In February 1998, when it was too late to make a difference, Kaczynski managed to persuade his attorneys to send his TAT answers, along with the answers of the twenty-one other study subjects, to a psychological testing expert, Bertram Karon, at Michigan State University. Because the individuals who gave these answers were identified only by code names, Karon could conduct a blind evaluation—measuring the answers without knowing who had given them. Karon found that on a scale of 0 to 10, with 0 a complete absence of illness and 10 the highest degree of illness, Kaczynski scored 0 for "Schizotypy" and 2 for "Psychopathy."

Kenny had been correct. Rather than setting off alarm bells, the Harvard data, according to Karon, showed Kaczynski to have been perfectly normal, at least until the end of his sophomore year, when this test was taken.

Nevertheless, throughout the fall of 1997 the defense team's mental defect defense preparations moved inexorably forward. And Kaczynski insists he was not aware of it. He seldom attended the pretrial hearings or jury selection and had missed those occasions during which his supposed mental state was discussed. Then, during jury selection proceedings on November 25, after the last prospective juror had departed, Kaczynski, overhearing a conversation between Burrell and the defense and prosecution attorneys on "neuropsychological testing," learned for the first time that the defense experts had diagnosed him as a paranoid schizophrenic and their conclusions had been released to the government and public.

On hearing this, Kaczynski at first seemed incredulous. His face grew red. He slapped his pencil on the table and glared at his attorneys. Until that time, he wrote the appeals court later, he "believed that his counsel would present, at most, evidence that he had relatively minor mental or neurological problems, and that he could control the mental-state evidence at least to the extent of preventing experts who had examined him from testifying." Now he discovered "that his attorneys intended to portray him as suffering from major mental illness, specifically schizophrenia."

Less than a week later—on December 1—Kaczynski wrote Judge Burrell, claiming that his attorneys were trying to portray him as "mentally ill without my consent" and seeking advice "from some source outside my present defense team that would help me to resolve my conflicts with my own attorneys." At Denvir's urging, however, the letter was not sent until December 18.

Then, along with his original letter to the judge, Kaczynski appended a second message, complaining that "I had been tricked and humiliated by people for whom I'd had warm affection" and explaining, "I would rather die, or suffer prolonged physical torture, than have the 12.2(b) defense imposed on me in this way by my present attorneys."

"I do not believe," he wrote then, "that science has any business probing the workings of the human mind, and that my personal ideology and that of the mental-health professions are mutually antagonistic." He asked Judge Burrell for permission to follow one of three courses of action: drop the 12.2(b) defense, allow him to represent himself, or allow him to hire new attorneys.

In response, Judge Burrell met in chambers with Kaczynski and his lawyers on December 22, where Kaczynski was told the court would not allow him to switch counsel, but Clarke and Denvir agreed to abandon the 12.2(b) strategy and not to use expert psychological testimony during the guilt phase of the trial.

Kaczynski mistakenly thought they had agreed not to submit *any* (expert or nonexpert) psychological testimony during the guilt phase. In return, he agreed to allow mental-state evidence during the penalty phase, because he thought this compromise was the best he could get. He was devastated, therefore, to learn on the evening of January 4,

1998, just a few hours before the trial had originally been scheduled to begin, that his attorneys still intended to present nonexpert mental-state testimony during the guilt phase.

Kaczynski, the ideologue, wanted his ideas to be taken seriously more than he valued his own life. Instead, his own attorneys planned to portray them as symptoms of mental illness. Such flaunting of the defendant's wishes greatly disturbed prosecutor Robert Cleary as well, who on December 24 warned that it "may raise important Sixth Amendment issues. . . . This is especially true because it appears that it is the defendant's right—not his lawyers'—to choose which defense to proffer."

By January 7, the judge and Kaczynski's legal team had put Kaczynski in a box. He couldn't stop his attorneys and he couldn't replace them. Burrell ruled that Denvir and Clarke would be permitted to submit mental-state evidence even against their client's wishes, but added that the defendant could, if he insisted, represent himself after all. By this time Kaczynski, exhausted, depressed, and contemplating suicide, declined the offer. He was "too tired," he told Burrell. When later that same day Kaczynski learned J. Anthony Serra was willing to represent him, he immediately asked Judge Burrell for permission to appoint Serra. But the judge refused. Changing defense counsel, the judge opined, would delay the trial and he refused to allow it.

Kaczynski had lost hope that he could avoid a trial in which he would be portrayed as crazy and his ideas dismissed as the ravings of a madman. Despairing, that evening he tried to hang himself in his jail cell with his government-issue underpants. The next morning sheriff's deputies found the underwear in the corner of his cell, "badly stretched out." Authorities put his cell under twenty-four-hour camera surveillance.

The trial resumed on Thursday, January 8. The room was packed. Kaczynski walked in wearing a cable-knit sweater and a face that gave nothing away. The judge opened proceedings by informing the court that the questions of Kaczynski's representation had been settled during meetings in chambers with Kaczynski and his lawyers over the preceding two days, and he was now determined to get the trial started.

Instead, a bizarre drama ensued, during which the defendant allied himself with the prosecution and quarreled with his own attorneys. Following Burrell's opening remarks, Judy Clarke announced that Kaczynski, deprived of other options, had changed his mind about self-representation and requested "that he be permitted to proceed in this case as his own counsel."

Now it was Judge Burrell's turn to change his mind. "I have a concern about the timeliness of the request," he responded, apparently ignoring the fact that Kaczynski had consistently objected to a mental defect defense ever since he first learned of its possibility. Desiring a speedy trial, the judge would not grant Kaczynski's request. Instead, he sought to reconcile Kaczynski with his defense team. He openly speculated on directing Clarke and Denvir to eschew insanity arguments, but they objected. They were convinced that Kaczynski suffered from a mental defect, they said, and they insisted on the right to choose the defense they deemed best.

This made the prosecution nervous. Burrell's action rendered it exceedingly likely that any conviction would be overturned by a higher court on appeal. "We look at this as a very, very serious matter," Cleary told the judge. Burrell had already expressed his opinion that Kaczynski was competent to stand trial, he reminded the court. And if he is competent, he has a right to direct his own defense.

"It's the government's position," Cleary declared, "the defendant is entirely competent to represent himself and to stand trial." Denying him this right "creates a potential for grave appellate error in this case. And that's been our major source of concern. . . ."

After a short recess, Burrell, along with prosecution and defense attorneys, agreed to have Kaczynski examined by a psychiatrist, to determine if he was competent to stand trial. If declared competent, everyone assumed, Kaczynski would be allowed to direct his own defense as he requested.

Within a week, the court had appointed Sally Johnson, a psychiatrist from North Carolina, to come to Sacramento to examine Kaczynski.

JOHNSON SPENT ten days interviewing Kaczynski and reading his writings. On January 19, she returned a verdict: a "provisional" diagnosis that Kaczynski suffered from "schizophrenia, paranoid type." But since this disease seemed now to be in "remission," she concluded that he was competent to stand trial and represent himself.

She wrote Judge Burrell: "It is my opinion that, despite the psychiatric diagnoses described in the attached report, Mr. Kaczynski is not suffering from a mental disease or defect rendering him mentally incompetent to the extent that he is unable to understand the nature or consequences of the proceedings filed against him or to assist his attorneys in his own defense."

Indeed, what seemed most notable about Johnson's conclusions was what she deemed Kaczynski *not* to be: he "does not show evidence of overt disorganization or psychotic symptomology at this time" and does not show "evidence of a mood disorder, obvious thought disorder, intellectual dysfunction." To be sure, he was "introverted, shy, and socially insecure" and had "strange thoughts, odd perceptions, and feelings of isolation and alienation"—behavioral traits, she observed, that are "consistent with individuals who have psychotic disorders that are mainly in remission at the time of test administration." But these traits are also shared by many who are not mentally ill.

Rather, Johnson's provisional diagnosis of schizophrenia, like those of the defense experts, rested almost entirely on what she considered two major categories of symptoms: Kaczynski's lifestyle and his ideas. He had chosen "a life of significant social isolation." And he harbored "delusional beliefs" about "the outcome of modern technology and the alleged (psychological) abuse by his family.

Specifically, she considered it "delusional" that Kaczynski thought he had been a victim of "psychological abuse by his parents" while growing up, that "he believed the system as it exists is bad and rebellion against it is justified," and that "freedom and personal dignity have greater importance than comfort and security." And she saw it as equally symptomatic that he "feels compelled to live a life of extreme isolation and to focus his energy against the aspects of a society that are attempting to control the masses."

These were weak threads on which to hang a diagnosis of mental illness. Beliefs are not "delusional" if they are true, and Johnson did not know whether Kaczynski's claims of psychological abuse were or not. Nor are political beliefs likely to be entirely irrational if they are shared by many people over a long period of time. And however delusional, the conviction that one's parents are responsible for our own unhappiness is so widely held that, although perhaps a symptom of neurosis, it can hardly be considered a sign of severe mental illness.

The national news media, however, noticed neither the specious reasoning that lay behind Johnson's tentative diagnosis nor her explicit caveat that it was "provisional" only. Instead, they hailed the report as proving Kaczynski insane.

William Glaberson wrote in the *New York Times* that Johnson had concluded Kaczynski "suffers from serious mental illness, including 'schizophrenia,' paranoid type." The *Sacramento Bee* reported that Johnson found Kaczynski suffered from "paranoid schizophrenia." The Associated Press said she dubbed him "a paranoid schizophrenic." The *Washington Post's* William Booth said that Johnson and the defense psychiatrists had concluded that Kaczynski "suffers from the grandiose fantasies and delusional rage of an unmedicated paranoid schizophrenic in deep denial." *Time* magazine's Tamala Edwards wrote that Johnson had "found that he was a delusional paranoid schizophrenic."

A January 23, 1998, *New York Times* editorial intoned that Kaczynski "suffers from schizophrenia and has delusions of persecution that can lead to violence. Dr. Johnson's diagnosis is in accord with the defendant's own psychiatric experts, who have said he is severely mentally ill."

ON JANUARY 22, just three days after Johnson delivered her report to Burrell, the trial resumed, and the judge—to everyone's astonishment—denied Kaczynski's request for self-representation. It was an Alice-in-Wonderland ruling. As William Finnegan observed in *The New Yorker*, there was "something odd" about Burrell's "flying a psychiatrist in from North Carolina for a week to determine the defendant's competency to represent himself and then, when she found him competent, ruling that he could not represent himself."

Michael Mello, a law professor and informal adviser to the Kaczynski defense, describes the decision as "bizarre." For whatever the merits of Johnson's diagnosis, her verification of Kaczynski's competency should have made Burrell's decision on the petition for self-representation an easy one. The law, suggests Mello, is clear: Any mentally competent defendant has a constitutional right to represent himself at trial, so long as he is warned what the risks of this strategy might be.

"How do we justify this travesty?" asked Thomas S. Szasz, the well-known professor of psychiatry at the State University of New York at Syracuse (now retired).

> *He offered to plead guilty and receive a life sentence in prison without parole. He has offered to go to trial, provided the "defense" . . . is anything other than that he is a madman. . . . He is willing to be represented by attorneys, provided the attorneys are willing to cooperate with him. He is willing to defend himself, if the judge will let him. . . . David Thoreau chose to live in a shack without electricity and water. Patrick Henry chose death over loss of liberty. Why can't we let Kaczynski choose his own defense? Why can't we acknowledge the dignity of his preferring to preserve his identity as a moral agent responsible for his deeds to the indignity of the benevolence we insist on inflicting on him?*

What happened? Mello writes that "Burrell seemed to be scrambling to find a reason, any reason, to keep Kaczynski's lawyers on the case and in control of the defense." The procedural pretext the court came up with was delay: Kaczynski had waited too long to invoke his right to self-representation.

Perhaps Judge Burrell had made up his mind not to grant Kaczynski's request even before he appointed Sally Johnson to examine Kaczynski. Perhaps, as Finnegan speculates, Burrell feared Kaczynski's representing himself would transform the trial into an O. J. Simpson–style courtroom circus, making the judge resemble the hapless Lance Ito. And certainly, he desired a speedy trial and knew that Kaczynski's self-representation would guarantee a lengthy one.

Whatever his motives, rather than clothing his decision in sound law, Judge Burrell now dragged in a red herring. Kaczynski's request, he said, was not serious. It was merely a tactic to delay the trial. The judge suggested Kaczynski had long known that his attorneys planned a mental defect defense, and stated that granting the defendant's request would be akin to turning the trial into a "suicide forum."

Neither the defense nor the prosecution chose to agree with Burrell. On January 8, Kaczynski's attorneys had repeatedly assured the judge that their client was ready to go to trial immediately, as soon as the issue of representation was settled. And the prosecutors observed that "we cannot say that the defendant's assertion of his right to represent himself was untimely or for the purposes of delay."

Burrell's decision nevertheless triggered a quick settlement. Within an hour of the ruling, defendant and prosecutors threw in the towel. Both reluctantly accepted a plea bargain offered by defense lawyers. Prosecutors became suddenly anxious to cut a deal because they realized that Burrell's denial of the defendant's right to self-representation vastly increased the risk that a guilty verdict would be overturned on appeal. And Kaczynski felt trapped. As he explained on January 26, the ruling "put me in such a position that I had only one way left to prevent my attorneys from using false information to represent me to the world as insane."

Faced with the prospect of a humiliating trial in which his attorneys would portray him as insane and his philosophy as the ravings of a madman, Kaczynski capitulated: In exchange for the government's agreement not to seek the death penalty, he pleaded guilty to thirteen federal bombing offenses that killed three men and seriously injured two others, and acknowledged responsibility for sixteen bombings from 1978 to 1995.

On May 4, 1998, Kaczynski was sentenced to life in prison without possibility of parole. "A few days ago," he said at that hearing, "the government filed a sentencing memorandum, the purpose of which was clearly political. By discrediting me personally, they hope to discredit the ideas expressed by the Unabomber."

AFTER THE TRIAL, Gil Murray's widow, Connie, would make a plea for full disclosure of all the evidence amassed against Kaczynski. "While we are relieved that the guilt phase of the trial process is over," she declared, "it is unfortunate that most facts of the case never saw the light of day."

What had been disclosed so far, Mrs. Murray went on, was "only the tip of the iceberg."

But instead, it seemed that America would never learn what lay beneath the still waters of this shy killer. "I must acknowledge that I don't really understand Ted," David Kaczynski confessed to me.

Perhaps no one did. So far as anyone knew at this time, Kaczynski may or may not have been insane. Johnson's examination had revealed just how complex and opaque his psyche is. Yet if there had been a trial, America might have learned why he killed. Without one, there would be no presentation of evidence, no cross-examination of witnesses, no disclosure of diaries, no information on how he chose his victims, no examination of possible ties to radical environmentalists, no arguments for or against his insanity, no revelations about what fueled his anger and at whom it was directed, no discussion of possible dysfunction within his family, no scrutiny of his early education or the environment in which he grew up, no accounting of why and when he conceived the manifesto philosophy, no questioning of the widely held assumption that he was "a product of the sixties," and no telling what had happened at Harvard.

Kaczynski would remain unknown. Not only would the key questions not be answered; they wouldn't even be asked. Few would be curious. The media had decreed there was no more to know. Public opinion dismissed him as a nut. America seemed to heave a collective sigh of relief that it would not have to confront this killer.

Why was virtually everyone so ready to dismiss him? Michael Mello suggests it is because his ideas are too extreme for us to contemplate without discomfort. The manifesto, Mello writes in his book on Kaczynski,

> *challenges the basic assumptions of virtually every interest group that was involved with the case: the lawyers, the mental health experts, the press and politics—both left and right. . . . Kaczynski's defense team convinced the media and the public that Kaczynski was crazy, even in the absence of credible evidence . . . [because] we needed to believe it. . . . They decided that the Unabomber was mentally ill, and his ideas were mad. Then they forgot about the man and his ideas, and created a curative tale.*

Scott Corey, in an article published in *Telos* (Winter 2000), concurs. Kaczynski's philosophy, he observes, not only embarrassed nearly everyone but, although flawed, was too cogent for many to confront. It reminded environmentalists that their revolution required "the virtual elimination of humanity." It showed "market ideologues" that "if libertarian individualism is what lends virtue to the merciless market, it lends itself all the more to anarchy," and that "if government control is illegitimate on libertarian grounds, there is no defense for the power of corporate bureaucracy either." It discomfited anarchists by implying that their revolution could not succeed without violence. It alienated intellectuals because "they found themselves . . . under attack by someone who was . . . 'one of us.'" It disconcerted his attorneys when it "became apparent that the defendant was bent on a political trial." And it alerted government that it was "in danger of being embarrassed by an enemy that might have something intelligent to say."

Altogether, Corey concludes, "the Unabomber episode . . . is a demonstration of how ill prepared modern society is for new, unfamiliar confrontations. . . . The awkward denials and embarrassed cringing . . . all flow from a central fear that modernity is not up to the argument."

So who *is* Ted Kaczynski?

PART TWO

THE EDUCATION OF A SERIAL KILLER

It is obvious that a high level of education in a general sense has often failed to protect twentieth-century minds from homicidal, or suicidal, aberrations. As we have seen, these have often been generated by men of high educational standing. And it has often been in colleges and universities that the bad seeds first bore fruit.

—Robert Conquest,
Reflections on a Ravaged Century

What are the radical defects from which modern European culture suffers? For it is evident that in the long run the form of humanity dominant at the present day has its origins in these defects.

—José Ortega y Gasset,
The Revolt of the Masses
from Kaczynski's cabin library

9

The Loneliness of the Blue-Collar Intellectual

The accumulation of the missed and compromised revolutions of modern times, with their consequent ambiguities and social imbalances, has fallen, and must fall, most heavily on the young, making it hard to grow up.

—PAUL GOODMAN,
Growing Up Absurd
from Kaczynski's cabin library

THE SOUTH Carpenter Street neighborhood is upscale now. Situated just two blocks from the University of Illinois Chicago Circle Campus where the Unabomber's first bomb had been placed in 1978, its attractively renovated row houses are occupied by Chicago's professional classes. Parked Volvos, Saabs, and BMWs line both sides of the narrow, dead-end street.

It was a Polish working-class community when Theodore Richard "Turk" Kaczynski and Wanda Theresa Dombek Kaczynski moved into the second-floor flat of a narrow, three-story frame house around two years after World War II. Ted, born on May 22, 1942, was almost five. David was born there two years later.

According to Ted, it was the third place the Kaczynskis had lived since Turk and Wanda's marriage, and it was a step upward. Here on Carpenter Street they owned their home (rather than renting it) for the first time.

Turk worked in the family sausage business near the South Side stockyards and followed politics passionately. But all who knew him say he loved books even more. Self-educated, he had an enormous appetite for learning. Gregarious, he liked to invite intellectuals to his home, to discuss and argue about authors, ideas, and politics. Neither he nor Wanda was religious and each looked to the rationalism of "experts" to give meaning to life. Their love of books and their agnosticism set them apart from blue-collar neighbors.

Turk liked the outdoors, too. But according to friends, he loved the *idea* of wilderness more than wilderness itself. He identified with non-conformists such as the Amish, who didn't fit into industrial society.

Turk's enthusiasms, friends say, overshadowed the quieter Wanda, and years later few would recall what, if anything, she had contributed to these discussions. Yet, as one family friend, retired Grinnell sociology professor Paul Carlston, told me, both Turk and Wanda believed that access to truth and insight came through contact with the best minds.

And the best minds in those days were very worried. Fear permeated the culture of the time. World War II had killed 60 million people. The bombing of Dresden, Leipzig, Hiroshima, and Nagasaki convinced many intellectuals just how technological knowledge might destroy the world. The grotesque "experiments" on human subjects by death camp doctors such as the notorious Josef Mengele of Auschwitz reminded them where science could lead. And no sooner had World War II ended than the Cold War began. The fear of totalitarianism and thermonuclear conflict spread.

In May 1946, just weeks after Winston Churchill had warned in Fulton, Missouri, that "from Stettin on the Baltic to Trieste in the Adriatic, an Iron Curtain has descended across the continent," Hungarian Communists, backed by the Red Army, seized power in a coup d'état. Within a year, Communists controlled all of Eastern Europe.

On July 24, 1948, Soviet troops cut off rail and highway traffic between West Germany and Berlin, igniting an international confrontation that came perilously close to war. In 1949, Communists took over China and the Soviets exploded their first atomic bomb. In June 1950, North Korea launched a surprise attack on South Korea. Three days later, U.S. troops, fighting under the United Nations flag, were rushed to the peninsula. And when, in November, Chinese forces crossed the Yalu River into North Korea, America found itself at war with China. By 1952, this war, which eventually would kill or wound nearly 150,000 Americans, reached stalemate, and no one seemed to know how to get the country out.

These events profoundly affected the social and intellectual climate. In response to the Soviet threat, America embraced technology. In 1946, Congress established the Atomic Energy Commission. In 1950, it created the National Science Foundation, which began pouring tens of millions of dollars into defense-related research. In 1958, a year after the Soviets had successfully placed *Sputnik I*, the world's first artificial Earth satellite in orbit, the United States established the National Aeronautics and Space Administration (NASA). The space race had begun and the prospect of thermonuclear war loomed large.

Meanwhile, the acceleration of technology during both the world war and the Cold War had a depressing effect on national culture. Many prominent writers began warning of the dangers of technology and the impending collapse of civilization. In 1944, Lewis Mumford's *The Condition of Man* appeared, warning that "Everywhere the machine holds the center and the personality has been pushed to the periphery."

In 1945, H. G. Wells would write that "the end of everything we call life is close at hand." Immediately after the war, the American public discovered Freud, who warned in his *Civilization and its Discontents* (first published in 1930), that the fundamental irrationality and aggressiveness of human beings threatened humanity's future. In his best-selling novels *Animal Farm* (1944) and *1984* (1949), George Orwell explored the terrors of totalitarianism. In other best-sellers, Jean-Paul Sartre and Albert Camus suggested that life is without meaning, the human situation fraught with angst and alienation, and that the only important philosophical question concerned suicide. The intellectual climate became an incubator for outsiders.

As an engaged and intellectually curious man, family friends say Turk followed these world events and literary developments closely. Among other writers, according to Paul Carlston, Turk studied Mumford and Freud, as well as Erich Fromm, whose *Escape from Freedom* (1941) noted that "certain factors in the modern industrial system . . . make for the development of a personality which feels powerless and alone, anxious, and insecure." Yet, like many second-generation Americans, the elder Kaczynskis were ambitious for their children and devoted themselves to their education.

SUCH WAS THE idealistic, passionate, bookish home into which Kaczynski was born. During their campaign to save Ted from death by convincing the media that he was insane, both Wanda and David said repeatedly that theirs had been a happy and normal home. The family, they said, was warm, loving, and close. The parents doted on Ted. As David summarized his and Wanda's perspective on *60 Minutes*, Ted's "feelings about our family bear no relationship to the reality of the family life that we experienced. These were loving, supportive parents." Turk took his sons camping. Wanda spent hours reading the *Scientific American* to them, and taking them to museums.

Yet David and Wanda also admitted that Ted had been "different"—abnormally quiet, ungregarious, and sometimes unresponsive—since he was a baby. They never explained how the family could have been so close if Ted was so distant.

According to this family version, Ted demonstrated exceptional academic ability early in life and became increasingly aloof as he grew up. He had almost no friends and would usually come directly home after school, closeting himself in his attic room. His mother would attract other children to their home by offering lemonade and cookies in an attempt to draw Ted out, but to no avail. He developed an irrational fear of doctors. Wanda fretted about what she saw as the "strange contradictions" in her older son's behavior—moody, rude, and unhappy one moment, pleasant and compassionate the next. "I would try to draw Ted out. 'What's bothering you?' I would ask him," Wanda told *Washington Post* reporters. "I don't know whether he knew himself what was bothering him. All he knew, I think, is that he felt rotten."

Despite Wanda and Turk's urging, David and Wanda claimed, Ted refused to join the Boy Scouts and almost never dated girls. He preferred to read a calculus text than to play with classmates. His parents began to fear he suffered from mental illness, but were too poor and fearful of the social stigma associated with such a disorder to seek medical help.

What had started young Ted's seemingly inexorable descent into isolation, according to Wanda, was a defining episode that occurred when the boy was only nine months old. At that time he contracted a severe case of hives and was rushed to the hospital. When Wanda brought him home five days later, his personality had changed entirely.

He was unresponsive, she told Leslie Stahl on CBS's *60 Minutes*—like "a little rag doll." And thereafter, Ted was periodically withdrawn and aloof.

In the "Baby Book" she kept during Ted's infancy, Wanda (using the third person) recorded her visit to Ted in the hospital: "Mother went to visit baby. . . . Mother felt very sad about baby. She says he is quite subdued, has lost his verve and aggressiveness and has developed an institutionalized look." After he returned home, she noted that he was strangely inert, "like a bundle of clothes." After that, she said, Ted was never the same.

That week, Wanda says, has haunted her ever since. "I ponder endlessly over it," she told the *Washington Post* reporters, "What could I have done to keep him out of the wilderness? What could I have done to give him a happier life? And yet there were so many happy, wonderful times with the family. I just don't, I just don't know."

This is a vivid, touching story, but according to Ted, almost entirely fictitious. Wanda invented it afterward, he says, when he was in high school, to explain why as a teenager he began rejecting her for the first time. Quoting from Wanda's own "Baby Book," he concedes that immediately after he was brought home from the hospital, Wanda had indeed written that he was as inert as "a bundle of clothes." What she failed to tell the media, he claims, is that three days after this incident she had also recorded in the "Baby Book" that he had returned to his usual animated and friendly self. And within three weeks, he was clambering to the front door in his walker whenever the buzzer rang, to greet whoever was there.

Indeed, Ted insists, most of what David and Wanda said about him, and the press embroidered and repeated, is false. His mother, he says, is terrified that people will think her a bad mother. So she and David invented the story of his early mental illness to protect her feelings. But it is just that: a story. Rather, his social isolation didn't begin in infancy, but much later. And it was caused, he insists, not by mental problems but by his parents, who pushed him too hard academically.

When families disagree about their past like this it is almost impossible for anyone—least of all an outsider—to know where the truth lies. It is not an issue of who's telling the truth. Rather, no two people experience the same events the same way. As adults, we view the episodes of our own childhood differently from the way our parents or siblings do because everyone's impression comes from a different perspective. Each portrays only part of a picture.

The same holds true of the Kaczynski family's conflicting accounts. While Ted viewed himself as shy and "socially reserved," Wanda saw him as antisocial. When Ted refused to play with the boy across the street because he didn't like him, Wanda fretted that he was "aloof." If Ted refused to stay in the Boy Scouts because he thought merit badges and uniforms dumb, his parents saw this as evidence that their young son was "different."

The letters and other materials Kaczynski sent me in the course of our correspondence—including his autobiography, "Truth vs. Lies," containing quotations from doctors, teachers, and college advisers—understandably reflect his own perspective. Nevertheless, in retracing Kaczynski's footsteps, I found much support for what he claimed. But not all. The environment in the Kaczynski household was not an entirely loving one. But it wasn't dismal, either. It was more unhappy than the family admits but less so than Ted declares. In short, it wasn't especially unusual. One might describe it as a typical, dysfunctional American home. In portraying himself as "abused" while growing up, Ted seems to forget that childhood is seldom easy and, sad to say, all too often miserable. And contrary to what David and Wanda claim, Ted, like millions of others, had much to complain about.

In only one way was the Kaczynski household unusual: in its intense intellectuality. This would become the leit motif of Ted's life. From the beginning, Turk's and Ted's intellectual interests would isolate the family from its neighbors and Ted from his peers. As the son grew older, his preoccupation with books and ideas would loom ever larger, until it created a social gulf too wide for him to cross.

KACZYNSKI SAYS, apparently accurately, that his early childhood was quite normal. At age two, his pediatrician wrote that he "plays well with other children." At eight, the medical records noted that Kaczynski, then attending nearby Sherman Elementary School, was "healthy" and "well-adjusted"; at nine, that he "plays well with children in school and neighborhood. Very happy"; at ten, "appetite, activity and general adjustment are all quite good"; at eleven, he "presents no behavior problems"; at twelve, he "does well socially." In the fifth grade, after the school guidance counselor, Vera Frye, had given him an IQ test, she observed that Ted was entirely normal, telling his mother (as Wanda told the *Washington Post*) that "he had a strong sense of security, which surprised me. . . . She said he could be whatever he wanted to be. . . . He was the cat's whiskers."

When he first moved to Carpenter Street, Ted says, he regularly played with the neighborhood boys and girls. Initially, he even took a "leadership" role in his small group of friends, once putting on a "carnival" and, with his comrades' help, advertising the production and selling tickets to it. In the fifth grade he had a brief crush on a girl named Darlene.

But Carpenter Street lay in a tough neighborhood, and as Ted grew older he began to realize that some of his friends were budding juvenile delinquents. When a group attacked an old homeless man, pelting him with garbage, Ted started drawing away. And his comrades, sensing his retreat, "saw me as too much of a good boy." His parents noticed that he was losing friends but didn't know why. They wondered if he kept to himself because he was so much smarter than they, or because there was something emotionally wrong with him.

The other forces propelling Ted's loneliness came from within the family itself. Even when he was small, Ted reports, his parents "always regarded themselves as a cut above their neighbors. They had intellectual pretensions. They—especially my mother—looked down on our neighbors as ignorant."

Turk was a self-educated freethinker living in a conventionally Catholic working-class community. Wanda corrected Ted's English, not allowing him to speak like the other kids in the neighborhood. Nevertheless, Kaczynski claims—and a close friend of Turk's confirms—that Wanda tended to be fearful their family would be perceived as different. Although nonconformist, Wanda wanted the family to be perceived as conforming. Thus, Ted records, although they were atheists, his parents instructed him to tell people they were Unitarians. And although he continued to seek the friendship of his peers, a gulf began to grow between them as he developed intellectual interests and they did not.

So, rather than allowing Ted to be himself, Turk and Wanda put conflicting demands on him. On the one hand, they saw themselves as intellectuals and freethinkers, not like their working-class neighbors. On the other, they feared being ostracized for their ideas. Ted grew up acutely aware that his family was different, but also cognizant that it was important for him to fit in.

And gradually, it seems, Turk began to turn cold—first toward his older son and eventually toward life in general. No one seems to know why. Perhaps he was being pushed to depression by the bleakness of his reading or world events. Perhaps he was becoming disappointed in Ted. Whatever the reason, Ted began to feel, as he recorded in "Truth vs. Lies," that "there was an undercurrent of scorn in his attitude about me."

Whenever Turk got angry at Ted, he would accuse him of being insane, or psychotic, using these words not in their clinical sense but merely as terms of derision. And over time, according to several sources, Turk became increasingly aloof and unfriendly toward his oldest son.

AFTER DAVID was born, claims Ted, Wanda began to change. She became increasingly irritable and the family atmosphere deteriorated. Everyone squabbled. Wanda became "crabby and irritable, Dad morosely passive." Then, in Ted's fifth grade year, something happened to set Ted on a downward course from which he never recovered.

The catalyst for this decline was the very same Vera Frye who had called him "the cat's whiskers." At the direction of school authorities, she gave him an IQ test on which he achieved a "genius" score of 167. At her suggestion, with the consent of the parents and school authorities, Ted was skipped into the seventh grade. And immediately the social isolation that Wanda feared and may up to that point have only imagined became real. He would never be accepted by his new classmates, who were at least a year older. The bigger boys bullied and teased him. The girls ignored him. He sank to the lowest social level, where he remained.

From then on, according to Ted Kaczynski and also to others who knew the family, his parents valued his intellect as a trophy that gave the family special status. Obsessed with the prospects of Ted's intellectual stardom, both parents pushed their son relentlessly toward academics.

On more than one occasion, Kaczynski remembers coming home with a report card showing all A's except for one B. And each time, his parents would lecture him about trying harder.

And while friends of the family confirm that Turk and Wanda did not apply this pressure consciously, there can be little doubt that, as Paul Carlston observed, "with Turk there was no question what the expectations were." In the Kaczynski family, rejection of books was simply unthinkable. And, as several friends observed, everyone was expected to keep personal problems to himself.

From the seventh grade onward, Ted felt increasingly outcast. He retreated into books. The harder he worked, the more his isolation grew. And as it did, his parents worried. Ted was too bookish. He was odd. So they pushed him hard socially as well, urging him to go out more, play with boys he did not like, and mix more. Soon a pattern emerged: Turk and Wanda put pressure on Ted to excel both socially and intellectually.

And Ted tried hard to please them. But as these were contradictory goals, he was bound to fail.

By the time Ted entered junior high, his parents had boxed him into a corner. If he did not succeed academically, they would be disappointed. Yet when he hit the books hard, they declared him a social failure. The seeds of the Outsider had been planted.

10

Growing Up Absurd

Postwar Silent youths came of age feeling an inner-world tension amid the outer-world calm.

—WILLIAM STRAUSS AND NEIL HOWE,
Generations

SOUTH OF CHICAGO, at the intersection of Kedzie Boulevard and 95th Street, lies the geographic center of the suburban community of Evergreen Park. Known as the "Village of Churches," it exudes outward calm and absence of strife and complexity. Less than three square miles in area, it reflects a determination to resist time and impose order, to remain a rock-solid island in a sea of suburban flux. The small retail establishments that in most towns change hands or go out of business regularly—the bowling alleys, dry cleaners, and Oriental takeouts—remain under the same ownership they had years ago.

In 1952, when Ted was ten, his parents moved the family from Chicago to Evergreen Park—in order, as they later explained to Ted, to provide him with a better class of friends. They settled into a neat, stone and frame house at 9209 South Lawndale. Small but not too small, their home was at once open and cozy. One could easily imagine teenage boys fifty years ago sitting at their desks by the dormer window, building model airplanes there.

The tree-lined street is immaculate—homes flawlessly kept, lawns carefully manicured. A park and playground stand just down the block, the perfect place for children to play tag or touch football. And beyond it lie two heavily wooded cemeteries. The effect is amazingly rural. Given such greenery, it is hard to realize that the area is surrounded by the urban jungle of greater Chicago.

Yet no children play in the playground. No toys can be seen in the yards. Few pedestrians walk the sidewalks. The surroundings reflect an iron order that does not tolerate the joyful anarchy of young people. Underneath this veneer of tranquility, Evergreen Park was, during Kaczynski's childhood, riven by divisions and even occasional violence. And by the time he left Evergreen Park, Kaczynski too, beneath his placid exterior, would be seething.

Originally settled by Dutch immigrants on what was once marshland, Evergreen Park had become, around the time the Kaczynskis arrived, a mixed neighborhood of Irish, Italians, Czechs, and Poles, who felt themselves under siege by yet another group of arrivals. On May 17, 1954, in a landmark case, *Brown* vs. *Board of Education of Topeka*, the U.S. Supreme Court ruled that segregated schooling was unconstitutional. To many people in Evergreen Park, this was tantamount to a declaration of war. For this town was, as several of Kaczynski's friends and teachers told me, an extraordinarily racist community. Even before the court decision, its citizens feared what they saw as black encroachment. African-American communities lay just outside, and black families came to town to shop and eat at Evergreen Park restaurants. Black teenagers hung around Evergreen Plaza.

The prospect of even a marginal number of minority families moving into town would eventually drive some locals to threaten insurrection. As Carlston reports, one would exclaim, "Them niggers will never cross 87th Street!"

The Kaczynskis had moved to Evergreen Park shortly before the Supreme Court ruling and soon found themselves under siege on the racial issue. As conscientious liberals, Turk and Wanda at first openly defended the rights of African Americans. And in these highly charged times, this was a brave and dangerous thing to do. Their views immediately drew fierce criticism. Eventually intimidated by this social pressure, Turk and Wanda, Ted says, started keeping their views on racial tolerance to themselves. But in one sense it was too late. Together with their religious skepticism and intellectual interests, their values, however quietly expressed, had already served to isolate the family from its neighbors.

Home life continued tense. Wanda, Ted says, would fly into rages at the slightest provocation. Turk, apparently consumed by a terrible metaphysical pessimism, retreated behind his newspaper.

Indeed, the Kaczynski family could hardly not be affected by the growing tension and despair of the period. For it was part of the air one breathed back then, putting its stamp on an entire generation. Kaczynski, like myself, is a member of what William Manchester dubbed "the Silent Generation"—that cohort of "depression babies" born between 1925 and 1942. "Never," Manchester wrote,

> *had American youth been so withdrawn, cautious, unimaginative,
> indifferent, unadventurous—and silent. The silent generation was
> a phenomenon of the 1950s, as characteristic of it as tailfins and
> white bucks. A vast hush had settled over the universities. . . .
> There seemed to be no indignant young men on campuses, no
> burning causes, and no militancy.*

Actually, our generation was not so much silent as ignored, repressed, and fearful. Growing up in a world on the brink of thermonuclear war, calmness became our facade, obscuring mounting anxieties. Born during the depression, we were fewer in number than either our predecessors, the GI generation, or our successors, the baby boomers. We weren't sufficiently numerous to have a major impact on politics, the economy, or popular culture. No one from our generation would become president. Advertising, consumer products, movies, popular fashions focused on the more numerous baby boomers.

Born during a time of economic collapse, we felt materially insecure. Born before the discovery of penicillin, we felt our own mortality. We saw our friends and siblings succumb to childhood diseases, such as whooping cough, measles, mumps, scarlet fever, chicken pox, meningi-

tis, pneumonia, and tuberculosis. We watched polio epidemics leap-
frog the country, claiming thousands of victims, leaving countless children and adults paralyzed or confined to iron lungs for the rest of their
lives.

Growing up during World War II, the Cold War, and the Korean
War, we had never known peace. In that pre-Pill culture, dread of
unwanted pregnancy poised like a sword over teenagers of both sexes.
Indeed, fear formed the backdrop of our lives: fear of poverty and unem-
ployment, fear of death from disease, fear that our fathers and brothers
would come home from the war in caskets, fear of unwanted pregnancy,
and perhaps most pervasive, fear of failing to measure up to our parents'
expectations of us.

Fearing that sickness might claim us, too, our parents were overly
protective and strict. Children were to be "seen but not heard." Pedia-
tricians and parenting books stressed strict discipline and warned that
"sparing the rod would spoil the child." We were constantly reminded
to conform, to "be good." As William Strauss and Neal Howe explain in
their book *Generations*,

> *Kids read stories about "Tootle" (a little train that always stayed on
> the track) and* Paddle to the Sea *(a little boat that reached its des-
> tination by floating safely with the current). At the movies, they
> watched Sparky, Alfalfa, and the "Little Rascals" scrupulously
> mind their manners whenever they encountered elders. As threats
> against national community deepened, children were bluntly told
> that older generations were making enormous sacrifices so they
> could grow up enjoying peace and prosperity . . . any day could
> bring devastating news—a layoff, a foreclosed home, the combat
> death of a father . . . a social and cultural no-man's land. Their
> worst school discipline problems ranged from gum chewing to cut-
> ting in line. The pressure to conform came more from adults than
> from peers.*

We tried so hard to behave! As Gail Sheehy has put it, the Silents
"were so good . . . they didn't know about drug raids, only panty raids.
In their day, grass was mowed, Coke was a cold drink and pot was something a girl asked for at her bridal shower." Alcohol, Sheehy implies, was

virtually their only vice. "As adolescents, they drank too much and drag-raced cars as big as tanks with tail-fins."

This repressive atmosphere and strict parenting made us turn inward. Silents "became teenagers when to be a teenager was nothing, the lowest of the low," the novelist Pat Conroy remembered. "Most of us kept quiet, attempting not to call attention to ourselves."

"We had no leaders, no program, no sense of our own power, and no culture exclusively our own," Conroy explained. Many were, like Kaczynski, "straight arrows," who neither drank nor did drugs and remained celibate into their twenties. But even those apparently dedicated to a frenzied pursuit of pleasure seethed beneath with anxieties and unexpressed emotions.

This was the meaning of the "quiet" fifties. It wasn't simply the period of carefree and innocent excess popularized by writers such as Sheehy and television sitcoms like *Happy Days*—a world of ducktails, "doo-wop," bobby socks, beer binges, drag races, Elvis, and piano-wrecking. Rather, frivolity was just half the story. For the decade was a schizophrenic one, of macabre contrasts. Domestically, the daily lives of ordinary Americans had never been better. The economy was booming. The country had recovered from the Great Depression and people, newly affluent, were seeing the USA in their Chevrolets. Yet civilization seemed to teeter on the brink.

The Cold War had triggered a technological race apparently leading toward global thermonuclear annihilation. Senator Joseph McCarthy's anti-Communist witch-hunt raised concerns of Communist subversion among some, while spreading the far more legitimate fear among many others that the Cold War's anti-Communist hysteria posed a grave threat to civil liberty. Confronted with the unthinkable, we Silents became escapist, living lives of quiet denial. We skated on the surface of life, in disconnected worlds infused with surreal juxtapositions of grim reality and mindless popular culture.

During this period, the Supreme Court ordered desegregation of public golf courses, parks, swimming pools, and playgrounds, and Ampex introduced the first tape recorder. Black civil rights leaders Lamar D. Smith and African-American minister George W. Lee were murdered by white gangs in Mississippi and America built its 1,800th shopping mall. William Golding's *Lord of the Flies*, with its bone-chilling portrayal of the darkness that lurks inside every human soul, became a best-seller and IBM introduced its first business computer. Mao Zedong launched the "Great Leap Forward," killing millions and dislocating a half a billion Chinese, and Texas Instruments introduced the first transistor. West Germany joined NATO and RCA introduced the first color television.

Fidel Castro launched "total war" against Cuba's corrupt Fulgencio Batista regime and the first tranquilizers—Miltown and Equanil—were put on the market. The Soviets denounced Boris Pasternak's *Doctor Zhivago* and the Wham-O Company introduced the Frisbee and the hula hoop. Soviet troops brutally suppressed Polish and Hungarian revolts against Moscow's rule and *Captain Kangaroo* debuted on national television. The Suez Crisis plunged the Near East into war and Disneyland opened. The United States built its first nuclear submarine and Elvis Presley made his debut, recording "That's All Right, Mama" and "Blue Moon of Kentucky."

THIS SAME SCHIZOPHRENIA infused the atmosphere at Evergreen Park High. In any public school such as this one, there had long been a gulf between the jocks and cheerleaders who formed the social elite, and the serious students—alternatively called "grinds" or "briefcase boys"—who occupied the lowest social stratum. The Cold War widened this gulf. The global struggle's emphasis on technology encouraged educators to push bright students more emphatically into mathematics and science. And the harder they worked, the more they were reviled by their peers.

Evergreen Park's fragmented school system further widened these divisions. The high school was not established until 1954, and its building not completed until the spring of 1955. Kaczynski, who became a member of the first class that spent all four years there, found himself in a school without cohesion or community, where few students knew each other. As Spencer Gilmore, a former science teacher, lamented, there was "no commonality in the student body." Howard Finkle, a former Evergreen Park High social studies teacher, describes Evergreen Park in those years as a school for strangers. Soon, the school was riven by cliques.

Until that time, students had been attending classes at various schools outside Evergreen Park, Finkle explains, and so moving to the new school meant leaving old friends behind and attending classes with students they did not know, although they may have been from the same neighborhoods. Thus they found themselves aliens in their own school. Many resented this enforced transfer, even if it meant they now had their "own" school.

These conditions, says Gilmore, made for an "odd school." He added that when the students who had been studying in outlying districts entered their new school, many of their friends and classmates from these other neighborhoods began hanging out in Evergreen Park as well. The "foreign" boys and girls cruised the neighborhood, drag-racing down Kedzie Boulevard in their souped-up '51 Mercs, firing zip guns (homemade firearms) and picking fights with the "natives." The local kids put white Band-Aids on their noses, so they could be easily identified by the police and by each other. Gilmore, who had been in charge of the high school detention hall, quickly had his hands full.

Meanwhile, the new school put unique pressures on the brighter students. "The fact to keep in mind about Evergreen Park," said Paul Jenkins, who taught Kaczynski mathematics and served as an administrator at the school for over forty years, "is that Gene Howard [principal of Evergreen Park High School at the time] enjoyed a big budget. He had combed the country for the best instructors he could find—folks who would be teaching junior college in most places. Yet most of the kids were incredibly naive. Some had never even been to downtown Chicago. The faculty was presenting them with ideas they'd never encountered before. Some hated the experience; others loved it. And it blew the minds of some, including perhaps Ted."

The students, according to Howard Finkle, were asked to read books ordinarily given to college undergraduates. The intellectually ambitious, like Kaczynski, adapted readily to these demands. But in a school where the most popular boys dressed like "The Fonz" and carried cigarette packs rolled up in the sleeves of their T-shirts, excelling at academics meant social exile.

Later, Eugene Howard would realize how dysfunctional Evergreen Park High had been during this period. The school was "highly authoritarian," he told me; the educational atmosphere "rigged" against the students.

The school system was a pyramid. At the top was the state board of education. Underneath in successive layers were the department of education, state school commissioners, local school boards, superintendents, principals, and assistant principals. At the very bottom were the teachers, who had virtually no authority at all.

State bureaucracies masterminded the choice of textbooks, curriculum, teacher education, and teacher certification. Unions controlled the teachers. At many schools (but not Evergreen Park) school board members were appointed, not elected. Specialists presided over myriad services from audiovisual instruction to special education.

It is not surprising, therefore, that student social life was dominated by cliques similarly rigid and hierarchical. As Howard wrote in 1989:

> *The clique composition of a school parallels, with some distortion, the clique structure of the community. It is there, in every school, always communicating a message of unworthiness to some pupils, always creating winners and losers. The composition of these cliques, the names given to them, and their place in the hierarchy varies from school to school. Most schools have equivalents of "eggheads," "greasers," "cowboys," or "jocks." Each clique has well-defined standards for admission to the group and each clique demands its own brand of conformity of its members. Members violate the groups' standards only at their peril. The valid threat of exclusion from all cliques is always there and always contributing to the process of freezing individuals into the cliques.*

Howard's reflections strongly paralleled those of other prominent educational reformers. Many, such as the social critic Paul Goodman, had complained eloquently that public schools were more concerned with turning youths into conformists than educating them.

Almost without exception, Goodman writes in *Growing Up Absurd*, alienated youths believed the enemy was "the system, with which they refuse to cooperate." The school system in particular, he says, was largely designed by social scientists who thought that

> *you can adapt people to anything, if you use the right techniques. [They] have become so accustomed to the highly organized and by-*

and-large smoothly running society that they have begun to think that "social animal" means "harmoniously belonging." They do not like to think that fighting and dissenting are proper social functions, nor that rebelling or initiating fundamental change is a social function. Rather, if something does not run smoothly, they say it has been improperly socialized; there has been a failure in communication.

Surrounding the school system lies the broader society itself, which also constitutes what Goodman describes as an "organized system" that has become a "technocracy," with

its role playing, its competitiveness, its canned culture, its public relations, and its avoidance of risk and self exposure. That system and its mores are death to the spirit, and any rebellious group will naturally raise a contrasting banner.

Now the organized system is very powerful and in its full tide of success, apparently sweeping everything before it in science, education, community planning, labor, the arts, not to speak of business and politics where it is indigenous. Let me say that we of the previous generation . . . have been sickened and enraged to see earnest and honest effort and human culture swamped by this muck.

In this environment, Goodman concludes, "the majority of young people are faced with the following alternative: Either society is a benevolently frivolous racket in which they'll manage to boondoggle, though less profitably than the more privileged; or society is serious . . . but they are useless and hopelessly out."

Feeling himself to be "hopelessly out," Kaczynski apparently agreed. The FBI found a copy of Goodman's book in his Montana cabin. And his manifesto attacks "the system" 210 times in its 232 paragraphs.

SUCH WAS THE polarized and autocratic regime that prevailed when Kaczynski matriculated at Evergreen Park High in the fall of 1955. He would find himself a stranger attending a school of strangers, where authorities sought to impose conformity from above.

The school had rules for everything. One advised, "You will act and dress in a more grown-up manner so that you can enjoy new privileges. Evergreen Park High School boys do not wear levies [sic] to school; nor do they wear juvenile haircuts." Another commanded: "Keep your grades high!"

Soon after Ted matriculated, Turk and Wanda joined this system too, serving on the PTA, as well as on the "caucus committee" that nominated candidates for election to the school board. Even at school, it seemed, Ted couldn't gain the distance from his parents every teenager craved. He became a "briefcase boy"—a member of the caste that comprised Evergreen Park's untouchables.

Ted's social rejection, in turn, fed Turk and Wanda's fears that the family might be perceived by others as different. They intensified pressure on their son to conform. When he woke to find a pimple on his nose on the day he was to have his photograph taken for his Harvard preregistration, Ted remembers that Wanda, fearful that this blemish would give a less than perfect impression to the admissions committee, scolded him roundly.

As Turk and Wanda's efforts to mold Ted into a boy at once socially popular and academically exceptional continued to fail, the parents took out their frustration by calling him "sick," "immature," or "emotionally disturbed." Whatever he did, Ted felt they interpreted as a sign of inadequacy or mental illness. When Wanda found him drawing war pictures, she concluded, he says, that he was obsessed with violence. When he refused to play with a neighbor's boy he considered a creep, she accused him of being antisocial.

AFTER KACZYNSKI'S arrest, the family would cement this image of Ted as an odd loner in the public mind. The *Chicago Tribune* reported that as a youngster, Ted had been "painfully shy." The Associated Press noted that he had walked around with "a pocket protector and briefcase." The *San Jose Mercury News* quoted a classmate as calling Ted "socially inept," and another as saying he was "a boy among men." The *New York*

Times suggested his childhood presented a "funereal portrait of loneliness, obsession and contradictions." As a teenager, the *Times* said,

> *his social handicaps were becoming increasingly apparent. By the time he entered Evergreen Park Community High School, Teddy was having more trouble fitting in . . . most classmates and [school activity] club members remember him as alien, or not at all. To Bill Phalen, Teddy was a nerd . . . Jerry Peligrano's fleeting memory was of a bespectacled kid with pencils in a pocket protector. Loren De Young remembered him as "a kind of non-person" . . . "Ted was technically very bright, but emotionally deficient," said Patrick Morris.*

Some reporters added another dimension: even in high school, they claimed, Ted had been fascinated with bombs. To gain the attention and acceptance of his peers, the *Chicago Tribune* reported, he helped his classmates build a bomb in chemistry class that was "so powerful that it broke windows in the chemistry lab"—an achievement that earned him a day's suspension from school. Another classmate, wrote the *Tribune*, saw Ted "set off a rocket back in the track." Associated Press added that Ted wasn't afraid of making bombs because he thought himself "too smart to get caught."

Kaczynski neither wore a pocket protector nor owned a briefcase and he hadn't been obsessed with making bombs. But once again, the media were deceived by their own methodology. By interviewing Kaczynski's classmates indiscriminately, they found many who did not know him. Yet his real friends and nearly all his teachers paint a very different picture.

"I probably knew Ted better than anyone else," one classmate of Ted's, Russell Mosny, told me. "And most of what media says about him is baloney.

"We were part of a group that hung out together," Mosny, now a computer consultant, went on. "Ted and I were much alike. Like him, I was an exceptional student. We were both members of the National Honor Society. We both had skipped a grade. We shared an interest in math and science. *Sputnik* had just gone up, kids were being pushed hard into science. It was a glamour discipline.

"And Ted was not a loner, not hostile, not obsessed with explosives. He was just two years younger than his classmates and immature to boot. True, he was socially inept, but studying math made all of us that way, at least a little. It required so much of our time we had little of it left for girls. And Ted's relations with the opposite sex were more of the 'putting pigtails into inkwell' variety."

As for the story about Ted's "obsession" with bombs, Mosny continued, "all high school kids want to make bombs. We were no exceptions. Ted, being bright, knew how to do it. Others badgered him, demanding that he show them how. They asked me, too, but being a year older than Ted and a bit more mature, I turned them down. So Ted, anxious to please, told one boy how to do it. The boy made the 'bomb.'

"It was a joke. I was standing six feet away and wasn't hurt. It didn't break a window, as has been reported. The principal called the boy in, who explained that Ted had told him how to make it. Ted was suspended for a day. But it was no big deal, since the principal knew Ted hadn't made the bomb and couldn't be responsible for what the other kid did."

"I know the stereotype of Ted," Paul Jenkins said to me. "He's supposed to have been an oddball his whole life. But that isn't so." Kaczynski, he said, was as typical as anyone with an IQ of 170 could be. He wasn't a loner or hostile or odd. He wasn't obsessed with making bombs. Since Jenkins as school administrator was responsible for enforcing discipline, if Ted had been a troublemaker, he'd have known it, he said. Ted had his circle of friends among the brighter students like himself and was something of a leader in this small group.

"The first week I had Ted as a [math] student," Jenkins went on, "I realized he was too advanced for my class. So to keep him challenged I made him my teaching assistant. He did this job very well. The other kids liked him, and appreciated his help."

How, then, could the media report that Kaczynski was so strange? "They made a natural mistake, I think," Jenkins replied. "After Ted was arrested, reporters poured into Evergreen Park and began interviewing at random those whose names appeared in Ted's high school yearbook. The most accessible were those still living in the vicinity. And quite by accident most of these had not been members of Ted's small circle. They were more the jock and cheerleader types, who didn't associate with the brainy kids anyway. To them, Ted was a 'grind.' And since Ted's own social circle had been a small one, reporters pretty much missed it entirely."

The very qualities that hurt Kaczynski with many of his peers made him a favorite of his teachers. Virtually all the former instructors I talked to who knew him well in those years saw him as studious and a member of the lowest-ranking high school clique, but otherwise entirely normal.

Kaczynski's former band teacher and friend, James Oberto, told me Ted "wasn't antisocial, just introverted." His physics teacher, Robert Rippey, described him as "honest, ethical and sociable.

"Ted was not a troublemaker, not a loner," Rippey added. "He was simply brilliant. One of the best students I ever taught." Kaczynski's American government teacher, Philip Pemberton, said Ted had many friends and indeed seemed to be their "ringleader." School reports regularly gave him high marks for "neatness," "respect for others," "courtesy," "respect for law and order," and "self-discipline."

No one was more lavish in her praise of Kaczynski than Lois Skillen, his high school counselor. "Of all the youngsters I have worked with at the college level," she wrote to Harvard in 1958,

> I believe Ted has one of the greatest contributions to make to society. He is reflective, sensitive, and deeply conscious of his responsibilities to society. . . . His only drawback is a tendency to be rather quiet in his original meetings with people, but most adults on our staff, and many people in the community who are mature find him easy to talk to, and very challenging intellectually. He has a number of friends among high school students, and seems to influence them to think more seriously.

By the late 1950s, the Cold War was still unabated. In the fall of 1956, the Soviets brutally suppressed a rebellion in Hungary against Communist rule, and Israel, supported by the British and French, invaded Egypt, triggering the Suez Crisis. And by 1958, real or potential conflicts between the Western and Communist powers—any one of which might be the trigger that started thermonuclear war—were proliferating around the globe. Following a Communist coup in Iraq, President Dwight Eisenhower sent U.S. Marines to protect Lebanon. The Chinese Communist regime began shelling the offshore islands of Quemoy and Matsu, occupied by Nationalist forces. Castro was poised to topple Cuba's currupt Batista regime. And Berlin became a flashpoint again.

Simultaneously, the space race heated up. On October 4, 1957, the Soviets launched the first successful artificial satellite. In response, America immediately accelerated its own space program. In 1958, Eisenhower signed into law the National Defense Education Act, allocating millions in aid for scientific and technological education. High school teachers pushed their brightest students toward scientific careers harder than ever. This momentum was well nigh impossible for bright young boys to resist, at Evergreen Park as everywhere else.

When Kaczynski was a sophomore, the high school administration recommended that he skip his junior year. James Oberto, the band teacher, remembers pleading with Kaczynski's father not to allow it. But Turk wouldn't listen. "Ted's success meant too much to him," Oberto says. Two years younger than his classmates, and still small for his age, Kaczynski became even more of an outcast in school. "There was a gradual increasing amount of hostility I had to face from the other kids," Sally Johnson reports Kaczynski as admitting. "By the time I left high school, I was definitely regarded as a freak by a large segment of the student body."

The pattern of outward calm and inner turmoil continued. Caught between acrimony at home and rejection at school, Kaczynski countered with activity. He joined the chess, biology, German, and mathematics clubs. He collected coins. He read ravenously and widely, excelling in every field from drama and history to biology and mathematics. He explored the music of Bach, Vivaldi, and Gabrieli. He studied music theory and wrote musical compositions for a family trio—David on the trumpet, Turk at the piano, and himself on the trombone. He played duets with Oberto.

Kaczynski tried hard to be good, to live up to the expectations of his family and teachers. But these efforts isolated him all the more. Most painful and irksome of all, they seemed to render him incapable of attracting female companionship. A sexual revolution was under way.

Freudian psychologists warned that suppressing sexual desire led to neurosis. In 1948, *Sexual Behavior in the Human Male*, known as "The Kinsey Report" after its author, University of Indiana zoologist Alfred Charles Kinsey, had rocked the nation with claims that pre- and extramarital sex were far more common than most people had hitherto thought. In 1953, Hugh Hefner launched a new magazine called *Playboy* and began to preach promiscuity as a kind of liberation theology he called "the *Playboy* Philosophy." In 1955, Vladimir Nabokov's satirical, erotic *Lolita* became the talk of the nation.

The climate of virtue had changed. Teenage boys who hadn't "done it" were ashamed to admit they were still virgins. And Kaczynski had almost never dated a girl. He lacked even elementary social skills.

Russell Mosny recalls one of Kaczynski's rare dates. Kaczynski borrowed his parents' car and took a girl to a movie. A half hour into the show, he excused himself and walked out of the theater, then returned a few minutes later. His date thought he had gone to the restroom. But thirty minutes later he left again, then returned. He repeated these mysterious exits twice more. But the last time he did not return. After the movie was over, the girl found Ted waiting for her on the street.

"Where have you been?" she asked.

"I parked the car at a thirty-minute meter and had to keep putting nickels in," he explained.

"But why didn't you come back the last time?" she persisted.

"I ran out of money for tickets to get back in the theater," he replied.

Inwardly, Kaczynski seethed. The seeds of alienation had been planted. Ashamed rather than proud of his academic achievements, furious at his own awkwardness, growing up during the Cold War in a town divided by racial issues, attending a high school where students were strangers to each other and the highest value was placed on conformity, pressured into mathematics so that he could serve the military-industrial complex, he had no chance to feel he belonged. In a blue-collar neighborhood where most kids' ambitions didn't go beyond meatpacking, Kaczynski had few opportunities for friendship. With parents who pushed him academically, then worried about his mental health when he didn't fit in socially, he felt a failure.

During his senior year, Ted Kaczynski was accepted at Harvard.

James Oberto pleaded with Turk not to let Ted go.

"He's too young, too immature, and Harvard too impersonal," Oberto said. "He could fall between the cracks."

But Turk wouldn't listen. "Ted's going to Harvard was an ego trip for him," Oberto observed.

And for Ted, Harvard would prove to be an educational experience.

11

The Religion of Reason

The madman is the man who has lost everything except
his reason.

> —G. K. CHESTERTON,
> *Orthodoxy*

The greatest intellectual capacity is only found in connection with a vehement and passionate will.

> —ARTHUR SCHOPENHAUER,
> *The World as Will and Idea*
> from Harvard's Gen Ed syllabus

NUMBER 8 PRESCOTT STREET in Cambridge is a well-preserved,
three-story, Victorian frame house, standing just outside Harvard Yard. Today, it houses Harvard's expository writing program. But in September 1958, when Ted Kaczynski, aged just sixteen,
arrived at Harvard, it was a more unusual place.

Earlier that year F. Skiddy von Stade, Jr., Harvard's dean of freshmen, had decided to use the house as living accommodations for the brightest, youngest freshmen. Von Stade's well-intentioned idea was to provide these boys with a nurturing, intimate environment, so that they wouldn't feel lost, as they might in the larger, less personal dorms. But in so doing he isolated the overly studious and less mature boys from their classmates and inadvertently created a ghetto for grinds, making social adjustment for them more rather than less difficult.

"I lived at Prescott Street that year too," Michael Stucki told me. "And like Kaczynski, I was majoring in mathematics. Yet I swear I never ever even saw the guy." Stucki, who recently retired after a career in computers, lived alone on the top floor, far from Kaczynski's ground-floor room. In the unsocial society of 8 Prescott, that was a big distance. "It was not unusual to spend all one's time in one's room and then rush out the door to library or class," Stucki said.

Francis Murphy, the Prescott Street proctor, was a graduate student who had studied for the Catholic priesthood, and to some students it seemed the house was intended to be run more like a monastery than a dorm. Whereas other freshmen lived in suites with one or two roommates, six of the sixteen students of Prescott Street, including Kaczynski, lived in single rooms. All but seven intended to major in a mathematical science. All but three came from high schools outside New England, and therefore knew few people in Massachusetts. They were, in Murphy's words, "a serious, quiet bunch."

Harvard had long been a notoriously anonymous place, where it was not unusual to live across the hall from someone for years and never know his name. High school graduates were especially isolated. Whereas most prep school alumni had grown up nearby, most public school graduates came from other states. They arrived at Harvard knowing no one and lived too far from home to visit during the shorter vacations of Thanksgiving and Easter. And Prescott Street was even more anomic than that. There were few of the bull sessions that usually characterized undergraduate life, and no hijinx. Most just stayed in their rooms and studied.

Much has been made of Kaczynski's being a "loner" and of his having been further isolated by Harvard's famed snobbism. Indeed, snobbism was pervasive at Harvard back then. Preppies saw themselves as patricians and high school graduates as lowly "wonks"—the Great Unwashed, whose worst offense was a failure to wear the right clothes.

The "correct" dress consisted of cordovan shoes, high, dark socks kept up with garters to hide the calf, a three-button tweed jacket (preferably from Brooks Brothers or J. Press), button-down shirt, regimental striped tie—and most important of all, the tie tied in a (narrow) four-in-hand knot. A single false sartorial step could brand one an outcast. And Kaczynski looked shabby. He owned just two pairs of slacks and only a few shirts. Although he washed these each week in the coin-operated machine in the basement of the house next door, they became increasingly ragtag.

Added to this were academic anxieties. Unlike preppies, many of whose parents and older siblings had attended Harvard and whose education at private schools had been second to none, arriving high schoolers often weren't sure they belonged academically. Thanks to the poor state of American public education, many were woefully unprepared for the academic challenges they would find. They arrived feeling that Harvard had probably made a mistake in admitting them. Consequently, during freshman year especially they hit the books hard, ignoring social life, while their upscale counterparts often made the opposite choice.

It is a mistake, however, to exaggerate Kaczynski's—or the average high schooler's—isolation. Most public school boys at Harvard in those days, including Kaczynski, viewed the tweedy in-crowd as so many buttoned-down buffoons who did not realize how ridiculous they looked. And the evidence is that Kaczynski was neither exceptionally a loner nor, at least during his early years at Harvard, especially alienated from his peers.

Harvard was a "tremendous thing for me," Kaczynski wrote in "Truth vs. Lies." "I got something that I had been needing all along without knowing it, namely, hard work requiring self-discipline and strenuous exercise of my abilities. I threw myself into this . . . I thrived on it. . . . Feeling the strength of my own will, I became enthusiastic about will power."

Freshmen were required to participate in sports, so Kaczynski took up swimming and then wrestling. He played the trombone, as he had in high school, even joining the Harvard Band (which he quit when he learned that he would have to attend drill sessions). He made a few friends. One housemate, Gerald Burns, remembers sitting with Kaczynski in an all-night cafeteria, arguing about the philosophy of Kant. After Kaczynski's arrest, Burns wrote to the anarchist journal *Fifth Estate* that Kaczynski "was as normal as I am now: it was [just] harder on him because he was much younger than his classmates." And indeed, most reports of his teachers, his academic adviser, his housemaster, and the health services staff suggest that Kaczynski in his first year at Harvard was entirely balanced. The health services doctor who interviewed Kaczynski as part of the medical examination Harvard required for all freshmen observed:

> *Good impression created. Attractive, mature for age, relaxed. . . . Talks easily, fluently and pleasantly . . . likes people and gets on well with them. . . . Exceedingly stable, well integrated and feels secure within himself. Usually very adaptable. May have many achievements and satisfactions. . . .*

And academically, Kaczynski seemed to fulfill this promise. By the end of the year, he had earned grades of B- and C in English composition, A's in German, physics, and mathematics, C and C+ in the first and second terms, respectively, of humanities ("Ideas of Man and the World in Western Thought"), and C and B- in social science ("The Role of Law in Anglo-American History").

In short, Kaczynski's freshman year seemed average. He kept to himself, but so did many of his classmates. He was awkward and illkempt, but so were they. He participated minimally in extracurricular activities—like many others. He was no more shy than one might expect of any sixteen-year-old living in a foreign environment a thousand miles from home.

But although Kaczynski didn't realize it, he had entered Harvard at a time when it, along with many other colleges and universities around the country, faced an intellectual crisis that would profoundly affect him and his generation. Kaczynski's encounter with this academic revolution, together with the other experiences that awaited him at the hands of Professor Murray, would transform this already emotionally fragile and angry young man into a full-blown Outsider.

✧ ✧ ✧

FOR MORE THAN 150 years, Harvard had been dedicated to what might be called the religion of reason. The college was founded as a Congregationalist institution by the Puritans in 1636. But as the Boston wing of that denomination turned toward secular rationalism during the eighteenth century, so did Harvard. And by the time the Congregationalist preacher William Ellery Channing broke from his church to found Unitarianism in 1819, the college was on its way to embracing the secular, rationalist idea that moral law could be proved objectively valid and rational, and that, conversely, pursuing scientific truth inevitably led to the promotion of virtue.

By the time Kaczynski arrived at Harvard in 1958, however, many of the faculty had lost faith in the idea that morality was rational. Harvard was experiencing a crisis in confidence. Although no one noticed, the religion of reason was giving way to something one could call the culture of despair.

All Harvard freshmen in the 1950s, including Kaczynski (and me), were immersed in what the college described as "general education" and students called "Gen Ed." This program of studies, which had been introduced in 1950, was part of a nationwide curricular reform that sought to inculcate a sense of "shared values" among undergraduates through instruction in the Judeo-Christian tradition.

Unlike the usual departmental offerings, which focused on methodological issues within a discipline, Gen Ed courses were intended to be interdisciplinary, with material arranged for students historically (chronologically) rather than analytically. Required Gen Ed courses focused on science, literature, philosophy, history, and Western institutions.

The undergraduate curriculum, therefore, was initially designed to be neatly divided into two categories, one general and one specialized, one emphasizing history and values, the other stressing the value-free methodologies employed by scholars in the various academic fields.

This curriculum was, in part, a very natural reaction to recent events—the Great Depression and World War II. The depression brought to the surface some weaknesses of U.S. democracy and its economic system. The Veterans' March on Washington, breadlines, bank failures, the halving of the income of the average American made many question American ideals and institutions.

The war reinforced these concerns. For it was an ideological conflict that convinced many of the need to reaffirm democratic values and to understand better why our soldiers fought and died. The bombing of Hiroshima and Nagasaki made scholars see just how knowledge, not guided by moral purpose, might destroy the world. The test of national survival galvanized the nation, bringing people together and making cooperation on campus, as well as elsewhere, possible. The Soviet threat—and the challenge to democracy that it posed—further cemented the conviction, held by many, that citizenship cannot be taken for granted but must be taught. Colleges and universities, fearing social fragmentation of their student bodies as enrollments swelled with veterans returning under the GI Bill, saw the need for promoting "shared values."

Between 1944 and 1947, curriculum committees throughout the country articulated this concern. The Dennison College faculty noted that general education would help the student "more intelligently assume his responsibilities as a citizen." In 1947, Amherst College adopted a curriculum dedicated to the ideal "that a man's knowledge and skill are his only to serve the good, public and private, of the community," University of Minnesota faculty Senate hoped general education would help the student learn to "work cooperatively," be "a responsible and informed citizen," and "develop a set of principles in the direction of personal and societal behavior."

These views found common expression in the 1946 report of President Harry Truman's Commission on Higher Education. This document advocated the expansion of higher education that took place in the postwar years. But it was equally intent on promoting general education. "Present college programs," it claimed, "are not contributing adequately to the quality of students' lives, either as workers or citizens. This is true in large part because the unity of liberal education has been splintered by over-specialization.

"Too often," the report continued, today's college student

> has acquired competence in some particular occupation, yet falls
> short of that human wholeness and civic conscience which the

cooperative activities of citizenship requires. The failure to provide
any core of unity in the essential diversity of higher education is a
cause for grave concern. A society whose members lack a body of
common experience and common knowledge is a society without a
fundamental culture; it tends to disintegrate into a mere aggrega-
tion of individuals. Some community of values, ideas and attitudes
is essential as a cohesive force in the age of minute division of labor
and intense conflict of interests. The crucial task of higher educa-
tion today, therefore, is to provide a unified general education for
American youth. Colleges must find the right relationship between
specialized training on the one hand . . . and the transmission of a
common cultural heritage toward a common citizenship on the
other.

Gen Ed, in short, was born of a lofty impulse: to establish in higher
education—as the Commission on Higher Education expressed it—"a
code of behavior based on ethical principles consistent with democratic
ideals."

But none of these calls for reform had as profound an effect on the
educational landscape as a report entitled *General Education in a Free
Society*, published by Harvard in 1945 and known for the color of its
cover as the Redbook. This work, considered the *locus classicus* of general education, was written by a Harvard committee convened in 1943
and charged by Harvard president James B. Conant with the task of
reviewing the Harvard curriculum. In his charge to the committee,
Conant wrote:

Unless the educational process includes at each level of maturity
some continuing contact with those fields in which value judg-
ments are of prime importance, it must fall far short of the ideal.
The student in high school, in college and in graduate school must
be concerned, in part at least, with the words "right" and "wrong"
in both the ethical and mathematical sense.

The committee's recommendation that Harvard introduce a general
education program "provided," as the historian Frederick Rudolph puts
it, "a new impetus to general education." Calling for what Rudolph

describes as "a submersion in tradition and heritage and some sense of common bond strong enough to bring unbridled ego and ambition under control," the Redbook's program of reform caught the imagination of educators across the country.

It was a bold idea, but not a new one. During the 1920s and 1930s, several colleges and universities had already embraced similar curricula, dedicated to the study of Western civilization—most notably Columbia University, which adopted its course of studies in "Contemporary Civilization" in 1919, and the University of Chicago, which instituted an ambitious program of classical education in 1939. But general education remained relatively rare.

"Until President James B. Conant of Harvard appointed a faculty committee on 'the objectives of a general education in a free society,' in 1943," says Rudolph, "college and university faculties were able to avoid the general education movement. . . . Once the Harvard Committee had issued its report in 1945, however, the prestige of the country's oldest and most influential university was committed to the search for some way to provide a general education for the citizens of an atomistic, necessarily specialized, and unavoidably complex society." Harvard's Redbook was, Rudolph concluded, "a landmark document."

By the mid-1950s, more than half the colleges in America were offering programs of general education modeled along similar lines. General education became a national phenomenon, pursued not merely at elite institutions such as Columbia, Harvard, and the University of Chicago but at every kind of college, including Brandeis, the City College of New York, New York University, Connecticut College, Washington and Lee, Washington University (in St. Louis), Bowdoin, Notre Dame, California Institute of Technology, Scripps and Harvey Mudd (both Claremont colleges), Stanford, Whittier, Grinnell, Massachusetts Institute of Technology, Mount Holyoke, and Tulane, among other places.

Although no two institutions adopted identical programs, their general education programs shared a definite family resemblance. All emphasized mandatory courses at the expense of electives, and many reduced the number of offerings listed in the catalogues. All offered interdisciplinary programs team-taught by faculty members from several departments. Most stressed Western history and literature. All placed great importance on the acquisition of basic skills in language, science, and mathematics, on encouraging ethical behavior, and on creating for faculty and students a sense of shared intellectual and social experience.

Yet, although at Harvard the name "Gen Ed" caught on, the philosophy behind it would not. Gen Ed was doomed from the start. It would become the latest victim of the long war between humanism and positivism—a conflict between two competing approaches to knowledge that had been raging since the Renaissance.

12

Is Intelligence Evil?

Where there is the tree of knowledge, there is always Paradise: so say the most ancient and the most modern of serpents.

—Friedrich Nietzsche,
Genealogy of Morals
from the Gen Ed syllabus

Civilization develops in man nothing but an added capacity to receive impressions—that is all. And the growth of that capacity increases his tendency to seek pleasure in spilling blood. You may have noticed that the most enthusiastic blood-letters have always been the most civilized of men.

—Fyodor Dostoevsky,
Notes from Underground
from the Gen Ed syllabus

A T THE HEART of this conflict lay a question about the nature of modern evil: Why are the most advanced civilizations also the most barbaric? Is intelligence evil? Or, more precisely, does reason undermine morality and does the accumulation of knowledge increase the prospects of cruelty and violence?

When Hitler came to power, Germany was perhaps the most scientifically and culturally advanced country on earth. In virtually every field of human endeavor, this country had produced some of the wisest and most creative people in history. Yet this same society launched the most diabolical, sickening, and widespread campaign of genocide in history.

How could a people so cultured, so advanced, have committed such unspeakable terror? Why did the land that gave us Beethoven also give us Hitler?

Nor was Germany the only "civilized" country to embrace terror. During the twentieth century, Stalin's Russia, Mao's China, and Pol Pot's Cambodia would kill, according to the best estimates, 87 million of their own citizens. The Japanese, another ancient, refined, and technologically-advanced culture, killed a further 30 million, often with sadistic relish. And America itself, a society founded on the highest moral and spiritual aspirations of mankind, half a century ago destroyed the city of Dresden, killing over twenty-five thousand men, women, and children in a series of firebomb raids for reasons so obscure that no one—to this day—knows what they were.

As terror escalated, people became inured to the sight of acts that once offended them. Early in the century, killing innocent civilians in war was considered a heinous crime. When, on May 7, 1915, a German submarine sank the passenger ship *Lusitania*, killing 1,195 civilians, many Americans supposed a sacred principle had been violated: No nation, it was then believed, had the right to kill noncombatants. It was to defend this principle, in part, that the United States entered World War I. Yet by the 1920s its own military planners were formulating strategies for future wars that required massive submarine warfare against civilian shipping and saturation bombing against cities. Today, targeting civilian populations remains a centerpiece of military planning.

Such killing, so unusual in earlier times, now became so commonplace that the twentieth century had to invent new words to describe it: expressions such as "concentration camp" (coined by the British in

1901, to describe the prisons where they kept Boer women and children); "saturation bombing" and "carpet bombing" (minted by the U.S. Army Air Corps during World War II); "gulag" (introduced by the Soviet Union in 1921, to describe its first forced-labor camp, in Archangel); "genocide" (according to the *Oxford English Dictionary*, first used in 1944); "holocaust" (again according to the *OED*, an ancient word originally meaning a burnt offering, first used to describe mass murder in 1942); "collateral damage" (an expression of recent coinage used to describe the unintentional killing of civilians during wartime); and "ethnic cleansing" (first used by the Serbs in 1992 to describe removal or elimination of Bosnian Muslims and Croats).

The more human beings advance, the greater their crimes. How is this possible? Could evil be increasing, not despite the progress of man but precisely because of this progress?

Clearly, technology increases our capacity for mayhem. But human beings are *conceiving* more ambitious ways to murder as well. The source of the problem lies in men's minds, not their machines. Could, therefore, the very advance of civilization be the source of modern evil?

On the surface, this question seems absurd, its answer obvious. After all, have not scholars always supposed intelligence, far from being evil, was good? Have they not long insisted that living the life of the mind—pursuing truth—is the highest, finest, most important thing we can do?

"Disinterested intellectual curiosity," suggested the English historian G. M. Trevelyan, "is the lifeblood of real civilization."

The aim of education, noted the nineteenth-century English educational reformer Cardinal John Henry Newman, was the cultivation of the intellect, an activity, he suggested, that was "beautiful, perfect and admirable, and noble in itself."

Knowledge, urged Robert M. Hutchins, founder of the general education curriculum at the University of Chicago, is the only thing that has intrinsic value. "The intellectual virtues," he said, "are good in themselves. . . . Material prosperity, peace and civil order, justice and the moral virtues are means to the cultivation of the intellect."

To recognize the intrinsic value of the intellect seems for scholars the mark of high refinement. But although such insight enjoys the status of conventional wisdom today, this was not always the case. Until the last century, few thinkers even believed it was true. For millennia they feared that intellect posed a grave threat, and knowledge, far from being good in itself, was only desirable when subjected to several important restrictions.

Early Greek mythology resonated with this theme. It was Prometheus, the Titan endowed with the gift of foreseeing the future, to whom the goddess Athena had taught all the wisdom of the liberal arts. Prometheus' sin, according to the myth, was passing this knowledge on to man. He taught man to walk on his hind feet, to use numbers and letters, to build ships and sail at sea, to cultivate the fields and to tame beasts of burden. He gave man the secret for making fire.

Prometheus gave man, in short, all the knowledge of the gods, and for so doing, Zeus sought to punish both. Prometheus was chained to a rock for a thousand years and man, having received these stolen goods, was sent the first mortal woman, the lovely Pandora, along with her dowry locked in a chest. The chest contained all the evils of the world, and although Pandora was forbidden to open it, her curiosity got the better of her. Wanting to know what it contained, she lifted the lid, unleashing upon mankind an eternity of suffering.

The same theme of the dangers of knowledge is woven throughout classical Greek drama, in the plays of Aeschylus, Sophocles, and Euripides. These Greek dramatists feared unlimited knowledge because they were aware of the limitations of man. Virtue lay in restraint. The cardinal virtues—wisdom, courage, temperance, and justice—were only possible through moderation. Yet the peculiar weakness of man, they knew, was his ability to exceed limits. Our intelligence was nearly limitless, our curiosity boundless. And whatever we knew how to do, we would eventually do. If we knew how to open the box, we would open it. Whatever restriction was placed on us—whether it was not to eat the apple or not to open that chest—we were tempted to trespass. And it was in trespassing, in our capacity for excess, that we did so much damage.

Thus, to the Greeks the worst crime of all—the crime of Prometheus—was what they called *hubris*: overweening pride or arrogance. The original meaning of the word *hubris* was "unlimited appetite," and it was this sense—the refusal to recognized one's limitation, the temptation to put oneself above others—that constituted the greatest danger to the human soul. And the way that hubris showed itself was in intellectual pride.

The sole prevention of hubris, the Greeks believed, lay in recognizing the existence of something greater than oneself. The only limit to human pride was humility inspired by reverence to the gods or for a higher good. The pursuit of knowledge, especially, had to be guided by the concept of *limit*, and this was done by requiring that it accord with the rules of virtue. "The highest object of knowledge," Plato wrote in *The Republic*, "is the essential nature of the Good. . . . Without that," he added, "knowledge to know everything else, however well, would be of no value to us. . . ."

So knowledge had to be permanently cemented to virtue. What would be the glue in this union? How could we justify limiting knowledge to the pursuit of virtue?

The key, suggested Aristotle, lay in the concept of *telos*, or "proper end." The universe, Aristotle believed, was one system kept in motion by God, the Unmoved Mover. Everything in the universe had a role to play in this system. This role was the thing's *telos* or proper end.

Such a universe was teleological because everything had its own *telos*, proper end or function. Like contemporary environmentalists, Aristotle believed that to know a thing is to understand its proper role in nature, and therefore to understand not only what a thing is, but also what it *ought to do*. In this way, in his world, fact and value remained fused tightly together. When things are behaving themselves, when they are doing what they are meant to do, he suggested, they aim at their proper end, propelled by love for the Unmoved Mover.

And while to Aristotle man's function is the exercise of his reason, the proper exercise of reason requires that it be done in moderation and in accordance with virtue. "The good of man," he said in the *Nicomachean Ethics*, "is the active exercise of his soul's faculties [i.e., reason] in conformity with excellence or virtue."

Thus, the vision of the Greek dramatists and philosophers rested on this insight: Only when knowledge is directed toward a virtuous purpose is it desirable.

This was also the vision of the early Catholic Church fathers. All human law and morality, argued St. Thomas Aquinas in his philosophical masterwork, *Summa theologica* (1266–73), rested on God's law, or "natural law," as he called it, which defined our proper end. Man's laws derived their legitimacy from natural law. And natural law was accessible by either reason or revelation. Only God, therefore, assured that knowledge would lead to virtue, and only He made virtue knowable. Faith was the glue holding reason and morality together.

Aquinas's insights would eventually be made official Catholic doctrine and his vision would, in turn, form the cornerstone of early programs of education. The forerunner of modern higher education, the thirteenth-century curriculum known as the *trivium* and *quadrivium*, was, in Frederick Rudolph's words, "permeated with the study of theology." Indeed, as another historian, Samuel Eliot Morison, observed, in its emphasis on the study of Latin, Greek, and Aristotelean metaphysics and ethics, it was "very nearly equivalent to a course on the works of Aristotle, in Latin translation."

But by the late sixteenth century this vision of the unity of faith, virtue, and knowledge began to come apart. Science was coming into its own, and the first idea it challenged was that of teleology. Scientists such as Tycho Brahe, Francis Bacon, Galileo Galilei, and Johannes Kepler discovered that they could understand the universe simply by observing the causes of things. Science, they came to believe, was the observation of quantitative patterns in nature, and the systematization of these patterns into "laws" or mathematical generalizations. Knowledge, therefore, was possible without knowing a thing's proper end, or *telos*.

Thus knowledge, based on observation alone, did not seem to need faith. Aristotle's and Aquinas's teleological and ethical views of the world, in which all things were to be understood in terms of their proper ends, could be replaced with one that was strictly causal and value-neutral.

But if the world could be understood without knowing its purpose, then the pursuit of knowledge, no longer a search for the proper ends of things, was also no longer a search for the Good. Intellect apparently stood on its own. And if knowledge neither rested on faith nor was guided by moral law, what would contain it?

By dropping teleology, Renaissance scientists had removed a major restriction to the pursuit of knowledge. The possibility of excess, of hubris, loomed larger. If the new science did not need religion, where would it lead? How would its pursuit be limited? For truth, they knew, was like light: it was everywhere dense. No matter how much we knew of a subject, we could always learn more. Would the desire of its pursuit turn out to be insatiable?

Even Sir Francis Bacon, regarded as the father of modern empirical science, the man who, as much as any other, had caused the world to doubt Aristotle, seemed to grasp the implications of what he had done. His new science had created a problem. If knowledge did not require faith, was it evil? "Some say," he wrote in *The Advancement of Learning* (1605),

> that knowledge is of those things which are to be accepted of with great limitation and caution; that the aspiring to overmuch knowledge, was the original temptation and sin, whereupon ensued the fall of man; that knowledge hath in it somewhat of the serpent, and therefore where it entereth into a man it makes him swell . . . that St. Paul gives a caveat, "That we be not spoiled through vain philosophy," that experience demonstrates how . . . learned times have been inclined to atheism, and how the contemplation of second causes doth derogate from our dependence upon God, who is the first cause.

Pure knowledge, Bacon conceded, was indeed dangerous if not guided and restricted. In all cases, he suggested, it must be infused with what he called a "corrective spice."

"This corrective spice," he wrote, "the mixture whereof maketh knowledge so sovereign, is charity (or love), which the apostle [Paul] immediately addeth to the former . . . for he saith, 'knowledge bloweth up, but charity buildeth up'; not unlike unto that which he delivereth in another place: 'If I spake,' saith he, 'with the tongues of man and angels, and had not charity, it were but as a tinkling cymbal.'"

Further, Bacon observed, to avoid the dangers of knowledge, it must be restricted in three ways: "the first, that we do not so place our felicity in knowledge, as we forget our mortality. The second, that we make applications of our knowledge, to give ourselves repose and contentment, and not distaste or repining. The third, that we do not presume by contemplation of nature to attain to the mysteries of God."

Here, then, the founding father of modern Western science set limits to his undertaking, limits which he felt necessary to set because his new empiricism made the limitless pursuit of knowledge a distinct possibility.

For the next two centuries—during the period philosophers call the "Age of Reason"—scholars continued to fret over the implications of the new science. Intellectual curiosity, they feared, could become insatiable. "The desire for knowledge," as Laurence Sterne put it in *Tristram Shandy* (1760), "like the thirst FOR riches, increases ever with the acquisition of it." Intellect was just another appetite. The Renaissance, in awakening the human mind, in conceiving the possibility of finding truth without God, had found Pandora's box. And who would open it?

Would it, asked Bacon's contemporary, Christopher Marlowe, in 1590, be Dr. Johann Faust, the mysterious German alchemist who sold his soul to the devil in return for knowledge and magical power? Indeed, thanks to Marlowe, and later to the poet Goethe—both of whom wrote plays about him—Faust came to symbolize this darker side of the Renaissance. He was the man who refused to accept limits. And Faust, he knew, lurked within all of us.

This fear of unlimited intellect not guided by morality and faith grew throughout the seventeenth century. The rules governing universities were written to ensure they could not, inadvertently, produce a Dr. Faust. The Laudian Code, established at Oxford University in 1634 (shortly after Bacon's death) and remaining in force until 1864, stipulated that "if the opinions of the philosophers are in any . . . respects altogether contrary to godliness, the lecturers shall earnestly remind their scholars or hearers of the feebleness of human sense to comprehend those things, the truth of which we know for certain by divine revelation."

Similarly, America's first universities were founded for the purpose of the propagation of the faith and the instruction of the young in the service of God. The purpose in founding Harvard University in 1636, for instance, was—according to the earliest known document—so that "every one shall consider the Mayne End of his life & studyes to know God & Jesus Christ, which is Eternall life."

But by the time the Laudian Code was written, by the time Harvard was founded, the genie was already out of the bottle. Dr. Faust was alive and well in the West, and his influence was growing. Science not guided by moral purpose had a momentum of its own and no one, it seemed, could stop it. By the eighteenth century—the period known as the Enlightenment—it seemed to some leading thinkers that the new science threatened to undermine morality. During this era philosophers such as Gottfried Wilhelm von Leibniz (1646–1716), George Berkeley (1685–1753), and Immanuel Kant (1724–1804) pursued what philosopher Alasdair MacIntyre called "the Enlightenment Project," namely, "the project of providing a rational vindication of morality." Attempting to reunited what Bacon and the Renaissance physicists had split asunder, they sought to reattach morality to science and demonstrate that science supported, rather than undermined, morality (i.e., Natural or "God's" Law) and religious faith.

But few were persuaded by their efforts. The claims of pure science were too seductive to be so easily dismissed. Like Humpty Dumpty, the neat Aristotelian universe was easier to break apart than to put together again. Science went on its merry way and became increasingly secular. It did not need religion. Invention, intellectual curiosity, the empirical techniques of observation, and the manipulations of mathematics and analysis were sufficient, it seemed, to follow the twists and turns of nature.

Western society became what Oswald Spengler, in *The Decline and Fall of the West* (1918), called the "Faustian" culture. It was a civilization that knew no limits, and its greatest minds went in search of far horizons.

Yet as reason and morality flew further apart, the reputations of both suffered. If knowledge and Godliness were no longer inseparable, then, many supposed, it would be possible to discover truth without finding virtue. And if virtue was not knowable, it was opinion, not truth. Moral judgments, no longer supposed to rest on anything objective—such as proper ends or moral law—came to be seen as entirely subjective. Right and wrong were matters of opinion. Morality was "relative."

Similarly, if knowledge was limited neither by God nor by natural law, then it was merely an instrument of the ego. No longer a handmaiden of theology, it came to be seen as the servant of the will.

A world dominated by egoism is not a pretty one, and modern novelists and dramatists in particular, no longer viewing reason as the stepping stone to virtue, came to see it as an instrument of destruction. The legend of Dr. Faust—the story of how too much knowledge leads to self-destruction—became a popular literary genre featuring the brilliant, cultured man who, out of a well-intentioned desire to make the world a better place combined with a naive idea of how to go about it, invented something, or created something—a machine, a chemical, a bomb, even a monster—that threatened to destroy the world and always—always—in the end destroyed its creator.

Such was the story of *Frankenstein*, written in 1818 by Mary Wollstonecraft Shelley, and subtitled *The Modern Prometheus*. The brilliant Victor Frankenstein, constructing a creature out of dead parts of human anatomy stolen from graveyard vaults, gives life to a monster which later destroys him. The creator, Frankenstein, a man described by the writer as possessing "unbounded knowledge and piercing apprehension," and, like Faust, believing himself "destined for some great enterprise," is in the end, for having created life, destroyed for usurping this role of God. "Are you mad, my friend," Frankenstein warns the reader at the end of the story, "Or whither does your senseless curiosity lead you? Would you also create for yourself and the world a demoniacal enemy? . . . Learn from my miseries and do not seek to increase your own."

As with Frankenstein, so with Mr. Kurtz, the avaricious, cruel, but once again brilliant character in Joseph Conrad's novella *Heart of Darkness* (1902). Kurtz, whom one critic described as "a god-devil who has power, intelligence and loyal followers—all but morality and responsible humanity," was, Conrad suggests, the model of modern man. "All Europe contributed to the making of Kurtz," Conrad tells us. "His was a gifted creature. He was a universal genius. . . . No fool ever made a bargain for his soul with the devil."

And what was Kurtz's sin? It was hubris. "The mind of man is capable of anything," Conrad warns us. Kurtz "had no restraint. . . . He was an extremist." What Kurtz forgot, Conrad suggests, was that strength does not come through intelligence but through faith. "You want deliberate belief," his narrator, Marlow, tells us. "Your strength comes in . . . your power of devotion, not to yourself, but to an obscure, backbreaking business."

BY THE END of the nineteenth century, it was clear that the Enlightenment Project had failed. Nietzsche was the first to see this and the first to look unblinkingly into the abyss. The pursuit of knowledge and science did not lead to virtue, he realized, but only to power. And if knowledge was the servant of the will, reason was irrational and morality a way of exerting power over others.

Few intellectuals could hide their disillusionment with the false hopes that the Renaissance had engendered, as the late nineteenth-century mind fell prey to a swarm of philosophies preaching various versions of irrationality. God, suggested Freud, was merely a father figure representing our childish subconscious desires to see the world, not as it is, but as we want it to be. Knowledge, suggested Schopenhauer, was the servant of the will, and science our way of dominating nature. Human behavior, suggested Marx, was not determined by the intellect, but by the material conditions of life.

The depths of the disillusionment in the Enlightenment's failure were dramatically demonstrated by the sudden pessimism evinced by H. G. Wells the year before his death in 1946. For most of his life, Wells had been, in Colin Wilson's words, "the scientific spirit incarnate." Best known for his science fiction, including *The War of the Worlds*, *The Invisible Man*, and *The Time Machine*, Wells had long been a leading proponent of the beneficial possibilities of science. But in his 1945 essay, *Mind at the End of its Tether*, he confessed his sudden realization that science offered no answers, only an unknown and dangerous future.

> *A frightful queerness has come to life. . . . To what will this lead? . . . There was always the assumption of an ultimate restoration of rationality. . . . Hitherto, events had been held together by a certain logical consistency, as the heavenly bodies have been held together by gravitation. Now it is as if that cord had vanished, and everything was driving anyhow to anywhere at a steadily increasing velocity. The pattern of things to come faded away.*

Wells had come face to face with the nature of evil in the modern era. It derives from our capacity to *theorize* and thereby dehumanize our enemies.

All the terrors, all the gulags, all the concentration camps and other forms of ethnic or ideological or class cleansing that killed tens of millions over the last two centuries were done in the name of ideas, conceived by well-intentioned philosophers. Just as surely as Rousseau's philosophy led to Robespierre and the Terror of the French Revolution, so did Karl Marx inspire Lenin, Mao, and Pol Pot, and Georg W. F. Hegel push all Europe down a slippery slope until it crashed into Mussolini and Hitler.

Guided by theories, philosophies, and ideologies, all the mass killers of modern history transformed their victims into depersonalized abstractions, making them easier to kill. Hitler was a vegetarian and animal rights advocate who banned vivisection in Germany. But by viewing history through the lens of racist theory, he was able to see Jews, not as flesh and blood like himself, but as an intellectual "problem" for which mass extermination was "the final solution." Stalin, citing Communist dogma, ordered the murder of millions of Ukrainian peasants to "eliminate the Kulaks as a class." The philosopher who served these states became not king but killer.

That abstract theorizing made mass murder easier to commit did not slow the advance of science. As atrocities followed one after the other while the twentieth century unfolded, the disillusionment with reason continued to grow.

At the beginning of the century, only the philosophers had come to believe that the Enlightenment's faith in reason was a delusion. In 1903, the Cambridge University philosopher G. E. Moore called attention to another implication of this epiphany, noting in *Principia Ethica* that it was a "naturalistic fallacy" to suppose ethical statements could be logically derived from factual or scientific ones. The implication was clear: science did not support the validity of moral law.

By the 1920s, the Austrian philosopher Rudolf Carnap and his colleagues—members of the so-called Vienna Circle—systematized these implications into a doctrine known as "logical positivism"—the doctrine that ethical judgments, being empirically unverifiable, were meaningless. In 1936, at Oxford University, A. J. Ayer introduced logical positivism to the English-speaking world with his, *Language, Truth and Logic*. In the same decade, an American philosopher, Charles L. Stevenson, expanded this doctrine into a theory he called "emotivism"—the doctrine that ethical statements, being unverifiable and lacking "cognitive content," were therefore merely expressions of emotional attitudes toward certain kinds of behavior.

After World War II, positivism's influence spread beyond philosophy departments and into the other university disciplines as well. Many scholars in academe came to the conclusion that the Judeo-Christian tradition that had persisted since the time of the seventh-century B.C. philosopher Thales, was now dead.

By the 1950s, professors of literature in the United States, hauling up the white flag of surrender, began to mimic the scientific method in their own fields. The positivist idea—that "value judgments lacked cognitive content" and that true scholars must remain "value-neutral"— became their mantra, too. And by the late 1960s literature would cease to be the study of "great books," since that would be a value judgment. Notions such as "moral fiction" and "art," also involving, as they do, value judgments, would disappear from humanities and aesthetics syllabuses. Eventually, freed from the need to debate what is a good book or a work of art, many humanities and arts professors would devote their courses to pet politics instead.

MEANWHILE, the march of positivism was having dramatic consequences in politics and world events. For, by undermining the objectivity of ethics, it eventually brought the legitimacy of everything into question, including the legitimacy of the state.

For nearly two thousand years, Western government was founded on natural law: the idea that, through reason, all men could come to know the law of God, and that only the law of God gave legitimacy to the state. The original rationale for American democracy, in particular, rested on the idea that all men, being rational, could know this natural law, and thus each had an equal right to govern. The Declaration of Independence explicitly stated that the individual's inalienable rights derived from "the laws of nature and of nature's God" and that the power of the state derived from consent of the governed.

But if man was irrational, if reason simply a tool of his will, if virtue another name for personal preferences, if God merely a symbol of infantile desires, then there could be no natural law. What, then, justified political authority? The answer was quick in coming: Nothing at all.

Governmental power came to be seen by many intellectuals in particular as simply a bald fact, to be used—exploited—by individuals or social classes. "Knowledge" and "virtue" were just words people used to give the exercise of this power the patina of respectability.

There was, suggested Karl Marx, no objective truth. Our beliefs, far from being "rational," merely reflected the interests of our economic class. God was an invention designed to keep the proletariat in their place, religion "the opiate of the masses." Therefore, the state, resting neither on God nor reason, had no standing. It was merely the way one class suppressed another.

Similarly, by the 1920s apologists for fascism argued that government had no legitimate foundation in reason or God. Its authority rested on power alone. Might made right. The rationale for democracy, many intellectuals believed, was bankrupt. It depended on assumptions about the rationality of man and the existence of God and natural law that few in the universities or the café societies believed. The choice, it was fashionable to think then, lay between fascism and communism.

These were the doctrines that propelled the world into World War II. Fascists thought their destiny lay in saving the world from communism. Communists thought their mission was to destroy capitalism. And although the war destroyed fascism as a political force and settled some questions of power, it did little to resolve the underlying crisis of Western democracy.

Such was the state of the intellectual world at the end of World War II: Most scholars believed that both God and secular humanism were dead. Reason reveals life to be without purpose or meaning. Science is the only legitimate exercise of the intellect, but that leads inevitably to technology and, ultimately, to the bomb. Democracy and human rights rest, not on natural law, but on power. The chief advantages of a free society are economic: free markets produce more wealth than managed ones.

In this atmosphere, Harvard's Gen Ed reformers were conflicted. On one hand, the war experience made many fear what science could do. The grotesque "experiments" on human subjects by death camp scientists such as the notorious Dr. Mengele of Auschwitz reminded them where "disinterested intellectual curiosity" could lead. Analyses of Naziism, such as Thomas Mann's novel *Doktor Faustus*, which appeared in 1947, revived and gave new relevance to the Faust legend, reemphasizing for these postwar educators what a short step lay between intellectual ambition and evil. "For long before I dallied with the poison butterfly," exclaims Mann's Faustus, Adrian Leverkuhn, in enunciating what could have been a call for educational reform, "my froward soul in high mind and arrogance was on the way to Satan."

On the other hand, while these scholars feared the unrestrained pursuit of science, they didn't believe in the alternatives to it, either. They could not accept the Enlightenment ideal—that the pursuit of knowledge be limited to the pursuit of virtue—because, being positivists themselves, they didn't accept that moral laws had rational foundation. Believing in neither God nor the rationality of virtue, they could not very well implement a curriculum that promised to "inculcate common moral standards."

So, rather than offering a ringing endorsement of these ideas, the Redbook committee remained ambivalent. Throughout, the Harvard report of 1945 revealed a tension between the felt need to teach virtue and the scholarly requisite for value-neutral scholarship. The very same body that had received Conant's charge to introduce all students to "those fields in which value judgments are of prime importance" would now back away, pleading that, as a later Harvard president, Derek Bok, would put it, "Ethical neutrality is the guiding rule for the historian or scholar."

Advocates of general education at Harvard and throughout the country also could not decide how to resolve the crisis of Western liberalism. They couldn't very well "reaffirm democratic values" once they had embraced "ethical neutrality." Nor could they justify democracy by appealing to "Nature's God" or "Natural Laws," as they didn't believe in these, either.

Faced with these irreconcilable conflicts, "Gen Ed" would become little more than an elitist effort to define a "corpus" or core set of "Great Books" that every "educated man" should read. Its curricula, Rudolph observes, became "an expression of 'the establishment.'" They "smacked of tradition and reliability, and to call them *general education* was to draw attention to the course of study as a school of certification for a predestined white, Anglo-Saxon, Protestant elite."

As such, Gen Ed was an anachronism at birth—an attempt to impose elite standards just as universities, flush with returning war veterans, were about to embrace a broad egalitarianism. And as an effort to inculcate "values," it would be a straw house built in a hurricane.

By 1950, THEREFORE, the split that had been growing ever since the Enlightenment, between positivism and the pursuit of science on one side and secular humanism and search for the foundation of morals on the other, had reached its culmination. At Harvard and elsewhere, faculties were divided between those who saw science and technology as threats to Western values and even human survival and those—a majority—who saw science as a liberator from superstition and an avenue to progress. Both these views found their way into the Harvard curriculum.

The dominant faction had little sympathy for the Redbook's concern to inculcate the Judeo-Christian tradition. They objected to Gen Ed's emphasis on presenting material within a historical context, preferring rather to organize studies around the methodologies of their own, mostly scientific disciplines. Desiring to recruit students to their own specialties (an instinct known in academe as "turf protection"), they favored a curriculum that emphasized departmental education rather than Gen Ed's "non-departmental" offerings. And, especially, they objected to the focus on morals, which they saw as violating the cardinal requirement for "value-free inquiry."

Thanks to this resistance, by the time that Gen Ed was phased into the Harvard curriculum in 1950, many Redbook Committee recommendations had not been fully implemented. And those that were put into the curriculum were quickly subverted by the people expected to teach them. These professors emphasized exactly the opposite lesson from the one Conant intended. Rather than inculcate values, they sought to undermine them. Soon the commandment, "Thou shalt not utter a value judgment," became the mantra for Harvard freshmen, in dorm bull sessions as well as term papers.

Superficially, this positivist message appeared an optimistic one, concerning the perfectability of science and the inevitability of progress. It taught that reason was a liberating force and faith mere superstition.

The advance of science would eventually produce a complete understanding of nature.

But even as positivism preached progress, it indirectly carried—quite in contradiction to the intent of Gen Ed's framers—a more disturbing implication: that absolute reason leads to absolute despair—or, as G. K. Chesterton wrote, "Imagination does not breed insanity. Exactly what does breed insanity is reason. Poets do not go mad . . . mathematicians go mad." For positivism implied that all the accumulated nonscientific knowledge of the human race, including the great religions and philosophies of the past, had been at best merely an expression of "cultural mores," and was at worst "lacking in cognitive content"—i.e., nonsense. The message's bottom line was that life had no purpose and morality no justification.

Science, in sum, seemed to paint a picture of a world in which few wanted to live—a sanitary place with no dark corners, no mystery, and no meaning. Besides, many of the individual scientific disciplines were leading in disquieting directions. Physics—the darling of the Cold Warriors—persisted in letting genies out of the bottle. The social sciences appeared bent on finding new ways for government to manipulate human populations. Economics already had a reputation as the "dismal science." And soon, ecologists would predict "the end of nature."

Hence, Gen Ed delivered to those of us who were undergraduates during this time a double whammy of pessimism. From humanists we learned that science threatens civilization. From the scientists we learned that science cannot be stopped. Taken together, they implied there is no hope. Gen Ed had created what would become a permanent fixture at Harvard, and indeed, throughout academe: the culture of despair.

13

Harvard's Culture of Despair

The last thirty years have been witnessing the active disintegration of Western civilization.

> —LEWIS MUMFORD,
> *The Condition of Man*
> from the Gen Ed reading list

Why does man feel so sad in the twentieth century?

> —WALKER PERCY,
> *The Message in the Bottle*

I N THE FALL OF 1959, Kaczynski moved into Eliot House, N-43. Located under the eaves at the top floor, it had once quartered the master's servants. Now it served as the stable where Harvard housed poorer scholarship students.

N-43 differed from most other undergraduate accommodations of the time. The typical suite, built in the 1930s during the era of gracious living, consisted of a living room, bath, and one or two bedrooms. It had been designed to encourage "gentlemen" to get to know one another in genteel surroundings. N-43, by contrast, resembled a cheap hotel. It offered six tiny single rooms, each separately opening onto a narrow hall. No one in N-43 had a "roommate." Each lived alone. It was Eliot's ghetto.

During Kaczynski's undergraduate years, Eliot House reflected the personality of its master, John Finley. A Harvard Ph.D. who had also studied in Athens and Berlin, Finley had been a co-author of the Redbook and was a leading authority on the poets, philosophers, and historians of ancient Greece. He taught one of the most popular courses at the college—Humanities 103, "The Great Age of Athens." But Finley was also a snob who embodied both the Redbook's WASPish lament for the declining Judeo-Christian tradition and a patrician's reverence for the gentleman-scholar. A graduate of Phillips Exeter Academy in New Hampshire, he believed in the Greek idea of *arete*, a concept from which we derive our word "aristocrat," but originally meaning excellence in achievement. And Finley clearly favored those students he saw as intellectual and social aristocrats.

Eliot House mirrored Finley's academic and social elitism. And although most Harvard houses in those days reflected the values of Boston Brahmin society (Elliott Perkins, the tall, balding master of my own house, Lowell, boasted an even more distinguished lineage), Eliot was more extreme. This house, noted a report of the Harvard Office of Research and Evaluation at about that time, "has long been called cold, snobbish, preppish, 'the clubby house,' and 'the home of the pseudo-intellectual.' All of these titles are, in a sense, true." Indeed, most undergraduates themselves agreed with this verdict, the report added. Even Eliot House residents viewed it as "aristocratic" and "snobbish." Residents of the other houses characterized the denizens of Eliot as "wealthy," "aristocratic," "snobbish," "white shoe," and "conservative." As Kaczynski's class yearbook, in 1962, noted:

"The member of Eliot House, the tale goes, is necessarily reserved and unfriendly with those he does not know very well; he is inordinately aware of his personal superiority, whether social, intellectual, or sartorial; he is totally apathetic to what goes on outside his own narrow sphere; he may well be insufferable, he is usually at least pretentious."

Kaczynski's impressions confirmed this image. The other Eliot House students, he wrote, were "unimaginative, conventional, suit-and-tie-wearing types," and "uninteresting, not to say dull." Years later, he would note in "Truth vs. Lies" that

> *there was a good deal of snobbery at Harvard. . . . The house master, John Finley, apparently was surrounded by an in-group or clique. . . . The house master often treated me with insulting condescension. . . . As a result, when my first attempts to make friends met with a cool reception, I just gave up and became solitary.*

Thus, Harvard's social environment, dominated by the values and fears of an elite in eclipse, merged with—and reinforced—an intellectual climate engendered by the Cold War and characterized by concerns about positivism and progress. The resulting mix was unusually potent.

Although I cannot say exactly what Kaczynski read, we took the same or closely similar courses in expository writing, German literature, deductive and inductive logic, Western literature and philosophy, and the history of science, and I know what books he encountered there. Indeed, it would have been impossible for him not to have encountered—at the dining commons, evening bull sessions, and tutorials as well as in course readings—the ideas that infused students' intellectual and emotional lives during this period.

The Gen Ed courses in social science quickly introduced us to the relativity of morals and the irrationality of religion. To establish that ethical standards were merely expressions of Western cultural mores, we were assigned to read works by anthropologists such as Margaret Mead (*Coming of Age in Samoa*), Edward Westermarck (*Ethical Relativity*), William Graham Sumner (*Folkways*), and Ruth Benedict (*Patterns of Culture*). We were introduced to logical positivism and emotivism through the works of A. J. Ayer (*Language, Truth and Logic*), Charles L. Stevenson (*Ethics and Language*), and countless other writers who had absorbed the messages of these doctrines.

In Humanities 5, or "Ideas of Man and the World in Western Thought" (also known as "Hum 5"), we read Freud's polemic against religious faith,

The Future of an Illusion, which dismisses the belief that life has purpose as a mere expression of infantile desires and as confirming that "man is a creature of weak intelligence who is governed by his instinctual wishes."

A life without God, meaning, or value is a difficult one to live. Not surprisingly, therefore, our reading lists were heavily laced with the works of existentialist philosophers and novelists—best-selling writers in the 1950s—such as Camus and Sartre, who sought to come to terms with the conclusions of science and thereby make sense of an existence science revealed to be "absurd."

In Hum 5, we read Karl Marx warn of "the intellectual desolation artificially produced by converting immature human beings into mere machines." We read Camus's observation in *The Myth of Sisyphus* that "The absurd is the essential concept and the first truth," as well as Sartre's bleak description of the human condition in *Being and Nothingness* that "I carry the weight of the world by myself alone without anything or any person being able to lighten it. . . . I am abandoned in the world . . . alone and without help, engaged in a world for which I bear the whole responsibility without being able, whatever I do, to tear myself away from this responsibility for an instant."

In expository writing, we encountered Thorstein Veblen's prediction that "so long as the machine process continues to hold its dominant place as a disciplinary factor in modern culture, so long must the spiritual and intellectual life of this cultural era maintain the character which the machine process gives it." We discovered Erich Fromm, complaining how technology contributes to the "insignificance and powerlessness of the individual." We read Norbert Wiener, developer at MIT of the new computer mathematics known as cybernetics, who warned that unless human nature changes, the "new industrial revolution . . . [makes it] practically certain that we shall have to face a decade or more of ruin and despair."

At least Mead, Westermarck, Sumner, Benedict, Ayer, Stevenson, Veblen, Fromm, and Wiener were, comparatively speaking, among the Harvard curriculum's optimists. They believed and even embraced the message of science. From writers who rejected science we heard even more powerful warnings of imminent cultural collapse. In *Modern Man Is Obsolete* (1945), we encountered Norman Cousins's cautionary remarks about "the power of total destruction as potentially represented by modern science. . . . The full dimensions of the peril must be seen and recognized. Only then will man realize that the first order of business is the question of continued existence."

In German R ("Intermediate German with Review of Fundamentals"), which both Kaczynski and I took, we encountered a whole corpus of pessimistic writers, from Nietzsche—"God is dead" . . . "Morality is the herd instinct of the individual" . . . "The thought of suicide is a great source of comfort"—to Spengler—"This machine-technics will end with the Faustian civilization and one day will lie in fragments, forgotten—our railways and steamships as dead as the Roman roads and the Chinese wall, our giant cities and skyscrapers in ruins like old Memphis and Babylon."

And no student could negotiate the Gen Ed curriculum without encountering the great Russian novelist Fyodor Dostoevsky, whose works suffused both the humanities and the social science curricula. In *Notes from Underground*, we met the distilled philosophy of alienation in the person of the Underground man, himself a victim of a civilization that had lost all values, who for twenty years had lived alone in his apartment, seldom going out, nursing his anger and plotting revenge against society. In passages eerily similar to Kaczynski's journal entries twenty years later, the Underground man expostulated:

> I am a sick man . . . I am a spiteful man. I am a most unpleasant man. . . . No hunchback, no dwarf, could be more prone to resentment and offence than I. . . . People who are able to wreak vengeance on an assailant, and in general to stand up for themselves—how do they do it? It can only be supposed that momentarily their whole being is possessed by a desire for revenge, and no other element is . . . in them.

In *Crime and Punishment*, we read what could have been a description of Kaczynski's thoughts while living in his Montana cabin twenty-nine years later: "I did not kill a human being, but a principle!" And in several courses we read Joseph Conrad, who would later become one of Kaczynski's favorite writers, and whose novel, *The Secret Agent*, he would adopt as a virtual Unabomber manual.

✧ ✧ ✧

MOST UBIQUITOUS of all in the Gen Ed curriculum were the writings of
the social philosopher and historian Lewis Mumford, who observed in
The Conduct of Life (1951) that "we have created an industrial order
geared to automatism, where feeble-mindedness, native or acquired, is
necessary for docile productivity in the factory; and where a pervasive
neurosis is the final gift of the meaningless life that issues forth at the
other end."

"The achievements of modern technology," Mumford wrote in *Science and Man* (1942),

> *have been part of a culture whose central theme was the seizure
> and exploitation of power.*
>
> *It . . . led to the ruthless exploitation of natural resources, the
> breakup of the natural balance of organisms, and the extermina-
> tion of many valuable cultural traditions. . . . The very illusion of
> moral progress that was fostered by the prevailing optimistic phi-
> losophy of the nineteenth century tended to conceal the vast hia-
> tus between technological and social achievements.*
>
> *Those who have put their faith in mechanical inventions and
> in the power theme have failed to see that only a modicum of our
> constant human needs is encompassed by the machine or included
> in the territory it conquers.*

And in *The Condition of Man* (1944), Mumford concluded that

> *The last thirty years have been witnessing the active disintegration
> of Western civilization. . . . Everywhere the machine holds the cen-
> ter and the personality has been pushed to the periphery. Western
> man has exhausted the dream of mechanical power which so long
> dominated his imagination . . . he can no longer let himself remain
> spellbound in that dream: He must attach himself to more humane
> purposes than those he has given to the machine. We can no longer
> live, with the illusions of success, in a world given over to devital-
> ized mechanisms, de-socialized organisms, and depersonalized*

societies: a world that had lost its sense of the ultimate dignity of the person. . . .

Along the way, some of us encountered Eugene O'Neill, several of whose plays, as we've seen, warned against the dangers of technology.

"I'm thinkin' he wouldn't use the telegraph or telephone or radio," a character remarks in *Dynamo*, "for they're contraptions that belong to His archenemy Lucifer, the God of Electricity." And we pitied another O'Neill character, Yank Smith in *The Hairy Ape*, who finds that technological civilization has no place for him. Talking to a gorilla through the bars at the zoo, Smith asks: "Ain't we both members of the same club—the Hairy Apes? . . . I was lookin' at de skyscrapers—steel—and all de ships comin' in, sailin' out, all over de oith—and dy was steel, too . . . on'y I couldn't get *in* it, see? I couldn't belong to dat. It was over my head. . . . Where do I fit in?"

Many undergraduates during that time would ask, "Where do I fit in?" Socially isolated by Harvard's elitist contempt for popular culture and depressed by the metaphysical angst of the readings, some would become what a later dean of the faculty, Henry Rosovsky, dubbed "lumpenstudenten"—the undergraduate underclass that fell through the cracks without leaving a trace.

14

"Lumpenstudenten": Falling between the Cracks

He had become so completely absorbed in himself, and isolated from his fellows that he dreaded meeting, not only his landlady, but any one at all. He was crushed by poverty.

—FYODOR DOSTOEVSKY,
Crime and Punishment
from Harvard's Gen Ed reading list

He was always alone. He never married, never had a mistress . . . Few people liked and supported him.

—COLIN WILSON,
The Outsider
(commenting on Nietzsche)

I N THE SPRING OF 1997, I shared an indigestible lunch of green pasta, stale bread, and cold cuts at the University of Colorado's Student Union with Patrick McIntosh. An owlish-looking man with round face and big glasses, McIntosh had "roomed" with Kaczynski at Eliot House—that is, the two both lived in singles that shared the same narrow, N-43 hallway. He is also prominent among those frequently quoted by the media in their portrayal of Kaczynski as an eccentric loner while at Harvard. But as it turns out, the media may have not entirely understood him.

McIntosh himself is an improbable combination, a self-taught astronomer. After graduating, he had been an instructor at a private high school in Massachusetts, then joined the staff of the solar astronomy and space environment forecasting division of the Environmental Sciences Service Administration in Boulder, Colorado. Writing in the Harvard class of 1962's tenth anniversary report, he explained: "I have chosen not to waste time in graduate school being molded into a professional scientist unable to be creative or responsive to life outside my profession." Nevertheless, he reported that he was earning "well above the median salary for Ph.D. astronomers."

In 1993, McIntosh took early retirement from his job of 29 years, in part because the dirt in the government office building was aggravating his allergies. He now ran his own consulting firm, specializing in solar studies.

After Kaczynski's arrest, McIntosh found his fifteen minutes of fame. "I am now known as The Roommate!" he wrote his classmates. The media beat a path to his door. He gave interviews to NBC, CBS, ABC's *Nightline* and *20/20,* Maury Povich, and Jenny Jones, among others. And the impression that these (in some cases edited) appearances left in viewers' minds was that Kaczynski had, indeed, been an eccentric loner at Harvard.

"Ted would not volunteer to join in the conversations with anybody," he said in an ABC *20/20* sound bite. "He would go in his room and shut the door, and I thought perhaps he just hadn't grown up yet."

Various magazines and newspapers invoked McIntosh quotations to make the same point: "Ted was one of the strangest people I met at Harvard" (*Newsweek*). "In three years, I don't recall more than ten words being spoken by Kaczynski" (*New York Times*). Kaczynski "would go to his room and slam the door" (*San Francisco Chronicle*). Kaczynski "had a special talent for avoiding relationships by moving quickly past groups of people and slamming the door behind him" (*Time*).

McIntosh confirmed these accounts to me, but added an important detail that most news media had missed: that Kaczynski's vaunted eccentricity had not been so unusual at Harvard. As he explained to his classmates (in the class of 1962's thirty-fifth anniversary report): "There were other roommates who were strange. . . . Kaczynski did not stand out as much as expected because Harvard had gathered a number of 'unusual' people in the class of 1962 and put an inordinate number of them in Eliot N-43! I am tempted to write my own book about those four years at Harvard, emphasizing the hardships inflicted on Kaczynski, myself and many other public school graduates who were used, abused and ignored by Harvard."

A MONTH AFTER I met with McIntosh, Keith Martin and I sat on the terrace of L'Enfant Plaza in Washington, D.C., eating sandwiches from Au Bon Pain off paper plates. A ferocious wind blew, threatening to dump our lunches on the heads of the stream of people pouring out of the Metro escalator below. Martin, too, had "roomed" with Kaczynski at Eliot House. And Martin was another Kaczynski classmate frequently cited by the media as a witness to Kaczynski's undergraduate isolation. But to me he portrayed Kaczynski as just another typical faceless Harvard introvert.

"Ted and I were wonks," Martin explained. "He wasn't shy. Arrogant maybe, since he was very condescending if you asked him a question. True, he never spoke when you met him in the hall, but then this was Harvard. Most undergraduates didn't speak to each other when they met, unless they were friends." Moreover, several people, including McIntosh and Martin, seemed somewhat in awe of Kaczynski. Both remarked that he exuded an air of superiority and would mock remarks he thought dumb.

Martin now worked at the Office of Housing and Urban Development. He read grant proposals from high schools. Upon graduating from Harvard, he taught English for a year at a high school in Germany. After studying at the Fletcher School of Law and Diplomacy, he joined the Foreign Service. In the early 1970s, he left the service and matriculated at the Wesley Theological Seminary. He was director of the Presbyterian Advocacy Project for a while, then lapsed into what he called a "midlife crisis" and quit that job too. He joined HUD in the early 1980s. Now he was looking forward to retirement and spending more time with his family.

"Do you remember me?" I asked Professor Andrew Gleason. "I took Natural Sciences 116 from you in 1956, 'Basic Concepts of Mathematics.'" Gleason, now retired, had no recollection of me at all. "Then do you remember Ted Kaczynski? You were his adviser in 1959." Gleason remembered him, though barely.

"I almost never saw Kaczynski," Gleason told me. Indeed, even in the adviser's report Gleason had been required to write at the end of Kaczynski's sophomore year, the professor admitted, "My acquaintance with Kaczynski has been slight. I have been his advisor but have never had him in class. . . . He has always struck me favorably at the personal level."

Welcome to Harvard, where lasting human relations are more rare than championship football teams. As this encounter with Gleason implies, Kaczynski's anonymity was not rare, but the norm. Even McIntosh and Martin, whose hints about Harvard anomie the media largely missed, had not been exactly social butterflies themselves.

Kaczynski says that the media exaggerated his isolation by interviewing only those classmates who did not know him well. His loneliness, while real, wasn't extreme. He did have some friends at Harvard. He snubbed McIntosh and Martin, he says, because he couldn't stand them, and McIntosh in particular mistakenly interpreted his coldness as shyness. This may be true. But even Kaczynski seems unaware how utterly typical his isolation and eccentricities were.

Besides Gerald Burns, only Napoleon Williams, identified to me by Kaczynski as one of his real friends, called attention to the obvious point: that Kaczynski's appearance and behavior during his undergraduate years had been unremarkable. A mathematics major, Williams, now

a Manhattan public-interest attorney, recalled Kaczynski sympatheti-
cally. Kaczynski was neither an oddball nor a loner, Williams told me.
Rather, "he was a typical mathematician. Most young, talented mathematicians tend to be unkempt, ascetic, awkward, shy, totally wrapped
up in their own world."

"Even a society depending on tradition-direction will have a certain
number of anomics," Harvard professor David Riesman wrote in *The
Lonely Crowd*, "those constitutionally and psychologically unable to
conform or feel comfortable in the roles such a society assigns to its regularly recurring deviants. . . . The anomics include . . . people of too
tight superego controls to permit themselves even the normal satisfac-
tions and escapes of their fellows."

And Harvard during that period was loaded with them. One of these
overachievers was Kaczynski, and another was an N-43 neighbor,
Robert Crosman. Although cited by Kaczynski as one of his friends,
Crosman can't remember Kaczynski today. A member of the class of
1964, he was two years behind Kaczynski and therefore closer to
Kaczynski's age than his own classmates. But as he left Harvard in the
middle of his sophomore year, Kaczynski and he overlapped at N-43
only very briefly.

Yet Crosman feels that he and Kaczynski were similar in their
unhappiness. Like Kaczynski, Crosman pushed himself too hard academically, to please his parents. "Harvard was using me up at an alarming rate," he wrote in his memoir of these times.

> *My problem was that I wanted to be* perfect: *the perfect student.
> . . . All around me, boys who had been valedictorians back home
> were getting D's and F's on chem exams and English papers. . . . I
> didn't feel excellent, I felt dull, muddled, and insecure. . . . I was
> simply taking the whole business of education—even of a Harvard
> Education—far too seriously. I worked too hard, studied too much
> . . . without knowing it, I was sitting on a volcano. Even I was
> beginning to suspect that something was wrong with me—you
> can't go around in a perpetual sweat of angst and feel normal.
> . . . [Crosman's emphasis]*

Immersed in Gen Ed's culture of despair and alienated from his roommates (whom he called "shallow jerks"), Crosman found himself depressed and angry most of the time.

> I would at times feel a vertigo, as if the world had fallen away beneath my feet, and left me standing exposed on some narrow ledge or tower. A physical dread would descend on me, and I would grip the arms of my desk-chair until the dizziness passed, or pace nervously about, picking up books and papers at random and laying them down again. . . .
>
> The best way to avoid these moods was to keep working, but . . . too much work would rouse me to angry rebellion, and then to truancy that would bring on my angst. . . . Like others of my generation I recognized myself in Camus' detached, affectless hero [in The Stranger]. . . . I have been reading a little Nietzsche in a book called Existentialism from Dostoevsky to Sartre. The purpose of this extract is to "live dangerously."

During his sophomore year, Crosman decided to leave college. His father, a college professor and philosopher, desperately tried to persuade him to stay.

"'What's bothering you?'" Crosman records his father asking.

"'Everything here is so wrong, so . . . *phoney*. . . . Just people with empty, wasted lives, talking their empty pointless talk, and waiting to die. I can't take it, I've got to get out.'"

" 'Get out! Where?'

"'Somewhere.' I paused. 'Somewhere where something makes some sense.'"

Crosman's father "thought for a moment, then spoke slowly, distinctly, avoiding my gaze as he spoke. 'There isn't any place where it makes sense,' he said, adding, 'We all lead lives of quiet desperation. But we have a choice. You can take the high road or the low road. Here at Harvard you're on the high road. . . . Leave and you'll be on the low road forever.'"

His father's remark "struck me like a blow," Crosman remembers. "I had been going on nerve, on verve, on a last-gasp, stoic-existentialist view of myself as someone who would neither wince nor cry aloud, no matter how bad the going got. Now my father had piled his own nihilism on top of mine, and I snapped."

A few weeks later, Crosman boarded a bus for California and never returned. Today, he is a professor of English Literature at the University of Alaska, in Anchorage.

CROSMAN'S ALIENATION was not unique. According to a study of Harvard and Radcliffe undergraduates that includes Kaczynski's class of 1962, conducted by William G. Perry, Jr., director of Harvard's Bureau of Study Counsel, the undergraduate curriculum had a profound impact on the emotions, the attitudes, and even the health of some students. Intellectual development for Harvard and Radcliffe undergraduates typically encompassed a progression, Perry explained, from a simplistic, "dualistic" view of reality to an increasingly relativistic and "contingent" one. Entering freshmen tended to exhibit "dualistic" attitudes toward truth and virtue. They favored simple over complex solutions and tended to divide the world into truth and falsehood, good and bad, friend and foe. Yet in most of their courses, especially the social sciences and the humanities, they were taught that truth is relative. Most accepted this; but a number could not. They reacted against relativism by clinging more fiercely to an absolute, or "dualistic" view of the world. To some of these students, in Perry's words, "science and mathematics still seem to offer hope."

Nevertheless, "regression into dualism" is not a happy development, for it "calls for an enemy." Dualists in a relativistic environment tend to see themselves as surrounded; they become increasingly lonely and alienated. This attitude "requires an equally absolutistic rejection of any 'establishment'" and "can call forth in its defense hate, projection, and denial of all distinctions but one," Perry wrote. "The tendency . . . is toward paranoia."

Other students gave way to loneliness, academic pressure, and the effects of a syllabus of despair by cultivating weird idiosyncrasies.

One of my undergraduate friends expressed his revolt by buttoning the bottom button of his Brooks Brothers suit instead of the middle button, as was the custom. Scion of a famous family, one of whose ancestors had signed the Declaration of Independence, he did not dare disobey his ultraconventional father, who insisted he wear the suit. Fastening the "wrong" button was as far as he risked showing his defiance. Later, he cemented his independence by taking up painting. But again, afraid to carry his revolt against authority too far, he painted very small pictures, becoming a miniaturist.

Other quests for independence were more obvious. Each evening, one of my classmates would dress ostentatiously as a Southern planter—donning a Pink hunting jacket, cavalry twill riding breeches, and a broad-brimmed Panama hat—even though he came from New York City. If his roommates teased him about this, he sought revenge by giving them the silent treatment. When this invariably caused them to collapse in delirious laughter, he would run out the door and head for Elsie's Delicatessen for solace. We became quite accustomed to seeing him walking down Mount Auburn Street late at night in his Peale boots, balancing a riding crop in one hand and a hot pastrami sandwich in the other.

Another of my classmates was expelled for dropping a bomb off the Anderson Bridge into the Charles River, setting off an explosion that shook windows throughout Cambridge. After leaving college, he was recruited by the CIA, which employed his incendiary talents during the successful, agency-sponsored 1954 putsch in Guatemala that ousted a democratically elected regime and brought a puppet of the United Fruit Company to power. As a reward for these "anti-Communist" exploits, Harvard readmitted him. Bombing got him expelled and bombing got him reinstated.

Crosman remembers other eccentrics. "One of the boys in my suite," he recalled in his memoir, "told me he had dreamed in high school of taking 'acid baths' to remove his acne. Another went to the Boston premiere of *Camelot*, and played the record album monotonously over and over in the living room we shared. . . .

"This wasn't reality," Crosman concluded, "this was a footlight and Clearasil delusion."

Sometimes, these delusions lasted far beyond graduation.

IT WAS A BEAUTIFUL fall day. The trees had turned gold and the buildings of Harvard Yard cast long shadows in the southerly sun. I sat on the steps of University Hall next to the statue of John Harvard, thinking about the lumpenalumni Harvard doesn't like to talk about. These are the invisible undergraduates who become invisible alumni. The one irreducible fact is that Kaczynski—and only Kaczynski—became a murderer. But we all bore scars earned from our vaunted Harvard experience, and perhaps those scars tell us something about Kaczynski's own spiral downward.

One of the great Harvard myths is that all its graduates live charmed lives. For generations, the university has sought to instill in its graduates the gospel that "Harvard is different." As students, we were told we were the best, because we went to Harvard. After graduation, we were deemed to be members of an elite society whose lives had more significance and importance than those of the unfortunate souls who lacked the intellect and strength of character to qualify for this rarified circle.

But in fact, we were just as likely to suffer failure, experience self-doubt, or live ordinary, even drab, uninteresting lives as anyone else. The only difference between us and other, ordinary mortals was that, as Harvard grads, we had been programmed to expect more from ourselves, and from life. So the realization of averageness or mediocrity hit us harder.

In *Remembering Denny*, Calvin Trillin writes about his classmate Denny Hansen, a member of the Yale class of 1957 (and coincidentally exactly my own age). A golden boy in college, Hansen was the Rhodes Scholar whose "million dollar smile" and bright future made him the subject of a feature in *Life* magazine. Yet by middle age Hansen found himself alone and thought himself a failure. He committed suicide at age fifty-five.

We have all known a Denny Hansen. As I worked my way through graduate school at Oxford and Princeton to become a college professor, I passed many who fell through the cracks along the way—the Princeton graduate school classmate who seemed to disappear after developing a psychological block that prevented him from completing his dissertation; the professor who let his hair grow, donned earrings, and developed the habit of laughing at inappropriate times, as though he were listening to a voice only he could hear; the colleague who after a promising early career began taking long sabbaticals to Mexico, where he wandered the streets of small towns, never writing another word.

And some of us see a little of Denny Hansen in ourselves. I went to graduate school without knowing why. I began teaching at Ohio State University—and hated it. Thinking I'd like a small college better, I took a position on the faculty of Macalester College, eventually becoming chair of the philosophy department. But I hated that too. At age forty, I gave up my tenure and escaped with my family to the Montana wilderness. Within a year, I was not only jobless but broke and virtually unemployable. Having five degrees from Harvard, Oxford, and Princeton didn't help find a job. In fact, it hurt. I was too well educated.

Most of Kaczynski's suitemates at Prescott Street and Eliot House would live similarly questing, unspectacular lives. None became a U.S. senator or a corporate CEO. They pursued quiet careers, without the glamour Harvard pretends is due its graduates. Indeed, several were remarkably like Kaczynski. As undergraduates, many had been mathematics or science majors. Most had gone to public high schools and had suffered from the class prejudices that ruled Harvard. After graduation, several, like Martin and myself, had trouble finding a congenial career. By the time they reached middle age, many found themselves still struggling, like myself. Not many would consider themselves especially successful in the conventional sense. Some still seem to be searching. McIntosh's wife had divorced him in 1987 and he was clearly lonely. "I am growing poorer," he wrote his thirty-fifth reunion classmates. "I hope my report for the fortieth reunion will be dull, brief and announcing me married and fully retired."

After graduating from Harvard and earning a master's in literature from Trinity College Dublin, Gerald Burns had embarked on a career as poet and teacher. But although winning a National Poetry Series award and writing several books, he long thought himself a failure. And he identified with Kaczynski.

In 1967, Burns wrote his classmates that he was teaching "ugly poetry" at Nassau Community College and thinking of writing a book entitled "Eminent Harvard Failures," prominently featuring himself. Burns died suddenly of a heart attack in August 1997, while working as a dishwasher in Arby's restaurant and as a clerk at Second Story Book Sellers, both in Portland, Oregon. Before his death, Burns wrote to the anarchist journal *Fifth Estate* expressing his solidarity with Kaczynski and commenting, "I too have ended up living way below the poverty line."

✧ ✧ ✧

ACROSS THE HARVARD Yard I could see the dark, northerly face of Hollis, the dorm where my friend and classmate, John King, had spent his freshman year. John and I were the only Carmel (California) High School students to attend Harvard that or any other year, so far as I know. An ebullient man with many enthusiasms, John was an avid pilot, photographer, sailor, hunter, fisherman, and sky diver. His love of life had been so infectious that it made people feel good just to be around him.

King's early career had been anything but average. He quit Harvard at the end of his freshman year to work for the Union Pacific Railroad. Two years later, he moved to Philadelphia, where he began studying English at the University of Pennsylvania. After one term, he quit that university too, to join the staff of the Lankenau Hospital, where he became assistant manager within a year. In 1957, he returned to Harvard, from which he graduated in 1959. Then drafted into the army, he attended officer candidate school, became a paratrooper, and was sent to the artillery/missile school at Fort Sill, Oklahoma.

There, King was introduced to computers and immediately fell in love with them. After leaving the service in 1962, he went to work as a data-processing technician for the Insurance Company of North America in Philadelphia. And in 1965, he moved to Boston, joining IBM. He met and married Juanita, an optometrist from Colombia, South America. By 1970, they had two children. "Family life is great," he wrote his classmates in 1972, "—especially raising a couple of dynamos."

But the longer King lived in New England, the more he yearned to return to Carmel. And by the late 1970s he managed to move his family there, establishing himself as an independent computer consultant.

I ran into King in 1982 at our twenty-fifth Harvard reunion. He was bubbling with joy over his life in Carmel—sailing in Monterey Bay, flying his light plane over the coast range. He even planned to build his own winery. He urged me to reestablish my ties to Carmel—that place, he told me, was paradise. Meanwhile, his infatuation with computers continued. In a letter to classmates that year, he marveled at how "computers are changing our lives."

Ted Kaczynski's Evergreen Park High School 1958 yearbook photo. He excelled in math, music, and history; belonged to the school coin, biology, chess, German, and mathematics clubs; and played in the band. (AP / Wide World Photos)

Henry A. Murray as lieutenant colonel in the Office of Strategic Services. Shortly after this photo was taken in early 1946, Murray returned to Harvard, soon to begin research on "the Dyad." (Psychology Archives, University of Akron)

Ted Kaczynski when an assistant professor of mathematics at the University of
California, Berkeley, in the late 1960s. By then he had already decided to quit teaching, escape to the wilderness, and "kill someone I hate." (AP / Wide World Photos)

Kaczynski's ten- by twelve-foot cabin near Lincoln, Montana, three days after his arrest. Crime-scene tape can be seen in the foreground. Contrary to media reports, it was hardly remote but, by Montana standards, virtually suburban. (FBI photograph)

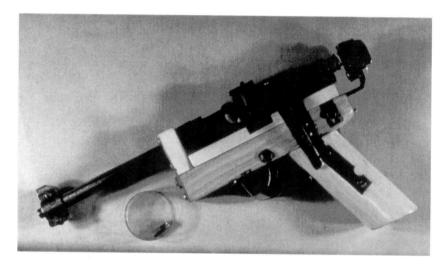

The pistol Kaczynski made from scrap in 1980. According to his secret diary he intended to use it as a "murder weapon." (FBI photograph)

(*Opposite, top*) FBI diagram of bomb #3 that caused a fire on board American Airlines Flight 444 on November 15, 1979. Its unique and elaborate design— use of a barometer as altimeter, multiple triggering and booby-trap mechanisms— impressed federal explosives experts. (FBI photograph)

(*Opposite, bottom*) FBI Crime Laboratory's reconstruction of the bomb that nearly killed Yale professor David Gelernter on June 24, 1993. Kaczynski had finally found "the perfect detonator." (FBI photograph)

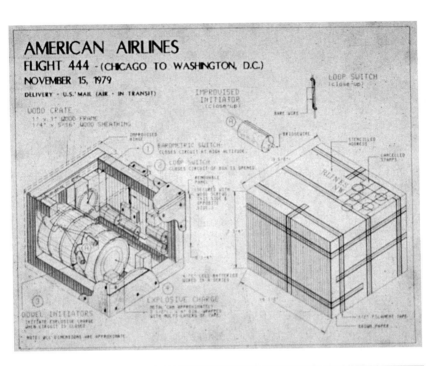

AMERICAN AIRLINES
FLIGHT 444 - (CHICAGO TO WASHINGTON, D.C.)
NOVEMBER 15, 1979

DELIVERY · U.S. MAIL (AIR · IN TRANSIT)

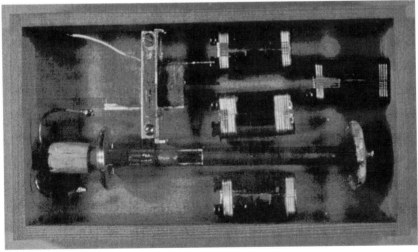

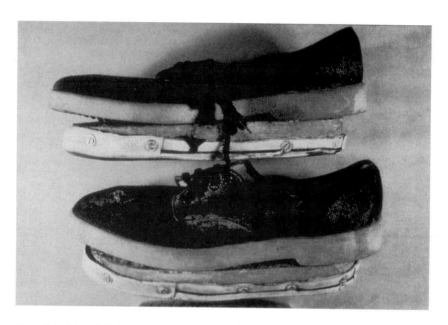

Pair of double-soled shoes Kaczynski designed to obscure his footprints and mislead investigators. Part of his large wardrobe of disguises, it is an example of the care he took to avoid detection. (FBI photograph)

Kaczynski's collection of "aviator" sunglasses, similar to the pair he was seen wearing when he planted bomb #12 behind the CAAMS computer store in Salt Lake City, Utah, on February 20, 1987. (FBI photograph)

Metal plates stamped with the Unabomber's "FC" signature, installed in many of his bombs and designed to survive the blast. He later explained that "FC" stood for "Freedom Club." (FBI photograph)

A coded page, or "matrix," from Kaczynski's secret journal. According to FBI experts, the code would have been virtually "unbreakable" had they not found Kaczynski's key for deciphering it. (FBI photograph)

(*Right*) A "list of meanings" constituting part of Kaczynski's key for encoding and decoding documents. (FBI photograph)

(*Below*) A page from the classification system Kaczynski used to organize documents according to the degree of secrecy they required. (FBI photograph)

LIST OF MEANINGS

0 = for
1 = bs (all present tense forms, including am, is, are, etc.)
2 = be (all past tense forms)
3 = be (future tense; i.e., will be)
4 = the
5 = a or an
6 = have (all present tense forms)
7 = have (all past tense forms; i.e. had)
8 = have (future tense)
9 = ed, or, when tagged onto the end of any verb, indicates the past tense, even if the past tense of that verb is not indicated by "ed" in ordinary English.
10 tagged onto the end of any verb indicates the future tense of that verb.

11 = ing	29 = I, me, mine, my	47 = E	68 = W
12 = er	30 = you, your, yours	48 = F	69 = X
13 = ly	31 = he, she, it, him, her,	49 = G	70 = Y
14 = tion	his, hers, its	50 = H	71 = Z
15 = there	32 = word spacer	51 = I	72 delete
16 = then	33 = word spacer	52 = J	73 delete
17 = and	34 = period	53 = K	74 = ch
18 = but	35 = comma	54 = L	75 = sh
19 = or	36 = question mark	55 = M	76 = th (unvoiced)
20 = to	37 = parenthesis (	56 = N	77 = th (voiced)
21 = from	38 = parenthesis)	57 = O	78 delete
22 = toward	39 = A	58 = P	79 = OM
23 = of	40 = A	59 = Q	80 = PLOD
24 = in	41 = B	60 = R	81 = ILL
25 = out	42 = C	61 = R	82 = ETONA
26 = no	43 = D	62 = S	83 = " (quotation marks)
27 = big	44 = D	63 = S	84 = when
28 = small	45 = E	64 = T	85 = where
	46 = E	65 = T	86 = what
		66 = U	87 = st
		67 = V	88 = that
			89 delete

Class 1. Hide carefully far from home.
Class 2. Hide carefully far from home, but can be destroyed at a pinch.
Class 3. Hide carefully, far from home, but can be burned at a pinch
Class 4. Burn away from home
Class 5. Burn in stove, eventually
Class 6. Burn with glass jars
Class 7. Destroy
Class 8. Treat to make safe
Class 9. Burn in stove, then dispose of remains
Class 10. Dump in trash far from home

QQ   Super queer
Q   Very queer
R   Moderately queer
S   Slightly queer

B   Burnable
NB   Not Burnable

(*Opposite*) Kaczynski's cabin interior, showing his books, bomb-making materials, and homemade chair. (FBI photograph)

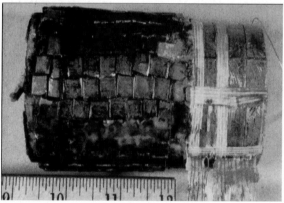

(*Above*) Location of bomb #17 under bunk (see arrow). (FBI photograph)

(*Left*) Close-up of the explosive charge of bomb #17. Note the shrapnel carefully glued to the bomb to increase its lethality. (FBI photograph)

Kaczynski's cabin interior, showing his bunk, under which agents found a completely assembled seventeenth bomb wrapped in a plastic shopping bag and wrapped in foil. It was identical to the one that killed Gilbert Murray. (FBI photograph)

Kaczynski being escorted by federal marshals from the Helena,
Montana, Federal Courthouse after his arraignment on April 4, 1996.
(Paul Dix)

But soon, signs of disillusionment showed. With uncanny prescience, in that same class report letter, King seemed to anticipate the "millennium bug" crisis. "My greatest concern for all of us," he wrote, "is what would happen if we lost our computers. Just imagine the collapse of the power grid, homes and businesses without power or communications. In a very short time, there would be no food, water or heat in most cities. Not only are modern societies dependent already on computers, but fall-back positions for individuals, families or countries suddenly without modern technology are difficult to imagine or plan."

Five years later, King's class reports evinced growing sadness. He complained of "trying to scratch out a living as a consultant and writer in the information/computer industry. I have to travel too much. . . ." Sailing in Monterey had become "somewhat boring," and "I've also lost most of my desire to operate a winery." He even seemed to have lost his faith in technology: "Sure," he wrote, "computers allow us to run a business more efficiently than without them . . . the unfortunate part is that many things that are possible today may turn out to be more harmful than useful. This obviously includes the capability to create civilization-ending weapons and to probe into individuals' lives on a scale that would make the Soviets proud."

King's business fortunes declined. Friends suspect that he got badly in debt. With a daughter at Wellesley, he faced heavy tuition bills. Yet Carmel, his friends would explain later, is an expensive place to live, where social pressures to keep up appearances are great. And King could neither give up his expensive lifestyle nor bear to face the humiliation of bankruptcy.

On October 10, 1991, King disappeared. His BMW was found parked at Moss Landing near Carmel, at the end of Sandholdt Road, on a spit of land known as "the island." Evidently, authorities surmised, late the night before he had driven his car to this lonely spot and, fully clothed, dived into the dangerous surf.

King's faith in technology had gradually turned into despair. Kaczynski's despair turned into hatred of technology. And if Kaczynski hadn't bombed and murdered he would have been simply another Harvard grad who fell between the cracks.

AFTER KACZYNSKI'S arrest, and shortly before he himself died, Gerald Burns wrote a poem entitled "Letter Bomb to Ted," which he sent to their Harvard classmates. In it, Burns sought to capture his and Kaczynski's shared anger:

> *Do I sentimentalize, writing you without*
> *invitation? You won't remember me but I remember you . . .*
> *whose threatened book,* Eminent Harvard Failures,
>> *can now include you . . .*
>> *you were one of*
>> *the last*
> *Berkeley professors to wear a jacket and tie to*
>> *work.*
>> *I could cry*
>> *over that,*
> *the Ivy League integument a casing for our*
>> *learning, or calling,*
>> *but not (in truth)*
>> *so far from middle management . . .*
> *Why'd you do it isn't interesting. I know why you did,*
> *pretty much. It's much the reason I write poems in sections.*
> *Cap the pen, cap the ends with copper. Bang, Ted.*

ONCE AGAIN, we find that Kaczynski's life was not particularly unusual. He grew up amidst world war and Cold War tensions, but so had the entire Silent Generation. He had been pushed hard academically by his parents, but so were many others. He was much younger than his classmates and had skipped two grades, but so had many other bright kids. He was a loner at Harvard, where "loner" was a virtual badge of honor. He was a mathematician, but so were others. He had been a victim of Harvard snobbism and its curricular culture of despair, but so had thousands of others. He espoused an antitechnology philosophy that is embraced by perhaps a majority of Americans. He remained an Outsider long after graduation, but so had many of his classmates.

In sum, in many ways Kaczynski closely resembled those who did not kill. The violence in him derived from the same thoughts and emotions that coursed through the veins of more peaceful classmates. Kaczynski, however, took his philosophy and anger further. He took, one might say, his averageness to extreme lengths. But why? Did his high IQ explain his extremism? Is there a "cognitive style" for murder?

Psychologists speak of different cognitive styles—distinct but equally rational ways of thinking. Mathematical reasoning is one such style. Napoleon Williams speculates that mathematics may have been the source of Kaczynski's later problems, but was insufficient in itself to explain his behavior. "It's possible to develop systems of ideas that are entirely consistent internally," Williams told me, "but have no relationship to facts. But most mathematicians are forced by circumstances to circulate in the real world after they graduate." Kaczynski, however, would choose never to face the "real world." So his mathematical bent alone cannot explain why his anomie became permanent—why, within a short time after graduating from Harvard he became and would remain a full-blown Outsider with a fully developed ideology of rage.

Our question remains: What drove him beyond the pale and kept him there? Did something besides his encounter with the culture of despair happen to him at Harvard to explain this?

As it turns out, the answer is yes.

15

The Experiment

Researchers who almost certainly knew better sometimes
employed unconsenting healthy subjects in research that
offered them no medical benefits.

> —*Final Report of
> the President's Advisory Committee
> on Human Radiation Experiments*

"I had been talked or pressured into participating in the
Murray study against my better judgment."

> —TED KACZYNSKI
> to attorney Michael Mello,
> August 24, 1998

I N THE FALL OF 1959, Harvard sophomores who had enrolled in a
popular psychology course received a curious invitation. "Would
you," it asked, "be willing to contribute to the solution of certain
psychological problems (parts of an on-going program of research in

the development of personality) by serving as a subject in a series of experiments or taking a number of tests (average about 2 hours a week) through the academic year (at the current College rate per hour)?"

The consent form failed to say that experiments would last not one, but three academic years. It did not reveal that students would be deceived. Nor did it provide information about the experiment's purpose or possible effects. Conducted by a team of psychologists headed by Henry A. Murray of the Department of Social Relations, this was the most elaborate in a series of three-year studies that Murray had undertaken during the 1940s and 1950s, entitled "Multiform Assessments of Personality Development Among Gifted College Men."

Around seventy students volunteered. Each was given a battery of psychological tests to determine his suitability as a study subject. Researchers were looking for a few "average" individuals as well as those representing extremes—some highly alienated and others exceptionally well adjusted. As Murray put it, they sought to enlist students who were "at the extreme of avowed alienation, lack of identity, pessimism, etc.," as well as those "at the opposite extreme (reporting nearly optimal physical, mental, and social well-being)."

Based on this prescreening, researchers picked twenty-two undergraduates, four or five of whom were deemed as belonging to each of the two polar opposite categories. Among those chosen was Ted Kaczynski. Of the nineteen people (not including Kaczynski) whose biographical data I reviewed at Harvard's Murray Research Center, eight were prep school graduates, two having attended Murray's alma mater, the exclusive Episcopal boarding school, Groton. At least ten were members of very wealthy families, some exceedingly prominent. The rest came from a solidly professional class background whose parents included a high school principal, an architect, a factory owner, the manager of an industrial plant, and an Ivy League professor. Kaczynski was the only blue-collar boy in the bunch.

To preserve their privacy, the experimental data referred to each student by a code name, carefully chosen by Murray himself. The pseudonym began with the letter that followed alphabetically immediately after the first letter of the student's last name, and was intended to capture the essence of the student's personality. "Murray was very good at this," one of his former assistants explained to me. "He was uncannily intuitive about people."

Murray dubbed Kaczynski, "Lawful."

Was this moniker meant to be taken literally or as irony? Was Kaczynski deemed exceptionally alienated or unusually well adjusted?

Probably both. At the time, Kaczynski gave off mixed signals: outwardly strait-laced and almost prudish, inwardly a time bomb. Murray was astute enough to see both dimensions. And that's probably why he wanted to study the boy.

So, "Lawful" was literally accurate. At the time, Kaczynski was trying hard to be a good boy. There was no outward sign of the rebel in him. His undergraduate behavior had been unremarkable. The reports of his housemaster, adviser, and the university doctors attested to his normalcy, as did the observations of classmates. And as we saw in chapter 8, Michigan State University professor Bertram Karon's blind scoring of Kaczynski's answers to the TAT, administered by Murray during the experiment, revealed a complete absence of mental illness.

But while Kaczynski may have been clinically sane, he was also clearly aloof. And as we shall see, Murray's preliminary screening would identify him as the most alienated of the entire cohort. That made him the perfect guinea pig for Murray's purposes. Perhaps as a sign of his eagerness to recruit Kaczynski, who had not enrolled in his course and couldn't have seen the flyer there, Murray may have disregarded the boy's fragility and approached him through an intermediary, persuading him to participate.

Not just Murray, but his assistant, Kenneth Keniston too, was interested in alienation. He focused on the most alienated subjects, and later put his observations into a book, *The Uncommitted* (1963).

According to Keniston, these youths exhibited "a strong sense of cosmic outcastness." They "spend less time with others; are less intimate with them, become less manifestly involved with groups than do many or most of their peers. To all but their closest friends and acquaintances these students are usually known as aloof and rather negativistic, somewhat scornful, unwilling to be drawn into the activities of others, perhaps condescending."

It would be a mistake, however, Keniston noted, merely to dismiss these young men as "disturbed" or "neurotic." Most of our definitions of mental health are based on what society believes is acceptable behavior, Keniston observed. And it would beg the question to call nonconformists mentally unhealthy simply because they rejected social norms. The alienated, moreover, "make a virtue, even a fetish, of complete and ruthless honesty with themselves about their most undesirable qualities," since "awareness and self-understanding are central goals." Hence, they can "show up poorly on personality tests partly because they lack the . . . desire to put up a 'good show' . . . to appear 'normal,' a classification they despise." So, "it often happens that an individual with extremely 'healthy' test scores can be in reality far more disturbed." Rather,

> what unifies the ideology of these alienated young men is their generalized refusal of American culture. . . . [V]irtually every alienated outlook can be seen as a rejection of (often unstated) American assumptions about life and the universe.

And most fundamental of these rejected assumptions is an unswerving faith in technology. As a people, Keniston argued, Americans "value scientific innovation and technological change almost without conscious reservation." Indeed, "though our own country is not unique in the role technology plays, it is distinguished by the intensity of, and the relative absence of restraint of technological change. Probably more than any other society, we revere technological innovation, we seldom seek to limit its effects on other areas of society, and we have developed complex institutions to assure its persistence and acceleration."

Yet, Keniston continued, it is precisely this scientific innovation and technological change that alienates individuals. They cut people off from their past, shatter communities and families, and create gulfs between children and parents. "What our society lacks, then," Keniston concludes, "is a vision of itself that transcends technology. It exacts a heavy human toll not because technology exists, but because we allow technology to reign."

Based on Keniston's book, Kaczynski seems the perfect example of a psychological type: the youth who is victimized by and rebels against technological society. As Jon Krakauer recounts in *Into the Wild*, the story of Chris McCandless, who escaped into the Alaska wilderness only to die there, such young men are common. They share a love of nature and a hatred for materialism, progress, and conformism. They all resemble, to some degree, Ted Kaczynski.

Yet, while he was certainly an Outsider, Kaczynski didn't fit Keniston's description in all respects. These uncommitted young people "lack clear affirmative goals and values"; their "main temporal goal is the present"; for them, "reason must play a secondary role to feeling"; they "go out with girls neither more nor less than any other group at college"; they are close to their mothers; "they find little self-definition or coherence in their intellectual interests"; and "they sense the impossibility of certainty."

By contrast, Kaczynski had clearly defined goals; he worried about the future of civilization; he possessed an absolute faith in reason; he seldom dated girls; he claimed to despise his mother; and he possessed consuming intellectual interests. Although alienated, unlike most such youths he was prone to action, not passivity. He was capable of feeling both despair and commitment. And this would prove a fatal combination. What Kaczynski would call his "highly unpleasant experience" with the Murray experiment would aggravate his despair and suggest a theory that seemed to demand drastic action.

Kaczynski had reached a turning point in his life.

THE CENTERPIECE of the experiments was something Murray called alternatively "stressful disputation," "dyadic interaction," "stressful dyadic episode," "stressful dyadic proceeding," "dyadic interaction of alienated subjects," or simply "the Dyad." Whatever its name, it was a highly refined version of the third degree. Its intent was to catch the student by surprise, to deceive him, bring him to anger, ridicule his beliefs, and brutalize him. As Murray explained in the only article he ever wrote about his experiment:

First, you are told you have a month in which to write a brief exposition of your personal philosophy of life, an affirmation of the major guiding principles in accord with which you live or hope to live.

Second, when you return to the Annex with your finished composition, you are informed that in a day or two you and a talented young lawyer will be asked to debate the respective merits of your two philosophies.

When the subject arrived for the debate, he was escorted into a "brilliantly lighted room" and seated in front of a one-way mirror. A motion picture camera recorded his every move and facial expression through a hole in the wall. Electrodes leading to machines that recorded his heart and respiratory rates were attached to his body. Then the debate began. But the students were tricked. Contrary to what Murray claimed in his article, Murray had lied to the students. He did not tell them they would debate a talented young lawyer. Rather, as Murray explained in an unpublished progress report, each student was led to expect he would confront "another undergraduate subject like himself." So when they were confronted with what Murray called "a law school student . . . our trained accomplice," they were caught completely by surprise and not prepared for what followed. This "well-prepared 'stooge,'" as Murray's biographer, Forrest Robinson, calls the law student, was talented indeed, and carefully coached to launch an aggressive attack on his younger victim, for the purpose of upsetting him as much as possible.

Robinson describes what happened next:

As instructed, the unwitting subject attempted to represent and to defend his personal philosophy of life. Invariably, however, he was frustrated, and finally brought to expressions of real anger, by the withering assault of his older, more sophisticated opponent . . . while fluctuations in the subject's pulse and respiration were measured on a cardiotachometer.

Not surprisingly, most participants found this highly unpleasant, even traumatic, as the data sets record. "We were led into the room with bright lights, very bright," one of them, code-named "Cringle," recalled afterward.

I could see shadowy activities going on behind the one-way glass. . . . [Dr. G] . . . started fastening things on me. [I] had a sensation

*somewhat akin to someone being strapped on the electric chair
with these electrodes . . . I really started getting hit real hard. . . .
Wham, wham, wham! And me getting hotter and more irritated
and my heart beat going up . . . and sweating terribly . . . there I
was under the lights and with movie camera and all this experimentation equipment on me. . . . It was sort of an unpleasant
experience.*

"Right away," said another, code-named "Trump," describing his
experience afterward, "I didn't like [the interrogator]."

*[Dr. G] . . . came waltzing over and he put on those electrodes but
in that process, while he was doing that, kind of whistling, I was
looking over the room, and right away I didn't like the room. I
didn't like the way the glass was in front of me through which I
couldn't see, but I was being watched and right away that puts one
in a kind of unnatural situation and I noted the big white lights
and again that heightens the unnatural effect. There was something peculiar about the set-up too, it was supposed to look homey
or look natural, two chairs and a little table, but again that struck
me as unnatural before the big piece of glass and the lights. And
then [Mr. R] . . . who was bubbling over, dancing around, started
to talk to me about he liked my suit . . . the buzzer would ring or
something like that, we were supposed to begin . . . he was being
sarcastic or pretty much of a wise guy. . . . And the first thing that
entered my mind was to get up and ask him outside immediately
. . . but that was out of the question, because of the electrodes and
the movie and all that. . . . I kind of sat there and began to fume
and then he went on and he got my goat and I couldn't think of
what to say. . . . And then they came along and they took my electrodes off.*

One subject, "Hinge," thought he was "being attacked." Another,
"Naisfield," complained: "The lights were very bright. . . . Then the
things were put on my legs and whatnot and on the arm. . . . I didn't like
the feel of the sticky stuff that was on there being sort of uncomfortable."

Although the "stressful dyadic proceeding" served as the center-piece of Murray's experiment (taking place during the winter of 1960), it was merely one among scores of different tests the students took in order to allow Murray and his associates to acquire, as Murray wrote, "the most accurate, significant, and complete knowledge and under-standing of a single psychological event that is obtainable."

Before the dyadic confrontation took place, Murray and his colleagues interviewed the students in depth about their hopes and aspirations. During this same period the subjects were required to write not only essays explaining their philosophies of life but also autobiographies, in which they were told to answer specific, intimate questions on a range of subjects from thumb-sucking and toilet training to masturbation and erotic fantasies. And they faced a battery of tests that included, among others, the Thematic Apperception Test (TAT), a Rorschach test, the Minnesota Multiphasic Personality Inventory, the California Psychological Inventory, a "fantasy inventory," a psychological-types inventory, the Maudalay Personality Inventory, an "inventory of self-description," a "temperament questionnaire," a "time-metaphor test," a "basic disposition test," a "range of experience inventory," a "philosophical outlook test," a food-preference inventory, analyses of their literary tastes and moral precepts, an "odor association test," a "word association test," an argument-completion test, a Wyatt finger-painting test, a projective-drawings test, and a "Rosenzweig picture frustration test." The results were then analyzed by researchers, who plotted them in numerous ways in an effort to develop a psychological portrait of each personality in all its dimensions.

Only after most of this data had been collected did researchers administer the stressful dyadic confrontation. Following this session, each student was called back for several "recall" interviews and sometimes asked to comment on the movie of himself being reduced to impotent anger by the interrogator. During these replays, Murray wrote, "you will see yourself making numerous grimaces and gestures" and "uttering incongruent, disjunctive, and unfinished sentences."

In the last year of the experiment, Murray made the students available to his graduate student assistants, to serve as guinea pigs for their own research projects. By graduation, as Keniston summarized the process, "each student had spent approximately two hundred hours in the research, and had provided hundreds of pages of information about himself, his beliefs, his past life, his family, his college life and development, his fantasies, his hopes and dreams."

WHY WERE THE students willing to endure this ongoing stress and probing into their private lives? Some who had assisted Murray confessed to me that they wondered about this themselves. But they—and we—can only speculate that a few of the students (including Kaczynski) did it for the money; that some (again probably including Kaczynski) had doubts about their own psychic health and were seeking reassurance about it; that some, suffering from Harvard's culture of despair, were lonely and needed someone to talk to; and that some simply had an interest in helping to advance scientific knowledge. But we do not know for sure. Alden E. Wessman, a former research associate of Murray's who has long been bothered by the ethical dimension of this study, said to me recently, "Later, I thought:'We took and took and used them and what did we give them in return?'"

Indeed, even by the standards of that day, these "stressful disputations" were unethical. For they violated what was and still is regarded as the holy writ of experimental ethics, known as the Nuremberg Code, which forbids deceiving participants.

The Code was inspired by the experience of jurists conducting the Nuremberg War Crimes Trials of Nazi concentration camp doctors following World War II. After the trial, the judges, concerned that there had been no clear guidelines available to them on which to base their condemnation of these defendants, promulgated ten rules of their own to be used in future such trials. The first and most important of these was what would become known as the requirement for "informed consent."

"The voluntary consent of the human subject is absolutely essential," the judges declared. And "the person involved should be so situated as to be able to exercise free power of choice, without the intervention of any element of force, fraud, deceit, duress. . . ."

These requirements, together with subsequent stipulations prohibiting unduly risky testing, formed the heart of the Nuremberg Code and would be quickly hailed as the golden rules for experimentation on human subjects. Even before the conclusion of the War Crimes Trials, in 1946, the American Medical Association adopted a distillation of the Code as mandatory for research on humans. And "by the late 1950s," stated *The Final Report of the President's Advisory Committee on Human Radiation Experiments* (published later), "many and perhaps even most American medical researchers had come to recognize the Nuremberg Code as the most authoritative single answer to an important Question: What are the rules for human experimentation?"

Nevertheless, as the Advisory Committee observed, "many researchers were not entirely happy with the prospect of living by the letter of the Code." In fact, the majority, while paying lip-service to the Code sought either to water it down or ignore it. Most prominent among the institutions contesting it was the Harvard Medical School, whose administrative board member, Henry K. Beecher, would in 1962 object to a U.S. Army proposal to require its research to conform to the Code by observing that it overlooked the fact that "valid, informed consent may be difficult to obtain in some cases." Eventually, the Advisory Committee reported, Harvard was able to persuade the army surgeon general to concede that "the 'principles' being inserted into Harvard's research contracts with the Army were 'guidelines' rather than 'rigid rules.'"

Before the ink was dry at Nuremberg, therefore, many researchers were already ignoring the Code. In a particularly infamous experiment conducted in 1962 by a Yale professor, Stanley Milgram, subjects (forty men recruited through mail solicitation and a newspaper ad) were led to believe that they were delivering ever more powerful electric shocks to a stranger, on orders from the researcher. Nearly two thirds of them continued to obey the orders even when they were asked to administer the highest level of shock, labeled: *Danger: Severe Shock.*

Some participants broke down on learning of their potential for cruelty. "I observed a mature and initially poised businessman enter the laboratory smiling and confident," Milgram wrote of one of his study subjects. "Within 20 minutes he was reduced to a twitching, stuttering wreck, who was rapidly approaching a point of nervous collapse."

Like Milgram, Murray had violated the Nuremberg Code. Why, then, did he undertake the experiment? His motives would remain obscure. No one seems sure what the "certain psychological problems" were that he sought to solve. The subjects were given almost no information and what they were told was in large part false. Murray's graduate assistants knew little more. In 1963, after the series was completed, Murray asked the National Institute of Mental Health for support "to finish writing a book" based on the data he had collected. But apparently he never even started it. Keniston, who assisted Murray in these experiments, told me that he wasn't sure what the goals were. "Murray was not the most systematic scientist," he explained.

Murray himself gave curiously equivocal answers. At times his explanations seemed circular—defining the Dyad in terms of the Dyad, for example, or when, without defining the term, he suggested his intent was to gather as much raw data as possible about one "dyadic" event, which could then be used in different ways to help "develop a theory of dyadic systems." At other times he recalled the idealistic goal of acquiring knowledge that would lead to improving human personality development.

Then, again, Murray at times suggested that his research might have no value at all. "Cui bono?" he once asked. "As [the data] stand they are nothing but raw data, meaningless as such; and the question is what meaning, what intellectual news, can be extracted from them?" In another context, he asked: "Are the costs in man-hours incurred by our elaborate, multiple procedures far greater than any possible gains in knowledge?"

Was his motivation not perhaps science at all, but what Germans call *Schadenfreude*—taking pleasure in others' discomfort? One of Murray's former assistants told Forrest Robinson, Murray's biographer, that the professor's real interest was just to see what happened when one person attacked another. Some of Murray's own comments seem to support this interpretation, such as his "Notes on Dyadic Research," dated March 16, 1959, stating that an ongoing goal of the research (which he admitted was focused heavily on "degree of anxiety and disintegration") was to "design and evaluate instruments and procedures for the prediction of how each subject will react in the course of a stressful dyadic proceeding."

Not only the purpose of his experiment but Murray himself would remain a puzzle. As the late psychologist Leopold Bellak explained to Robinson, Murray, while personally gracious and generous, could also be "elusive, exasperating." Even the normally sympathetic Robinson would describe Murray as "mysterious and ungraspable."

To the end of his long life (he died in 1988 at the age of ninety-five), Murray kept two secrets. One of these secrets few would learn until his death. The second is only now being revealed for the first time. The key to unlocking both lies in fathoming Murray's obsession with what he called "the Dyad."

16

The Dyad

Murray's most telling contribution to method is that of using the same subjects for the whole program of the research group. . . . [T]he subjects quite naturally become friendly with the investigators, and the investigators with the subjects. . . . But Murray has also been much occupied with creating concrete situations of an emotionally involving character.

> —ROBERT W. WHITE,
> *The Study of Lives* (1963)

We were told that we were to engage in a debate about our personal philosophies, and then found that our adversary in the debate subjected us to various insults that, presumably, the psychologists helped him to concoct. It was a highly unpleasant experience.

> —TED KACZYNSKI
> to attorney Michael Mello,
> September 19, 1998

A T THE TIME Kaczynski reluctantly agreed to participate in the Multiform Assessment experiments, Henry Murray was a towering figure in the world of psychology, approaching the end of a remarkably distinguished career. His *Explorations in Personality* (1938), defining a whole new field of personality assessment that he called "personology," is considered a classic by many. Murray, with his friend and colleague Christiana Morgan, conceived the Thematic Apperception Test, or TAT, which became widely used by psychologists as a tool for probing the psyche.

During World War II, while working for the Office of Strategic Services (precursor of the CIA), Murray helped develop a system for testing recruits' capacity for clandestine warfare that inspired an entirely new technology of employee evaluation, widely used by government and business today.

Murray is also deemed the co-founder of humanistic psychology, a discipline dedicated to expanding human potential, that gave birth to a variety of alternative therapies of the 1960s and 1970s.

Despite Murray's august reputation, however, those who knew him disagree widely about how to assess his science and character. Some still idolize him. These consider the TAT a lasting achievement and the *Explorations*, as one former colleague, Edwin Shneidman, described it to me, "the most important book in psychology since William James's *Principles of Psychology* appeared in 1890."

Others, while attesting to Murray's charm and creative imagination, say he didn't accomplish much. They dismiss the *Explorations* as brilliant for its time but of no enduring value. And despite Murray's repeated claims throughout his professional career that he was working on many more books, he never completed another.

Rather, say these critics, Murray's major contribution was his influence on students. He was "a great initiator, with marvelous ideas but little follow-through," as Morgan's biographer, Claire Douglas, puts it.

Some suggested that he feared to publish because this would expose him to criticism, which he couldn't tolerate. For he did, indeed, have very thin skin. Invariably, he made a charming initial impression. An extraordinarily good listener, he could appear utterly enthralled by someone he'd just met. Yet at the first sign that this worship was not requited, he turned, often treating the other cruelly.

"The great Murray," wrote another former colleague, Frank Barron, "didn't like anyone to leave him, he liked to be the one to leave." The late psychologist David McClelland told Robinson in 1970 that Murray

hurt people by his consistent paranoia, that people didn't love him enough, or something . . . he is extremely sensitive, super-sensitive, and the kind of games he plays always end up with all the people his own age very irritated and withdrawing from the game. With younger people it can be extremely damaging. . . . [T]here wasn't anybody that he was close to, that I know of, really close to, that didn't end up bleeding when he left. . . . Harry is so super-sensitive that even hinting [criticism] during his lifetime would be disastrous, in terms of your relationship with him.

In short, Murray took everything personally. He couldn't keep his feelings and science apart, and was unable to decide whether he was a humanist exploring his own soul or a scientist studying the psyches of others. He embodied the conflict, ongoing in academe at the time, between humanism and science.

As a humanist, Murray was for many years among Lewis Mumford's best friends, until the two—which was not unusual for Murray—drifted apart. Politically liberal, Murray feared for the future of civilization and advocated implementing the agenda of the United World Federalists, which called for a single world government as the only way the human race could be prevented from extinguishing itself. The atomic bomb, he wrote Mumford, "is the logical & predictable result of the course we have been madly pursuing for a hundred years." The choice for human-ity was "One World or No World."

Yet, unlike Mumford, Murray, who not only had a medical degree but a Ph.D. in biochemistry, maintained a deep faith in science, which he saw as the key to reforming humanity. Crucial to achieving this change was learning the secret of successful relationships between peo-ple, communities, and nations.

This tension between Murray's humanism and science affected his research profoundly. To ensure objectivity, scientific protocol demands the investigator keep distance between himself and his study subjects, so that personal relations do not affect the outcome. Otherwise, the subject's feelings about the experimenter, or the experimenter's feelings about the subjects, could "contaminate" (i.e., skew) the conclusions.

Murray, however, invited contamination. He wasn't careful about protocol. He liked to feel that the student subjects liked him. His research lacked the objective controls that the scientific method demanded. As one of his former colleagues, Henry Riecken, told me, "Murray was no scientist, no experimenter. One could hardly call the exercises to which he subjected Kaczynski and his cohort 'experiments.'"

This mingling of the personal and professional, the humanistic and scientific, was more than accidental. It was the essence of the Dyad. Seemingly scientific, "the Dyad" was in fact a personal concept, signifying to Murray the strange, and secret, forty-year love affair he had with Christiana Morgan. "It became clear," Robinson writes, "that the secret love affair was the key to it all. It everywhere energized and informed the public career; was the hidden center, the focus, the source of inspiration and direction."

In short, Murray's science was an extension of his private life. The two intersected in the Dyad, and the key to understanding both lay in his past.

Born in New York City on May 13, 1893, into a wealthy and well-connected family, during his early years Murray seemed destined to live an utterly conventional life. His father was a descendant of John Murray, 4th Earl of Dunmore, and his mother was the scion of a distinguished New England family. Murray attended Groton, then Harvard, where he was a member of the elite A.D. Club, graduating in 1915. A year later he married Josephine Rantoul, herself from an old New England family. In 1919 he was awarded a degree in medicine from Columbia University and in 1927 a Ph.D. in biochemistry from Cambridge University.

Yet, like so many privileged people whose outwardly conventional lives hide eccentricities, Murray's seeming propriety masked a private life bordering on the bizarre. Feeling rejected by a hypercritical mother and tormented by his domineering older sister, Murray grew into a complex and conflicted man: narcissistic, sexually ambivalent, angry, repressed, and alternately loving and cruel toward others, desperately longing to rebel from the Puritanical restrictions of his childhood.

When, in 1923, he read Herman Melville's *Moby-Dick* for the first time, he became virtually obsessed with the novel and its author. He closely identified, not just with Melville but with Captain Ahab himself, the half-mad sea captain who sought revenge against the great white whale that had taken his leg. To Murray, the whale embodied the cruel and unforgiving God of Calvinism; and Ahab, by seeking to slay it, was a tragic hero. By battling the whale, the sea captain sought to strike a blow for psychic and sexual freedom.

From that time forward, Murray would pursue the whale. In 1949 he named the Harvard Psychological Clinic—that he had directed since 1928—"the Baleen," adopting a spouting sperm whale as its logo. And his identification with Melville and the author's fictional character would stay with him. "Harry Ahab-Murray Melville," as Frank Barron described him. " . . . It was all Harry; the whole universe was inside him; the outside world had no reality, it was mere spectacle."

It was in 1923, during an intermission at the Metropolitan Opera, that Murray met Christiana Councilman Morgan, a stunning beauty, and the wife of a World War I veteran, William Morgan. Like Murray, she came from privileged surroundings and chafed under them. Nevertheless, there was something about Harry that frightened her.

"I wish that with Harry I didn't have this feeling of a snake in the grass somewhere," she recorded in her notebook two years later, in 1925. "It always seems to be interfering with my sensing of his personality. Its head always crops up immediately after I think it is not there. This snake is the desire for power, always present."

In 1926, Murray and Morgan became lovers. After accepting an appointment at the Harvard Psychological Clinic that spring, he arranged for Morgan to come as his assistant. The couple rented an apartment above a tobacconist's shop on Massachusetts Avenue for their assignations. By entering discreetly through the shop, they supposed, they could meet unobserved.

They were mistaken. Murray's wife, Jo, discovered their secret almost immediately from her cook, who was a friend of the tobacconist's janitor. It wasn't a secret from Bill Morgan, either. Both betrayed spouses were terribly hurt and their pain endured. Murray's daughter, Josie, Douglas reports, "would wonder in coming years, why her mother now cried so often behind closed doors." Bill Morgan sank into a lasting depression. Seeking solace in the bottle, he died in 1934 of tuberculosis before he reached the age of forty.

Murray and Morgan's affair would last more than forty years. She became Murray's muse and collaborator. In 1929, the clinic's founder and director, Morton Prince, died and Murray was made its head. Soon he had moved it into larger premises at 64 Plympton Street. The couple's interest by now focused on "personology," which Claire Douglas describes as "a complete survey of human personality through examining individuals in depth." In 1935, Morgan's name would be listed above Murray's as co-author of the famed Thematic Apperception Test, which they had conceived and intended, they said, to measure the "deeper layers of personality." The TAT would take psychologists by storm, becoming the second best-selling publication ever issued by Harvard University Press.

Murray led a double life. In summer, he spent six weeks with Jo at their place in the Thousand Islands on the St. Lawrence; then six weeks with Christiana in Massachusetts. When together, the lovers threw themselves into the task of what Carl Jung called "completing the self"—which included exploring the darkest parts of their souls. Attacking Calvinist taboos with gusto, they explored the limits of their libidos.

They gave themselves pet names. He became "Mansol," she "Wona." During the summer of 1936, Morgan records that "Mansol returns from 1000 Islands wearing red finger nails and a beard." Then the following November: "discovered that our life was in the whip—the black whip that hurt. Without that there is no passion for us now."

"They chronicled their sexual psychodramas," Douglas writes,

> in a book called the "Red and Gold Diary," which Harry destroyed in the 1980s when he was going through his papers. Christiana had excerpted passages, which she kept in her files. The diary started as early as 1936, when Christiana recorded that Harry wore a green Hindu shirt and a black velvet skirt and whipped her before they made love.

Elsewhere in the "Red and Gold Diary" "Wona" records that "Mansol's lust knew only obedience, ultimate, sensual submission. . . . Mansol fixed the handcuffs and laid me down across the bed spread. Tonight Mansol wore the rose skirt and gold bracelet." Then Mansol asks, "Could you love anyone but a Sadist? You suspected it, didn't you? Infinite kindness and compassion first, final sadism behind it."

And Wona speaking again, in January 22, 1938:

> *Mansol returned. Came on narrow shoes*
> > *bringing bed spread.*
> *He told me he loved my cunt.*
> *He brought chains, handcuffs, a whip, a knife.*
> > *He asked me if I was ready for a year of submission.*
> *He explained to me the sacrifice he demanded.*
> *He told me of his blood lust.*
> *We told each other of our masturbations and*
> > *the dreams thereof.*
> *He told me that I would submit to him as to*
> > *the God of my trances.*
> *At night he wore the orange shirt and green*
> > *skirt. Pearl bracelets on his wrists.*

Meanwhile, in 1937, Murray helped Christiana build a stone tower on land she had purchased in 1927, above a tidal river in Rowley, Massachusetts. It was modeled after Carl Jung's retreat in Bollingen, Switzerland, which Murray and she had always wanted to replicate. It became her retreat and their trysting place, where they explored their subconscious selves in elaborate sadomasochistic rituals they called "Walpurgis evenings."

Murray's longtime assistant, Ina May Greer, told Robinson that "The tower gave [Murray] . . . a place that he could put his evil and find it accepted." When asked, what evil? she replied, "Anger, frustration, aggression, hostility, need to punish, need to explode, need to let go of all the controls of society and live out whatever mood was there, whatever instinct or impulse was there. . . . [This] was stronger [in him] than it is in most people."

Murray, she went on, needed "to be in control. In control of himself, in control of his life. At the same time he had from time to time to let go all barriers, all constraining structures, and explode."

In 1938, Murray's *Explorations* appeared, instantly making his reputation. Morgan was listed as a co-author too, but although they didn't realize it, she was already headed toward the periphery of his life.

A year later, at Christiana's urging, Murray took a two-year sabbatical, staying at the tower to write a book on Melville. By 1941, he had a manuscript over 1,000 pages in length. But it was an embarrassing dud and Murray never sought to publish it. For it had been undermined by his own narcissism. As much autobiography as biography, it revealed just how closely Murray identified with Melville. Rather than offering an objective portrait of the novelist, it was, as Robinson observed, a "mirror of its maker." The work exposed, with painful clarity, Murray's own obsessions. Publishing it would bare his most private self to scrutiny.

This was the turning point in the affair. Murray returned from his sabbatical, Douglas says, angry at Christiana for exposing his failure by encouraging him to write the book. Two years later he went to work with the OSS and moved to Washington with his wife, where their lives and military protocol allowed no room for Christiana. She became seriously ill and had a major operation. Depressed by their separation, she turned increasingly to drink.

By that time, many others around Murray were suffering. "Christiana got the short end of the deal, she was used," Murray's old friend, Carl Binger, told Robinson. "Jo was used, too. . . . Christiana was being exploited. . . . She drank more and more and became increasingly slovenly and unattractive."

After the war, Murray returned to the Harvard Psychological Clinic. But now Christiana felt like a fifth wheel. The younger graduate students, not knowing who she was, regarded her, says Douglas, as an "elegant but distant lady." Christiana spent less time there, retreating more frequently to the tower. Harvard University Press, with Murray's consent, dropped her name as the co-author of the TAT. Her drinking, never light, grew worse.

In 1958, the clinic moved yet again, to Divinity Avenue. The series of experiments in which Kaczynski participated—the last Dyad—would begin the next year and be completed in 1962, the same year that Murray retired and Kaczynski graduated. Jo died in 1962, reviving Christiana's hopes that Murray would at last marry her. But she would be disappointed. Murray was approaching the end of his rope, as well. In 1959, he was introduced to LSD by Timothy Leary, then a young professor in his department, who would soon become infamous as the Johnny Appleseed of psychedelics. Long addicted to amphetamines, now Murray became infatuated with acid and introduced Christiana to the drug as well.

According to Claire Douglas, Murray "had at least eleven unfinished books he was planning alone or with co-authors." He became

> *increasingly difficult to work with and somewhat erratic in the late fifties and early sixties, partly because of his brief investigations of LSD with Timothy Leary . . . and because of Murray's continued use of amphetamines. The stimulants helped Murray get through his days and the enormous amount of work that multiplied around him, but Benzedrine also fueled both its chaotic and its perfectionist character, projects proliferated into endless others, Sorcerer's Apprentice-like, each seeming to take on a life of its own. The effort to duplicate the initial studies foundered under a mammoth accumulation of material.*

As Murray pursued his experiments on Kaczynski and his cohort, this decline continued. He "took amphetamines and got himself whipped up to the point where he could work," one former colleague observed, "and then he worked feverishly for as long as he could at a stretch and knocked himself out, and then he had to take sedatives to sleep." And Morgan joined him. Both, said Ida May Greer, "were on a weird combination of sedative and pepper-up pills."

The affair continued until Christiana's death in 1967. She and Harry had been vacationing on St. John in the Virgin Islands. Apparently, she drowned in the tidal pool just below their cottage, but the exact circumstances remain obscure. Murray, the sole witness, gave widely varying accounts to different people. And some didn't believe him. A former friend, the poet Conrad Aiken, suspected that Murray had somehow been responsible for her death. Lewis Mumford, writes

Douglas, "perhaps as suspicious of Harry's treatment of Christiana in death as in life, refused to attend" her funeral.

SHORTLY BEFORE his death. Murray finally wrote frankly about Christiana and the Dyad. "I have been asked," he noted, "why Christiana and I started a separate dyad and what kept our marriages going as best as possible under the circumstances." Among the reasons he gave was that "I had a wish to develop my theory in which two people (not just one personality) are incorporated into one system, a dyadic system," and that "we wanted also to experiment with different types of combinations in play and work."

The affair, in other words, was an experiment—and his experiments were, at least partly, surrogates for his affair. "Stressful dyadic interactions" such as those Murray arranged for Kaczynski and his classmates stood for his relationship with Morgan, but also for his sadism, sexual fantasies, desire for power, anger, need to explode and cause pain. Murray had so intermingled his personal and professional selves that he could no longer tell them apart. He both idealized the relationship and tried to keep it secret. And while he may have romanticized the personal dimension of the Dyad, he also tried to hide it. "To the very end of his life," Robinson notes, "Murray was reluctant to go public with that information [about the affair]." For he must have known in his heart of hearts that evil was its leit motif. An old friend, Alvin Barach, recalled that there is a portrait of Murray on the thirteenth floor of Harvard's William James Hall. "Harry doesn't like the picture," he told Robinson. "Someone else said, and I think they're wrong, 'the reason he doesn't like it is because it brings out too much of the Satan.' Harry would be the first one to admit to Satan. I think he takes a kind of perverse pride in being prepared to make the admission."

The Dyad, in short, was, in its personal dimension, Murray's first and biggest secret, an extension of his complex character, representing his feelings for and treatment of Morgan and others. But this wasn't its only significance. It would have wartime uses as well, where Murray's obsession with stressful interrogations would play a role in the conflict with Germany and Japan. Later, it would figure in the Cold War. This would be his second big secret. Together, these formed the two aspects of the Dyad that a naive young undergraduate from Evergreen Park, Illinois, would encounter in 1959.

17

The Old School Tie

The candidate . . . was given a grilling cross-examination on the details of his story in an attempt to confuse and disquiet him as much as possible.

—HENRY A. MURRAY AND DONALD W. MACKINNON,
"Assessment of OSS Personnel,"
Journal of Consulting Psychology (1946)

All subjects became, to a varying degree, both anxiously and angrily involved in this stressful situation. . . .

—HENRY A. MURRAY,
Progress Report on "Dyadic Interactions"

I N THE SPRING of 1954, six Harvard seniors gathered in a room at the Boston Psychopathic Hospital with the hospital's number two man, Dr. Robert Hyde. They weren't sure why they were there, other than that they had volunteered for an experiment and would be paid $15 an hour to participate. They couldn't even agree who suggested they enlist in the first place.

One of the students, Ralph Blum, recalled that another participant, Charles Platt, had asked him if he'd like to earn big money being a psychopath for a day. "I said to myself, Wow!" Blum told me. "Imagine getting paid for what we do anyway!"

Platt thinks it was the other way round—that Blum first told him about the experiment. Others recall hearing about it from graduate students or the undergraduate employment bureau, or seeing a notice on the Social Relations Department bulletin board.

After initial screening by technicians from the Department of Social Relations, that included testing their capacity to tolerate frustration and taking the TAT and other personality inventories, they reported to the Psychopathic Hospital, a Harvard institution. There, a graduate student in social relations passed around a tray containing little vials of a clear, colorless, and odorless liquid, which they were told to drink. They were told the glasses contained something called "lysergic acid" and might produce an "altered state," but otherwise they had no idea what to expect.

Each had different recollections of what happened next. Some believe the investigators tried to sow discord between them, to see how they would react. Blum says that one volunteer had a bad trip and tore a telephone off the wall. But none can remember doing it. They all seem to remember some became paranoid, but can't recall who. Before dying in an automobile accident in 1966, Robert Worth Bingham, Jr., another participant, told me that he had a bad trip, too. The experience scared him. Platt remembers being "mildly schizophrenic." Bingham and Platt never took LSD again. But the experience changed Blum's life. He stayed with the program and has been marching to his own drummer ever since. Today, he lives in Hawaii, where he sells what he calls "oracular things" such as tarot cards and the *Book of Runes* for a living.

These students did not know that Dr. Hyde had dosed them with LSD for the CIA. Quite unwittingly, they had become combatants in the Cold War, a conflict in which America's covert intelligence agencies, with the complicity of hundreds of university professors, pursued ethically questionable research—some involving drugs, others not—often using students as guinea pigs.

By employing money as the carrot, defense agencies hijacked the chemical, biological, and social sciences. They lavishly supported research projects they wanted, while allowing those in which they had no interest to languish for lack of funds. And what they wanted were new tools for controlling, transforming, and directing human behavior—whether for purposes of propaganda, interrogation, screening spies, training military recruits, analyzing enemy countries and their leaders, or creating a new "democratic man."

The psychological research establishment would lead the way in this co-optation, forging an alliance with government that would transform the field, empower its practitioners, and set in motion events contributing to the culture of despair in the 1950s, the student counterrevolution of the 1960s, and terrorism in the 1990s.

Murray's personality theory would be central to the whole endeavor. Throughout this disturbing history, the professor's name keeps popping up. Like Zelig, the title character in Woody Allen's movie, at nearly every critical juncture Murray can be seen in the picture, largely unnoticed, somewhere in the back row, staring enigmatically at the camera.

It all started with the best of intentions . . .

In July 1940, a small group of social scientists began meeting informally in New York City at the home of a neighbor of Murray's to discuss how they could help prepare America for the war they saw coming. Declaring that "in the present crisis Morale will probably be the decisive factor and that the United States must employ her tremendous morale resources to the fullest extent for a long time to come," they called themselves the Committee for National Morale.

It was an elite assemblage. Three well-known cultural anthropologists—Ruth Benedict, Margaret Mead, and Gregory Bateson—attended. So did a veritable *Who's Who* of leading psychologists, among them Karl Menninger, co-founder of the Menninger Clinic; Hadley Cantril, who just that summer had established Princeton's Office of Public Opinion Research; as well as Harvard's Harry Murray and Gordon Allport.

Soon the group was conducting research, Forrest Robertson explains, "often on request from the federal government, on various aspects of strategy and propaganda." But many attending had a more ambitious mission in mind. As Mead put it in 1942, "We must see this war as a prelude to a greater job—the restructuring of the culture of the world." Yet, however well intentioned the participants' hubris, these meetings also signaled the beginning of the transformation of psychology into a new intellectual technology whose primary mission, during the coming world war and Cold War, would be to serve the covert military establishment.

The Committee for National Morale was merely one of many cooperative efforts between the social sciences and government during the years leading up to the war. In 1939, the Emergency Committee in Psychology was formed "to prepare the profession for a great national crisis," which the following year would be reorganized under the auspices of the Division of Anthropology and Psychology of the National Research Council. During this same pre-war period, the Social Science Research Council would sponsor various studies on how the war would affect the civilian population.

When these organizations sprang to life, the social sciences were relatively new fields. In academe, psychology had been considered merely a branch of moral philosophy until 1876, when William James began teaching a course on the physiology of psychology at Harvard. Not until World War I did this new discipline gain prominence. When the shooting started in August 1914, both the Allies and the Axis discovered the need for experts to evaluate the suitability of military recruits for warfare and to develop propaganda that would boost national, and undermine enemy, morale. The United States embraced this new science in 1917 when President Woodrow Wilson established the Committee of Public Information, aimed at directing America's propaganda efforts.

Between the wars, private social science think tanks proliferated: Morton Prince's (later Murray's) Psychological Clinic, founded at Harvard in 1926; John Dollard's Institute of Human Relations at Yale in 1929; Hadley Cantril's Public Opinion Research Project at Princeton in 1940; and Harold Lasswell's Experimental Division for the Study of Wartime Communication at the Library of Congress (with private funds), also in 1940.

These social scientists were convinced that their new discipline could save democracy from both its enemies and itself. Freud had persuaded them that, rather than being rational, people are captives of their instinctual desires, and that human survival depended on strengthening the cultural forces that redirected these impulses in constructive directions.

"The fateful question for the human species," Freud had observed in *Civilization and its Discontents*, is "whether and to what extent their cultural development will succeed in mastering the disturbance of their communal life by the human instinct of aggression and self-destruction." Freud explained in a letter to Albert Einstein that we must make whatever "psychical modifications" are necessary to bring about "a progressive displacement of instinctual aims and a restriction of instinctual impulses. . . . Whatever fosters the growth of culture works at the same time against war."

Adolf Hitler showed what happened when these aggressive instincts were exploited rather than controlled. The success of his propagandist, Josef Goebbels, in using psychology to manipulate Germans to commit barbaric acts offered additional evidence of humanity's fundamental irrationality. Psychology came to be seen as a powerful tool that could be used for good (when employed by an enlightened elite) or for evil (when used by Hitler).

The rise of psychology in public policy was, then, yet another manifestation of the culture of despair. Psychological techniques of manipulation were thought necessary because people are ruled not by reason, but by dark, inchoate emotions. The masses could not be trusted; or, as the historian Ellen Herman puts it, summarizing the thinking of this time, "mass opinion was dangerous as well as fickle. . . . [It] was a real threat to rational planning."

But if the people could not rule wisely, how would democracy survive? This was what New York Law School Professor Edward A. Purcell, Jr., termed the "crisis of democratic theory" that many intellectuals believed they confronted. And it led to uncomfortable conclusions.

Most scholars were politically liberal. They voted for Roosevelt, publicly praised "the common man," and wanted to save democracy. Yet in their heart of hearts they had lost faith in people and embraced a new paternalism. They became what historian Brett Gary calls "nervous liberals," beset by "propaganda anxieties." Saving democracy, these scholars concluded, required new psychological techniques that would point public opinion in "correct" directions. Social science was seen as not just a way to understand man, but to control him as well. It would provide the means by which an enlightened elite would encourage proper democratic behavior.

A leading proponent of this elitist view was Harold Lasswell, a University of Chicago communications theorist who had written his doctoral dissertation on the use of propaganda during World War I and who Archibald MacLeish, with financial support from the Rockefeller Foundation, had covertly ensconced by 1940 at the Library of Congress.

Managing populations, Lasswell argued, required every kind of tool, from assassination to indoctrination. "Successful social and political management," he wrote in 1933, "often depends on proper coordination of propaganda with coercion, violent or non-violent, economic inducement (including bribery); diplomatic negotiation; and other techniques." For "the modern propagandist, like the modern psychologist, recognizes that men are often poor judges of their own interests."

Lasswell's lack of faith in people's ability to govern themselves reflected the opinion of many intellectuals of the era, including Walter Lippmann, the former editor of a propaganda unit with the American Expeditionary Forces during World War I, author of several important books on public opinion, and later a renowned columnist. "Representative government," Lippmann observed in 1922, "cannot be worked successfully, no matter what the basis of election, unless there is an independent, expert organization for making the unseen facts [of the new world] intelligible to those who have to make the decisions." For Lippmann, "decision makers had a responsibility to repair the 'defective organization of public opinion.'"

But in the long term, saving democracy required more than mere propaganda and coercion. It also needed the new science of personality development, pioneered by Murray, to provide a blueprint for transforming people into better citizens.

The ultimate goal, Murray explained in *Explorations in Personality*, was to reform human nature and save civilization.

> *Man is to-day's great problem . . . by what means can he be intentionally transformed? . . . If it is true, as some reasonable men affirm, that culture—the best of man's high heritage—is in jeopardy, and that to save and further it man, its creator and conserver,*

*must be changed—regenerated or developed differently from
birth—then the immediate requisite is a science of human nature.*

After the war, Murray would evince hope that psychology might
avert international catastrophe by weaning humanity off its neurotic
attachment to violence. He advocated creation of a world government—
a task, he wrote Lewis Mumford, that "involves transformations of personality such as never occurred quickly in human history; one
transformation being that of National Man into World Man."

In the future, Murray wrote in 1962, "the formidable task assigned
to the social sciences" will be "that of designing a system of practices of
child rearing, education, and self-development which, under favorable
conditions, would produce generations of adult personalities who would
prove progressively more fit, emotionally and intellectually, to live and
(if called upon) to govern in a world capable of producing genocidal
weapons."

DURING THE interwar years, the Rockefeller Foundation took the lead in
promoting psychology in public policy, underwriting research by Cantril,
Dollard, Erik Erikson, and Murray. And once hostilities began, psychologists jumped on the bandwagon, anxious to prove that their expertise
was essential for victory. By early 1942, one third of all psychologists in
America had volunteered for the war effort. By war's end, a quarter of
U.S. psychologists—a total of 1,700—were serving in the military. And
the more psychologists it hired, the more jobs the government found
that psychologists could do.

The Department of Defense (DOD) put these people to work in
myriad ways. Many helped conduct psychological evaluations of the 15
million military recruits, to determine their suitability for combat, using,
among other things, the TAT as a screening tool. Others became so-
called sykewarriors of the Psychological Warfare Division under General
Eisenhower's command, where they devoted themselves to undermining
German and Italian morale. Still others went to work for the Sociologi-
cal Research Project at the Japanese-American Relocation Center in the

Colorado River valley, established by the War Relocation Authority (the bureaucracy responsible for the forced relocation of Japanese Americans) for the purpose of developing "techniques of human management that would prove useful to internment management."

The Office of Strategic Services, or OSS, established a Psychological Division which employed eighteen psychologists. Headed by President Franklin Roosevelt's charismatic friend, General William "Wild Bill" Donovan, the OSS also relied heavily on consultants from the American Psychological Association and the Society for the Psychological Study of Social Issues, as well as from the universities, to provide a variety of services, including propaganda planning, screening of newly recruited secret agents, monitoring civilian morale, analyzing foreign-language publications, collecting clandestine intelligence, and drawing psychological profiles of Axis leaders.

The former master of Harvard's Adams House, James Phinney Baxter, became head of the OSS's Office of Research for the Coordination of Information, where, wrote former Harvard administrator Sigmund Diamond, "military personnel on the committee were outnumbered by professors of history, political science, economics, geography and law from Harvard, Yale, Michigan, Duke, and other universities." And "in the fall of 1942, the Research and Analysis Branch of the OSS began to contract out research projects to specialized institutes at various universities, first at Stanford and Berkeley, then at Denver, Columbia, Princeton, Yale and others." William L. Langer, the Harvard historian who replaced Baxter, established a committee to coordinate work between the OSS and the universities, further cementing this relationship.

The OSS was particularly anxious to develop a system for determining if recruits were suited for clandestine operations. The Germans, it was felt, were ahead of the Allies in this department, having developed extremely thorough and arduous methods of testing soldiers for elite, *Waffen-SS* units. The British Secret Service, too, led the Americans, having established an estate in the countryside known as Camp X for training and evaluation of agents who would work behind enemy lines. So, in 1943, the OSS created its own assessment program, which it called Station S, located at a large country estate outside Washington, D.C.

Receiving a commission as captain in the OSS in 1943, Murray joined the staff of Station S, where he helped devise procedures for evaluating trainees being prepared as saboteurs, spies, or propagandists. He put together an assessment system, John Marks reports in *The Search for the "Manchurian Candidate,"* that "tested a recruit's ability to stand up under pressure, to be a leader, to hold liquor, to lie skillfully, and to read a person's character by the nature of his clothing. . . . Murray's system became a fixture in the OSS."

One of these tests was intended to determine how well applicants withstood interrogations. As Murray and his colleagues described it in their 1948 report, *Selection of Personnel for Clandestine Operations*:

> *The candidate immediately went downstairs to the basement room. A voice from within commanded him to enter, and on complying he found himself facing a spotlight strong enough to blind him for a moment. The room was otherwise dark. Behind the spotlight sat a scarcely discernible board of inquisitors. . . . The interrogator gruffly ordered the candidate to sit down. When he did so, he discovered that the chair in which he sat was so arranged that the full strength of the beam was focused directly on his face. . . .*
>
> *At first the questions were asked in a quiet, sympathetic, conciliatory manner, to invite confidence. . . . After a few minutes, however, the examiner worked up to a crescendo in a dramatic fashion. . . . When an inconsistency appeared, he raised his voice and lashed out at the candidate, often with sharp sarcasm. He might even roar, "You're a liar."*

Even anticipation of this test was enough to cause some applicants to fall apart. The authors wrote that one person "insisted he could not go through with the test." They added, "A little later the director . . . found the candidate in his bedroom, sitting on the edge of his cot, sobbing."

During this period, writes Robinson, Murray "flourished as a leader in the global crusade of good against evil." Eventually made chief of Station S and promoted to lieutenant colonel, he would become one of the Psychological Division's most valued officers, later earning the Legion of Merit for his contributions. In March 1943, he was sent to England to study the English assessment system. Then he helped to organize another assessment center in the Washington area (Station W), and others in California (Station WS) and Potomac, Maryland (Station F, to assess personnel being reassigned from the European to Pacific theaters).

In July and again in October 1944, Murray traveled to the front lines in France, to evaluate OSS operatives in the field. In the spring of 1945, the OSS sent him on a highly secret mission over "the Hump" (Himalayas) to Chungking, China, to supervise the evaluation of Nationalist Chinese special forces being trained to operate behind Japanese lines. Finding himself in China when the war ended in August, Murray was flown home in General Donovan's private plane.

Murray loved this work. He even became infatuated with war, toying with the idea of asking for a transfer to a combat unit. And his assessment experiments would prove widely influential. After the war, Murray and his Station S colleagues published their findings in a book, *Assessment of Men*, which became the inspiration for yet another field of psychology that would be known as the Assessment Center Method and used to evaluate personnel by more than two thousand private and governmental organizations. It was this work that provided Murray with the idea for a new line of research called "the Dyad."

As we've seen, "the Dyad" had a double meaning. It referred both to his affair with Christiana Morgan, which began in 1926, and to his research on "stressful disputations." And it would be his assessment work for the OSS, involving interplay between an interrogator and his captive, that gave shape to the later research. After the war, these interrogations would become the centerpiece of Murray's experiments.

Personality assessment was merely one of many feathers in Murray's war bonnet. He advised psychologists in the other military branches on administering the TAT to recruits. Together with the psychoanalyst Walter Langer, he produced a psychological study of Hitler for the OSS that greatly pleased the brass.

"What is required is a profound conversion of Germany's attitude," he wrote in this assessment. Germany started the war in Europe because it was mentally ill. After the war, it would be psychology's job to heal it.

We must realize that we are dealing with a nation suffering from
a paranoid trend: delusions of grandeur; delusions of persecution;

profound hatred of strong opponents and contempt of weak oppo-
nents; arrogance, suspiciousness and envy—all of which has been
built up as a reaction to an age-old inferiority complex and a
desire to be appreciated. . . . Paranoids cannot be treated suc-
cessfully if they are not impressed (consciously or unconsciously)
by the ability, knowledge, wisdom, or perhaps mere magnetic force,
of the physician. . . . The indwelling burning hunger of the para-
noid is for recognition, power and glory—praise from those whom
he respects. This hunger should be appeased as soon as possible, so
that the paranoid thinks to himself: "The great man appreciated
me. Together we can face the world." It is as if he thought: "He is
God the Father and I am his chosen son." . . . Having attained a
measure of satisfaction by winning the respect and friendship of his
physician and then having gained some insight and control, the
patient is ready for group therapy. [emphasis in the original]

Murray's portrayal of himself, the psychologist, as a healer whom patients view as a "great man," and even God, may have exposed his own narcissism, but after the war it would also sufficiently impress the newly created Central Intelligence Agency to establish a whole division dedicated to Murray's novel use of psychology. By March 1953, CIA officials would propose "a Division of Personality Analysis to serve intelligence and psychological operations."

"The classic psycho-political analysis in World War II was made by Prof. William [*sic*] Langer and Prof. Henry Murray of Harvard," the proposal said. "Is it possible to produce comparable psycho-political analyses of Soviet leaders?" To do so, this new division

should be staffed by clinical psychologists, who have been trained
and experienced in making individual biographic studies, but who
have also had intelligence experience, political sophistication and
intimate personal knowledge of at least one foreign area and mas-
tery of at least one foreign language. There has been talk about the
need for this sort of thing since the end of World War II, and some
progress has been made in this direction through increased atten-
tion to personality data. But a more systematic attack on this prob-
lem now seems warranted and practicable.

As WORLD WAR II ended and the Cold War began, the tight bonds between the intelligence establishment and university scholars that had been forged by the global conflict became even tighter and more multifarious. Each military branch established its own network of consultants. Christopher Simpson (author of *Science of Coercion*) reports that by 1952 the National Science Foundation found "that over 96 percent of all reported federal funding for social science at that time was drawn from the U.S. military. By 1960, federal agencies were providing 83 percent of the research budget of the California Institute of Technology and 78 percent of the budget of the Massachusetts Institute of Technology. And they were contributing $13 million out of Harvard University's $65 million total operating expenses.

Psychology was among the biggest beneficiaries. "Between 1945 and the mid-1960s," Ellen Herman writes, "the US military was, by far, the country's major institutional sponsor of psychological research . . . the DOD spent more on social and behavioral science than all other federal agencies combined." From 1945 to 1950, the Office of Naval Research (ONR) led in funding university research, spending around $2 million annually on psychology. But as the Cold War wore on and covert intelligence funding increased, so did the number of federal agencies sponsoring research and the methods of indirection by which they channeled it into academe.

One of these covert sources of university funding was the Department of the Army's Human Resources Research Office (HumRRO), which, along with the U.S. Army Personnel Research Office and the Special Operations Research Office, had been dedicated, according to a congressional subcommittee report, to "improved performance in counter-insurgency, military assistance, unconventional types of warfare and psychological operations through social and behavioral science studies of methods for predicting the reactions of indigenous troops and populations in foreign areas; and other studies as may be needed for direct support of stability operations."

Throughout this period, Murray could be seen dipping into these troughs. At one point, he was approached by HumRRO to serve as a "consultant" for clandestine research. And although the nature or extent of his participation remains unclear, the record reveals it did require him to apply for security clearance. In 1958, he joined longtime CIA consultant Hadley Cantril on an agency-sponsored tour of the Soviet Union, done, Simpson explains, "under private, academic cover to gather information on the social psychology of the Soviet population and 'mass' relationships with the Soviet elite."

In the early 1950s, Murray served as adviser on a U.S. Army project conducted at Boston's Peter Bent Brigham and Robert Breck Brigham hospitals, in which patients were given experimental doses of the steroids ACTH and cortisone to determine their "pharmacological effect."

"A certain number of patients," the team later reported, "had become psychotic or otherwise emotionally disturbed in response to treatment with these drugs. . . . Other patients became anxious, restless, wakeful, and complained of irritability, distractibility, and racing thoughts."

For the next decade, Murray apparently would help with similar army-sponsored studies. Some sought to correlate Harvard rowing crew members' chemical and psychological responses to stress caused by competition. Others looked for similar physical/emotional correlations in randomly chosen students subjected to sleep, sensory, or food deprivation. All the studies included administration of the TAT and other personality tests. And at one point the interviewing psychologist would comment that "we were sometimes surprised at the degree of emotional turmoil encountered during our interviews with some of the men."

Throughout the postwar period, the biggest employer of college professors would be the Central Intelligence Agency, whose "ties to the academic world," University of Georgia historian Loch Johnson writes

*extended back to the day the agency opened its doors in 1947. . . .
Each of the four CIA directorates and several subsidiary units
within them have been involved in a wide range of associations
with colleges, universities, research groups, think tanks, technical
schools, secretarial schools and even high schools throughout the
country and abroad. The relationships defy simple description. . . .*

Eventually, the CIA would have so many professors on its payroll at hundreds of different universities, serving in so many different capacities, that even the agency itself couldn't keep track of them. In 1967, according to John D. Marks and former CIA officer Victor Marchetti, Director Richard Helms

> *asked his staff to find out just how many university personnel were under secret contract to the CIA. After a few days of investigation, Helms immediately ordered a full study of the situation, and after more than a month of searching records all over the agency, a report was handed in to Helms listing hundreds of professors and administrators on over a hundred campuses. But the staff officers who compiled the report knew that their work was incomplete.*

Even so, the committee found:

> *hundreds of college professors who had been given special clearances by the agency's Office of Security to perform a wide variety of tasks for different CIA components . . . the Directorate of Science and Technology employed individual professors, and at times entire university departments or research institutes, for its research and development projects.*

The old school tie sustained this CIA-university connection. Recruited during the war, mostly from the Ivy League, OSS veterans stayed in touch with each other, as some joined the CIA and others returned to the universities. They became a kind of shadow fraternity in which brothers in government and those in the universities continued to help each other.

The psychologists in this fraternity formed what Carnegie Corporation president John Gardner called the "behavior science network," in which philanthropies such as the Ford, Rockefeller, and Russell Sage foundations and Carnegie Corporation—at the behest of their friends in the CIA, Department of Defense, and executive branch—supported secret research with their private funds, thus ensuring that this research would remain "off-budget" and would never be exposed to congressional oversight. Or individuals such as Nelson Rockefeller, who served both in government and on the board of powerful foundations, simply arranged the funding themselves.

To further conceal its support, the CIA employed other channels as well. It contracted with private, "twilight zone" research think tanks, such as the RAND Corporation, to hire professors for specific research. It relied on legitimate federal funding agencies, such as the National Institute of Mental Health and the National Science Foundation, to support favored projects. It channeled monies through "cooperators"— legitimate philanthropies and other nonprofit organizations. And it made grants through entirely bogus foundations set up for the purpose.

As the *Congressional Quarterly* explained:

> *The CIA probably used at least 50 foundations in an involved method of funneling funds to certain organizations. Under a method of transfer known as the "triple pass," the usual procedure was for the CIA to convey funds to "dummy" foundations it had established to act as fronts for its activities. The "dummy" foundations then made grants to legitimate foundations. These foundations, which also handled other funds, then made grants to certain CIA-designated organizations, using the funds from the "dummy foundations."*

Thanks to this indirection, often a professor didn't know he was working for a defense intelligence agency. The CIA called these people "unwitting agents," as, for example, in the following 1958 agency memo: "funding and nominal supervision of this project will be handled by the [name of conduit redacted] in the regular manner. Accounting for the funds expended will be according to the procedures previously established for the [redacted] relative to grants to unwitting agents."

In these ways, the CIA enlisted the talents of many on the Harvard faculty, which in 1952 found itself the beneficiary of no less than 160 clandestine defense contracts. By 1960, according to one Harvard history, "three-quarters of all [Harvard] university research was funded by the government, much of it at the behest of the Defense Department." Between 1953 and 1963, federal support for Harvard research increased from $8 million to $30 million. By 1959, these monies exceeded tuition revenues. And while Harvard was not the only beneficiary, many of its professors were among the most loyal friends of the covert intelligence establishment.

Two of Murray's colleagues in Harvard's Department of Social Relations, in particular, would perform prominent services for the CIA: the sociologist Talcott Parsons, and Murray's closest friend on the faculty, the cultural anthropologist Clyde Kluckhohn.

Sigmund Diamond, author of *Compromised Campus*, reports that Parsons, as one actively engaged with the CIA throughout the postwar period,

> *approved attaching universities to the intelligence apparatus of government—covertly; bringing persons accused of collaboration with the Nazis to the United States—covertly; using Harvard connections to influence government officials to ease their entry to the United States—covertly; breaking down the distinction between research and intelligence. As late as 1974 he was serving as consultant to the CIA on the effects of the student rebellions of the 1960s and on the personality of potential CIA recruits.*

But Clyde Kluckhohn was the CIA's big man on campus. As the first director of Harvard's Russian Research Center, founded in 1949, he forged links between the university and the agency that would endure throughout the postwar period. Indeed, according to Diamond, Kluckhohn had been instrumental in cementing "the CIA-Harvard connection" through negotiations with Harvard's president, James B. Conant himself. This was, Diamond adds, "one of the best kept of Harvard's academic secrets."

Yet not until 1967, after *Ramparts* magazine published a series of stories exposing CIA covert funding of research at various campuses, would this relationship become known. Asked by Dean of the Faculty Franklin Ford (yet another OSS alumnus) to investigate the extent of CIA involvement in research on campus, Ford's assistant, Humphrey Doermann, reported that, based on unclassified data alone, between 1960 and 1966 the CIA had contributed $456,000 to thirteen Harvard programs and individual professors in the departments of Psychology, Philosophy, and Social Relations.

But while Doermann's report would partly expose Harvard's covert connections, Murray's role remained hidden. His second big secret was still safe.

18

Murray,
the Zelig

Drugs that affect the mind are only one example of the
new methods of controlling human behavior that modern
society is developing.

—TED KACZYNSKI,
"Industrial Society and Its Future"

The LSD movement was started by the CIA. I wouldn't be
here now without the foresight of the CIA scientists.

—TIMOTHY LEARY, 1977

I N GIVING the six unwitting Harvard seniors LSD that spring of
1954, Dr. Hyde was motivated by the highest ideals. He and his
colleagues believed that by studying the effects of this drug on the
brain, they might find a cure for mental illness. But the CIA was paying
his bills, and it had a different agenda in mind. The agency wanted a
drug, as LSD historians Martin A. Lee and Bruce Shlain put it, that
would "blow minds and make people crazy."

University researchers would soon discover that, like Dr. Faustus, the legendary Renaissance magician who sold his soul to the devil in exchange for knowledge and power, they had signed a contract before reading the fine print. And the fine print contained an ethical trap: Saving the world required the sacrifice—of others. In the name of the highest ideals, some would commit the lowest of crimes. Others, while not quite doing evil, simply lost their ethical direction. For both, this journey from high to low was such a gradual descent that many did not notice.

And among these fellow travelers would be Professor Murray himself.

THE AGENCY'S interest began with its precursor, the OSS, in 1942, when General Donovan, anxious to perfect interrogation techniques for captured spies, established a "truth drug" committee of prominent psychologists, including Dr. Winfred Overholser, superintendent of St. Elizabeth's hospital in Washington, D.C., and Dr. Edward Strecker, president of the American Psychiatric Association. The committee began testing a wide variety of chemicals on test subjects, from peyote and marijuana to "goofball" concoctions of sedatives and stimulants.

The following year, an obscure Swiss chemist named Albert Hoffmann, working for the Sandoz pharmaceutical company, accidentally imbibed a concoction he had created while looking for a circulation stimulant. The chemical was D-lysergic acid diethylamide, better known today as LSD. Without warning, Hoffmann found himself experiencing what was the world's first acid trip. Coincidentally, at the same time, across the Rhine River in Germany, Nazi doctors were testing another hallucinogenic drug, mescaline, on inmates at the Dachau concentration camp.

The discovery of the Nazis' Dachau notes after the war by U.S. Navy investigators triggered intense interest in mescaline in American intelligence circles. But it also generated alarm. The field of psychoactive drugs, it seemed, was yet another defense-related area in which the Nazis had been ahead of the Allies. To snatch up these Nazi experts in the dark sciences before the Soviets got them, the Pentagon launched

"Operation Paperclip," a highly secret program to bring some of these German scientists into America. As most had been Nazis, their entry into the United States was prohibited by law. So Paperclip officials smuggled them in, forging, deleting, and doctoring documents to erase evidence of their Nazi past.

Some Paperclip scientists, such as the famous rocket specialist and Nazi Party member Werner von Braun, went to work in the U.S. space program. Others were chemical warfare specialists, experts on everything from sterilization to mass extermination. Among these were members of the former team of doctors already wanted by the U.S. Army war crimes unit for having conducted the ghoulish "high-altitude" (oxygen and pressure deprivation) experiments on Dachau inmates that killed at least seventy. These men would carry on similar research for the U.S. Air Force. Still other Paperclip scientists were sent to Edgewood Arsenal in Maryland, where they were put on the CIA payroll and began testing Nazi nerve and mustard gases on unwitting American GIs, seriously injuring several.

Soon, the very same Nazis who had helped to develop nerve gas and "Zyklon B"—the gas used to exterminate Jews at Auschwitz—were helping to perfect America's own "Psychochemical Warfare" program, testing everything from alcohol to LSD on unsuspecting American soldiers. At Edgewood and Fort Holabird, Maryland (where I was stationed as a young second lieutenant in intelligence in 1957–58) at least one thousand soldiers were given up to twenty doses of LSD. Some, locked in boxes and then given LSD, went temporarily insane. Others had epileptic seizures.

In 1949, a Viennese chemist named Otto Kauders gave a lecture on LSD at the Boston Psychopathic Hospital, claiming that this newly discovered drug artificially and temporarily induced psychosis. This claim would later be found false—acid trips are not at all like psychosis—but Kauders's account impressed the hospital staff. If LSD reproduced the symptoms of psychosis, they reasoned, this proved that the disease had a chemical base. So studying LSD's effects might lead them to drugs for treating mental illness.

Shortly after Kauders's talk, one hospital staffer, Max Rinkel, ordered a supply of LSD from Sandoz and then persuaded his colleague Robert Hyde to test it on himself. Hyde's ensuing trip—the first by an

American—fired his enthusiasm for further experimentation. Research on one hundred subjects began at Harvard's Boston Psychopathic under Hyde's direction in 1950.

Meanwhile, the CIA was in hot pursuit of the elusive truth drug. After the Soviets' 1949 show trial of the Hungarian prelate Cardinal József Mindszenty, this pursuit turned into a race. At the trial, the cardinal confessed to crimes he clearly didn't commit, and acted as though he were sleepwalking. Other Soviet show trials demonstrated the same apparent "brainwashing" of prisoners. Later, it would be learned that the Soviets didn't use drugs at all to accomplish this. Their major weapon was psychology—and sleep deprivation. But at the time, the CIA suspected the Soviets had some super-mind-control drug. And they had to have it too.

In 1949, according to John Marks, who first broke the story of CIA experimentation with LSD, the agency's head of Scientific Intelligence went to Western Europe to learn more about Soviet techniques and to supervise experiments of his own, in order, this official explained, to "apply special methods of interrogation for the purpose of evaluation of Russian practices." By the spring of 1950, the agency established a special program under its security division named "Operation Bluebird" to test behavior-control methods, and started recruiting university scholars to work for the program. Bluebird scientists began experimenting on North Korean prisoners of war and others. They tried "ice-pick lobotomies," electroshock, and other "neural-surgical techniques," as well as a host of drugs including cocaine, heroin, and even something called a "stupid bush," whose effects remain classified to this day.

To pursue these shadowy endeavors, the government enlisted the elite of the American psychological establishment, either as conduits, consultants, or researchers. According to a later agency review, these helpers included at least ninety-three universities and other governmental or nonprofit organizations, including Harvard, Cornell, the University of Minnesota, the Stanford University School of Medicine, the Lexington, Kentucky, Narcotics Farm, several prisons and penitentiaries, the Office of Naval Research, and the National Institutes of Health.

Project Bluebird was renamed "Project Artichoke" in 1951, and in that same year the CIA discovered LSD. When the Korean War drew to a close the following spring, the CIA's interest in the drug became an obsession.

As American prisoners of the Chinese were repatriated, authorities discovered to their horror that 70 percent had either made confessions of "guilt" for participating in the war or had signed petitions calling for an end to the U.S. war effort in Asia. Fifteen percent collaborated fully with the Chinese, and only 5 percent refused to cooperate with them at all. Clearly, the Chinese had found new and formidable brainwashing techniques that could transform American servicemen into "Manchurian candidates" programmed to do Communist bidding. America faced a brainwash gap!

Pushing the panic button, in April 1953 the CIA replaced Project Artichoke with a more ambitious effort called MKULTRA, under the direction of Sidney Gottlieb, a brilliant chemist with a degree from Cal-Tech. Gottlieb was the ultimate dirty trickster, having personally participated in attempts to assassinate foreign leaders. And he immediately put his talents to work, this time against Americans.

Once MKULTRA was established, say Lee and Shlain, "almost overnight a whole new market for grants in LSD research sprang into existence as money started pouring through CIA-linked conduits." Among these conduits was the Josiah J. Macy Foundation, whose director was an ex-OSS officer named Frank Fremont-Smith. And among the beneficiaries of this covert funding would be Harold Abramson, an acquaintance of Gregory Bateson's, who was an allergist at New York's Mount Sinai Hospital and a CIA consultant to Edgewood Arsenal's Paperclip scientists. Another was Hyde's group at Boston Psychopathic.

The aim, Gottlieb explained, was "to investigate whether and how it was possible to modify an individual's behavior by covert means." LSD, he hoped, would turn out to be the Swiss Army knife of mind control— an all-purpose drug that could ruin a man's marriage, change his sexual behavior, make him lie or tell the truth, destroy his memory or help him recover it, induce him to betray his country or program him to obey orders or disobey them.

Soon, MKULTRA was testing all conceivable drugs on every kind of victim, including prison inmates, mental patients, foreigners, the terminally ill, homosexuals, and ethnic minorities. Altogether, it conducted tests at fifteen penal and mental institutions, concealing its role by using the U.S. Navy, the Public Health Service, and the National Institute of Mental Health as funding conduits. During the ten years of MKULTRA's existence, the agency's inspector general reported after its termination in 1963, the program experimented with "electro-shock, various fields of psychology, psychiatry, sociology, and anthropology, graphology, harassment substances, and paramilitary devices and materials."

Its brainwashing research also took the CIA to Canada, where the agency hired an eminently prestigious psychologist, Dr. D. Ewen Cameron, president of the Canadian, American, and World Psychiatric associations and head of the Allen Memorial Institute at McGill University (which had been founded with money from the Rockefeller Foundation). Cameron's studies centered on what he called "depatterning" and what one CIA operative described as the "creation of a vegetable." This entailed giving unwitting test subjects bevies of drugs that caused them to sleep for several weeks, virtually straight, with only brief waking intervals. This was followed by up to sixty-five days of powerful electroshock "therapy," where each jolt was twenty to forty times more intense than standard electroshock treatment. After this program, some were given LSD and put in sensory deprivation boxes for another sixty-five days.

By the late 1950s, the CIA and LSD had become virtually inseparable. The advent of LSD, Timothy Leary would declare later, "was no accident. It was all planned and scripted by the Central Intelligence."

Indeed, it was. As Lee and Shlain explain:

Nearly every drug that appeared on the black market during the 1960s—marijuana, cocaine, heroin, PCP, amyl nitrite, mushrooms, DMT, barbiturates, laughing gas, speed and many others—had previously been scrutinized, tested, and in some cases refined by CIA and army scientists. But of all the techniques explored by the Agency in its multimillion-dollar twenty-five-year quest to conquer the human mind, none received as much attention or was embraced with such enthusiasm as LSD-25. For a time CIA personnel were completely infatuated with the hallucinogen. Those who first tested LSD in the early 1950s were convinced that it would revolutionize the cloak-and-dagger trade.

To push its drugs, the CIA sought help from the university elite. In 1969, John Marks reports,

> *the Bureau of Narcotics and Dangerous Drugs published a fascinating little study designed to curb illegal LSD use. The authors wrote that the drug's "early use was among small groups of intellectuals at large Eastern and West Coast universities. It spread to undergraduate students, then to other campuses. Most often, users have been introduced to the drug by persons of high status. Teachers have influenced students; upperclassmen have influenced lower classmen." Calling this a "trickle-down phenomenon," the authors seem to have correctly analyzed how LSD got around the country. They left out only one vital element, which they had no way of knowing: That somebody had to influence the teachers and that up there at the top of the LSD distribution system could be found the men of MKULTRA.*

Fremont-Smith and Abramson were the links between the universities and MKULTRA.

> *Fremont-Smith organized the conferences that spread the word about LSD to the academic hinterlands. Abramson also gave Gregory Bateson, Margaret Mead's former husband, his first LSD. In 1959 Bateson, in turn, helped arrange for a beat poet friend of his named Allen Ginsberg to take the drug at a research program located off the Stanford campus.*

And Murray was part of this drug-testing pyramid. During this time, according to Frank Barron, he had supervised experiments "on the subjective effects of psycho-active drugs, injecting adrenaline . . . into naive subjects to study changes in their subjectivity." And in 1960, even as the "Multiform Assessments" on Kaczynski and his classmates were underway, Murray had, according to Leary, given his blessing to the latter's testing psilocybin, an hallucinogen derived from mushrooms, on undergraduates.

In his autobiography, *Flashbacks*, Leary, who would dedicate the rest of his life to "turning on and tuning out," described Murray as "the wizard of personality assessment who, as OSS chief psychologist, had monitored military experiments on brainwashing and sodium amytal interrogation. Murray expressed great interest in our drug-research project and offered his support."

Leary had taken LSD for the first time at Harvard in 1959, where, traveling in Abramson's orbit, he had attended Fremont-Smith's Macy Foundation conferences on the drug. And Murray, write Lee and Shlain, "took a keen interest in Leary's work. He volunteered for a psilocybin session, becoming one of the first of many faculty and graduate students to sample the mushroom pill under Leary's guidance."

By that time, Gregory Bateson was working at the Veterans Administration Hospital in Palo Alto, California. While he was introducing Allen Ginsberg to the drug, a colleague began testing it on Stanford undergraduates. One of these students was Ken Kesey, who would later write *One Flew over the Cuckoo's Nest* and was soon to be immortalized by Tom Wolfe as a "Merry Prankster" and LSD missionary in *The Electric Kool-Aid Acid Test*.

Meanwhile, Murray, already addicted to amphetamines, continued to flirt with hallucinogens. At Leary's suggestion, according to a former colleague, he took psilocybin again, this time with Aldous Huxley and Ginsberg. He introduced Morgan to LSD. And in 1961 he spoke at the International Congress of Applied Psychology in Copenhagen, which, thanks to Leary and Huxley's presence, turned into a virtual psychoactive circus. His talk there, wrote Forrest Robinson, featured "a highly literary rendering of a psilocybin 'trip' that he took with Timothy Leary a year earlier. . . . 'The newspapers described it as the report of a drug-induced vision,' he wrote [Lewis] Mumford, with obvious delight."

Not all scientists worked for the CIA. And many did so unwittingly. Nor was this agency the only covert intelligence bureaucracy sponsoring Cold War studies. The U.S. Army, Navy, Air Force, and other defense agencies financed their own experiments as well, often duplicating each other's efforts, sometimes at the same institutions. (The Harvard Medical School, for example, conducted LSD research on unwitting subjects for the Department of the Army in 1952–54, even as Hyde continued with similar work at Boston Psychopathic for the CIA.)

And although LSD may have been the most sensational subject, Lee and Shlain make clear that it was far from the only field in which the government was prime mover. Cold War research ran the gamut, from investigations of sleep deprivation to perfecting anthrax delivery systems. It co-opted nearly an entire generation of scholars in the physical, social, and health sciences. This work was so various, so widespread, and so secret that even today it is impossible to grasp its full dimensions.

Among MKULTRA papers that later came to light, Lee and Shlain write, were

> *CIA documents describing experiments in sensory deprivation, sleep teaching, ESP, subliminal projection, electronic brain stimulation, and many other methods that might have applications for behavior modification. One project was designed to turn people into programmed assassins who would kill on automatic command. Another document mentioned "hypnotically-induced anxieties" and "induced pain as a form of physical and psychological control." There were repeated references to exotic drugs and biological agents that caused "headache clusters," uncontrollable twitching or drooling, or a lobotomy-like stupor. Deadly chemicals were concocted for the sole purpose of inducing a heart attack or cancer without leaving a clue as to the actual source of the disease. CIA specialists also studied the effects of magnetic fields, ultrasonic vibration, and other forms of radiant energy on the brain. As one CIA doctor put it, "We lived in a never-never land of 'eyes only' memos and unceasing experimentation."*

As university professors and hospital researchers pursued their devil's bargain with the intelligence community, victims accumulated.

On January 8, 1953, Harold Blauer, a professional tennis player, reportedly died from a massive overdose of a mescaline derivative at the New York State Psychiatric Institute. The drug, say the investigative journalists H. P. Albarelli, Jr., and John Kelly, was administered "as part of a top-secret Army-funded experimental program . . . code named Project Pelican, in which Blauer was used as a guinea pig." The supervisor of the project was Dr. Paul H. Hoch, director of experimental psychiatry and, according to Albarelli and Kelly, an associate of Harold Abramson's.

Project Pelican, write Albarelli and Kelly, was part of a larger cooperative venture between the CIA and the army's Chemical Corps Special Operations Division at Fort Detrick, Maryland, called MK-NAOMI —reputedly named after Abramson's assistant, Naomi Busner. The project's purpose, according to CIA documents, was to develop biological weapons that could be used on "individuals for the purposes of affecting human behavior with the objectives ranging from very temporary minor disablement to more serious and longer incapacitation to death." At the behest of the Chemical Corps, the New York medical examiner conducted no autopsy of Blauer, kept the army's name out of its report, and described the death as an accidental overdose.

Eleven months later, the CIA claimed another victim. On November 28, 1953, a Fort Detrick biochemist fell—or was pushed—from a thirteenth-floor window of New York's Statler Hotel on Seventh Avenue, falling 170 feet to the sidewalk. He was still alive and trying to talk when the night manager, Armond Pastore, reached him, but died a few minutes later.

Frank Olson, a chemist and joint employee of the CIA and Army Chemical Corps, had worked his entire professional life at Fort Detrick. An expert in germ warfare, during World War II he had designed clothing intended to protect Allied soldiers from possible German biological attacks during the Normandy invasion. In 1949 and 1950, he worked briefly on "Operation Harness," a joint US-British effort to spray virulent organisms—so-called BW antipersonnel agents—around the Caribbean, decimating untold thousands of plants and animals. At the time of his death, Olson was developing a new, portable, and more lethal form of anthrax that could be put into a small spray can.

By 1953, Olson was acting chief of Fort Detrick's Special Operations Division, which, according to a Michael Ignatieff article in the *New York Times Magazine*, had become "the center for the development of drugs for use in brainwashing and interrogation." But he was becoming increasingly disillusioned.

The turning point came during the summer of 1953. Olson had traveled to England and Germany to observe the use of mind-control drugs on collaborators and German SS prisoners considered "expendable." Some died. While in Europe, according to his son, Eric, Frank Olson also learned that the Americans were deploying Anthrax against enemy troops in Korea. When returning American POWs reported this—the first use of bacterial weapons by the United States in war—authorities in Washington dismissed their claims as products of brainwashing. Returning to America shaken, Olson resolved to quit.

On November 19, Gottlieb met with six MKULTRA personnel, including Olson, at Deep Creek Lodge in rural Maryland. The CIA would claim twenty-two years later that during the retreat, on Gottlieb's order, his deputy, Robert Lashbrook, spiked the after-dinner Cointreau with LSD. Olson and all but two of the others (one a teetotaler, the other abstaining because of a headcold) drank it. In fact, Eric Olson believes that only his father's drink was spiked, and that the substance he imbibed was probably not LSD but something stronger. In any case, soon, Olson was experiencing disorientation.

When he came home, his wife, Alice, found him withdrawn, saying repeatedly that he "had made a terrible mistake." The next day he told his supervisor, Vincent Ruwet, that he wanted to resign from the agency. But officials couldn't afford to let him leave. He knew too much. Once outside, he could be an acute embarrassment. So Ruwet and Lashbrook took Olson to New York, supposedly to see a psychiatrist. In fact, they brought him to Harold Abramson, who prescribed nembutal and bourbon.

According to the CIA, Ruwet and Lashbrook had earlier taken Olson to see John Mulholland, a magician hired by the CIA to advise on "the delivery of various materials to unwitting subjects"—i.e., on how to spike drinks with drugs or poisons. Olson was suspicious of Mulholland and asked Ruwet, "What's behind this? Give me the lowdown. What are they trying to do with me? . . . Just let me disappear."

That evening, Olson wandered the streets of New York, discarding his wallet and identification cards before returning to the Statler. And the next day, the CIA claims its experts decided Olson must be institutionalized. Yet he seemed to be feeling better. After he and Lashbrook ate a dreary Thanksgiving meal at a Horn & Hardart restaurant, the two men returned to their room at the Statler, which they shared, and Olson called Alice to say he "looked forward to seeing her the next day."

Around 2:00 A.M. the next morning, Pastore found Olson on the sidewalk. Olson tried to tell Pastore something, but his words were too faint and garbled to be understood. He died before the ambulance arrived. Immediately afterward, Pastore asked the hotel operator if she'd overheard any calls from Room 1081A. Yes, she said, two. In one, someone from the room said, "He's gone," and the voice at the other end of the line said, "That's too bad."

The CIA hushed up Olson's death. The medical examiner made no mention of the CIA, did not do an autopsy, and ruled the death a suicide due to depression. The family didn't believe this story, as Olson had never seemed depressed until after the retreat at Deep Creek Lodge. Yet it would not be until 1975 that they would learn some of the circumstances of his death, and even then not apparently the whole story.

At the request of Frank Olson's son, Eric, an autopsy was performed in 1994, revealing that Olson had apparently been struck on the left side of the temple and knocked unconscious before going through the window. In 1998, the Manhattan District Attorney's office reclassified Olson's death "cause unknown."

WITH OLSON'S DEATH, the culture of despair had come full circle. Having experienced what Ellen Herman called "a collapse of faith in the rational appeal and workability of democratic ideology and behavior," the generation of scholars that emerged from World War II had sought to perfect the tools of social control by which the elite would save democracy. Following the rubrics of positivism, they believed that good and evil are fictions. People aren't bad, merely sick. By curing them, psychologists can prevent war. All problems can be fixed by the alchemy of the mind sciences.

But a world in which morality has no meaning is one in which eventually everything is permitted. The same narrow focus on value-free science that led Nazi concentration camp doctors to commit atrocities encouraged many of these well-meaning scholars to cross ethical lines. By following a path of moral agnosticism, they reached a dead end. Rather than saving democracy, they created tools for coercion, and many people were hurt.

Murray was a product of these times, a man whose career and ideas embodied the development of his discipline and its role in American culture. Like other leading psychologists of his generation, he was a beneficiary of the Rockefeller Foundation's efforts to promote psychology in public policy. He was intensely patriotic and served on the Committee for National Morale. He flourished during World War II and he was a star in the OSS.

After the war, Murray's contributions to personality theory, including the TAT, personnel assessment, and techniques for analyzing foreign leaders and countries, became virtual Cold War institutions. Throughout this undeclared conflict he continued to serve, albeit quietly, America's defense efforts. And among the services he performed would be the experiments on Kaczynski and his cohort.

Even today, however, neither Murray's friends, his widow, nor even some historians believe this. Murray, they argue, was a world federalist who, in Herman's words, was "transformed into a militant pacifist and peace activist after the U.S. dropped the atomic bomb on Hiroshima and Nagasaki."

Their skepticism is understandable. It is rare when even spouses know of these connections. The CIA never reveals the identity of its "assets." Often the professor himself doesn't know the originating source of research monies he receives. And Murray made much of his supposed transformation into "peace activist" following Hiroshima.

Nevertheless, they are mistaken. Hiroshima did not convert Murray to world federalism. Even in 1943, during the same period when he was seeking combat duty in Europe, he wrote in his analysis of Hitler that "there is a great need *now* rather than later, for some form of *World Federation*" (Murray's italics).

Rather, like so many "nervous liberals" of his generation, Murray was both hawk and dove. He resembled his contemporary, Cord Meyer, the war hero and onetime president of United World Federalists, who eventually became a top officer in the CIA. Such ambivalence characterized virtually the entire elite clique of East Coast professionals to which he belonged. Theirs was a world in which everyone knew each other, and many worked for the CIA. Murray was so surrounded by agency people he couldn't have moved without bumping into one.

In fact, as we have seen, Murray was indeed a Cold War warrior—not, perhaps, as prominent a player as some, but a player nonetheless. He received steady funding from the Rockefeller Foundation, which had served as cover for his trip with Cantril to the Soviet Union for the CIA in 1958, and from the National Institute of Mental Health, also known to be a covert funding conduit. He apparently worked for Hum-RRo. He served as an adviser on army-sponsored steroid experiments. He helped found Harvard's Social Relations Department, which had been generously funded by covert intelligence agencies. He served the U.S. Army Surgeon General's Clinical Psychology Advisory Board and the National Committee for Mental Hygiene with the CIA's propagator of LSD, Frank Fremont-Smith. Along with Fremont-Smith, Abramson, and Leary, he occupied a spot on the agency's LSD pyramid.

And in 1959, Murray would cap off a long and distinguished career with the last of a series of studies inspired by his OSS assessments and originally undertaken for the U.S. Navy Department. And Ted Kaczynski would participate.

19

The Cognitive Style of Murder

I found the experience devastating . . .

> —Former undergraduate participant
> in deceptive psychologicalexperiment
> at another college

After breaking off my participation in a state of extreme anger (including a highly elevated heart rate), I met with [Stanley] Milgram on several occasions . . . arguing that the methods were totally unacceptable.

> —HERBERT I. WINER,
> thirty-eight years after
> participating in the Milgram experiment
> while a Yale professor

I N 1948, Henry Murray wrote the Rockefeller Foundation requesting support, in part for "development of a system of procedures for testing the suitability of officer candidates for the navy." He was awarded the grant. After some delays, research commenced in 1949. This would be the first of four such studies, each three years in length, conducted after the war on selected Harvard students. Eventually, they, along with a more rudimentary version first launched in 1941, would be called "Multiform Assessments of Personality Development Among Gifted College Men." All postwar efforts focused on stressful dyadic confrontations akin to those mock interrogations Murray had helped to orchestrate for the OSS.

Kaczynski's was the last and most complex of these, involving, Murray claimed, "over 1,000 variables." At its conclusion, he would retire. It was, one might say, his last hurrah, embodying all that he was: his brilliance, narcissism, charm, creativity, snobbery, patriotism, energy, idealism, sadism, love for Christiana, testy relations with assistants and colleagues, desire to perfect the human personality, susceptibility to writer's block, and the inability to decide whether he was a humanist, physician, or scientist. And virtually every one of these traits would touch, directly or indirectly, the twenty-two undergraduate study subjects—especially those, like Kaczynski, who were particularly vulnerable.

Indeed, in their essays, test answers, and interviews at the outset of the experiment, many of these young men exhibited attitudes of anger, nihilism, and alienation—reflecting, perhaps, just how pervasively the culture of despair had already affected them.

"Bulwer" admitted that "right now I have sort of a nihilistic outlook on life. . . . How do you justify studying if you regard yourself as an ant crawling through a great huge anthill with millions of others?"

"Ives," speaking of living a conventional life, confessed:

And for doing all this I will hate myself. I mourn the world in which I live because for me there is no place unless I compromise. All I can do is gather up the shattered remains of my hope and love and in the debris of the world keep at least one small blaze of poetry burning. . . . I most feel akin to . . . the artists and the philosophers and have a hatred for the scientists. The scientists I hate because they are pursuing goals which are destined to remove man even further from himself.

"Naisfield" averred, "I don't feel that there is any purpose in my being alive. . . ."

To describe his philosophy of life, "Oscar" claimed to quote Bertrand Russell (whose writings were assigned in Gen Ed): "Only on the firm foundation of unyielding despair, can the soul's habitation henceforth be safely built."

"Quartz" announced that there were "no such things as objective values."

"Dorset" wrote simply, "Society as I see it stinks."

"Sanwick," as one researcher put it, is "basically distrustful of the whole enterprise of life." Researchers found analyzing him "almost impossible," because "his whole life is conceptualized within a bombastic framework of philosophical concepts: being, life, death, transcendency, preservation, liberation, repetition, chaos. . . . One feels . . . a great tumult and chaos of awarenesses, perceptions, and feelings."

And so on. Another (not Kaczynski) was deemed to be "a young man in a state of considerable distress, depression, and confusion . . . extremely alienated," and still another as prone to "withdrawal, silence."

Such thoughts were bound to magnify the impact of the dyadic proceeding. And indeed, the experiment clearly affected some profoundly. According to a source on Kaczynski's defense team, more than one of the subjects experienced emotional problems afterward. And their responses to questionnaires sent after the project ended confirm that certain students found the experience searing. Even twenty-five years later, several recalled the unpleasantness.

In 1987, "Cringle" remembered the "anger and embarrassment . . . the glass partition . . . the electrodes and wires running up our sleeves."

Twenty-five years later, "Drill" still had "very vivid general memories of the experience. . . . I remember someone putting electrodes and blood pressure counter on my arm just before the filming. . . . [I] was startled by [his interlocutor's] venom. . . . I remember responding with unabating rage."

What "Hinge" remembered most vividly was being "attacked" and hating "having all my movements and sounds recorded . . . we were led over to the chairs and strapped in and as the wires were attached to us . . . I began to get more involved in the situation and I began to realize that . . . there I was, actually was going to be in front of the movie camera. . . . I was surprised by how strongly he was attacking me. . . ."

Twenty-five years, later "Locust" wrote:

> *I remember appearing one afternoon for a "debate" and being hooked up to electrodes and sat in a chair with bright lights and being told a movie was being made. . . . I remember him attacking me, even insulting me, for my values, or for opinions I had expressed in my written material, and I remember feeling that I could not defend these ideas, that I had written them not intended for them to be the subject of a debate. . . . I remember being shocked by the severity of the attack, and I remember feeling helpless to respond. . . . So what I seem to remember are feelings (bewilderment, surprise, anger, chagrin) sensations (the bright lights used for the filming, the discomfort of the arrangements) reactions (how could they have done this to me; what is the point of this? They have deceived me, telling me there was going to be a discussion, when in fact there was an attack).*

At his twenty-fifth college reunion, "Ives" wrote,

> *My memories of the encounter 25 years ago*
> *The young lawyer was surprisingly hostile*
> *He had wavey jet black hair*
> *The subject was the nature of love.*
> *I argued that love could only be for a specific person.*
> *He argued that one could love all mankind.*
> *We talked about Natasha from* WAR & PEACE.
> *I did not enjoy the experience.*

To be sure, not all students recall the experiment as unpleasant. Although the contractual conditions under which Harvard allowed me access to the "data sets" prohibit me from contacting the study subjects, two individuals, obviously fond of Murray, did write *The Atlantic* or my book publisher. And both, along with other friends and former assistants of the professor's and, reportedly, a third former participant, denied that the experiment was unethical or harmful in any way. One described it as "fun," another as "highly agreeable."

These opinions are obviously sincere. But they are hardly surprising. Different people react differently to the same experiences. Even the data sets confirm that not all students were bothered by the Dyad. But neither the retrospective testimonials nor the protestations of Murray's supporters constitute proof, one way or the other, of how the experiment may have affected Kaczynski. Both are, as scholars would say, purely anecdotal.

Harvard's secrecy apparently discourages a more scientific evaluation. The university forbids contacting study subjects, except as part of a research plan it reviews and approves. Yet even though it is possible to conduct follow-up studies that preserve participants' privacy, apparently no thorough such study was proposed or approved. And as we've seen, after publication of my article "Harvard and the Making of the Unabomber" in *The Atlantic* in June 2000, the Murray Center permanently sealed its records of Kaczynski's participation in the experiment.

Nevertheless, we do know that Murray's experiment, despite the protests of his allies, was indeed unethical. Like so much research by Cold Warriors of that era, his violated the Nuremberg Code's requirement of "informed consent."

By defending the experiment and by failing to implement a thorough review of it, both Murray's defenders and the Murray Center reveal they share a tolerance for deceptive research with virtually the entire psychological research establishment. Bias in favor of this practice—despite the Nuremberg Code's condemnation—was not only pandemic among professionals in Murray's day, but is still with us today. Even the American Psychological Association's current draft guidelines do not condemn it, but merely require that "the use of deceptive techniques is justified by the study's significant prospective scientific, educational, or applied value. . . ."

That is, the prospective experimenter (or research review committee) is asked to weigh the benefits to his or her career (or what the committee deems to be the possible benefit to the public or research institution) against the risks to the student volunteer. Thanks to this permissive attitude, few professionals seem interested in measuring, objectively, the long-term effects of such deceit on participants. Indeed, not many will even discuss the subject. When I raised it, most responded, "Those are good questions," then terminated the conversation. The research community, as one explained, "is afraid what it might find out."

Some defenders of the practice point to Stanley Milgram's follow-up questionnaire, which reported that 84 percent experienced no untoward effects. Some cite a handful of other such retrospective studies, which on average suggest that "only" around 20 percent of participants in deceptive research were harmed by it. According to the most cited survey of this kind—a questionnaire administered to 195 former participants in deceptive research—"only" fifty-six people, or 29 percent, say they suffered.

And this "low" percentage, say these apologists, justifies the dishonesty. If a majority remains unharmed, they conclude, deceit is justified.

Such is the bizarre reasoning that passes for ethics in contemporary psychological research. Fortunately, not everyone feels this way. "The harm the minority of subjects report they have suffered," writes Diana Baumrind, a research psychologist at the University of California, Berkeley, and one of the few critics of the practice, "is not nullified by the majority of subjects who claim to have escaped unscathed, any more than the harm done victims of drunk drivers can be excused by the disproportionate number of pedestrians with sufficient alacrity to avoid being run over by them."

Moreover, Baumrind notes, the self-reporting questionnaires typically used to collect this data are notoriously unreliable because the most alienated might not respond at all or be reluctant to offend the experimenter by admitting they had been harmed. "It takes well-trained clinical interviewers to uncover true feelings of anger, shame, or altered self-image in participants who believe that what they say should conform with their image of a 'good subject.'"

"My own belief," Baumrind explains, " . . . is that subjects are less adversely affected by physical pain or stress than they are by experiences that result in loss of trust in themselves and the investigator and, by extension, in the meaningfulness of life itself. College students, who are the most frequently used subject pool, are particularly susceptible to conditions that produce an experience of anomie."

Such experiments, she goes on, can "impair his or her ability to endow activities and relationships with meaning," "reduce trust in legitimate authority," and "impair the individual's sense of self-esteem and personal integrity."

Several surveys confirm that deceitful experiments sow distrust. According to a 1972 summary of such research, one found that "deception led to increased suspiciousness." Another that "deceived and debriefed subjects were 'less inclined to trust experiments to tell the truth.'" Still others have noted that "deception . . . increases negativistic behavior."

One person whose self-esteem was profoundly undermined by apparently innocuous deceptive research was Baumrind's own former secretary. "I found the experience devastating," the secretary wrote later.

> I was harmed in an area of my thinking which was central to my personal development at that time. Many of us who volunteered for the experiment were hoping to learn something about ourselves that would help us to gauge our own strengths and weaknesses, and formulate rules for living that took them into account. When, instead, I learned that I did not have any trustworthy way of knowing myself—or anything else—and hence could have no confidence in any lifestyle I formed on the basis of my knowledge, I was not only disappointed, but felt that I had somehow been cheated into learning, not what I needed to learn, but something which stymied my very efforts to learn.

And it only takes one. Deceptive research is wrong even if no one is hurt, because lying is wrong. And if just a single individual suffers—or worse, is prompted to commit suicide or murder—then the research was doubly indefensible. Yet, in virtually every deceitful experiment, *someone* is harmed.

Could Kaczynski have been one?

Yale University professor Robert Levine, generally regarded as one of the world's leading experts on human subject experiments, thinks so. Although cautioning that his field is internal medicine and not psychology, he nevertheless confirmed to me that his "gut feeling" is that "such an experiment would prove traumatic to a subject who went into it already psychologically unstable." Paul Appelbaum, a professor of psychiatry at the University of Massachusetts, concurs. "Could such experiments have a negative effect on vulnerable persons?" he asks rhetorically. "Since many forms of psychological trauma can lead to symptoms at a later point . . . it is certainly not beyond the realm of possibility."

As we shall see, Kaczynski was especially vulnerable in precisely the ways Baumrind describes. Murray's own analysis, which was obtained from sources other than the Murray Center, verified that Kaczynski had been more severely affected by the experiment than any of the other subjects.

THE DYAD FORMED the nexus where Murray's and Kaczynski's lives intersected. Given the professor's powerful personality and reported "contamination" of research through personal relations with students, it should not be surprising if he made a strong and negative impression on the boy.

It is hard to imagine two more different people: Kaczynski, the son of working-class Poles, and Murray, the scion of a rich and well-connected family. Murray did not hide his privileged background. He featured his ancestor, the 4th Earl of Dunmore, prominently on his curriculum vitae. He helped to finance the Harvard Psychological Clinic with his own funds, and it showed. One former colleague called him "the squire" and "ruler of a latifundial estate," exhibiting "aristocratic demeanors."

Murray was, commented Leopold Bellak, "a man of style, in living, not just writing . . . the understated elegance . . . he feels very much an aristocrat, makes me feel a plebeian and an uninformed lout. . . . Harry always struck me as a person with an aversion to the common people. . . ."

Some of Kaczynski's experimental cohort may have been charmed by this patrician demeanor. But to a boy of sixteen who had only two pair of trousers to his name, this suave New Yorker, who supervised these tests, who boasted aristocratic ancestry, who summered in the St. Lawrence, occasionally vacationed in the West Indies, and has been described as leaving friends "bleeding when he left," must have seemed formidable indeed.

Kaczynski was acutely sensitive to snobbery. It is hard to imagine him at the Annex, sipping tea with graduates of Groton and enjoying the experience. In "Truth vs. Lies," he reports on the pain he felt when an assistant of Murray's snubbed him, apparently because "this man didn't want to be seen socializing with someone who wasn't dressed properly and wasn't acceptable to the clique of which he was a member."

Anger at such perceived slights found fertile ground in Kaczynski, whose philosophy of life, as expressed in the essay Murray asked every student to write at the outset of the experiment, revealed him to be the most nihilistic of all the participants.

Murray had divided these essays into three categories. The first set expressed "vague or unformed philosophies"; the second, more developed ideas; and the third—the most mature of all—"generally formed or nearly formed philosophies containing statements on personal ideals, principles, goals which conceivably can be lived by."

Within the first group, Murray wrote, some rejected the need for a philosophy of life. Others betrayed strong pessimism. Still others expressed only ill-formed opinions either because, he hypothesized, the student wasn't interested in the exercise, or had never thought about the question, or didn't want to cooperate, or rejected the whole idea of having a philosophy of life.

Murray consigned Kaczynski's paper to the most solipsistic subset of this "vague or unformed" category—of "negative approaches to life which precluded any positive philosophy of life." In these, Murray observed, "self-centeredness appears to be a common attribute."

But Kaczynski's opinions reflected more than mere egoism. They also revealed how thoroughly he had absorbed Gen Ed's message of despair.

"I can't find any objective basis for accepting any set of values, any philosophy, etc. rather than any other," Kaczynski wrote.

If I say something "should be" or that a person "should be" this or that it is my own personal emotional reaction to the question; I don't really see any reason why anything should be this way or that.

. . . The most important parts of my philosophy: The desirability of competition and struggle. There is no morality or objective set of values. The importance of independence. We can know nothing for certain.

"*There is no morality or objective set of values.*" These words not only constitute a symptom of alienation. They also show that Kaczynski had learned his Harvard lessons well. He was merely expressing the positivist view of ethics—omnipresent in the curriculum—that philosophers call the "emotive theory."

"The main contentions of the emotive theory," the *Macmillan Encyclopedia of Philosophy* explains, "may be described . . . as consisting of a negative and a positive claim. The negative claim . . . is that . . . ethical convictions can neither be demonstrated, like propositions of arithmetic, nor tested by observation or experiment. . . ." The positive claim is that "ethical terms function typically to express emotion. . . ."

Emotivism, in short, is nothing more than the view that only science matters, and that ethical opinions, not being science, are merely emotional utterances. It was a recurring theme that students of the period encountered every day, at lectures, bull sessions, and in assigned reading.

Some first met it in Ayer's *Language, Truth and Logic*, a book frequently assigned in introductory philosophy courses. An ethical judgment, Ayer announced, "is purely 'emotive.' It is used to express feeling about certain objects, but not to make any assertion about them. . . . Sentences which simply express moral judgements do not say anything. They are pure expressions of feeling."

Some were introduced to it by the author of the emotive theory himself, Charles L. Stevenson, who explained that "the sentence, 'X is good,' means 'we like X.'" And some learned it from a freshman Gen Ed English composition sourcebook, *Toward Liberal Education*, in which a contributor advises that to use "words implying moral judgments in the course of argument is very generally an attempt to distort the hearer's view of the truth by arousing emotions."

Kaczynski, therefore, was clearly vulnerable. While the results of the TAT test rated him as sane at the outset of the experiment, given this social insecurity and philosophic nihilism, the Murray experiment was bound to affect him badly. And it did. The research team's own analysis of student reactions to the Dyad—in which their philosophies of life were attacked by the interrogator (whom Murray called "the Alter")—rated Kaczynski's as the most extreme, by every measure.

"Lawful," the team found, scored highest in the three categories: (1) "Intensity of Criticism in Alter's Philosophy"; (2) "Intensity and frequency of criticism of Alter's Philosophy"; and (3) "Rank Order of Dissension in the Dyad." In other words, Kaczynski had the most traumatic experience of all. In his own handwriting next to "Lawful's" scores, Murray scrawled: "Overt expressions of Low Evaluations. Lawful—low, underlying resentment and contempt."

As KACZYNSKI's college life continued, outwardly he seemed to be adjusting to Harvard. By the end of his junior year, John Finley, the Eliot housemaster, would write with characteristic condescension that Kaczynski's

> *midyear performance of three A's and a B begin to justify the curious act of imagination that got him here. He turned nineteen only at the end of May and has had to overcome both youth and simple upbringing. His excellent and mounting marks reveal high inner strength; he should begin to find himself fully in graduate school. All very gallant, touching, and memorable.*

But while Finley was speaking of Kaczynski's "high inner strength," inwardly the student began to worry about his health. He slept fitfully and started having terrible nightmares. Like Nietzsche, Kaczynski began to feel like "one of those machines that sometimes explode. The intensity of my emotions makes me tremble." As he told Sally Johnson later, he started having fantasies of revenge against a society that he increasingly perceived as evil and obsessed with enforcing conformism through psychological controls.

These daydreams upset him all the more because they exposed his own ineffectuality. He would become horribly angry with himself because he could not express this fury openly. "I never attempted to put any such fantasies into effect," he told Johnson, "because I was too strongly conditioned . . . against any defiance of authority. . . . I could not have committed a crime of revenge even a relatively minor crime because my fear of being caught and punished was all out of proportion to the actual danger of being caught."

He was a good boy, and his goodness had prevented him from finding harmless outlets for his anger. His over-developed superego allowed the pressure to build until he thought he would burst. Kaczynski's attempts to live by society's rules, to live up to the expectations of his parents and teachers, had driven him into utter loneliness and misery. Bit by bit, society—the system—was destroying him.

Justice demanded he take revenge. But he lacked the courage to do so. So, instead, he would seek escape. He started to daydream about breaking away from society and living a primitive life. According to Johnson, he would soon spend time "learning about the wilderness." And like many American intellectuals before him, from Thoreau to Edward Abbey, he would form a plan to seek personal renewal in nature.

In 1999, KACZYNSKI would tell the *Green Anarchist* that (as the journal summarized his remarks) "It was in 1962, during his last year at Harvard . . . when he began feeling a sense of disillusionment with the system." And there is little doubt that this period marked a critical point in Kaczynski's life. The Murray experiment had made a strong impression on him. More than thirty-six years later he would still recall it as "unpleasant" and had kept a copy of Murray's article about it.

As Johnson reported, Kaczynski began to experience emotional distress then, and to develop his antitechnology views. Lois Skillen, Kaczynski's high school counselor, is among those who believe that the Murray experiment could have been the crucial factor. Ralph Meister, one of Turk Kaczynski's oldest friends and a retired psychologist who has known Ted since he was a small boy, also raises this possibility. And one of Murray's research associates expressed the same opinion to me.

For it was the confluence of two streams of development that transformed Kaczynski into the Unabomber, one psychological, the other philosophical; and the Murray experiment seems to have contributed to both. One stream was fed by his anger toward his family and those he felt had slighted or hurt him in high school and college—including, perhaps, Murray, his colleagues, or the other students in the experimental cohort. The other reflected the culture of despair Kaczynski first encountered at Harvard, as well as his philosophical critique of society and its institutions, including psychology.

Gradually, while he immersed himself in his Harvard readings and in the Murray experiment, Kaczynski put together a theory to explain his unhappiness and anger: Technology and science were destroying liberty. The system, of which Harvard was a part, served technology, which in turn required conformism. By advertising, propaganda, and other psychological techniques, this system sought to transform people into automatons, to serve the machine.

As he continued to suffer through Murray's experiments, Kaczynski began to worry about society's use of "mind control." In the context, this was not a paranoid delusion. Kaczynski was not only rational but right. In Murray he had encountered the quintessential Cold War warrior, bent on perfecting behavior modification. The university and the psychiatric establishment had been willing accomplices in an experiment that treated human beings as unwitting guinea pigs, and had treated them cavalierly. Here was a powerful, logical foundation for Kaczynski's latterly expressed conviction that academics—and in particular, scientists—were thoroughly compromised servants of "the system," employed in the development of techniques for the behavioral control of populations.

It is evident from his writings that Kaczynski rejected the complexity and relativism he found in the humanities and the social sciences. He embraced both the dualistic cognitive style of mathematics and Gen Ed's despairing message. And perhaps most important, he absorbed positivism, which demanded value-neutral reasoning and preached that, as Kaczynski would later put it in his journal, "there was no logical justification for morality."

In 1971 or 1972, Kaczynski told *Green Anarchist*, he encountered Jacques Ellul's *Technological Society* for the first time, and its message that society served technology, not vice versa. Individuals, Ellul argued, were valued only insofar as they served this end. All social activities, but especially mathematics, education, and psychology, were shaped by and devoted solely to technological progress. Yet, as Kaczynski would explain later, these ideas did not surprise him. He had already encountered very similar ones at Harvard.

"I had already developed at least 50 percent of the ideas of that book on my own," he recalled in 1998. "And . . . when I read the book for the first time, I was delighted, because I thought, 'Here is someone who is saying what I have already been thinking.'"

Thus, Kaczynski's Harvard experiences shaped his anger and legitimized his wrath. By graduation, all the elements that would ultimately transform him into the Unabomber were in place: the ideas out of which he would construct a philosophy; the dislike of mathematics and psychology; the unhappiness and alienation. Soon after, too, would come his commitment to killing. Embracing the value-neutral message of positivism—morality was merely emotion—made him feel free to commit murder. Within four years after leaving Harvard his life's plan would be firmly fixed.

PART THREE

THE DESCENT OF TED KACZYNSKI AND THE IDEOLOGY OF MODERN TERRORISM

The values of this Western civilization under the leadership of America have been destroyed. Those awesome symbolic towers that speak of liberty, human rights, and humanity have been destroyed. They have gone up in smoke.

—OSAMA BIN LADEN, October 2001

[S]uch men . . . could not bear to be contradicted or shown to be wrong; this also threatened their image of themselves as a kind of god or superman.

—COLIN WILSON AND DAMON WILSON,
The Killers Among Us

20

Nightmares about Psychologists

So far . . . is reason from being the source of morality that it is reason alone which makes us capable of being rascals. . . . It is reason which enables us to form an evil resolution and to keep it when the provocation to evil is removed; it enables us, for example, to nurse vengeance. . . .

—ARTHUR SCHOPENHAUER,
On Human Nature

Real prowess in wrong-headedness, as in most other fields of human endeavour, presupposes considerable education, character, sophistication, knowledge, and will to succeed.

—RONALD HINGLEY,
Russian Studies scholar,
Oxford University

K ACZYNSKI graduated from Harvard in June 1962, less than a month past his twentieth birthday. For the country, it was the beginning of a new era, and for Kaczynski, the beginning of the end.

The cultural sea change symbolized by the 1960s had begun. The space race and technological progress; escalation of the Cold War; the sexual revolution, birth of the drug culture, and emergence of television as a national medium; the civil rights revolution, spreading violence; ubiquitous consumerism; and the environmental awakening—all combined to trigger a transformation in the nation's consciousness.

That year, John Glenn became the first American in space. James Meredith enrolled at the University of Mississippi under armed guard, after the U.S. Supreme Court ordered the university to admit him. Television networks began broadcasting in color three and a half hours a week. The Cuban missile crisis erupted, nearly triggering thermonuclear war. Media pundit Marshall McLuhan's *The Gutenberg Galaxy* appeared, predicting that television would turn the world into a "global village." Anthony Burgess's *A Clockwork Orange* and Ken Kesey's *One Flew Over the Cuckoo's Nest* were published. The Esalen Institute, a countercultural psychotherapy center, was founded in Big Sur, California.

The Manchurian Candidate, a fictional movie about brainwashing and mind control, was released. The first Wal-Mart store opened. Rachel Carson's environmental classic, *Silent Spring*, appeared. The birth-control pill first became readily available. On campus, professors and graduate students had begun to emulate Timothy Leary, who was to be fired by Harvard the following spring for indiscriminately promoting psychedelic drugs. Also in 1963, Betty Friedan's *The Feminine Mystique* would launch the women's rights movement.

But Kaczynski tried to ignore these events. If he read newspapers regularly, he told Sally Johnson later, "I would build up too much tense and frustrated anger against politicians, dictators, businessmen, scientists, communists, and others in the world who were doing things that endangered me or changed the world in ways I resented."

He lived in his own cocoon. It was time to get on with his life. He applied to three graduate schools to continue his studies in mathematics. But judging from his grades, he didn't seem especially enthralled with the subject. If anything, he seemed more interested in history, or evolutionary theory. He failed to graduate with honors from Harvard, receiving a damning C in Mathematics 101, a C+ in "Differential and Integral Calculus," and a modest B in "Functions of a Real Variable."

Nevertheless, Kaczynski decided to continue his studies in mathematics because he still sought to please his parents. Perhaps also, like many young men of his time, he worried about the draft, and graduate school attendance would extend his deferment. Thanks to his low grades, however, only one of the graduate schools to which he applied— the University of Michigan—offered him a teaching fellowship. And according to a former member of the graduate admissions committee, even Michigan would not have accepted him had he not received a glowing recommendation from a visiting professor who had been his instructor in Modern Higher Algebra, John G. Thompson.

Kaczynski says he remembers Thompson, and fondly. The older man is, Kaczynski told me, a "true mathematical genius." But what Kaczynski liked most about Thompson is that he wasn't a snob. Thompson, Kaczynski added, didn't act like "a typical member of the Harvard math department. Like me, he dressed like a slob and went around unshaven. . . . I found Thompson very likeable because he was a 'regular guy.' Other Harvard professors, in a subtle way that is hard to explain, made it clear to you that they were in a superior station, whereas Thompson always dealt with you as a complete equal."

And Thompson was also "generously helpful to students. I showed him my first attempt at original research . . . and he praised me generously for it." It was this research, says Kaczynski, that so impressed Thompson that he wrote a strong recommendation for him to Michigan. That 1962 endorsement "was much too generous. . . . I've always remembered him with affection."

AT MICHIGAN, where he arrived in the fall of 1962, Kaczynski lived a double life. Outwardly, he shone, achieving professional success most graduate students can only dream of. Inwardly, he despaired. The streams that had begun to converge at Harvard finally intersected. His undergraduate Gen Ed studies had already formed the foundation for a philosophical critique of industrial society, thereby providing a rationale for revenge against those he blamed for his misery. But until he got to Michigan these ideas were inchoate, not fully developed. There, he would refine them. Meanwhile, personal misery drove him to the breaking point.

A double epiphany occurred—one emotional, the other philosophical. Emotionally, for the first time he resolved to abandon efforts to be "a good boy." Philosophically, he now had a fairly complete theory to explain both his alienation and the ills of society. And the connecting links between his personal suffering and social critique would be psychology and mathematics. These were fields with which he had firsthand experience. They were also the enterprises that lay at the very heart of the industrial society which Kaczynski had come to hate. Together, these emotions, experiences, and ideas focusing like a laser on revenge and revolution would propel him to hatch a plan of terrorism and murder.

But on the surface, this turmoil remained invisible. As a graduate student, Kaczynski's accomplishments at Michigan weren't merely good but off the chart. Students graded his work as a teaching fellow highly. He fulfilled the language requirements in French and German easily. Required to take a course outside the field of mathematics, he chose to study human evolution under the physical anthropologist Frank B. Livingstone. Kaczynski "was brilliant," Livingstone told the *Ann Arbor News*, "He got the first A-plus I ever awarded."

But it was in mathematics that his genius really flowered. Peter Duren, who taught Kaczynski a course in real analysis, described him as "one of the best students I've ever taught. He had a very powerful analytical mind." His thesis adviser, Allen Shields (now dead), marveled about his "high standards" and "impressive" work. He has, Shields wrote his colleagues, "a lot of native power." Another former math instructor, George Piranian, described his mind simply as "first-rate."

"I remember Kaczynski," observed a fellow graduate student, Joel Shapiro, "as a quiet, private, unassuming sort of person who, at least to his classmates, didn't seem to stand out from the crowd. Our interactions were limited to occasional conversations about the classes we shared. During the course of these it became clear that Ted was a very smart guy."

And Kaczynski achieved an honor rare for graduate students: to publish papers in professional mathematics journals. Yet, characteristically modest, he didn't bother to tell his professors about his successes.

Shapiro, now a professor at Michigan State University, remembers:

I didn't appreciate how good he really was until one day . . . I came across a recently arrived journal in the mathematics library that featured an article written by "T. J. Kaczynski." So while most of us were trying to learn how to arrange logical statements into coherent arguments, Ted was quietly solving open problems and creating new mathematics. It was as if he could write poetry while the rest of us were struggling to learn grammar!

After that I was enormously impressed by the quiet demeanor with which Ted carried his mathematical ability.

But it was Kaczynski's doctoral dissertation, and the challenges that had to be overcome in completing it, that finally revealed his brilliance and character. This thesis, entitled "Boundary Functions," was, says Duren, "an extraordinary dissertation, a spectacular paper." Indeed, it provided the solution to a fundamental problem of mathematics that had stumped the best minds for years, and not surprisingly would be awarded the Mathematics Department's Sumner Myers Prize as the most outstanding doctoral dissertation of 1967.

But the road to this success was a rocky one. It began in Piranian's class, where Kaczynski had been a student. To pique his pupils' interest in mathematics, the professor described a boundary functions problem that no one had been able to solve. A few weeks later, Piranian told me, Kaczynski came into his office and dumped 100 handwritten pages on his desk.

Kaczynski had solved the problem. Without telling Piranian or anyone else, he submitted it to a professional journal, where it was accepted and published. But although Piranian urged him to do so, Kaczynski declined to submit it as his doctoral dissertation.

Meanwhile, Kaczynski was enrolled in a course taught by Allen Shields, who also challenged his students to find the solution to a long-unsolved problem. And sure enough, one day in September 1965,

Kaczynski dropped by Shields's office with a long manuscript containing a solution. He and Shields decided it should be his thesis.

"During that fall he developed these ideas further," Shields recalled, "till one day early in 1966 he came in and announced sadly that the work had already been done." A graduate student at Stanford had solved the problem. But as that student had never published his results and had left the field of mathematics entirely, Shields told Kaczynski that his paper would still be accepted as the dissertation.

But, Shields says, Kaczynski "wanted no part of that. He has high standards and simply dropped the whole thing." Instead, Kaczynski turned his attention to another problem, which he solved, and which again Shields said would make an acceptable dissertation. But after reworking his proof over the summer of 1966, Kaczynski returned to tell Shields that "there was a serious gap in his proof" and that therefore he was withdrawing the paper from consideration. When Shields suggested submitting it for publication as a short note, Kaczynski refused; "he felt it was too trivial."

It was only after all these false starts that Kaczynski decided to submit the original "Boundary Functions" paper he had written for Piranian, as his thesis.

Kaczynski "works almost entirely on his own," Shields commented in a memorandum. "I rarely saw him. He believes in doing everything himself, and he dislikes learning and applying elaborate machinery developed by other people. I tried to steer him more toward what I consider the main stream, but I was not very successful." Duren observed that Kaczynski, "a loner," was "a very serious person, not one to get involved in bull sessions."

"He went very much his own way," Duren continued, "was very independent, extremely meticulous. When he'd write a proof, he'd put in every possible explanation. He couldn't leave anything to imagination. He was very careful in everything, to a fault."

At Michigan, Kaczynski revealed character traits shared by most successful people: intellectual pride, perfectionism, independence of mind, and a willingness to pursue a thought wherever it took him, regardless of what people would think or the consequences. Among scholars, such obsessiveness and independence are deemed highly laudable, indeed, trademarks of genius. As Piranian remarked, speaking of Kaczynski's fixation with the ideas of his manifesto, "Anyone who becomes obsessed with one book—whether it be the Bible, Koran, or *Das Kapital*—is, in a sense, a madman. In that sense, Ted may be crazy. But in that sense half of academe is, too."

But, as the ancient Greek dramatists warned, these same qualities, possessed in extreme, lead to tragedy. The step from intellectual pride to egoistic arrogance or from obsession with an idea to deifying it may be small but nevertheless is fraught with risk. Kaczynski differed from other geniuses only in degree; but that small degree was enough to set him on a dangerous course.

By demonstrating what Shields called "high standards," Kaczynski revealed how hard he still tried to be good. He was still outwardly "lawful," exuding the utmost intellectual honesty. But he had set his standards so high that maintaining them was impossible. What doesn't bend, breaks. And there in Michigan, Kaczynski broke.

KACZYNSKI'S SUCCESSES at Michigan offered little personal satisfaction. To those who either didn't read or couldn't understand his work—which is to say virtually everyone—he seemed utterly insignificant. He even looked funny, wearing, as the *Ann Arbor News* would report later, "a sport coat and tie to class at a time when that was considered outlandish garb for a student."

Kaczynski had discovered just how much knowledge and learning can isolate, how they can cut a person off from others. The more one knows about something, the fewer people there are with whom one can share one's thoughts. He had conquered a field of mathematics so narrow that only a handful of geniuses around the world could appreciate what he had done. And where was the satisfaction in such an obscure victory?

Desperately lonely, Kaczynski still wished to get away from it all. He began studying wild edible plants and, during summers, taking frequent hikes in the Cook County Forest Preserves.

He worried about everything, from his health to his ability to attract women. He had trouble sleeping. His isolation almost absolute, he continued to refine the ideas first encountered at Harvard. He longed for wilderness. He longed for justice. He longed for revenge.

Anger coursed through his veins unabated. But he was too conscientious, too inhibited to vent these feelings. Only in nightmares did his
anger fully express itself. And after his experiences with the Murray
experiment, many of these dreams seemed aimed at psychology and
psychologists.

"During my years at Michigan," he later explained to Sally Johnson,

> *I occasionally began having dreams of a type that I continued to
> have occasionally over a period of several years. In the dream I
> would feel either that organized society was hounding me with
> accusation in some way, or that organized society was trying in
> some way to capture my mind and tie me down psychologically or
> both. In the most typical form some psychologist or psychologists
> (often in association with parents or other minions of the system)
> would either be trying to convince me that I was "sick" or would
> be trying to control my mind through psychological techniques. I
> would be on the dodge, trying to escape or avoid the psychologist
> either physically or in other ways. But I would grow angrier and
> finally I would break out in physical violence against the psychol-
> ogist and his allies. At the moment when I broke out into violence
> and killed the psychologist or other such figure, I experienced a
> great feeling of relief and liberation.*
>
> *Unfortunately, however, the people I killed usually would
> spring back to life again very quickly. They just wouldn't stay dead.
> I would awake with a pleasurable sense of liberation at having bro-
> ken into violence, but at the same time with some frustration at
> the fact that my victims wouldn't stay dead. However, in the course
> of some dreams, by making a strong effort of will in my sleep, I was
> able to make my victims stay dead. I think that, as the years went
> by, the frequency with which I was able to make my victims stay
> dead through exertion of will increased.*

In the fall of his fifth year at Michigan, 1966, Kaczynski's dreams of
violence coalesced into a real plan for revenge. The catalyst was sex.

At the time, he was living in a typically grubby off-campus student
apartment house at 524 South Forest Street in Ann Arbor. Through the
thin walls of his room, Kaczynski, already suffering from insomnia,

could plainly hear the sounds of the couple in the next room as they engaged in frequent and noisy sex. Not surprisingly, around that time, Johnson reports, "he describes experiencing a period of several weeks where he was sexually excited nearly all the time. . . ." The frustration was almost too much to bear. So he conceived a bizarre remedy.

Having failed to find a woman he could touch, he decided to turn himself into one. One can only speculate what previous experience—homosexual, transvestite, or transgender, at Harvard or earlier—may have triggered this decision, but Kaczynski claims that his reason for contemplating the change was not that he saw himself as a woman in a man's body, but rather that only by becoming a woman could he hope to touch one.

Realizing that a sex-change operation would not be performed without the approval of a psychiatrist, Kaczynski made an appointment with one at the University Health Center. He hoped that "by putting on an act," as Johnson put it, "he could con the psychiatrist into thinking him suitable for a feminine role even though his motive was exclusively erotic."

While sitting in the Health Center waiting to see the psychiatrist, however, Kaczynski suddenly realized what a self-destructive act he was contemplating. And simultaneously, he sensed how he had been driven to this point: He had sought too hard to please others. Pressure from his parents, school authorities, and math department professors had brought him to the point of contemplating, literally, an act of self-emasculation. The realization filled him with self-loathing. How he hated "the system" that had pushed him to this brink.

When he saw the doctor, therefore, he didn't explain the real, original reason for making the appointment. Instead, he concocted a story about being depressed over worry about the draft. He then left the clinic quickly, feeling "rage, shame and humiliation."

"As I walked away from the building afterwards," he explained to Johnson,

> I felt disgusted about what my uncontrolled sexual cravings had almost led me to do and I felt humiliated, and I violently hated the psychiatrist. Just then there came a major turning point in my life. Like a Phoenix, I burst from the ashes of my despair to a glorious

new hope. I thought I wanted to kill that psychiatrist because the future looked utterly empty to me. I felt I wouldn't care if I died.

Then it occurred to him: If trying hard to be good drove him to despair, his salvation lay in being bad! By obeying society's ethical standards, that positivism had taught him were subjective anyway, he had created a prison for himself. Freedom lay in throwing the rules away and not caring what other people thought. And throwing off the yoke of these moral scruples would allow him to do what he really wanted, namely, to take revenge on all those who had built this cage around him.

With this thought, Kaczynski realized that he could have what Johnson calls "the courage to behave irresponsibly."

And so I said to myself why not really kill the psychiatrist and anyone else whom I hate? What is important is not the words that ran through my mind but the way I felt about them. What was entirely new was the fact that I really felt I could kill someone. My very hopelessness had liberated me because I no longer cared about death. I no longer cared about consequences and I said to myself that I really could break out of my rut in life an [sic] do things that were daring, irresponsible or criminal.

Kaczynski describes that his first thought was to kill someone he hated and then kill himself, but then he determined that he would not give up his life so easily. At that point, he decided, "I will kill but I will make at least some effort to avoid detection so that I can kill again."

Henceforward, he resolved to ignore the strictures of society and do only what he wanted. What he wanted was to take a rifle and flee to some remote place in Canada, where he would live off the land. And "if it doesn't work and if I can get back to civilization before I starve then I will come back here and kill someone I hate."

All this, writes Johnson, "went through his mind in the time it took to walk about one block." He now had a plan. He would accept the offer of a tenure-track professorship from the University of California, Berkeley, but only to save money to buy land in some remote area. Then he would retreat to the wilderness and carry out his revenge.

21

Dawn of the Age of Aquarius

Force is becoming a popular student tactic, because students are learning that it works.

—*New York Times Magazine*, May 26, 1968

History shows that very often [violence] does work.

—TED KACZYNSKI,
"Truth vs. Lies"

E VENTUALLY, May 15, 1969, would be known as "Bloody Thursday" in Berkeley. But until things got out of hand, it seemed like just another campus riot.

Three blocks down Telegraph Avenue from the campus, around three thousand students, faculty, and off-campus revolutionaries from the Free Speech Movement and Students for a Democratic Society (SDS) chanted, carried placards, and jeered as helicopters vibrated overhead, dumping tear gas on them. A convoy of soldiers and policemen, some with bayonets, charged a scruffy band milling around a pathetic little vacant lot the students called "People's Park."

The lot belonged to the university. But administrators had shown no interest in it until a month earlier, when the *Berkeley Barb* urged folks to claim the land as their own and start growing things there. The idea caught on. Students, professors, their families, and street people trooped to the lot, planting grass and flowers and claiming to "expropriate" it. But no sooner was this land reform underway than the university decided to assert its suzerainty. At 4:00 A.M. that fateful Thursday morning, it sent contractors to put an eight-foot chain-link fence around the lot. Within hours, a throng of protesters marched down Telegraph Avenue, prepared to counterattack.

In response, Berkeley authorities asked police from neighboring cities to help evict the trespassers. Governor Ronald Reagan called in 2,200 National Guardsmen. Soon the place was a war zone. A police officer was stabbed. Three students suffered punctured lungs, thirteen protesters were hospitalized with shotgun wounds, and one was killed by police gunfire. Eventually, a thousand people would be arrested, two hundred of whom were charged with felonies.

All this happened just a few short blocks from the apartment where Ted Kaczynski lived, and along the route he walked to and from campus.

But if Kaczynski noticed the commotion, he paid no attention, just as he apparently never noticed the activists haranguing crowds at the university's Sproul Plaza, through which he walked daily. In fact, he apparently passed through the entire decade of the 1960s unaware of the tumult around him.

Controversy over the wisdom of pursuing the war in Vietnam was splitting the country asunder. Thanks to the draft deferment system, which exempted young men from the military so long as they stayed in school, college campuses became bubbling cauldrons of discontent, populated by students seeking sanctuary rather than learning, who seethed with resentment against the war, the government, and their own universities.

His own University of Michigan thesis adviser, Allen Shields, was already deep into antiwar politics, having even participated in street protests at the Democratic National Convention in Chicago the previous year. But not Kaczynski. He didn't even join in the politics of his own mathematics department, which its chairman, John W. Addison, described as having been at that time "one of the three most radical departments on campus."

Kaczynski ignored the riot because he had his own agenda. And that involved a different plan of action.

Just ten weeks earlier, on March 2, Kaczynski wrote Addison to say that he would resign his position as assistant professor of mathematics, effective in June. Addison was astounded. Although he thought Kaczynski "pathologically shy" and not a good teacher, nevertheless he recognized the young man's brilliance. And Kaczynski published prolifically. Why leave?

On hearing of Kaczynski's decision, his former professor at the University of Michigan, Peter Duren, wasn't entirely surprised. It reflected, Duren told me, Kaczynski's greatest weakness: intellectual pride. Duren and Kaczynski's other mentors at Michigan had hoped that when their prize student got to Berkeley, he would branch out, exploring other fields of mathematics. Boundary functions, the subspecialty in which Kaczynski made his reputation, was too narrow. He had accomplished all that could be done with it. Too few people could appreciate his work. If he was to continue to grow professionally, he needed to find new challenges.

Instead, Kaczynski stuck to his specialty. He was too proud, Duren felt, to take the advice of others. So naturally, his learning curve flattened out. Mathematics ceased to excite him. In contrast to Michigan, where students valued his performance as an instructor highly, Berkeley undergraduates gave his teaching skills a failing grade. Some accused him of ignoring questions put to him; others rated his lectures "useless."

Duren may have been right about Kaczynski's intellectual pride, but he is wrong about his motivation. Kaczynski didn't give up mathematics because he got bored. Neither was it because, as so many media commentators suggested after his arrest, he had become radicalized by the student activism of the 1960s. Rather, his decision to leave academe was made in Michigan that fateful fall of 1966, as he left the University Health Center psychiatrist's office. He took the Berkeley job not to launch an academic career, but to earn a grubstake sufficient to support himself later, in the wilderness. When he arrived at Berkeley in 1967, his ideology and life's plan were fixed. He would teach for a couple of years, then get out and find wilderness somewhere.

So, Kaczynski had merely been marking time. He had no interest in politics. Mathematics no longer intrigued him. He made no effort as a teacher. Wearing chinos, tie, and tweed jacket to work, he still looked like a fish out of water in a subculture where most students didn't even wash their Levi's. And this disdain was apparently requited. Berkeley was a left-wing place, and he didn't like leftists.

Yet, however aloof, Kaczynski was not entirely immune to the ideas circulating at the time. The political philosophies of the era, and their infatuation with violence, had an indirect effect. For these ideas weren't new. They derived from the very same culture of despair which Kaczynski and his generation encountered on campus during the previous decade.

According to conventional wisdom, the period 1961 through 1970 was a revolutionary decade. And on the surface, if one only paid attention to events, this insight seemed right.

Within that ten-year frame came the assassinations of Jack and Bobby Kennedy, Malcolm X, and Martin Luther King, Jr.; the Great Society, Mississippi Summer, and the Civil Rights Act; Haight-Asbury's "Summer of Love;" anti–Vietnam War protests in Washington and campuses throughout the country; riots in hundreds of cities and countless college campuses; moon landings and Woodstock, the Kent State massacre, and Earth Day.

The Cold War had turned hot. In 1961, the Berlin Wall went up, igniting a confrontation between NATO and the Soviets. A year later came the Bay of Pigs fiasco, soon followed by the Cuban missile crisis. In 1964, Congress passed the Tonkin Gulf resolution, dramatically escalating the "police action" in Vietnam. In 1968, Soviet tanks crushed the "Prague Spring" reformers in Czechoslovakia. In 1969, the United States bombed Cambodia for the first time, and in 1970, U.S. forces invaded the country, sparking protests at college campuses across the country.

But these dramatic events concealed a deeper truth: that while politically revolutionary, the 1960s were, philosophically speaking, still rooted in the 1950s. Ideas drive history, and it was the philosophies germinating on college campuses in the earlier decade that triggered the events which appeared on television screens later.

Indeed, the chaos of the sixties seemingly proved earlier pessimists right: the Age of Reason had come to an end. Humanists and others who predicted that positivism would undermine faith in the moral uses of reason believed they saw their worst fears realized. The SDS and its allies were merely, they thought, driving the last nails in the coffin of a Western civilization already terminally ill. Science had fueled governmental hubris and destroyed the liberal arts and faith in authority, and now a new generation of barbarians was turning it against itself.

By the time Kaczynski left Berkeley in 1969, Harvard's Gen Ed program and its equivalents on other campuses had undergone metamorphoses from within and would eventually be scuttled entirely. The faculty opponents of this pedagogy carried the day. The value-neutral approach to scholarship won the battle for the academic mind, and professors began to see their role, not as making good citizens but as training their own replacements. Universities, competing with each other to hire the freshly minted Ph.D.'s needed to teach the burgeoning ranks of baby boomers, gave in to the demands of the newly hired professors who wanted to teach, not general courses, but their own subspecialties.

The undergraduate curriculum became value-neutral and superspecialized just as the country was swept into the maelstrom of moral and political conflict over civil rights, the war in Vietnam, the environment, feminism, and (a little later) Watergate. By the middle of the decade students had realized that this new, desiccated curriculum was irrelevant to the critical moral issues of the day, and rejected it. In response, colleges jettisoned any pretense of promoting serious scholarship and began to pander to activists' cries for "relevance" by offering openly political courses.

A generation of college students had been taught that all values are subjective. Therefore, many reasoned, the state's authority is subjective, too. Government lacks objective moral foundation. It rests on power alone. Might makes right. It seemed to follow that the object of politics is not to promote virtue or justice but to capture the coercive powers of the state to work on one's own behalf. Lobbying, public protests, and even violence are justified so long as they achieve their objectives to overthrow the established order.

If this sounded vaguely Marxist, it was. Karl Marx taught that the state is a tool by which the bourgeois class exploits the proletariat. So it wasn't surprising that many professors embraced similar, quasi-Marxist ideas that suggested "the system" was responsible for our ills.

"Whatever the specifics of their ideologies," writes Norman Cantor of the intellectuals of this era,

> *this new breed shares a faith in the authenticity and power of systems as opposed to the consciousness and values of the individual. They believe that the individual is imbedded in a cultural, intellectual, moral structure, and that he is the end product, the object of the system that animates it. In their view, the individual cannot claim a separate identity and private value outside this system.*

Among the emerging systems theories popular in academe, Cantor says, was structuralism, which preached that human beings are mere pawns—without free will—of their intellectual and material environments; and deconstructionism, which carried structuralism one step further, suggesting that all aspects of culture, including political and social institutions, art, and literature—even reason itself—are without objective value.

Most popular among deconstructionists was the influential French philosopher Michel Foucault who, in Cantor's words, had "come to the conclusion that there was morality nowhere. Foucault's culture is a culture of political despair. He sees only a struggle for power, a manipulation of ideas and ethical values by all groups of society through all moments of time, including the present."

The shift of emphasis from the individual to the system of which he was a part reinforced feelings of helplessness: the system ruled and everyone was its victim. And Foucault's would not be the only theory to say so. In place of old canons rose a host of new "system" dogmas. As they filtered down from faculty to students, they were distilled into one crude thought: That "the system" rested on power alone and therefore must be destroyed.

Simplistic ideologies proliferated, each dedicated to destroying one "system" or another. Of course, activists disagreed about which system to destroy. To groups such as the Young Americans for Freedom and others on the right, it was the media, or government, or public education. To leftists, it was the legal system, the military-industrial complex, male chauvinism, liberalism, fascism, elitism, or—that perennial favorite—capitalism. Indeed, Marxist doctrines in particular ran rampant across the campuses of America, challenging the moral authority of the state.

Meeting in Fort Huron, Michigan, in 1962, the Young Democrats and Young Socialists joined with the Americans for Democratic Action under the leadership of a young Berkeley student named Tom Hayden to form the Students for a Democratic Society. Their founding document, known as the Fort Huron Declaration, declared (as Richard Norton Smith summarizes it), that nowhere was "modern life devouring humane values more rapaciously than in the university—once the shrine of the liberal arts, now a market stall dispensing the latest hardware to business, government, and the military."

"The revolutionary idea," one Fort Huron participant, David Horowitz, wrote, "was not to attain a new place in the old order of things, but to change the world itself. Marxism was about a new creation that would begin with a 'new man' and 'new woman.' It was about remaking the world. About going back to Eden and beginning again. It was the romance to end all romances.

"We were proud to be socialists, Marxists, and revolutionaries," Horowitz added. "We scorned the Old Left's dishonesty in hiding its agendas behind liberal and progressive masks. Liberals were the real enemy. . . . We were, in our own eyes, the self-conscious vanguard of a social revolution, not a collection of spiritual idealists."

Call it a seismic generational shift. Opposing these boomers stood the older Cold Warriors of the Johnson and Nixon administrations, who had lost faith in the common man but not in themselves. Many were Harvard graduates, including National Security adviser McGeorge Bundy, his brother William at the CIA, and Defense Secretary Robert F. McNamara, who clung to the idea that they knew what was best for us. Indeed, Harvard remained the last redoubt of the elitist ideal that former student activist John Trumpbour called "reason in the service of empire." Staunchly positivist, they believed, as Bundy put it, that "gray is the color of truth." Seeing themselves as the custodians of technology and rational planning, they pursued an ugly and unnecessary war.

"The Best and the Brightest," as David Halberstam dubbed them, "knew the right path and they knew how much could be revealed, step by step along the way. They had manipulated the public, the Congress and the press from the start, told half truths, about why we were going in, how deeply we were going in, how much we were spending, and how long we were in for."

And when things began to go wrong, the establishment circled its wagons. "When their predictions turned out to be hopelessly inaccurate," Halberstam writes, "and when the public and the Congress, annoyed at being manipulated, soured on the war, then the architects had been aggrieved. They had turned on those very symbols of the democratic society they had once manipulated, criticizing them for their lack of fiber, stamina and lack of belief."

Yet their thinking was already out of date. Deceived by their own hubris, the elite did not realize that the new generation of students and young professors had already discarded the very premises for their authority—notions of the supremacy of science, the importance of academic expertise, and the fairness of government.

Having used positivism to scale the walls of authority, the student revolutionaries then threw this ladder away, invoking systems theories to demolish what remained. Others embraced not ideas but feelings—of rage, love, reverence for nature, and need for commitment. Many turned to drugs as tokens of their rebellion, unaware that by doing so they were embracing tools of behavioral control concocted by their mortal enemy, the establishment. "Drug-taking," as Richard Norton Smith puts it, "became classified as a political act."

Like the pigs in Orwell's *Animal Farm*, the revolutionaries increasingly resembled the reactionaries they opposed. For although promising a brave and better world, they were actually mirror images of the ruling elite. They too believed that morality is subjective and only power counts. They too were willing to lie in the name of truth and resort to violence in defense of virtue. What both sides forgot was the message of the liberal arts, passed down from the ancient Greek philosophers until it disappeared from college curricula in the 1960s: that knowledge without virtue is dangerous and that virtue demands humility and restraint.

WITHOUT MORAL buffers, an irresistible force had collided heavily with an immovable object. And with this contact came violence. Protests escalated, as the establishment responded to force with a ferocity of its own. A deadly kind of tit-for-tat ensued, where one extreme act triggered another.

In 1967, around 150,000 people marched against the Vietnam War in New York and San Francisco. Later that year, another 150,000 protestors marched against the Pentagon. As opposition to the war grew, the CIA launched "Operation Chaos," a plan to spy on American citizens that would eventually collect the names of 300,000 people. Meanwhile, race riots rocked 127 cities, killing at least 77, injuring over 4,000.

In January 1968, North Vietnam launched the Tet Offensive, and two months later an American platoon massacred civilians at My Lai. In March, FBI director J. Edgar Hoover initiated a "Counter-intelligence program" against "Black-Nationalist-Hate-Groups." Two weeks later, the assassination of Martin Luther King, Jr., triggered race riots in 125 cities, causing 46 deaths, 21,270 arrests, and involving 55,000 National Guard and federal troops. In April, students at Columbia University in New York seized five buildings to protest, among other things, the university's ties to the federally supported Institute of Defense Analysis. In June, Senator Robert Kennedy was murdered after winning the California Democratic presidential primary. In August, the SDS and other student revolutionaries staged street riots at the Democratic National Convention in Chicago, provoking the city police into bloody retaliation. In November, students at San Francisco State College began a strike against the war that would last five months.

And so it continued through 1969 and beyond, as Kaczynski left in search of wilderness. During this period, reports Ted Robert Gurr in *Violence in America* (a work found in Kaczynski's cabin library), "The United States unquestionably experienced more widespread and intense civil conflict . . . than all but a very few other Western democracies." Twenty percent of the protests of this era became violent.

All told, "more than six million Americans resorted to demonstrations, riots, or terrorism" during this decade, Gurr adds. "An estimated 350 people died and more than 12,000 were reported injured. Nearly 100,000 people were arrested . . . Americans averaged 5,400 man-days of participation in protests (demonstrations and riots) per 100,000 population. This figure is about eight times the median value for other

Western democracies and six times the median value for all 87 countries in the survey."

UNTIL APRIL 9, 1969, Harvard, the very citadel of the establishment, seemed the calm at the center of this storm. But that day, everything changed. Without warning, three hundred students charged the steps of the administration building, University Hall. Fanning through the building, they hung the red and black banner of the SDS from a second-story window, then began hustling the deans, assistant deans, and other staffers out the doors.

Dean of Students Robert B. Watson "was pushed and dragged through the halls," wrote Roger Rosenblatt, then a young faculty member. Dean of Freshmen F. Skiddy von Stade, a man then in his sixties with a bad back, and Archie C. Epps, assistant dean of freshmen and the only black man in the Harvard administration, were "roughed up and hustled down the steps." Assistant Dean James E. Thomas was "tossed over somebody's shoulder and carried from the building." On the wall of Dean of the College, "someone had scrawled with blue crayon, 'fuck authority.' Others tried to obliterate the message unsuccessfully with white spray paint."

In response, Harvard's president, Nathan Pusey, wasted no time. At 5:00 A.M. the next morning, police retook the hall. After breaking down the door with a battering ram, they clubbed the occupiers and dragged them out by the hair. It was over in minutes.

Altogether, forty-one students were injured. And of the 135 who had been identified as occupiers, 16 were expelled, 3 received the more severe punishment of "dismissal" (they could only be readmitted upon a two-thirds vote of the faculty), and the rest received lesser punishments. No student was expelled permanently or "expunged" (having their names permanently erased from the college record).

The students had aimed to stop the war. But with curious logic, they attacked not the White House but the university, which they deemed to be part of "the system." In so doing, they kept the bathwater and threw out the baby. They didn't stop the war; but they did change the university and American culture forever.

It was, Rosenblatt lamented in 1997,

the most disruptive and wrenching time in the university's modern history. . . . What began with a single explosive incident in the Yard exposed an entire generational rift and touched upon antagonisms that have not been mended to this day. For the country as a whole, "fuck authority" would become "fuck" business contracts, institutional loyalties, a broad liberal arts education, the liberal tradition itself, and the ideal of the melting pot, even human contact. It would become . . . "Fuck everybody."

And for once Kaczynski was listening.

22

The Two Diasporas

We now seem to be approaching a point at which the changes generated within a single generation may render inept for the future the skills, the institutions, and the ideas which formed that generation's principal heritage.

—SIR GEOFFREY VICKERS,
Value Systems and Social Processes (1968)

American colleges and universities are in trouble. . . . Columbia, Michigan State, Northwestern, Stanford, are only where the lightning has happened to strike. The disorders on these campuses are reflections in part of disorders in the larger society—disorders in our social arrangements, and disorders in the ways in which we think about these arrangements.

—CHARLES FRANKEL,
Education at the Barricades (1968)

"AHEAD FOR the country," Roger Rosenblatt later recalled about that spring of 1969,

> were Kent State and the Christmas bombing of Cambodia and Watergate and all the sadness, wildness, and disintegrations that characterized the era. . . . I never felt the same after that spring, and it was not because of anything that I had brought about or that happened to me. I did not feel that I belonged in my time, or that I knew my country anymore. . . . There had been a great eruption in the earth, and the grass and rocks were upturned everywhere. No matter how smoothly the land might be restored, one knew what it was like underneath, and one's stomach churned.

Many felt as he did. On America's campuses, gloom deepened. Despite a booming economy, the war refused to end. While their own living conditions were good, students were convinced that disaster loomed ahead. Everyone, it seemed, had to choose—between hawks and doves, scholarship and politics. There was no middle ground. For those many professors and students who opposed the war but still wanted to teach and learn, it was a terrible time. Unable to stop the Vietnam conflict and equally powerless to prevent destruction of the houses of intellect, they were swept away by colliding forces of violence and ignorance.

The culture of despair changed. Whereas the 1950s feared that science and technology would destroy civilization, the 1960s fretted that science and technology were destroying nature. Another systems theory emerged, called "ecology," whose practitioners predicted that the earth faced environmental collapse.

> We poison the caddis flies in a stream and the salmon runs dwindle and die. We poison the gnats in a lake and the poison travels from link to link of the food chain and soon the birds of the lake margins become its victims. These are matters of record, observable, part of the world around us. They reflect the web of life—or death—that scientists call ecology.

Until 1962, when Rachel Carson's landmark *Silent Spring* opened with these words, most Americans had never heard of ecology. Henceforward, it would become a household word, seemingly infused with spiritual magic and awesome, unstoppable political power. It signaled the opening of a modern environmental awakening that would do much good, from reducing smog to protecting wetlands. But it would also ensure that the culture of despair, engendered by the Cold War and infecting colleges and universities throughout the 1950s, would not die but merely undergo a transformation, from worry about society to worry about nature. And amazingly, the same agencies and foundations that had funded experiments in mind control and behavior modification would play a prominent role in promoting this new bleak outlook.

Like psychology, ecology's rise began during World War II. At that time, Norbert Wiener, a professor at Massachusetts Institute of Technology, had developed the new mathematics called cybernetics to aid in the design of antiaircraft guns and missiles. It was the science of self-regulating systems, where feedback mechanisms keep the system in a preset equilibrium state. Thus, it applied to things that operate like house thermostats. When the temperature rises beyond a certain point, the furnace cuts off; when it drops below a certain degree, the furnace turns back on.

Cybernetics was an exciting idea. And almost immediately, both the government and its allies in the foundations began to look for other uses for this new mathematics of self-regulating systems, particularly for the purposes of control and movement of large populations in the event of atomic war.

In 1946, the Josiah J. Macy Foundation—the same philanthropic institution that would later serve as a CIA conduit for funding LSD research—sponsored the first of a seven-year series of conferences on the application of the concept of feedback loops to other sciences. At this first conference, the Yale ecologist G. Evelyn Hutchinson suggested applying Wiener's model of the self-regulating system to nature. "Ecosystems," as Hutchinson called his new hypothetical creation (borrowing a word coined in 1935 by Oxford botanist A. G. Tansley), could be conceived as behaving like the self-regulating machines, or feedback loops, that Wiener had designed. They were capable of maintaining themselves in a state of equilibrium.

By applying Wiener's mathematical model to nature, Hutchinson had helped to invent the new field of systems ecology. Living communities, according to this view, were organized into self-regulating negative feedback loops, in which every part plays a role in keeping the system in balance. But if the system loses parts—that is, loses species diversity—the feedback mechanism might be impaired and the system would then become unstable, even perhaps suffering "ecological collapse."

Guided by this reasoning, ecologists searched for signs of balance in nature. But they could find few. Nearly everywhere they looked they discovered not balance but instability. Therefore, by the 1960s they would conclude that natural systems virtually everywhere faced imminent ecological collapse. A global environmental crisis, it seemed, was at hand.

Hutchinson saw the self-regulating idea as useful in biology; but the government had different applications in mind. It wanted to manage human populations, not plants and animals. "The new systems theory," writes the English historian Peter J. Bowler, "offered the prospect of social control through the setting up of stable feedback loops of human interactions. In an atmosphere of post-war optimism, science seemed to offer the prospect of creating a new and more secure world."

It was not long, therefore, before the federal government began backing ecology heavily. Beginning in 1946, the Atomic Energy Commission launched ecosystem research programs at its Oak Ridge, Tennessee, atomic research facility; at Brookhaven National Laboratory in New York; at the nuclear research site in Hanford, Washington; and at the Savannah River nuclear facility in Georgia. At Savannah River, it hired University of Georgia ecologist Eugene Odum to study the impact of a nuclear power plant on surrounding farmland. Meanwhile, the Office of Naval Research (the same agency that had sponsored so much covert Cold War psychology) contracted with Eugene's brother, Howard, to study mineral springs in Florida. And in 1954, the commission sent the Odum brothers to Eniwetok, an atoll in the Pacific, to study, in their words, "the effects of radiation on whole populations and entire ecological systems in the field."

Fueled by generous transfusions of federal defense monies, this field would become by 1970 what some historians came to call "Big Ecology." Public agencies forged associations with think tanks at the universities, expanding ecological teaching and research. Private philanthropies inaugurated grants programs designed to promote the idea.

In 1970, President Richard M. Nixon would approve funding for U.S. participation in the International Biological Programme, a multi-year effort to develop comprehensive models for understanding ecosystems. And in 1974, the National Science Foundation would launch a generous long-term, grant program to promote the idea.

Unfortunately, the idea of the self-regulating ecosystem was based on a mistake. It had been derived more from Weiner's abstract mathematics than from empirical data. And by the mid-1980s, most ecologists would realize that the fundamental assumption of this mathematics—the notion of self-regulation—was false. There is no balance of nature. Living systems aren't like thermostats. They don't "self-regulate." They experience constant, random, and extreme change. The biologists of this era failed to find balance, not because ecosystems everywhere were on the verge of collapse but because there never had been any balance to find.

However mistaken, the idea remained popular, spreading unwarranted pessimism. The truth about declines in environmental quality—from air and water pollution and resource depletion to urban sprawl and species extinctions—was bad news enough. But the new theory unnecessarily carried this gloom to a deeper, almost metaphysical level of despair. A flawed theory had been superimposed on dispiriting facts, compounding a sense of decline.

Thanks to its imperfect reasoning, ecology seemed to forecast the end of nature. Such was the bleak view brought by Rachel Carson in introducing the new science to a broader public. Soon, the same young people who had declared war on the "military-industrial complex" were flocking to its banner. But as with drugs, they did not realize that their own agenda had been in part launched by their very enemies in government. They rioted to bring an end to ROTC, but never picketed the offices of those promoting ecology as the science of social control, at the Office of Naval Research. They failed to see the connection between their own visions of nature and a mathematical model advanced by defense technology.

Despite his apparent aloofness, Kaczynski absorbed these intellectual currents. He was conscious of the violence around him. He was already obsessed with psychology. And in the manifesto, he would espouse a systems theory of society. This "system," he decided, could be blamed for everything. It lacked moral foundation and rested on "power" alone. And its chief engineers, whose assigned role was to keep people in line, were psychologists. The word "power" appears in the manifesto 193 times, "system" 210 times, and "psychology" and "psychologists" more than 65 times. "Freedom" Kaczynski defined as "participation in the power process." And despite his professed dislike of leftists, he shared with them the view that individual freedom could only be achieved within a "system" (i.e., the "power process"). Like them, he saw individuals as cogs in a machine.

Although Kacyznski did not read Ellul until the early 1970s, he claims to have reached many of the same conclusions before the encounter. Therefore, Ellul's philosophy gives us a glimpse into Kaczynski's thinking during the 1960s. In particular, although Ellul didn't espouse deconstructionism (which is an atheistic doctrine), he did blame systems for the evils of the world.

For Ellul, technology—or "technique," as he calls it—doesn't just refer to machinery. Rather, it stands for a way of thinking—a system of knowledge, if you will—that often involves "the extensive application of mathematics." For Ellul, everything from politics and public relations to education and engineering is technique. And Ellul's main point is that while techniques may originally have been intended merely as a means to create products, they were now treated as ends in themselves.

In other words, Ellul said we serve techniques; they don't serve us. And among these techniques is psychology, whose "first goal" is to help ensure people will continue to serve the technological system. It is possible, he wrote, "through psychological means to draw from man his last measure of effort and at the same time compel him to bear up under the disadvantages with which the new society hinders him."

This kind of behavior control Ellul called "propaganda," whether manifested as advertising, public information, or education. And propaganda itself "is based on scientific analyses of psychology and sociology."

Such insights exactly fit Kaczynski's predilections. Their message seemed clear. He had experienced a close encounter of an unfortunate kind with a professor dedicated to transforming people by psychological techniques. And now he, Kaczynski, was himself guilty of advancing the field of mathematics—the very discipline Ellul exposed as lying at the heart of virtually every modern technique. By trying to be good he had unwittingly served the very machine that sought to destroy his freedom. To paraphrase Walt Kelly's comic strip character Pogo, he had met the enemy, and it was he.

Like the character of the carpenter in Geoffrey Chaucer's "The Miller's Tale" (in *Canterbury Tales*), whom Kaczynski would later obliquely refer to in Unabomber letters, he discovered he had been duped, and went "wood." At the heart of this anger lay fury at his own gullibility. "The system" had seduced him, and he wanted out.

He was not alone. During these chaotic times, many sought escape. Not a few turned to psychedelics. But these were only the beginning— the "entry point," as Marilyn Ferguson described it in *The Aquarian Conspiracy*, "drawing people into other transformative technologies." For psychology itself had become a technology, a science of inner retreat. And in those violent times, retreat seemed increasingly appealing. Among the fruits of cooperation between the military and the social sciences, it would infuse the national culture, giving birth to what Ellen Herman calls "America's romance with psychology."

The Age of Aquarius had dawned. Many were willing to try anything—and everything—that promised to ease pain or produce a "higher" level of consciousness. As Ferguson reports, they attended Esalen retreats and underwent Erhard Seminar training. They dabbled in "sensory isolation and sensory overload," biofeedback, "autogenic training," hypnosis and self-hypnosis, various meditation methods from Zen, Tibetan, and Buddhist to transcendental, Kabbalist, and tantric yoga. They embraced "psychosynthesis," Sufi stories, koans, dervish dancing. They studied Silva Mind Control, underwent rebirthing and primal scream therapies, kept dream journals, studied Arica, theosophy, Gurdjieffian systems, logotherapy, Gestalt therapy, Reichian psychology, T'ai Chi Ch'uan, aikido, karate, running, dance, Rolfing, bioenergetics, Feldenkrais, Alexander and applied kinesiology.

And while some turned inward, others turned outward, seeking escape not within themselves but in nature. By 1969, two great diasporas had begun.

The most famous of these were baby boomers seeking Ecotopia in the backwoods. As Charles Reich has described their beliefs in *The*

Greening of America, these young people found themselves at war with "the corporate state." They longed for "freedom from the domination of technology." Motivated by idealism and driven by a new ideology of nature, they weren't so much seeking escape as hoping to construct new, model communities, supported by the economy of marijuana. Abandoning Haight-Asbury and other countercultural enclaves, they trekked to rural towns like Garberville, California, and Cave Junction, Oregon, to grow pot and stop logging. After Nixon ended the draft in 1973 and male students no longer felt constrained by the deferment system to stay in college, the flight to wilderness accelerated. Ever optimistic, they took their militancy with them. Within a few short years they had embraced a form of terrorism they called "ecotage," dedicated to saving nature.

The second, less well known back-to-the-land movement was populated by trekkers of the Silent Generation, such as myself. In the 1950s, our professors warned us that the Judeo-Christian heritage faced imminent collapse. Like Rosenblatt, himself of the Silent Generation, by the late 1960s we believed that that collapse had occurred. We were not prepared for the chaos. Our world had simply disappeared.

As campuses split asunder, it seemed the literary and philosophical tradition in which we had been reared came to an abrupt halt, and we could not cope. The life of the mind for which we had prepared became irrelevant. We ourselves had become irrelevant just as we came of age. The 1960s should have been our salad days, when we assumed the baton of leadership. Instead, it passed over our heads, directly from the World War II generation before us to the boomers who followed. In the 1950s, we were too young; by the 1960s, too old. We found ourselves, as Gail Sheehy puts it, "grown up just as the world went teenage."

No longer fitting in, we opted out. Some simply kept low profiles, sticking to job and family. Others sought escape, either by moving to the wilderness or by finding new careers in small niches or specialties where they could avoid public life altogether.

In short, while the younger back-to-the-landers were motivated by a desire to get close to nature and build a new, ecologically pure society, the Silents were driven by an urge to get away from a world they saw disintegrating. Boomers rejected science, authority, and the past. Silents embraced classical civilization and history. Boomers remained optimistic activists. Silents were too pessimistic to believe in the efficacy of action.

Kaczynski's birth date—1942—lay at what demographers consider the cusp between Silents and boomers. And he seemed to combine the perspectives of these two generations. Like many other Silents, he had been immersed in a college curriculum that warned of the dangers technology posed to society. He went into wilderness to escape. But like boomers he also wanted action.

He therefore represented a curious synthesis of despair and commitment. This would be a deadly combination. Like the drugs phen/fen, these different generational visions, while less harmful in themselves, would prove lethal when combined.

23

Bonbons and Bombs

There is a sense among today's undergraduates that they are passengers on a sinking ship, a *Titanic* if you will, called the United States or the world. Perhaps this is part of the reason why suicide has become the second leading cause of death among students in the 1970s, exceeded only by accidents.

> —ARTHUR LEVINE,
> *When Dreams and Heroes Died:*
> *A Portrait of Today's College Student* (1980)

The erosion of our confidence in the future is threatening to destroy the social and the political fabric of America.

> —PRESIDENT JIMMY CARTER,
> so-called National Malaise speech, July 15, 1979

Nestled in the northern end of the Big Belt Mountains, Raynesford, Montana, population 208, is little more than a wide spot on the road—or more accurately, two roads. State Route 427 to Monarch intersects U.S. Highway 87 connecting Great Falls with Lewistown there. There's nothing much to the town, besides the Kibbey-Korner Kafe and truck stop, the Mint Bar, and the local school.

One wintry night during the fall of 1974, a waitress in the restaurant, Nancy Hepburn, was getting off work late. It was cold and dark outside, and she worried that her car wouldn't start. The mother of four children, Hepburn had gone to work at Kibbey-Korner to earn money to buy a color television set. But darn, here she was, working into the night while her husband and children were snug at home watching the tube.

The guys who worked in the garage were really helpful, though. Hepburn grew up just down the road, in Belt, and had known some of them since they were kids. They offered to warm up her car in the garage before she left. So, at 9:00 P.M., Hepburn climbed behind the wheel, ready to leave. She started the car and shifted into gear. Nothing happened. The engine revved, but the car just sat there.

Meanwhile, Hepburn's mechanic "buddies," as she called them, were laughing themselves silly, waiting for her to figure out what they'd done. And what they'd done was to jack the rear wheels off the ground just enough to prevent the tires from gaining traction.

It was a fun joke. And leaning against the wall and enjoying it most was Ted Kaczynski, who'd been working in the garage only a few weeks. It was the first time she'd ever seen him laugh.

Kaczynski had lived in Montana only three years by then and was already discovering that wilderness offers few job opportunities. One might call this the paradox of paradise. Each year, thousands of well-educated, twentysomethings come to the state in search of scenery and solitude. But they soon discover that wilderness means no work. Some promptly leave. The rest take blue-collar jobs for which they are either overqualified or underskilled. It is not unusual to find fishing guides with law degrees and waiters who had been Fulbright scholars.

But it takes humility to migrate downscale like this, and that was a quality Kaczynski utterly lacked. Not only was he too well educated and deficient in patience for available jobs; he felt insulted by them. His intellectual arrogance had remained intact. He was too proud.

> *I tended to feel that I was a particularly important person and superior to most of the rest of the human race [an undated entry in his journal records]. It just came to me as naturally as breathing to feel that I was someone special.*

It galled him that no one appreciated his brilliance. He was too superior to be a mere mechanic or bag boy. No matter what job he took, eventually he would lose his temper, get fired, or quit.

Like the man who said, "I only want the love and respect of the people I hate," Kaczynski both wanted to say, "Fuck you!" to the world and to be appreciated by it. So he was unemployed and broke most of the time. He seethed with anger, not only at society and people who slighted him but also, increasingly, at his family. Relations with his parents and brother would soon reach the breaking point. Like a rebellious teenager, he wanted nothing to do with his family but still counted on them for an allowance. As the seventies wore on, he grew more desperate. Thoughts of murder and revolution haunted him. He read obsessively, visiting the library several times a month, perfecting his rationalization for revenge.

But revenge against what? Ultimately, against himself. He revered the scientific method, yet blamed science for the world's ills. He feared technology, but would employ it to make bombs. He deplored mathematics for serving technological society, but was a mathematician himself. He feared psychology, but obsessively used its concepts to understand himself. In short, he hated everything about himself. And he blamed his parents and "the system" for making him so detestable.

KACYZNSKI'S LIFE PLAN was not working as he had hoped. After he left Berkeley in June 1969, he and David drove to Canada, looking for land. They filed a request with the Canadian government to lease a remote plot in northern British Columbia, then drove to their parents' new home in Lombard, Illinois. And when that fall David returned to Columbia University for his senior year of studies, Ted stayed in Lombard, waiting for word from Canada. Eventually, his application was denied. Disappointed, he returned to Canada again the following summer, to continue his search for real estate. But, as he confessed later in "Truth vs. Lies," he was already discouraged and didn't look very hard.

Meanwhile, in June 1970, David graduated from Columbia and spent the summer touring the West with college friends. After returning to Lombard for a short time, he moved to Montana, where he rented an inexpensive apartment at 1001 Sixth Avenue North in Great Falls. He took a job at the Anaconda Company smelter, across the Missouri River in Black Eagle. The next spring, he invited Ted to visit.

Shortly after arriving in Great Falls, Ted resumed his search for land. Soon he found 1.4 acres four miles south of Lincoln. After he'd shown the spot to David, the brothers decided to buy, each contributing $1,050 toward the purchase. Immediately after the sale was completed, on June 19, 1971, Ted set to work building a cabin.

If Kaczynski had been looking for peace and quiet, the Lincoln land was an odd choice. It offered little of the solitude he craved. It lay smack in the middle of an area dotted with summer and hunting cabins and teeming with snowmobilers, hunters, gold prospectors, and loggers. And comparatively speaking, it was expensive. If he'd continued shopping, he could have found a more remote place costing a tenth as much. There was plenty of real estate in Montana those days selling for less than $100 an acre.

Why did he buy? Kaczynski admitted the lot "was not nearly as isolated as I would have liked," but explained, " . . . I'd decided that I was going to have to settle for something that was less than ideal." His choice ensured that, rather than enjoy soothing solitude, he would encounter aggravating distractions. Rather than becoming more at peace, he would become increasingly angry. The location virtually guaranteed noisy neighbors who would keep him perpetually agitated, pick at the scabs of his emotional wounds and keep them fresh, open, and sore.

But in one respect, the Lincoln lot was ideal: It was the perfect place from which to launch a campaign of terror. By this time Kaczynski's antitechnology philosophy was already developed. He was completing the untitled essay in which he praised Ellul's *Technological Society*, warned of the dangers of "psychological manipulation," and predicted that "continued scientific and technical progress will inevitably result in the extinction of individual liberty." And he had already resolved to do something about it.

But terrorism required travel. A truly remote cabin would have been infeasible. Lincoln, however, was more convenient. It had good bus connections to Helena, Great Falls, and Missoula. By buying this lot, therefore, Kaczynski had taken a giant step toward murder. The venue would offer plenty of excuses for anger as well as opportunities for venting it.

Thanks to the baby boomer diaspora, during the early 1970s primitive became chic and living without plumbing a sign of heightened spiritual consciousness. In the context of these times, Kaczynski's lifestyle in Lincoln hardly seemed unusual.

Like other back-to-the-landers of the era, he threw himself into the rustic life. But unlike most, he pursued his primitivism scientifically, carrying it to extremes. He read books on woodcraft, botany, organic chemistry; on poison antidotes, nutrition, pesticides, Indian customs, rifle shooting, and first aid; on wilderness medicine, seeds, controlling weeds, and identifying trees, shrubs, animal tracks, mushrooms, and edible and poisonous plants, as well as both wildflowers and non-flowering plants.

He built a ten- by twelve-foot cabin, dug a root cellar, and planted a garden. Rather than dig a well, he merely siphoned water out of Canyon Creek with a hose. And inspired by a passage about rural life in India from V. S. Naipaul's *An Area of Darkness*, he didn't build an outhouse. Instead, each day he carried his solid waste on a newspaper to the garden and buried it. When his only motorized vehicle, a dark blue Chevy pickup truck, broke, he gave it away rather than try to fix it.

Meanwhile, in 1972 David quit the smelter job and began studying for a degree in education at the College of Great Falls. After receiving the degree in 1973, he moved back to Lombard.

But even when the brothers were separated, they continued their philosophical arguments—what David would later describe to the FBI as a "discussion and debate—a dialectic"—via the mails. Ted ridiculed his younger brother's ideas as romantic, fuzzy-minded, and unscientific. Only empirically verifiable beliefs, he insisted, were meaningful.

By this time, David told the FBI, Ellul's *Technological Society* had become Ted's "Bible." And the "core argument" of these discussions

> *concerned TED's belief that scientists had a truer picture of the universe than artists did, because of their reliance on the "Verifiability Criterion." Ted defined this criterion as holding that a "fact" was valid only insofar as it could be proven "true or false." Dave on the other hand, believes that reality is not necessarily "black and white," but includes many "mystical unknowables" which are a part of human experience not easily quantifiable, or even identifiable. Dave includes "Art" as part of this type of experience. Dave emphasized that Ted has long been committed to rationality as a guiding principle, and noted that a particular characteristic of Ted's debating style was that he placed special emphasis on making his arguments compelling. In doing this, Ted characteristically stressed that since his ideas were based on a "rational ideal," any action in support of them was justifiable. Dave expressed sadness in commenting that this type of justification would enable Ted to feel fully justified and even visionary in killing people to accomplish his "rational objectives."*

Kaczynski not only believed in reason, he was obsessed by it. He had what Don Richard Riso and Russ Hudson describe in their book *Personality Types* as an "investigator" personality—the mind-set of an intellectual.

Emotionally healthy individuals of this type, the authors explain, are "mentally alert, curious [and] have searching intelligence." They "attain skillful mastery of whatever interests them." They are "excited by knowledge" and "often become expert in some field."

This characterization is based on an ancient system of analyzing personalities, called the Enneagram, whose origins remain largely unknown. Yet while neither scientific nor of proven diagnostic or therapeutic value, it shares a central insight with many modern personality theories: that mental health requires balance.

Those who allow one aspect of the personality to dominate—whether it be thinking, feeling, or intuition—gradually decline. Their personal foibles become more extreme. When intellectuals in particular lose balance, their fascination with ideas and theories progressively isolates them.

Such studious temperaments, say Riso and Hudson, can lead this type to be "increasingly detached, as they become involved in complicated ideas. . . . [T]hey are willing to entertain *any* thought, no matter how horrible, unacceptable, or taboo it may seem to others" (authors' italics). They "value their independence very highly." Totally absorbed in their own thoughts, they eventually become "reclusive" and in some cases "explosively self-destructive."

When Kaczynski arrived in Montana, his personality had already become a concentrated distillation of this intellectual type. Thenceforward, it would become ever more extreme, ultimately fulfilling some dire forebodings of the Enneagram.

As THE 1960S ENDED and 1970s began, the national diaspora to wilderness continued. Thousands of young and middle-aged people, having given up on mainstream America, sought escape. Writers and novelists extolled the simple life. *Desert Solitaire*, Ed Abbey's ruminations about his short stints as a seasonal ranger in Arches National Monument, Utah, in which he poetically depicted living alone in wilderness, caught the national imagination. E. F. Schumacher's *Small Is Beautiful* launched a new ethic, opposed to big-scale technology and favoring the simpler life.

Meanwhile, a sense of doom saturated literary, academic, and popular culture. Paul R. Ehrlich's best-selling *Population Bomb* flatly (and mistakenly) predicted that "in the 1970s and 1980s hundreds of millions of people will starve to death." Similarly, Barry Commoner's blockbuster, *The Closing Circle*, declared that the earth was already experiencing an "environmental crisis," which exposed "the hideous fraud hidden in the vaunted productivity and wealth of modern technology-based society." While apologizing for the "bleak cynicism," of his

Where the Wasteland Ends, Theodore Roszak in 1972 nevertheless lamented the "psychology of science and culture of industrialism" which had triggered the "flight from the primitive." The same year, the Club of Rome's *Limits to Growth* predicted that the world was about to experience a "sudden and uncontrollable decline in both population and industrial capacity."

"If present trends continue," the *Global 2000 Report* to President Jimmy Carter announced in 1980, "the world in 2000 will be more crowded, more polluted, less stable ecologically and more vulnerable to disruption than the world we live in now."

On campuses, pessimism spread like mononucleosis. As Carnegie Foundation senior fellow Arthur Levine reported on the empirical findings by the University of Michigan's Institute for Social Research, "with each succeeding year, students have grown slightly more pessimistic about the country, until 1979, when pessimism increased a full fifth.

"When asked what they were apprehensive about," Levine continued,

> *undergraduates listed everything under the sun—and that, too, if one counts solar energy. They were fearful of the economy, pollution, energy, crime, morals, and nuclear war. They were concerned about nuclear power, corporations, greed, illegal aliens, and the right wing. Anita Bryant and her anti-homosexual campaign, Phyllis Schlafly and her anti-equal-rights-amendment campaign, and California and its anti-tax Proposition 13 were mentioned; so were waste, the poor, foreign policy, self-centeredness, divorce, money, authoritarianism, and prices. Students were worried about drugs, increased regulation, permissiveness, reduced standards of living, the environment, and the justice system—these and much, much more were on their list.*

By 1979, this gloom had become so thick that even Jimmy Carter— whose *Global 2000 Report* would soon add fog of its own—couldn't ignore it. On July 15, in an address that would later be known as his "national malaise" speech (although it never used the expression), Carter warned that America faced a "crisis of confidence."

"It is a crisis that strikes at the very heart and soul and spirit of our national will. We can see this crisis in the growing doubt about the meaning of our own lives and in the loss of a unity of purpose for our Nation. The erosion of our confidence in the future is threatening to destroy the social and the political fabric of America."

Indeed, the fabric was rent—and terrorism began to fill the hole. As Ted Robert Gurr defines it, terrorism is "the use of unexpected violence to intimidate or coerce people in the pursuit of political or social objectives." In this sense, terrorism had been an isolated part of the American scene since the Ku Klux Klan appeared in the South soon after the Civil War. But in the 1960s it began to flourish. Right-wing and leftist terrorist groups, including southern white segregationists, black militants, and Marxist revolutionaries, multiplied like killer bees.

On the right, the Minutemen, a violently anti-Communist paramilitary group, appeared in the early sixties. The American Nazi Party flourished until its leader, George Lincoln Rockwell, was murdered in 1967. By that year, the Klan would have 700 local Klaverns and 17,000 members. In 1969, the militant, loosely knit Posse Comitatus appeared. Others followed in fast succession: the Order (an offshoot of Posse Comitatus); California Rangers; the Covenant, the Sword, the Arm of the Lord (CSA); and Church of Jesus Christ Christian of the Aryan Nations. Many of these were so-called survivalist organizations which advocated that their members retreat to the wilderness and stock up on food and other necessities. To prepare for what they saw as the inevitable revolution, they sought to establish their own, "autonomous" governments with standing armies.

Meanwhile, new black militant and Marxist terrorist groups were appearing almost annually, including the Black Panthers, the Black Nationalists of New Libya, the Black Liberation Army, the Revolutionary Action Movement, the Republic of New Africa, the Weather Underground, the Weather Bureau, extreme elements of the Students for a Democratic Society, the New World Liberation Front, and the Symbionese Liberation Army (SLA).

While most of these were short-lived, as Gurr notes, throughout the seventies and into the eighties "other groups have continued to act out similar fantasies, though with much less media attention." In the eighties and nineties, they would be joined by abortion clinic snipers, bombers, and arsonists, who with unintentional irony called themselves advocates of the "right to life."

Nor were these the only terrorists. The early 1970s saw the rise of a new tactic soon known as "monkeywrenching," after Ed Abbey's novel *The Monkey Wrench Gang* (1975), extolling a band of supposedly lovable misfits who roamed the West destroying roadside signs, sabotaged construction machinery, and ultimately plotted to blow up a major hydroelectric dam. And although at first blush these hijinx seemed innocent enough, they would eventually become more serious.

Monkeywrenching was inspired by tactics student activists had developed during their campaigns against the war in Vietnam. When that war ended and they left for the boondocks, they took their tactics with them. They staged picturesque protests, featuring costumes and made-for-television staging they called "guerrilla theater." And they invented monkeywrenching: ruining bulldozers by pouring sugar into their gas tanks, pulling up survey stakes, and "billboarding" (destroying roadside signs). And they "spiked" trees (hammering ten penny nails into the trunks that would cause chain or band saws that encountered them to virtually explode in the operator's hands, sending potentially lethal shrapnel in all directions).

In 1970, someone known as "the Arizona Phantom" began sabotaging heavy equipment at the Black Mesa strip mine. In Kane County, Illinois, "the Fox" capped smokestacks he thought caused too much air pollution. In Tucson, Arizona, a group calling itself the "Eco-Raiders" sabotaged subdivision sites. On the East Coast, the mysterious "Lobo" went on a billboarding spree. And in Blaine County, Idaho, unnamed activists sawed down virtually every outdoor sign on Route 93, from Hailey to Ketchum.

By the time *The Monkey Wrench Gang* appeared, the idea had caught on, particularly among backwoods boomers. They were not terrorists, they insisted, because they only harmed property, not people. So the national media, following Abbey's lead, depicted these saboteurs as lovable ragamuffins, treating their exploits as harmless fun. But such innocence would not last. Like all historical movements, ecotage came to have its imitators, who didn't shy from real violence.

IN THESE GROUPS, America was for the first time encountering the mind of the modern terrorist. For despite their differences, they shared essential similarities:

They saw themselves as actors on a large, historical stage. Militiamen sought to relive the Revolutionary and Civil wars, pursuing struggles against what they saw as the tyranny of central government. Black militants thought they were righting the wrongs of slavery; antiwar activists carried the torch for Marxism and sought to remove imperialism and capitalism from the dialectical process of history. Environmentalists declared their goal was nothing less than to "save the planet."

They all sought revenge for perceived injustices that had occurred long ago: the Confederacy's defeat in the Civil War (militiamen); slavery (black militants); French rule in Indochina (antiwar activists); the "rape of the Great Plains" by early American settlers (environmental extremists).

They all had given up on America; and indeed, despised everything modern and Western. Militiamen and environmentalists rejected industrialism as well as technology, and embraced a primitive, late Pleistocene lifestyle. Leftist revolutionaries declared war on "bourgeois" (or "white, Anglo-Saxon," "male chauvinist," "free-market capitalist," or "imperialist") values. Black extremists, rejecting Christianity as the slaveowner's religion, converted to Islam and gave themselves Muslim names.

They all killed or terrorized in the name of an ideology, transforming their victims into abstractions representing ideas rather than flesh and blood. And they all were convinced that their theories made violence not only acceptable but necessary.

Violence, in short, was in the air. And Kaczynski was breathing it. He was already acutely sensitive to noise, and had discovered there was plenty in his new neighborhood. The sounds of chain saws, snowmobiles, jet planes, prospectors, and helicopters drove him to new heights of rage. So he, too, took up monkeywrenching—stringing wire across trails in hopes of garroting backcountry bikers, shooting at helicopters, and destroying logging and construction equipment.

"Few years ago," he wrote in his coded journal,

some fuckers built a vacation house just across Stemple Pass Road. Motorcycle and snowmobile fiends. They would buzz up and down road past my cabin on most weekends, summer and winter. Last summer seemed they were worse than usual. Sometimes made it a three day weekend. When they were not buzzing up this road I would hear those cycles growling and growling over by their place, all day long. It was getting absolutely intolerable. My heart is going bad. Takes exercise OK, but any emotional stress, anger above all, makes it beat irregularly.

So he decided to take action.

Risky to commit crime so close to home. But I figured if I did not get those guys, the anger would literally kill me. Anyway, so one night in fall I sneaked over there, though they were home, and stole their chainsaw, buried it in a swamp. That was not enough, so couple weeks later when they had left the place, I chopped my way into their house, smashed up interior pretty thoroughly. It was a real luxury place. They also had a mobile home there. I broke into that too, found silver painted motorcycle inside, smashed it up with their own axe. They had four snowmobiles sitting outside. I thoroughly smashed engines of those with the axe.

Nor was Kaczynski content merely with property damage. By the summer of 1977 he would write:

I set a booby-trap intended to kill someone, but I won't say what kind or where because if this paper is ever found the trap might be harmlessly removed.

As "INVESTIGATORS" DECLINE, note Riso and Hudson of this personality type, they become "intellectually arrogant." They "love to take ideas to their furthest limits [to] . . . use their entire lifestyle as a statement of their views and as a rebuke of the world. They may choose to live an extremely marginal existence to avoid 'selling out.' . . . [B]ecause they are not participating as actively in the world, they are getting fewer 'reality checks.'" Eventually, "they can be terse, cryptic, or totally uncommunicative." They become "extremely Spartan and minimal in their existence."

This was true of Kaczynski. No sooner had he settled in his Eden than serpents appeared. He had trouble sleeping and began to worry about his health. Money problems loomed. To replenish his grubstake, in the fall of 1972 he took a job as carpenter's helper in Salt Lake City, returning to Lincoln the following June. In 1974, he worked at Kibbey-Korner.

And the noise! Even after building himself a "secret cabin" in the wilderness, he couldn't escape the noise. He recorded in his coded journal:

> Last summer dynamite blast was booming all over the hills. Occasionally audible at my cabin. . . . Exxon conducting seismic exploration for oil, couple of helicopters flying all over the hills, lower a thing with dynamite on cable, make blast on ground, instruments measure vibrations. Early August I went and camped out, mostly in what I call diagonal gulch, hoping to shoot up a helicopter in area east of crater mountain. Proved harder than I thought, because helicopters always in motion, never know where they will go next. Tall trees in way of shot. Only once had half a chance. Two quick shots, roughly aimed, as copter crossed space between two trees. Missed both. When I got back to camp I cried, partly from frustration at missing, but mostly grief about what is happening to the county. It is so beautiful. But if they find oil, disaster. Even if not find oil, the blasts and helicopters ruin it. Desecration. Where can I go now for peace and quiet?

During the 1970s, Kaczynski's life in Lincoln settled into a curious rhythm of anger at motorcycles and snowmobiles, interspersed with monkeywrenching, short stints at odd jobs, philosophical exchanges with David, and planning a campaign of terror.

And although he lived nearly two thousand miles from Illinois, he couldn't stop quarreling with his family. He desperately wanted Turk and Wanda to leave him alone, but simultaneously depended on them for occasional gifts of money. So, despite repeated threats to do so, he could not quite bring himself to break with them. Instead, he lobbed accusations at them through the mail, demanding repeatedly that they apologize for their "treatment of me during my adolescence."

Turk seldom replied. But Wanda, distressed at her son's decision to abandon his career and worried about the risks he faced in the Montana wilderness, infuriated Ted by clinging to him tightly. During the winter of 1973–74, Ted claims in "Truth vs. Lies," Wanda threatened to contact local authorities if he didn't write more frequently. He became so enraged, he says he broke off contact with her for a year.

Yet Wanda's love was not easily rejected. She regularly sent him packages of candy, fruit, or magazines, but these gifts only infuriated him further. They were just what he didn't want—too sweet or too unhealthy. He became apoplectic when she insisted on sending him boxes too big for his mailbox, thereby requiring him to bicycle to the post office to pick up something he didn't want. And although he laid down strict rules about the sizes of boxes he would permit her to send, and what was allowed in them, she kept disobeying him.

October 1972:

DON'T SEND ME ANY MORE MAGAZINES. I mean it.

March 1975:

> *You sent me a Reader's Digest. Look, stupid, how many times must I tell you not to send me magazines. I have told you over and over not to send them, and you promise not to send them, then you go and send them anyway!*

November 1975:

> *Please don't send me so many packages, and please don't send smoked oysters. . . . I don't like smoked oysters. . . . The sunflower seeds you sent me were salted.*

December 1976:

> *You put some cookies in that package. Remember I said any food*
> *packages are supposed to contain only dried fruit and unsalted*
> *nuts.*

And yet again in November 1977:

> *If you want to send me a package you had better keep it down to*
> *the 4.5" width. Permissible items for package: Dried fruit, nuts,*
> *cheese.*

Anyone who has raised adolescent children can sympathize with Turk and Wanda. Blaming parents is a teenage affliction, like acne. But it is rarely justified. If parents are responsible for how their children turn out, then *their* parents are responsible for how they turn out, and the great-grandparents are responsible for how the grandparents turned out, and so on. According to this reasoning, no one is ever responsible for anything.

In fact, everyone except the clinically ill is accountable for his or her own behavior. Learning to accept responsibility is a rite of passage, called "reaching adulthood." Kaczynski, however, never reached adulthood. Emotionally, he remained a teenager. Although detesting psychology, he embraced the therapeutic mind-set, invoking psychological theories to justify blaming his parents and society, thereby excusing himself. They were guilty, he kept insisting, of "psychological abuse" or "verbal abuse."

And as his personal rage against his family and philosophical rejection of society grew, he had increasing difficulty separating the two. Although he would later deny Sally Johnson's claim that he could "direct his anger from one set of ideas to the other quite fluidly," she was, in fact, right. In explaining his motives for murder, his journal did, indeed, move fluidly between citations of his twin desires of "personal revenge" to "revenge against the system."

As he wrote on April 6, 1971, more than two months before he bought the Lincoln land,

My motive for doing what I am going to do is simply personal revenge. I do not expect to accomplish anything by it. Of course, if my crime (and my reasons for committing it) gets any public attention, it may help to stimulate public interest in the technology question and thereby improve the changes for stopping technology before it is too late; but on the other hand most people will probably be repelled by my crime, and the opponents of freedom may use it as a weapon to support their arguments for control over human behavior. I have no way of knowing whether my action will do more good than harm. I certainly don't claim to be an altruist or to be acting for the "good" (whatever that is) of the human race. I act merely from a desire for revenge. Of course, I would like to get revenge on the whole scientific and bureaucratic establishment, not to mention communists and others who threaten freedom, but, that being impossible, I have to content myself with just a little revenge.

By THE FALL of 1977, Kaczynski was extremely discouraged—disappointed in himself for failing to carry out his revenge and depressed that he had not found greater solitude. He wanted to take another trip to Canada, to look for a more remote place to live. But that required money he didn't have. So he decided to return to the Chicago area, work and save money, then go to Canada.

And at last, his secret journal records:

I think that perhaps I could now kill someone.

While in Illinois, he would plant a bomb.

I emphasize that my motivation is personal revenge. I don't pretend to any kind of philosophical or moralistic justification. The concept of morality is simply one of the psychological tools by which society controls people's behavior. My ambition is to kill a scientist, big businessman, government official, or the like. I would also like to kill a Communist.

On February 17, 1978, he wrote Turk to arrange employment at Foam Cutting Engineers near Lombard, Illinois, where his father and brother worked, explaining it was to earn money for "the northern trip." That done, in May he traveled by Greyhound bus to Illinois, arriving earlier than his parents expected and without telling them.

Before leaving Montana, I made a bomb in a kind of box, designed to explode when the box was opened. This was a long, narrow box. I picked the name of an electrical engineering professor out of the catalogue of the Rensselaer Polytechnic Institute, and addressed the bomb-package to him.

The package was too big to fit into a postbox, so Kaczynski took it to the University of Illinois Chicago Circle Campus, placing it between two parked cars in the lot near the science and technology buildings.

I am proud of what I did.

But he was also bitterly disappointed not to see any mention of a bomb explosion in the newspapers. As he wrote later that summer,

I did make an attempt with a bomb, whether successful or not I don't know.

After leaving the package, he appeared at his parents' house in Lombard as though he had just arrived from Montana. And in June, he started at Foam Cutting Engineers. But the job didn't last long. In mid-July, he fell in love with another employee named Ellen Tarmichael. When the couple had gone on a couple of dates together, however, she told him she didn't want to see him again. Devastated, on August 22 Kaczynski retaliated by posting an obscene limerick about her in the lavatories and on the walls around the factory. And when he continued doing this even after David, who was his supervisor, demanded he stop, he was fired.

While it might seem Kaczynski had reached the end of his rope, in fact the Tarmichael fiasco buoyed his spirits. The affair, he would write in his journal, *has done strange things to me. In the first place, it aroused in me hope—a hope for something worthwhile. Perhaps foolishly, I did hope that I might win, if not her love, then at least a reasonable amount of affection—physical sex too, of course, but it would have been more important to me to have her care for me than to have physical sex with her. I could get by with just holding her hand if necessary, if I thought she really cared for me. Of course, kissing her was immensely pleasurable. . . .*

Within a week, Kaczynski found new employment, with Prince Castle, a manufacturer of restaurant equipment in nearby Carol Stream, Illinois. By fall, Turk and Wanda made the first of what would be annual gifts of money to Ted and David, in preparation for reducing inheritance taxes. Initially $1,000 a piece, the amounts increased slightly until by the 1990s they reached $1,500. Now Ted could afford to make better bombs.

During the last few months [he recorded on May 6, 1979] . . . I have been troubled by frustrated hatred much less than usual. I think this is because, whenever I have experienced some outrage (such as a low-flying jet or some official stupidity reported in the paper), as I felt myself growing angry, I calmed myself by thinking—"just wait till this summer! Then I'll kill!"

And indeed, he tried. On May 9, 1979, while still working at Prince Castle, he placed a bomb in a graduate student common room at Northwestern University's Technological Institute, in Evanston, Illinois.

The bomb. . . used match-heads as an explosive. . . . The bomb was in a cigar box and was arranged to go off when the box was opened. According to the newspaper, a "graduate researcher" at northwestern [John Harris] was "hospitalized with cuts on the arms and burns around the eyes" . . . unfortunately, I didn't notice anything in the article indicating that he would suffer any permanent disability. . . .

KACZYNSKI STAYED at Prince Castle until the summer of 1979. By then he'd saved $3,000 and, his family thought, he could finally afford to take his Canada trip. In the fall, he borrowed David's car and was gone for around eight weeks—they assumed to Saskatchewan—before returning to Lombard. Later, early in December, he went back to Montana.

In "Truth vs. Lies," however, Kaczynski says that "the Canadian wilderness trip never came off." So it appears he didn't drive to Saskatchewan as his family thought, but instead returned to Montana to make another bomb. After building it, he probably returned to Lombard, mailing the device a few days later from Chicago. This was the bomb that nearly brought down American Airlines Flight 444 on November 15, 1979.

Plan to blow up airline in flight. Late summer and early autumn I constructed device. Much expense, because had to go to Gr. Falls to buy material, including barometer and many boxes of cartridges for the powder. I put more than a quart of smokeless powder in a can, rigged barometer so device would explode at 2000 FT. or conceivably as high as 3500 FT due to variation of atmospheric pressure. Late October mailed package from Chicago priority mail, so it would go by air . . . newspaper said was "low power device." Surprised me. . . . I will try again if can get better explosive. Bomb did not accomplish much. Probably destroyed some mail. . . . At least it gave them a good scare . . . the papers said FBI investigating incident. FBI suck my cock. So I came back to Montana early December now work on other plans.

24

Jihad

This is Jihad, pal. There are no innocent bystanders. . . .
We'll broaden our theater of conflict. . . . Everything, every
assumption, every institution needs to be challenged.
Now! . . . Go and get them suckers, fill-em full of steel.

> —MIKE ROSELLE,
> *Earth First! Journal* (December 1994,
> the month Thomas J. Mosser was murdered)

The amount of noise which anyone can bear undisturbed
stands in inverse proportion to his mental capacity, and
may therefore be regarded as a pretty fair measure of it.
. . . Noise is a torture to all intellectual people.

> —ARTHUR SCHOPENHAUER,
> *The World as Will and Idea*

THE PARK HOTEL on Last Chance Gulch in Helena, Montana, exists no more. In an irony Kaczynski would not appreciate, my son Sidney and his partners bought the building after Kaczynski's arrest and turned it into a state-of-the-art office complex, complete with high-speed Internet connections and other business amenities.

While Kaczynski lived in Montana, however, the Park Hotel was a local landmark. Redolent with the atmosphere of the old frontier, it was inexpensive and plain, but clean and very neat. The rooms were just big enough to hold a bed, bureau, chair, and washbasin. The bathroom was down the hall. In their simplicity and functionality, they reminded me of rooms at the Harvard Club of New York, but with better views.

Kaczynski stayed at the hotel frequently, but not for the amenities. Rather, thanks to the transportation options it afforded, it was an excellent launch pad for bombing runs. On some of these trips, according to the FBI, Kaczynski took the Rimrock Trailways bus from Lincoln to Missoula or Great Falls. On others, he hitched a ride with his postman, Dick Lundberg, directly to Helena, staying overnight at the Park Hotel. All of these places—Great Falls, Missoula, and Helena—offered bus connections to the places where he planted or mailed his bombs.

As the 1980s dawned, Kaczynski was about to become a very busy traveler indeed.

ON APRIL 18, 1980, after spending four nights at the Park Hotel, Kaczynski apparently took the bus to Chicago. He would be gone most of the summer. In Chicago on June 3, he mailed the bomb to United Airlines president Percy Wood, inside a hollowed-out copy of Sloan Wilson's *Ice Brothers*.

Kaczynski would write later,

I feel better. I am still plenty angry. I am now able to strike back! I can't strike back to anything like the extent I wish to, but I no longer feel totally helpless, and the anger duzzent gnaw at my guts as it used to.

It felt so good to be a bomber! He wrote later that year,

Since acquiring the ability to commit revenge crimes, I have found vast relief from these problems now my anger need no longer be held in. Also, I have made a change of attitude . . . my revenge crimes, because since I can strike back.

On returning to Montana, Kaczynski resumed monkeywrenching. Once he had dared to be bad, anything seemed possible. In early September, he wrote in his journal that he had finished making a pistol and resolved,

I want to use the pistol as a murder weapon.

Having taken the first steps on the slippery slope, Kaczynski now began his long slide to the bottom. There would be no turning back. His ambition to kill gave him a purpose in life, fueled his energies, and in a curious way inflated his ego. Murder represented the triumph of his will. He had broken the rules and gotten away with it. He had liberated himself from what society calls morality and he saw as "propaganda." And how sweet the revenge, when a bomb maimed or killed someone!

But Kaczynski would find that rather than offering relief, his crimes ultimately made him feel worse, not better. He had become addicted to violence. Killing and maiming produced only a temporary rush. Soon, he needed another fix. So, his campaign of terror did not cheer him up. Rather, it aggravated his rage. It forced him to avoid neighbors and lie to his family, thereby isolating him further. And it consumed money, increasing his financial dependency on his family just as he sought to break with them.

This irreconcilable conflict would take its toll.

As "INVESTIGATORS" DETERIORATE further, write Riso and Hudson, "They become extremely isolated and prey to growing eccentricity and nihilistic despair." They "take delight in deflating what they see as the bourgeois illusions by which others get through life so comfortably." They "'burn their bridges behind them,' ending friendships, quitting jobs, and emptying out all but the barest necessities in their lives. . . . They neg-

lect themselves physically, paying no attention to their appearance, eating poorly, and going unwashed. . . . They are filled with rage at a world
which they believe has rejected them. . . ."

Kaczynski picked up the pace. In October 1981, he planted his fifth
bomb in the Bennion Hall Business Building at the University of Utah,
which authorities intercepted. In April 1982, he mailed his sixth bomb
to Professor Patrick Fischer of Vanderbilt University, seriously injuring
Fischer's secretary, Janet Smith. On July 2, 1982, he took a bus to
Berkeley and placed bomb number seven on the floor of Room 411 of
the Cory Hall Mathematics Building at the University of California,
maiming Professor Diogenes Angelakos.

As these murderous peregrinations continued, Kaczynski's already
strained family relations worsened. He and his brother had become so
estranged by May 1982 that he bought David's share of the Lincoln
property, so that they wouldn't have to do business with each other any
more.

The incessant, acrimonious correspondence with Wanda continued.
She kept sending him food he didn't want. He became livid when, in May
1982, she sent him a package of nuts and dried fruits. Although these
items were on his "permitted" list, he explained to David, "the package got
me very upset, because I've asked her repeatedly—a thousand times!—
not to send me any packages without my permission beforehand."

Ted still demanded an apology from his parents for their alleged
treatment of him as a teenager. But Turk was silent and nothing Wanda
said seemed to satisfy him. On Christmas Eve 1984, she gently advised
him that he needed to learn to forgive and to keep on loving. But this
triggered another round of white-hot anger: Kaczynski charged that she
never acknowledged the "vicious insults" his parents had hurled at him.
She was just looking for an excuse not to accept responsibility for her
"psychological abuse."

Wanda sought to keep and love her son. Turk remained aloof. Ted
wanted independence, but also an apology. David played peacemaker.
Yet, despite repeated threats to do so, Ted could not bring himself to
make a clean break. He needed the stipend the family provided to pay
for his bombs.

✧ ✧ ✧

As "INVESTIGATORS" NEAR the bottom, say Riso and Hudson, "They have reduced their activities and living conditions to the point where there is nowhere left to retreat." They cannot sleep and "are unable to stop the destructive force of their distorted thinking because they have cut themselves off from almost all of the constructive outlets for their tremendous mental energies." They "would like to destroy *everything*, so detestable has the world become in their eyes. . . . Life becomes unbearable . . . their minds are devouring them. . . . When others question their self-destructive escapism, their responses can be abusive and infantile" (italics in original).

Kaczynski's life had become a living hell. Everything bothered him—the neighbors, the noise, Wanda's uninvited parcels, David's fuzzy thinking—because he was so busy. Busy making bombs. The interruptions interfered with his mission of revenge. He ate less, became increasingly unkempt. His insomnia and heart arrhythmia grew worse. He began taking antidepressants, but with little effect.

By 1985, the pace had become feverish. In May, he traveled to Berkeley, placing bomb number eight in Cory Hall, which nearly killed Air Force captain John Hauser. The same month, he mailed bomb number nine from Oakland to the Boeing Aircraft Company's Fabrication Division in Auburn, Washington, but it failed to explode. In November, he again traveled to Salt Lake City, where on the 12th he mailed bomb number ten to James V. McConnell, injuring both McConnell and his assistant, Nick Suino. And even before the McConnell bomb was on the way to its target, Kaczynski was at work on a bigger bomb that, as his coded journal recorded, he hoped would fulfill all his dreams of murder.

His secret notes explain how he filled his days:

In the morning of October 3rd [1985], we placed under the igniting wire the first part of the #3 mixture. In the morning of October 6th, we added a little more of the #3 mixture, in order to bring the top of the black powder mass closer to the igniting wire.

In the afternoon of October 8th, the paste of #2 mixture was placed on the igniting wire. In the afternoon of October 9th, another paper

cone was correctly placed on the ignitor, the powder paste was fin-
ished, and the cone was filled with the paste of #3 mixture.

On the afternoon of October 11th, the paper was removed from
the ignitor. At noon on October 24th, the ignitor was covered with
a layer of a 5-minute epoxy, and later with a layer of brown wrap-
ping paper glued with a 5-minute epoxy.

At noon on October 25th the ignitor was covered with a layer of
paraffin. The paraffin was then scratched with a razor blade, so
there was only a very thin layer left.

[October 29], we put in the pipe the lid with the ignitor and we
sealed everything well with epoxy. On the afternoon of November
15th, 7.639 units of #4 mixture were prepared and placed in the
pipe.

[November 16] . . . the lid was placed on the open end of the pipe
and everything was sealed well with epoxy . . . the device itself
(that is, the pipe with its contents and cover) is now finished.

On December 8th, around 10:00am (official time) the last con-
nection was soldered (fig. 13). The device was deployed on Decem-
ber 11th, 1985.

December 11, 1985, Rentech bomb placed in Sacramento.

[Last entry, December 27] . . . the device detonated [December
11] with very good results.

Bomb number eleven eviscerated Hugh Scrutton, owner of Rentech
Computer Rental Company in Sacramento, on December 11, 1985.

WANDA, TURK, AND DAVID were the only people who really loved Ted.
Without them, he was totally alone. But he rejected them, not only

because he could not control his anger but also because his crimes forced him to lie to them:

> *I recently wrote a letter to my brother, that the inhibitions that have been trained into me are too strong to permit me ever to commit a serious crime. This may surprize reader considering some things reported in these notes but motive is clear. I want to avoid any possible suspicion on my brother's part!*

His guilt also added to his isolation. For despite repeated denials, Kaczynski did indeed have a conscience. And every time pangs of remorse arose, he fought to dismiss them. They were, he kept reassuring himself, signs of weakness. A sense of guilt was a failing, a symptom that one had been brainwashed. Superior persons such as himself could and should, by exercising intelligence and will power, overcome such feelings. As a man of science, he knew that there is no morality.

But try as he might, Kacynski could not erase these feelings altogether. "Guilty feelings?" he asked himself after the Percy Wood bombing.

> *Yes, a little. Occasionally I have bad dreams in which the police are after me. Or in which I am threatened with punishment from some supernatural source. Such as the Devil. But these dont occur often enuf to be a problem.*

After his bomb had maimed Captain John Hauser, he recorded:

> *I must admit I feel badly about having crippled this mans arm. It has been bothering me a good deal. This is embarrassing because while my feelings are partly from pity, I am sure they come largely from the training, propaganda, brainwashing we all get, conditioning us to be scared by the idea of doing certain things. It is shameful to be under the sway of this brainwashing. But donot [sic] get the idea that I regret what I did.*

In February 1987, Kaczynski traveled yet again to Salt Lake City, planting bomb number twelve behind the CAAMS computer store on the 20th. Nearly an exact replica of the Rentech bomb, it was potentially very deadly. But the would-be victim this time, CAAMS vice president Gary Wright, was lucky. Wright was seriously injured but not killed. Further, Kaczynski was seen placing the bomb by an employee of a neighboring business.

The bomber, the FBI reported, was "a white male, approximately 25–30 years old, 5'10" to 6' in height, 165 pounds, lean, wiry build, with a reddish, rough looking complexion and strawberry blond colored moustache and no other facial hair." It was a good portrait of Kaczynski and it gave him a fright.

Description (several versions). The "composite drawing" did not show any beard, although it did show a small mustache.

Sobered by this narrow escape, and determined to find a more perfect detonator, between 1987 and the summer of 1992, Kaczynski took a sabbatical from bombing. At secret sites in the wilderness behind his cabin, he tested new mixtures and devices. He continued monkey-wrenching. And he carried on his verbal war with David and Wanda.

He reacted with fury when David wrote him in 1989 to say that he planned to live with his future wife, Linda Patrik. Please don't write me again, Ted responded, except in emergency. In that case, he instructed David to place a red line on the envelope beneath the stamp to indicate its importance. He would destroy unread any missive lacking the red line.

In 1990, David wrote Ted to invite him to his July wedding. Ted didn't answer. In September, David wrote again to announce that Turk was seriously ill. Ted replied that their father's illness was an appropriate use of the red line. When Turk, terminally ill with cancer, shot himself on October 2, David wrote Ted to invite him to the memorial service. Ted didn't come.

Eleven days later, Ted finally did write to David, saying that he hadn't "shed any tears" over their father's death. Expressing sorrow for Wanda, he confessed, "I never resented her quite as much as I resented Dad." Turk's intelligence had turned the man against life. And, Ted believed, he vented this bleak disillusion by tormenting his oldest son.

Turk's death, however, did not bring the familial bickering to an end. Ted would repeatedly announce he was breaking ties with his family forever, then ask for money. Early in 1991, he wrote to David proposing he relinquish his share of Turk's estate in exchange for $60,000. He was turned down, but according to the FBI, Wanda did send him $7,000 somewhat later. Yet he treated her no better. When, in June 1991, Wanda wrote to apologize for whatever errors she may have made in raising him and to say she and Turk still loved him, Ted became furious that she would call their treatment of him an accident and not intentional.

Yet again, Ted insisted on terminating contact with his family.

> *I have got to know, I have GOT TO, GOT TO, GOT TO know that every last tie joining me to this stinking family has been cut FOREVER and that I will never NEVER have to communicate with any of you again. . . . I've got to do it NOW. I can't tell you how desperate I am. . . . It is killing me.*

By now, everyone close to Kaczynski saw a change in him. He was more doggedly reclusive than ever. His neighbor Chris Waits, the piano teacher and logger, noted that he seemed to be getting thinner, less kempt. Even his library friends—Sherri Wood and Mary Spurlin—while still fond of Ted, noticed a decline. He came to the library less frequently, "and he looked awful," Spurlin told me.

"Thinner every time he came in," Wood said.

"Something worrying him," Spurlin added.

UNHEALTHY INVESTIGATORS who reach the final stage of disintegration, write Riso and Hudson, "feel as though they had no space left, even in their own minds . . . they have collapsed into one continuous experience of pain and horror." Those "who do not take their own lives may end up living a life of helplessness, dependency, or incarceration—the very situation they most feared. . . . Fearing that they have reached some sort of horrible dead end, they may compulsively do permanent harm to themselves or someone else."

By the summer of 1992, after much experimentation at his secret wilderness testing sites, Kaczynski had developed his "perfect detonator," which the following June, 1993, he "tested" on Dr. Charles Epstein in San Francisco (bomb number thirteen) and on David Gelernter (number fourteen) at Yale, nearly killing both men. Once he found the formula, he began making two devices at a time. But this meant more expenses. The cost of materials, travel, and disguises ate into his meager resources, leaving him almost nothing to live on.

In May 1994, Kaczynski started simultaneously on what would become bombs number fifteen and sixteen that would kill Thomas Mosser and Gilbert Murray. And by October, both were complete. But he was out of cash. Once again, he was forced to ask his family for money.

In November he wrote to David requesting a $1,000 loan. After his faithful brother sent him a cashier's check for this amount, he was off again, this time to San Francisco, where he mailed the bomb that killed Burson-Marsteller vice president Thomas J. Mosser on December 10.

By now, his need to kill was out of control. After returning from San Francisco, Kaczynski wrote David, this time asking for $2,000. His brother responded with a cashier's check for that amount in January 1995. Then, on March 27, Ted sold David's original half interest in the Lincoln lot back to his brother, either as collateral for the earlier loans or for yet further sums. By that time, according to the FBI, Kaczynski had received over $16,000 from his family since 1985.

Supplied with the necessary funds, in April, Kaczynski journeyed to Oakland, where on the 20th—the day after McVeigh and Nichols blew up the Alfred P. Murrah Federal Building in Oklahoma City—he mailed the bomb that would kill Gil Murray four days later. It didn't matter that Murray was not his intended target. He was pleased anyway. He was proud of what he had done and wanted to boast about it.

It was at this point that Kaczynski began writing to newspapers and prominent scientists more frequently—taunting, boasting, threatening. In June 1995, he sent off his manifesto to the *New York Times*, the *Washington Post*, and *Penthouse*, with his promise that if they published, he would "permanently desist from terrorism." And when, in September, the *Post* did publish his essay, it seemed that his reign of terror had indeed come to an end.

Yet on June 24, 1995, the very same day Kaczynski mailed the manifesto with its accompanying "publish or perish" threat to the three publications, he mailed a new threat to the *San Francisco Chronicle*:

> WARNING: *The terrorist group FC, called Unabomber by the FBI,
> is planning to blow up an airline out of Los Angeles International
> Airport sometime during the next six days. To prove that the writer
> of this letter knows something about FC, the first two digits of
> their identifying number are 55 [referring to the false Social Secu-
> rity number].*

The note made national news and prompted aviation authorities
to install what were then extreme security measures, slowing air traffic and disrupting travel. The airmail system was shut down while
postal inspectors checked packages. Then on June 28, just four days
after he had sent the manifesto to the *Times*, the *Post*, and *Penthouse*,
Kacynski mailed yet another missive, explaining that the airline bomb
threat had been "one last prank" on the public, "to remind them who
we are."

It should have been clear that Kaczynski wasn't through. He had
finally achieved the "revenge" and recognition that he long craved. He
relished the attention. Simultaneously, physically and emotionally, he
had reached the end of his rope. Terrorism and serial murder had
become his raison d'etre. If he gave them up, what would he do with
himself?

The rewards for murder had become too great. Almost certainly he
would not stop killing, whether he had made a promise to do so or not.
For him, breaking a promise would not have been hard. He lied about
his crimes continually to his family and others. And his analytical mind
was good at finding technical excuses—fine print that only he could
read—for his deceptions and violence. Surely, it was capable of finding
a rationale for breaking his commitment to the newspapers.

When authorities arrested Kaczynski on April 3, 1996, they found a
fully prepared bomb, identical to the one that had killed Murray, under
his bed. Wrapped and ready to go, all it lacked, one FBI agent told me,
"was the address label."

Who would have been next? A few weeks before his arrest Kaczynski recorded ominously:

> *My opposition to the technological society now is less a matter of a bitter and sullen personal revenge than formerly. I now have more of a sense of* mission.

The personal motives may have changed, but the political objectives remained the same. Ted Kaczynski had found his calling.

25

Ted Kaczynski and the Rise of Modern Terrorism

We therefore advocate a revolution against the industrial system, This revolution may or may not make use of violence; it may be sudden or it may be a relatively gradual process spanning a few decades.

—THEODORE J. KACZYNSKI,
"Industrial Society and Its Future"

The battle has moved to inside America. We will work to continue this battle, God permitting, until victory.

—OSAMA BIN LADEN,
Interview on Al Jazeera television, October 2001

Today, Ted Kaczynski is serving four consecutive life sentences in a maximum-security prison in Florence, Colorado. And although his plea bargain with the government specifically waived the right of appeal, immediately after sentencing on May 4, 1998, he began preparing one anyway. Unable to find an attorney, he filed the brief himself, claiming that his guilty pleas had been coerced.

By formulating a "mental state" defense against his wishes, Kaczynski argued, his attorneys sought to put his sanity on trial—a prospect he claimed so unendurable that he had no choice but to plead guilty, to avoid a trial altogether. And by refusing to allow him to fire his attorneys and hire replacements or represent himself, the court, he said, had violated his constitutional right to direct his own defense.

This pleading revealed Kaczynski's passionate suspicion of psychologists as well as his strong desire to be judged on his ideas, not his psyche. If he had been granted a new trial, he would have argued that his killings were necessary in order to save the world from a greater evil—namely, the growing threat of industrial civilization. And while most legal experts believe this would have been an unpersuasive and even suicidal defense strategy leading directly to a guilty verdict and a death sentence, it was apparent that Kaczynski preferred to die a martyr for his ideas rather than live the rest of his life in prison.

But he lost the appeal. Although the Ninth Circuit Court agreed to hear it, the judges ultimately refused to grant him a new trial. And when in March 2002 the Supreme Court declined to hear the case, his options had run out.

So Kaczynski will remain confined alone in a small cell whose narrow window affords no view of the mountains he loves so much. But while out of sight, he is not out of play. Through letters, he maintains relations with many people he knew before his arrest.

And although most scholars continue to ignore his manifesto philosophy, Kaczynski has attracted a large following of new admirers among political activists. Indeed, he has become an inspiration and a sort of leader in exile for the burgeoning "green anarchist" movement. In a letter to me, Kaczynski made clear that he keeps in contact with other anarchists, including John Zerzan, the intellectual leader of a circle in Eugene, Oregon, who was among the few people to visit Kaczynski while he was in jail in Sacramento, awaiting trial. Theresa Kintz, one of Zerzan's fellow anarchists, was reportedly the first writer to whom Kaczynski granted an interview after his arrest. Writing for the London-based *Green Anarchist*, Kintz quoted Kaczynski as saying, "For those who realize the need to do away with the technoindustrial system, if you work for its collapse, in effect you are killing a lot of people."

The *Los Angeles Times* reported that in June 1999 two thousand of Zerzan's comrades rioted in Eugene, smashing computers, breaking shop windows, throwing bricks at cars, and injuring eight police officers. According to the *Seattle Times*, followers of Zerzan's also arrived in force at the December 1999 "Battle of Seattle" at the World Trade Organization meeting, where they smashed shop windows, flattened tires, and dumped garbage cans on the street. Kaczynski continues to comment approvingly on the violent exploits of environmental radicals. In a letter to the Denver television reporter Rick Sallinger, he expressed support for the Earth Liberation Front's 1998 arson of the Vail ski resort, which destroyed more than $12 million worth of property.

"I fully approve of [the arson]," he wrote Sallinger, "and I congratulate the people who carried it out." Kaczynski went on to commend an editorial in the *Earth First! Journal* by Kintz, who wrote: "The Earth Liberation Front's ecosabotage of Vail constituted a political act of conscience perfectly in keeping with the sincere expression of the biocentric paradigm many Earth First!ers espouse."

So Kaczynski remains to some a political prisoner, to others mentally disturbed or just plain evil. But however problematic these characterizations, one thing remains clear: He is a terrorist.

IN AN ARTICLE published in *The American Scholar* in 1960, while assisting Murray's experiments on Kaczynski and his cohort, Kenneth Keniston asked:

> *Why are young people increasingly unwilling to accept what their culture offers them? And, closely related to this, why do we lack positive visions of the future? . . . Psychological accounts alone are seldom adequate to explain attitudes and stances which characterize large numbers of people simultaneously. To understand these as*

social phenomena, we must trace the complicated interplay of cul-
tural and historical forces which, by their influence on individual
families and other agencies of "socialization," produce individuals
who are unusually sensitized to special aspects of their environ-
ment.

If Kaczynski's life and psyche were entirely unique, then a purely personal analysis of his biography might be sufficient to understand him. But he is not unique. Psychological compulsion alone did not drive him to this point. Rather, his turn to terrorism fits a pattern. He is a child of his time, shaped in part, to be sure, by his personal history and even perhaps his genes, but also by his embracing, of his own free will, ideas that make the era in which we live a time of terror.

The ideas that Kaczynski embraced were products of two historical trends: a crisis of reason and the Cold War. Together, they helped pro-duce the culture of despair, inspiring not just Kaczynski's philosophy but countless other ideologies of rage as well.

The crisis of reason was a loss of faith in what the Declaration of Independence called the "self-evident" truths that individual rights and the legitimacy of government derived from "the laws of nature." By the 1950s, this belief had been undermined in academic circles especially (as we have seen) by the success of science and its companion philoso-phy, positivism. And this philosophy convinced many—including Kaczynski—that as only empirically verifiable statements are meaning-ful, moral and political beliefs, such as those expressed in the Declara-tion, being untestable, are nonrational as well. Government rests, they concluded, not on "laws of nature" as the founding fathers supposed, but on power alone. By removing ethics from the equation, positivism laid the foundation for radical ideologies—including Kaczynski's—which preached that "the system" was illegitimate and violent overthrow acceptable.

The Cold War accelerated this evolution. It created a climate of fear. It stimulated technological progress, provoking an antimodernist backlash in environmentalists and religious fundamentalists of various faiths. By equating scientific progress with national survival, it encouraged researchers to abuse the rights of students and others. It fed the hubris of some psychologists, encouraging them to seek ways of modifying behavior, to make people "better" citizens. It gave birth to the drug culture and to a generalized disillusionment with America and it government.

Kaczynski's brilliant mind proved fertile ground for these thoughts. Although clearly neurotic, the best clinical evidence suggests he is quite sane. He willingly chose to kill, and his prideful intellect provided the rationale for doing so. It shaped and directed the powerful fury he felt toward his parents and toward a society that ignored him. As Tom Wolfe remarked, the human psyche is not a boiler room but a computer. "Letting off steam" does not reduce anger but encourages it, by allowing it to feed on itself, thus forming a feedback loop that spins faster and faster until the computer crashes. And Kaczynski crashed.

He despised what he believed was a cold, distant, and morose father, a controlling and ambitious mother, a conformist and intellectually hostile high school environment, pressures to excel, and ensuing social isolation. Countless other bright young students suffered similar hurts, but Kaczynski among the few, being more brilliant than most, transformed his frustrations into an ideology. And his experiences at Harvard proved to be crucial.

It was at Harvard that Kaczynski encountered the culture of despair and found the ideas he would put into the manifesto. It was there that he became a true believer in the scientific method and its philosophy, positivism, which allowed him to think that morality was meaningless. It was there that, by his own admission, his developing alienation bloomed into disillusionment with society. It was there that he endured Professor Murray's deceptive experiments—an experience that triggered a suspicion of psychology and "the system" of which it is a part, and would soon be followed by nightmares about psychologists.

And it was in all probability this professor—an establishment persona who fancied himself a father figure to students—who became the catalyst for transforming Kaczynski's anger at individuals into philosophical fury against industrial society, and the central role that psychology plays therein.

Indeed, perhaps the charming professor was "Big Daddy Lombrosis," the nightmare figure whom Kaczynski describes as "kindly, paternal, dignified," looking "like a man whom one could respect," yet nevertheless fearsome, who sought to dominate him psychologically through "some sort of deception." In Lombrosis as in Murray, Kaczynski's hatred toward his father and suspicion of "the system" come together. While Lombrosis may, as Professor Donald Foster suggests, have stood for Turk, more likely he embodied both Turk (the father whom Kaczynski feared and hated—and Murray (the father figure who symbolized social authority). As the only leading psychologist Kaczynski knew personally, Murray represented the establishment. And this establishment, Kaczynski thought, threatened liberty. Like Lombrosis, he thought it demanded *"submission."* And so his intelligence transformed familial anger into a philosophical screed calling for retaliation.

Of course, he didn't have to retaliate. Curiously, Kaczynski revered Joseph Conrad and Jacques Ellul, both of whom deplored violence and advocated the spiritual life.

Action, Conrad warns in *Nostromo*, "is the enemy of thought and the friend of flattering illusions." What Kurtz forgot—the narrator, Marlow, reminds readers in *Heart of Darkness*—is that survival does not come through intelligence but through faith. "You want deliberate belief," he advises. " . . . Your strength comes in . . . your power of devotion, not to yourself, but to an obscure, backbreaking business."

In *Autopsy of Revolution* (the English-language edition that Kaczynski read was published in 1971, the year Kaczynski arrived in Montana), Ellul argued that political revolutions cannot topple technology, because even revolutionaries must make use of it. Such a revolution, he wrote, "still serves technology . . . and will be forced to restore society through technology." So the "'revolution' will not have happened at all."

"If you would be genuinely revolutionary," Ellul suggested,

> . . . be contemplative: that is the source of individual strength to break the system. It would represent a vital breach in the technological society, a truly revolutionary attitude, if contemplation could replace frantic activity. Contemplation fills the void of our society of lonely men.

And Ellul continued, quoting the Nobel Prize–winning Mexican writer Octavio Paz:

> "I write to discover, because contemplation is the art of discovering things that science and technology cannot reveal. Contemplation

restores to man the spiritual breadth of which technology divests him, to objects their significance, and to work its functional presence. Contemplation is the key to individual survival today."

Kaczynski, however, paid no attention. Blinded by scientism and rage, he missed the message of Ellul, Paz, and Conrad altogether. And so would many of his and later generations. For the same social and intellectual conditions that influenced him continue to flourish today.

Bright youths now are no less alienated than they were when Kaczynski was growing up. High schools still incubate alienation, particularly among brighter students, as the authoritarian and antiintellectual atmosphere of Kaczynski's generation continues. Colleges, high schools, even grade schools still propagate the culture of despair, scaring youth with tales of impending ecological collapse. In the universities, the crisis of reason deepens as traditional disciplines of the liberal arts—literature, philosophy, and history, the very disciplines that promote the contemplation Ellul and Paz felt was essential for human survival—are subverted by politicizing methodologies or give ground to social sciences such as psychology, sociology, and political science, all dedicated, according to their practitioners, to "prediction and control" of human behavior.

Deceptive psychological research, such as Kaczynski experienced, is more common today than it was in Murray's time, and remains, as one recent scholarly article put it, "an extremely popular methodological tool." In 1946, according to one survey of this practice, only 18 percent of all psychological experiments on human subjects involved deception. By 1963, the figure had risen to 38 percent. By 1996, according to an updated review, it reached 42 percent.

Perhaps not coincidentally, adolescent alienation is more common. In the earlier era, youthful anomie attracted widespread concern among educators. Today, it goes largely unremarked. Meanwhile, high schools are even less dedicated to learning than they were, choosing instead to ensure that students conform to the canons of political and behavioral correctness, by the administration of drugs such as Ritalin and Luvox and what teachers call "behavior modification."

The anger that motivated Kaczynski bears an uncanny resemblance to the rage that drove the schoolboys who in recent years have gone berserk, shooting classmates. Like Kaczynski, the Columbine High School killers, Eric Harris and Dylan Klebold, were motivated by rage, not only against those they saw despoiling the environment but also against the dominant school culture that ridiculed them. *Newsweek* reports that, tormented by classmates for being different, they would walk through the halls of the school "with their heads down, because if they looked up they'd get thrown into lockers and get called a 'fag.'" Physically threatened and jeered as "dirt bags" and "inbreeds," their rage exploded.

Not surprisingly, many middle-class Americans, especially among the educated elite, remain gripped by despair. Alienating philosophies, offering the false promise of quick solutions through violence, proliferate.

Meanwhile, many people turn a blind eye to violence in their own midst. Although condemning terrorist acts committed in the name of political agendas of which they do not approve, they ignore the savagery prompted by ideals they share. Indeed, some seem reasonably comfortable with mayhem short of murder, as long as it is done for a cause they support: just as some conservatives are untroubled by antiabortion bombings or by the rise of armed militias, others condone violence putatively committed on behalf of animals or the environment. Extremist animal rights groups continue to receive support from many celebrities. The national media still depicts monkeywrenching as humorous "guerrilla theater," performed by lovable idealists. And trendy philanthropies still support some extreme groups, thereby conferring respectability on them.

With these social forces at work, it should not come as a surprise that, as the *Wall Street Journal* noted after a bomb exploded at the 1996 Atlanta Olympics, "Terrorism for the U.S. now has many faces."

Over the past five years, FBI director Louis J. Freeh told Congress in May 2001, "the level of [terrorist] acts committed in the United States have [sic] increased steadily," including "the number of cases or incidents involving use or threatened use of [weapons of mass destruction]."

According to the FBI, explosive and incendiary bombings doubled during the first four years of the 1990s. And what the agency calls "single-issue" terrorism (that would include Kaczynski's) has become increasingly prominent. As Freeh told Congress in 1999, "The most recognizable single issue terrorists at the present time are those involved in the violent animal rights, anti-abortion, and environmental protection movements . . . the potential for destruction has increased as terrorists have turned toward large improvised explosive devices to inflict maximum damage."

Eco- and animal rights excesses continue. As James F. Jarboe, domestic terrorism section chief of the FBI's Counterterrorism Division told Congress in February 2002, the Animal Liberation Front (ALF) and the Earth Liberation Front (ELF) have "become the nation's most destructive domestic extremist groups," committing "more than 600 criminal acts in the United States since 1996, [which resulted] in damages in excess of $43 million."

Even as Kaczynski was being arraigned, according to Reuters news service, just a few miles from his home, "Bands of Khaki-outfitted, armed warriors traverse the forests and mountains in order, they say, to save the land from destruction by logging and mining interests." Ric Valois, leader of these "Environmental Rangers," "roams the land along the Blackfoot river of Montana, a 9mm pistol strapped to his hip, on the lookout for any signs of encroachment by 'outsiders.'"

"We are armed to the teeth," he reportedly said. "We carry semiautomatics and combat shotguns because we are determined to win."

After concluding a ten-month investigation of this phenomenon, *The* (Portland) *Oregonian* reported in 1999:

> *Escalating sabotage to save the environment has inflicted tens of millions of dollars in damage and placed lives at risk . . . Arsons, bombings and sabotage in the name of saving the environment and its creatures have swept the American West over the last two decades, and Oregon is increasingly the center of it. At least 100 major acts of such violence have occurred since 1980, causing $42.8 million in damages.*

The Oregonian found that "during the last four years alone, the West has been rocked by 33 substantial incidents, with damages reaching $28.8 million." And although these crimes started nearly two decades ago, "they have escalated dangerously, sometimes with the use of bombs, in the last six years."

Indeed, between January 1999 and March 2002, the Earth Liberation Front and its allies, according to *The Oregonian*, are suspected in
sixty-nine more major arson attacks. Among them were the May 2001
destruction of a horticultural research center at the University of Washington; the July 2001 burning of an oil company building in suburban
Detroit; and the early 2002 destruction, by ELF, of a University of Minnesota genetic research center under construction, which caused
$630,000 in damages.

And although no one in America—other than three of Kaczynski's
victims—has yet been killed by earth, animal, or anarchist fanatics,
investigators consider it merely a matter of time. "I think we've come
very close to that line," one federal agent told *The Oregonian*, "and we
will cross that line unless we deal with this problem."

LAW ENFORCEMENT agencies still distinguish between "domestic" and
"international" terrorism, yet such movements have never recognized
national boundaries. Both the ALF and the ELF were founded in England, where many of their American operatives were trained. Before he
was captured in the Sudan in 1994 and turned over to French authorities, one of the most infamous terrorists of all time, Ilich Ramirez
Sanchez, alias "Carlos the Jackal," had worked for Libya, Iraq, Syria,
Cuba, the Popular Front for the Liberation of Palestine, Italy's Red
Brigade, Columbia's M-19 Movement, and Germany's Baader-Meinhof
Gang.

Thanks to the Internet, cell phones, and air travel, today many terrorist organizations maintain a truly global presence. Some join together
to form alliances for the purposes of trading in drugs and guns or laun-
dering money. Others, such as Kaczynski's allies, the anarchists, already
form a global network. Osama bin Laden's henchmen hail from scores
of countries—including, as the case of John Walker Lindh attests,
America itself.

Driving this convergence is a startling universality of philosophy. All
terrorists, homegrown or foreign, see themselves as players in a broad
historical drama, whether it be Islam's fight against Christianity, the proletariat's war against imperialism, or a people's struggle for liberation

against foreign oppressors. They all have long memories: Al Qaeda seeks to avenge what it views as acts of Western imperialism dating back to the Crusades. The IRA hasn't forgotten centuries of English occupation. South American guerrillas seek to undo Cortés and Pizarro's sixteenth-century conquests of Mexico and Peru.

There are indeed distinctions to be made among these philosophies. Some claim to fight for national liberation or an interpretation of the Koran, Bible, or the U.S. Constitution, others for anarchism, Marxism, animals, or the environment. But there is one idea they all share: hatred of modernity. They all endorse, in one form or another, what Arthur Lovejoy and George Boas called "cultural primitivism" and described as "the discontent of the civilized with civilization, or with some conspicuous and characteristic feature of it."

Call it the crisis of modernism. What began as an academic problem—a loss of confidence in ancient Western notions about reason—has transmogrified into a vast political assault on contemporary civilization. "Industrialism is a *system*, an entire, inescapable net of social organization," writes an editorialist in the February 16, 1998, "Industrial Civilization Collapse" issue of the radical environmentalist paper, *Live Wild or Die!* "The Machine is, or soon will be, everywhere. . . . It is the industrial empire—its technological, mechanical, political, social, psychological and economic apparatus combined into a unified operation, the Machine—that is responsible for the state of the planet and our daily living conditions. . . . So don't recycle this paper, use it to start a sawmill on fire!"

"I tell you, freedom and human rights in America are doomed," Osama bin Laden prophesied in a television interview. "The U.S. government will lead the American people—and the West in general—into an unbearable hell and a choking life."

These people, like Kaczynski, feel threatened by civilization. They despise the contemporary nation-state, which they see as big, repressive, and unresponsive to the needs of people. In response, they would destroy everything. And they perceive the enemy not merely as governments but as entire societies. So, in their eyes, everyone is fair game. As bin Laden put it, there is no "differential between those dressed in military uniforms and civilians. They are all targets in this fatwa."

✧ ✧ ✧

THE REAL STORY of Ted Kaczynski and contemporary terrorism is one of the nature of modern evil—evil that results from the corrosive powers of intellect itself, and its arrogant tendency to put ideas above common humanity. It stems from our capacity to conceive theories or philosophies that promote violence or murder in order to avert supposed injustices or catastrophes, to acquiesce to historical necessity, or to find the final solution to the world's problems—and by this process of abstraction to dehumanize our enemies.

Mass and indiscriminate murder is the crime of educated people, not because they are worse than others but because intelligence leads some to commit hubris, the sin of intellectual pride. It seduces them into believing that they have a right to decide what is best for others. It prompts them to ignore Immanuel Kant's advice—to "treat humanity, whether in your own person or that of another, always as an end and never as a means only"—and instead tempts them to view others as merely the means to fulfillment of theories.

And although the vast majority of educated people never turn to crime, history reveals that intellect is, indeed, a prerequisite for accomplishing mass murder. During the twentieth century, movements founded or led by intellectuals killed nearly 200 million people. General Tōjō Hideki, whose Japanese regime murdered an estimated 15 million, mostly Chinese, graduated at the top of his class at the Imperial Army Staff College and headed the military's so-called Control Faction, an association of officers promoting technological modernization.

The Nazi Party, responsible for the death of over 40 million, was conceived and led by Germany's best and brightest: IQ tests given their leaders on trial at Nuremberg after the war ranked the most senior leadership—including Hermann Goering, Rudolf Hess, and race theorist Alfred Rosenberg—in the 90th percentile, in other words, higher than nine out of ten people. The concentration camp doctors who performed sadistic experiments on inmates were educated men, devoted to science.

All twentieth-century Communist movements—which collectively murdered 100 million souls, according to the *Black Book of Communism*, a compilation of their crimes by leading French scholars—were conceived or led by educated or exceptionally brilliant men. Vladimir Ilich Ulyanov, otherwise known as Lenin, whose Russian Communist regime he established would murder 20 million of its own people, was a certified genius, voracious reader, and exceptional linguist, who graduated top in his high school class. Banned from the universities because his brother had been executed as a terrorist, Lenin taught himself law, completing a four-year program in one year, then took the top grade in the bar exam.

Mao Zedong, whose government murdered 65 million Chinese, was an avid reader and former teacher, historians tell us, who valued education highly. Pol Pot, who orchestrated the "killing fields" in Cambodia that extinguished the lives of another 2 million, converted to Marxism while studying in Paris on a government scholarship.

And so it continues. "Carlos the Jackal" earned a degree at Patrice Lumumba University in Moscow, the Soviet school of ideology and terrorism. Osama bin Laden has a degree in economics and business administration. Even Timothy McVeigh, who dropped out of the Bryant and Stratton Business College in New York, in part for financial reasons, was an exceptionally bright student who received a near-record score on one of his last exams at the college.

The September 11, 2001, attacks by Al Qaeda suicide killers on the Pentagon and the World Trade Center in New York City were indeed barbaric. But although greater in scale than most terrorist atrocities, they were far from unique. Nor will they be the last. Indeed, the worst may be yet to come. For it is not at all clear whether we understand what the conflict is really about.

This isn't "war" in the conventional sense. It cannot be won by the military, or by better propaganda or public relations. The foe is not just bin Laden. The real enemy is all around us, and sometimes within us as well. Terrorism is as much a product of our own history, ideas, and values as those of other peoples. It is about what we consider education, the intellect, ethics, and even civilization to be. Defeating this enemy will require that we come to terms with modernism—not just science and technology but also, especially, its political thinking. A flawed conception of reason created the culture of despair, which in turn transformed our time into an age of ideologies, and these ideologies are now killing us. By politicizing everything, we leave ourselves no sanctuary.

Until the nations of the world condemn terrorism in every form, no matter what the apparent political rationale, until they recognize that despite apparently disparate agendas all terrorists follow the same logic and share similar goals, until they see that their ultimate aim is the destruction of modern life itself, no one is safe. And until the cognitive styles that encourage these crimes—the moral confusion, despair, perversion of religious faiths, hubris of science, and proliferation of ideologies—cease, more people will die.

In short, to win this war, the society must mend itself, too. Bright school students must be made to feel prized. Educators should end their efforts to engineer social conformity. Despair should be replaced by an optimistic faith in our highest ideals, and the liberal arts, representing the best of civilization, should be returned to college curricula. The public and media must rethink the role of ideologies in modern life. Until then, America and the West generally will remain a source as well as a victim of terrorism.

Unfortunately, in reacting to the dreadful events of September 2001, our government, not having learned from history, may condemn us to repeat it. For its version of the "war on terror" is taking on all the trappings of the Cold War. Once again we hear calls for more governmental secrecy, more intrusions into the private lives of ordinary Americans, more restrictions on travel and public behavior, more emphasis on military solutions, more "sykewarriors" and propaganda experts, and less accountability by public officials. These are precisely the trappings of modernity that trigger alienation. By taking these steps, government may in fact increase terrorism rather than reduce it.

As we await the outcome of society's response, Kaczynski's ideology of choice—anarchism—continues to gain converts at an alarming rate. The spring 2002 *Green Anarchist*, which lists Kaczynski as a "prisoner of war," published an article by him in which he urged the movement to "eliminate the entire techno-industrial system." To "hit where it hurts," he advised would-be revolutionaries to "attack the vital organs of the system," such as the electric power grid, communications, computers, "the propaganda industry," including "the entertainment industry, the educational system, journalism, advertising, public relations . . . (and) the mental health industry." But "the best target" would be the leadership of the biotechnology industry. "You have to strike at its head," he explained.

Meanwhile, Kacynski's antiglobalist allies were already taking to the streets. In July 2001, in Genoa, Italy, 300,000 protesters clashed with police at what *The Guardian* called a "Blood-soaked G8 Summit." The September 2001 meeting of representatives from the European Union and the United States, held in Gothenburg, Sweden, to discuss Kyoto global warming protocols, turned into a "night of violence" in which six hundred people were detained. And in March 2002, protests against a meeting of European Union ministers in Barcelona again turned ugly.

May Day, 2001, was the occasion for violent anarchist and antiglobalization protests in France, Germany, Australia, England, and many other countries. It took ten thousand police to quell a riot in London that day.

Kaczynski remains, therefore, a bellwether. In a September 1998 letter to me, he wrote:

> *I suspect that you underestimate the strength and depth of feeling against industrial civilization that has been developing in recent years. I've been surprised at some of the things that people have written to me. It looks to me as if our society is moving into a pre-revolutionary situation. (By that I don't mean a situation in which revolution is inevitable, but one in which it is a realistic possibility.) The majority of people are pessimistic or cynical about existing institutions, there is widespread alienation and directionlessness among young people. . . . Perhaps all that is needed is to give these forces appropriate organization and direction.*

When Henry Murray spoke of the need to create a new "World Man" this was not what he had in mind.

Chronology

1942   Theodore John Kaczynski, first son of Theodore Richard (Turk) Kaczynski and Wanda Theresa Dombek Kaczynski, born on May 22, 1942.

1947   Family moves to Carpenter Street, Chicago.

1949   Second son, David, is born on October 3, 1949.

1952   Family moves to 9209 South Lawndale, Evergreen Park, Illinois.

1955   Ted enters the new Evergreen Park High School.

1958   Ted enters Harvard in the fall at age 16; lives at No. 8 Prescott St.

1959   Fall, Ted moves into Eliot House, N-43. Enrolls in Henry A. Murray's "Multiform Assessments of Personality Development" experiment, along with 21 other students from the Harvard class of 1962.

1962   Ted graduates from Harvard in June with weak grades, later reflects that his Harvard years were a critical period of his life.

Ted is accepted at the University of Michigan graduate program to study mathematics.

1966   Ted formulates plan to save money, then buy land in wilderness and "if it doesn't work and if I can get back to civilization before I starve then I will come back here and kill someone I hate."

Turk and Wanda Kaczynski move to Lisbon, Iowa.

1967   Ted, living at 524 South Forest St., Ann Arbor, receives the Sumner Myers Prize for his doctoral dissertation on "Boundary Functions."

Ted receives Ph.D. from Univ. of Michigan; moves to Univ. of California at Berkeley to teach math.

1968   Turk and Wanda Kaczynski move from Lisbon, Iowa, to Lombard, Illinois, where Turk goes to work for Foam Cutting Engineers.

1969   June, Ted resigns from Berkeley math department.

Summer, Ted and David drive to Canada to look for land; they file government request to lease a plot.

Fall, David returns for his senior year at Columbia. Ted returns to his parents' home in Lombard, Illinois to await Canadian govt. decision.

1970   June, David graduates from Columbia, spends summer touring West with friends.

Summer, Ted learns that his application for land has been denied and returns to Canada to continued to look for wilderness property, but has become disheartened.

Late summer, David returns briefly to Lombard, then moves to Great Falls, Montana, and starts work at Anaconda Co.

1971   Ted completes his untitled essay on the evils of technology.

April, Ted writes of taking "personal revenge" in his journal.

June, Ted visits David, resumes search for land; he finds 1.4 acres south of Lincoln, Montana, which the brothers purchase. Ted starts building cabin.

1972   Christmas, Ted determines "to murder a scientist"; he starts undertaking minor sabotage—monkeywrenching, etc.

1978   February, Ted asks his father to organize a job at Foam Cutting Engineers in Addison, Illinois, where his father works.

Mid-May, Ted arrives in Chicago.

May 25, Ted leaves bomb #1 in parking lot of the Science & Engineering Building at the University of Illinois, Chicago Circle campus, where it is found by Mary Gutierrez and taken to Evanston.

May 26, Terry Marker, campus security officer at Northwestern University in Evanston, is slightly injured.

June, Ted goes to live with his parents in Lombard, Illinois, and begins work at Foam Cutting Engineers.

June–August, Ted falls in love with Ellen Tarmichael, who spurns him. He posts obscene lyrics and is fired by David. Ted gets new job at Prince Castle, Inc.

1979   May 9, Ted places bomb #2 at Northwestern University's Technological Institute in Evanston. It slightly injures graduate student John Harris.

November 14, Ted mails altitude-sensitive bomb (#3) from Chicago to an address in Washington, D.C. The next day, it explodes in mail carrier inside American Airlines flight number 444, forcing plane to make an emergency landing at Dulles airport.

1980   June 10, bomb #4: Percy Wood, United Airlines president, at home in Lake Forest, Illinois, receives package. He is seriously injured.

1981   October 8, bomb #5: A Univ. of Utah student picks up large package in Bennion Hall Business Building, Salt Lake City; no injuries.

1982   May 5, bomb #6, mistakenly addressed to Professor Patrick Fischer at Penn State University, then forwarded to Fischer at Vanderbilt University in Nashville, Tennessee. Janet Smith, Fischer's secretary, is badly injured.

July 2, bomb #7: Diogenes Angelakos, director of Univ. of California Electronics Research Laboratory at Berkeley picks up package in Room 411, Cory Hall Mathematics Building; receives serious injuries.

1985   May 15, bomb #8: Air Force captain John Hauser enters the same Room 264 of Cory Hall and picks up a spiral binder that explodes; very severely injured.

June, bomb #9, postmarked May 8, opened at Boeing Aircraft Fabrication Division, Auburn, Washington. Bomb does not explode.

November 15, bomb #10 addressed to Univ. of Michigan professor James V. McConnell at Ann Arbor. Nick Suino, his assistant, opens it. Both men are injured.

December 11, bomb #11 is planted in parking lot behind Rentech, a computer rental store in Sacramento, California. The same day, Hugh Scrutton, the store's owner, picks up the package and is killed.

1987   February 20, bomb #12 is placed in parking lot of CAAMS, a small computer store in Salt Lake City. Gary Wright, the store's owner, picks the device up and is badly injured.

1987–93 Kaczynski perfects a new type of bomb using a powerful explosive.

1990   October 2, Turk Kaczynski commits suicide.

1993   June 22, bomb #13 received at the Tiburon, Marin County, California, home of Dr. Charles J. Epstein, world-renowned geneticist. He is severely injured.

June 24, bomb #14 received by Yale professor David Gelernter at the Computer Science Department of Yale Univ. He is severely injured.

1994   December 10, bomb #15 received at the home of Thomas Mosser in North Caldwell, New Jersey. Mosser, executive at the public relations firm Burson-Marsteller, opens the package and is killed.

1995   April 24, bomb #16, addressed to William Dennison, former president of California Forestry Association in Sacramento, California, is opened by his successor, Gilbert Murray, who is killed.

June 24, Ted mails copies of "Industrial Society and its Future" by "FC," which the FBI dubs, "The Manifesto," to the *New York Times*, the *Washington Post*, and *Penthouse*.

September 19, *Post* publishes the manifesto.

1996   January, David approaches the FBI through his attorney, Anthony

Disceglie. FBI begins surveillance of Ted's cabin.

April 3, FBI arrests Ted, who is removed to California in June to stand trial.

1997   November, Ted's trial begins, with jury selection.

1998   January 8, Ted requests permission of the court to fire his attorneys and represent himself.

January 22, Ted pleads guilty.

May 4, Ted is sentenced to life in prison without the possibility of parole.

1999   June 16, Ted appeals his sentence to the Ninth Circuit Court.

2001   February 12, 2001, the Ninth Circuit rejects Ted's appeal. Judge Stephen Reinhardt dissents. Ted appeals to the Supreme Court.

2002   March 18, Supreme Court rejects Ted's appeal.

Notes

Chapter 1

page

18   From the fall of 1959: Henry A. Murray, "Multiform Assessments of Personality Development Among Gifted College Men, 1941–1962," data set (made accessible in 1981, raw data files), Henry A. Murray Research Center of the Radcliffe Institute for Advanced Study, Harvard University, Cambridge, MA.

18   "vehement, sweeping": H. A. Murray, "Studies of Stressful Interpersonal Disputations," *American Psychologist*, vol. 18, no. 1 (January 1963).

18   "has intertwined his two": Sally C. Johnson, Psychiatric Competency Report. Submitted to the court on January 17, 1998; unsealed September 11, 1998.

19   "the most intellectual serial killer": Michael Rustigan, San Francisco State criminology professor, quoted by Karyn Hunt of Associated Press, April 4, 1996.

21   Dubbed "the Unabomber": Various interviews with James C. Ronay between 1997 and 2001.

21   Terry Marker: Government's Trial Brief, November 12, 1997; Government's Sentencing Memorandum, May 4, 1998.

22   "acknowledged responsibility": Sentencing Memorandum, May 4, 1998. Kaczynski pled guilty on January 22, 1998, and was sentenced on May 4, 1998.

22   "is a rational man": Sale's comments quoted in Steven Marcus, "Rebels Against the Future: The Luddites and Their War on the Industrial Revolution: Lessons for the Computer Age," book review, *The New Republic*, June 10, 1996.

22   "is subtle and carefully developed": James Q. Wilson, "In Search of Madness," *New York Times*, January 15, 1988.

23   a "prisoner of war": See, for example, *Green Anarchy*, no. 8 (Spring 2002), p. 20.

23   The conservative columnist: Tony Snow, "Unabomber 'Gores' Technology," *Detroit News*, September 21, 1995.

23   "rooted in the overheated passions": "Brilliant Misfit Caught in Changing Times," *Boston Globe*, April 6, 1996.

23   "a 1960s indictment": Stephen Budiansky, "Academic Roots of Paranoia," *U.S. News & World Report*, May 13, 1996.

23   the "extreme radicalism": Maria Puenta, "Berkeley May Have Radicalized Kaczynski. Unabomber Suspect Lived Near Hot Spot of Campus Activism," *USA Today*, November 13, 1996.

23   "Ted's fear that his students": William J. Broad, "Did Antiwar Tumult in '60s Ignite Unabomber?" *New York Times News Service*, June 3, 1996.

23   "is a man whose reading": Pierre Thomas and Serge F. Kovaleski, "FBI Itemizes Evidence from Kaczynski's Cabin," *Washington Post*, April 16, 1996.

23   "one of the most crucial decades": David Gelernter, *Drawing Life* (New York: Free Press, 1997), p. 62.

24   the difference between murderers: See Robert I. Simon, *Bad Men Do What Good Men Dream* (Washington, DC: American Psychiatric Press, 1996), pp. 2, 11–12.

25   "great evil can be perpetrated": *Ibid.*, p. 12.

25   as Hannah Arendt observed: Hannah Arendt, *Eichmann in Jerusalem: A Report on the Banality of Evil* (New York: Penguin Books, 1964).

25   During the seventeen years: Simon, *Bad Men Do What Good Men Dream*, p. 1; National Crime Victimization Survey, 1973–95.

26   John White Webster: *The Harvard Guide*, 2001 available at: www.news.harvard.edu/guide/lore//lore9.html.

26   Harvard dropout Harry Kendall Thaw: Suzannah Lessard, *The Architect of Desire: Beauty and Danger in the Stanford White Family* (New York: Bantam Doubleday Dell, 1996).

26   Kennedy School fellow Ira Einhorn: Steven Levy, *The Unicorn's Secret* (New York: Penguin Putnam, 1990); and Associated Press, "Einhorn back on U.S. Soil to Face Trial," *Bozeman Daily Chronicle*, July 21, 2001.

26   Harvard undergraduate, Sinedu Tadesse: "Satan Goes to Harvard," book review by Mary Gaitskill of Melanie Thernstrom, *Halfway Heaven: Diary of a Harvard Murder*, *Salon*, October 13, 1997.

27   "Is he an Outsider" and the quotes that follow: Colin Wilson, *The Outsider* (Boston: Houghton Mifflin, 1956), pp. 13–15, 20.

29   "The madman is the man": G. K. Chesterton, *Orthodoxy* (San Francisco: Ignatius Press, 1995), p. 25.

31   "*omertà*": T. J. Kaczynski, letter to the author, September 17, 1998.

31   "permanently removed": Kirsten G. Studlien, "Murray Center Seals Kaczynski Data," *Harvard Crimson*, July 14, 2000.

32   "There's a little bit of the Unabomber": Robert Wright, "The Evolution of Despair," *Time* magazine, August 28, 1995.

PART I
Chapter 2

38   Sixty miles north: Interview with Don Sachtleben, April 30, 2001.

39   "The Unabomber sees a loss of life": Patrick Hoge and Jane Meredith Adams, "Bomber Seen as Arrogant Crusader," *Sacramento Bee*, April 28, 1995.

39   an omnivorous reader: Book list from author's files. Interview with Sherri Wood, Lincoln town librarian, May 22, 1997. Also interview with staff of Aunt Bonnie's Bookstore, May 25, 2000.

41   relied on his "literary pursuits": Donald Foster, "The Fictions of Ted Kaczynski," *Vassar Quarterly* (Winter 1998), pp. 14–17. See also, Don Foster, *Author Unknown* (New York: Henry Holt and Company, 2000), chap. 3, "A Professor Whodunit," pp. 95–142.

41   "no one, not even NASA computers": Interview with Tom Mohnal, April 30, 2001.

41   He was very careful: Interview with FBI agents Don Sachtleben and Tom Mohnal, April 30, 2001. See also Turchie Affidavit, submitted April 3, 1996, by FBI agent Terry D. Turchie in support of the government's request for a search warrant for Theodore Kaczynski's Montana cabin, and Sentencing Memorandum, May 4, 1998, exhibits attached to Appendix A.

42   "A while back": Sentencing Memorandum, May 4, 1998, Exhibits 88 and 89.

43   provided a Social Security number: Robert Graysmith, *Unabomber: A Desire to Kill* (Washington, DC: Regnery Publishing, 1997), p. 321–22; Sachtleben, Mohnal interview.

43   "The only constant and universal element": William Monahan, "Ceci n'est pas une bombe," *New York Press*, vol. 8, no. 29 (July 18–25, 1995).

45   "had an advanced degree": Graysmith, *Unabomber*, pp.173–74. John Douglas and Mark Olshaker, *Unabomber: On the Trail of America's Most-Wanted Serial Killer* (New York: Pocket Books, 1996), pp. 122–30.

45   "Boyz-in-the-hood hood": "On the Internet, the Unabomber Is a Star," *New York Times*, April 6, 1996.

Chapter 3

47   "Get to Dulles Airport": Interviews with James C. "Chris" Ronay, October 10, 1997, and May 30, 2001.

48   a graduate student named John Harris: Turchie Affidavit, April 3, 1996.

49 When the officer, Terry Marker, started: Government's Trial Brief.

50 why the "Eugene O'Neill" stamps?: See Louis Sheaffer, *O'Neill: Son and Playwright* (Boston: Little, Brown, 1968), p. 125.

50 After dropping out of Princeton: *Ibid.*

50 odd jobs in Argentina: Arthur and Barbara Gelb, *O'Neill* (New York: Harper & Bros., 1960), pp. 133ff.

51 "my brains were wooly with hatred": *Ibid.*, p. 690.

51 "mainly for one reason": Sentencing Memorandum, Exhibit 15.

52 "I had hoped": Sentencing Memorandum, Exhibit 23.

52 "In some of my notes": Sentencing Memorandum, Exhibit 25.

52 "continued scientific and technical progress": Theodore J. Kaczynski, untitled essay dated 1971, attached as exhibit to Turchie Affidavit.

53 "About a year and a half ago": Sentencing Memorandum, Exhibit 13.

53 he received a package: Turchie Affidavit.

54 as Sloan Wilson suggested to me: Interview with Sloan Wilson, May 31, 2001.

54 "If life was all that rotten": Sloan Wilson, *Ice Brothers* (New York: Arbor House, 1979), p. 199–202.

55 After the Wood bombing: Ronay interview, April 30, 2001.

55 "was particularly satisfying": Government's Motion in Limine for Admission of Evidence under Fed. R. Evid. 404(B), Exhibit B, p. 7.

56 "My projects for revenge": Sentencing Memorandum, Exhibit 28.

56 "Juan Darien": Foster, "The Fictions of Ted Kaczynski," p. 16.

57 "There was nothing personal about this attack": George Lordnes and Lorraine Adams, "To Unabomber Victims, a Deeper Mystery," *Washington Post*, April 14, 1996.

57 "Sent a bomb to a computer expert": Sentencing Memorandum, Exhibit 29.

58 "I went to the U. of California": Sentencing Memorandum, Exhibit 30.

58 "Success at last": Government's Motion in Limine, Exhibit B, pp. 10–12.

59 "Experiment number 82": Sentence Hearing, January 22, 1998. See also Sentencing Memorandum, Exhibit 32.

59 "the reductionist assault": Theodore Roszak, *Where the Wasteland Ends* (New York: Doubleday, 1972), pp. 242–44.

61 "Experiment 100": Sentencing Memorandum, Exhibit 33.

62 used "J. Konrad" as an alias: Graysmith, *Unabomber*, p. 79.
    "an inadequate human being": Frederick R. Karl, *A Reader's Guide to Joseph Conrad* (New York: Noonday Press, 1966), p. 199.

62 "is the sacrosanct fetish": Joseph Conrad, *The Secret Agent* (New York: Doubleday, 1953), p. 40.

62 The theme is moral decay: See Karl, *A Reader's Guide to Joseph Conrad*, p. 202.

63 "Winnie Verloc's story to its anarchistic": Conrad, *The Secret Agent*, p. 13.

63 In a letter to *Penthouse*: "The Unabomber Speaks," *Penthouse*, vol. 27, no. 2 (October 1995), pp. 57–59.

Chapter 4

65 Hugh Scrutton owned: U.S. Department of Justice, *Ex Parte and in Camera*, documents submitted to court, November 7, 1997.

65 "an inherent student": Cynthia Hubert, "Hugh Scrutton Led Life Full of Joy, Adventure," *Sacramento Bee*, December 20, 1985.

66 "Experiment 97": Sentencing Memorandum, Exhibit 34. Note this is one of the rare times Kaczynski gets his dates wrong. Scrutton was killed on December 11, 1985, not December 12.

66 "Experiment 121": Government's Motion in Limine, Exhibit B, p. 18.

68 Epstein and his team: Mara Bovsun, "Down Syndrome Mouse Points to Better Alzheimer Research Model," *Biotechnology Newswatch*, February 3, 1992; David Perlman, "UCSF Researchers Find New Clue to Treatment for Alzheimer's," *San Francisco Chronicle*, February 15, 1992; *Business Wire*, "Mouse Model for Down's Syndrome Suggests Possible Role for Growth Factors in Treating Alzheimer's," February 14, 1992.

68 On Tuesday, June 22: U.S. Department of Justice, *Ex Parte and in Camera*, documents submitted to court, November 7, 1997.

69 Two days later, David Gelernter: *Ibid.*

69 In his latest book: David Hillel Gelernter, *Mirror Worlds: Or the Day Software Puts the Universe in a Shoebox. . . How It Will Happen and What It Will Mean* (New York: Oxford University Press, 1991). See also Hugh Kenner, "The Ultimate Database Might Mirror Reality," *Byte*, March 1, 1992; Steve Courtney, "Author Sees Computer as Window to World," *Hartford Courant*, May 28, 1992; and Jack Schofield, "Computer Book Reviews," *The Guardian* (London), January 21, 1993.

70 The consequences of technology: Gelernter, *Mirror Worlds*, pp. 216–20. Gelernter's italics.

71 "Bombs must be going off": U.S. Department of Justice, *Ex Parte and in Camera*, documents submitted to court, November 7, 1997.

72 "Experiment Log, Experiment 225": Sentencing Memorandum, Exhibit 52.

72 "Call Nathan R": Ronay interviews, October 10, 1997, and May 30, 2001. See also Graysmith, *Unabomber*, p. 259.

72 "In the epilog of your book": *Sacramento Bee*, "Text of Letter from

Unabomber to Gelernter," April 24, 1995, at www.unabombertrial.com; Douglas and Olshaker, *Unabomber*, pp. 181–2. See also Graysmith, *Unabomber*, p. 301.

73 "Native Forest Network": Native Forest Network Second International Temperate Forest Conference, "Focus on Multinationalism," University of Montana, Missoula, MT, November 9–13, 1994. See also Native Forest Network, *Native Forest News—Special Edition* (Winter 1993–94), p. 1.

73 "Eco-Fucker Hit List": "Eco-Fucker Hit List," *Live Wild or Die!* (undated, but early 1990).

73 was the charge: Scot Greacen, "B.C.," *Earth First! Journal*, June 21, 1993, p. 4.

73 would later confess: *United States* vs. *Theodore Kaczynski*, Trial Transcript, January 22, 1998.

73 On December 10, 1994: U.S. Department of Justice, *Ex Parte and in Camera*, November 7, 1997.

75 "Experiment 244": Sentencing Memorandum, Exhibit 40.

75 "We blew up Thomas Mosser": Sentencing Memorandum, Exhibits 37–38.

76 The mention of testing bombs: Cynthia Hubert and Patrick Hoge, "Rangers Comb Sierra for Unabom Test Sites," *Sacramento Bee*, May 16, 1995.

77 "Suggestions for Earth First!ers" and "How to Hit an Exxon Exec.": Sentencing Memorandum, Exhibits 90–92.

77 Back in May 1990, Earth First! leaders: See Alston Chase, *In a Dark Wood: The Fight Over Forests and the Myths of Nature* (Boston: Houghton Mifflin, 1995), chap. 24.

78 The Mosser bombing gave them: Interview with Judi Bari, April 25, 1995, and Sachtleben interview, April 30, 2001.

78 On April 24, 1995: Interview with Bob Taylor, October 22, 1997.

79 In a covering letter to the *New York Times*: Sentencing Memorandum, Exhibits 37, 48.

81 According to Foster: Foster, "The Fictions of Ted Kaczynski," p. 17; and Serge F. Kovaleski, "Kaczynski's Letters Reveal Tormented Mind," *Washington Post*, January 20, 1997.

82 "I threw myself at his feet": Quoted in Foster, "The Fictions of Ted Kaczynski," p. 17.

Chapter 5

83 a prolific correspondent: Turchie Affidavit.

84 In the last week of June: *Ibid.*; Corey, "On the Unabomber," p. 157.

84 "Do you think our analysis": "FC" to Tom Tyler, mailed June 24, 1995, received June 30, 1995, see Douglas and Olshaker, *Unabomber*, pp.

189–90. See also Turchie affidavit; and *San Francisco Chronicle*, July 4, 1995.

84 "If the enclosed manuscript is published": Author's files. Letter has also appeared from time to time in various redacted forms on the Internet. See also Turchie Affidavit.

84 On the 19th of September: "Industrial Society and Its Future," A Supplement to the *Washington Post*, September 19, 1995; Cynthia Hubert, "Treatise May be Unabomber's Undoing," *Sacramento Bee*, September 20, 1995.

85 "The Industrial Revolution and its consequences": by "FC." (Note: Kaczynski has never admitted to being FC. But by convicting him of FC's crimes, the court has determined that he is.) Theodore John Kaczynski, "Industrial Society and Its Future" (cited hereafter as Manifesto), paragraph 1, reproduced in Turchie Affidavit, Attachment 2.

87 Within hours: Marc Fisher, "The Terrorist Tract That's Hot Reading," *Washington Post*, September 23, 1995.

87 "I've never seen the likes": Cynthia Hubert and Kate Rix, "Notorious Unabomber Draws Fascination—Even Fans," *Sacramento Bee*, July 11, 1996.

87 "We may not share": Robert Wright, "The Evolution of Despair," *Time* magazine, August 28, 1995.

87 Kirkpatrick Sale announced: Quoted in Marcus, "Rebels Against the Future," book review, June 10, 1996.

87 "extraordinarily well-written": Cynthia Hubert, "Scientists: Unabomber Lacks Formal Schooling," *Sacramento Bee*, August 4, 1995.

88 "certainly not the rantings": *Ibid*.

88 "vision of things": *Ibid*.

88 "a long, tedious screed": Grant Buckler, "Unabomber Manifesto Draws Limited Comment Online," Newsbyte News Network, October 24, 1995, and Marc Fisher of *Washington Post*, "Manifesto Strikes Chord with Many Readers," in *Arizona Republic*, September 24, 1995.

88 "it sounds like": Snow, "Unabomber 'Gores' Technology."

88 "is turning the public off": "Ecologists Tell Unabomber to Get Lost," *Washington Times*, July 9, 1995.

88 a "diatribe": Tony Fremantle, "Arrest Thrusts Private Man, Private Town into Limelight," *Houston Chronicle*, April 10, 1996.

88 "obsessively repeated theme": Walt Wentz, "Unabomber May Be Crazy, but the Points Made in His Manifesto Aren't," *The Oregonian*, October 11, 1995.

88 "impenetrable": Ellen Goodman, "The Kaczynski Conundrum," *Boston Globe*, January 8, 1998.

88 "narcissistic personality disorder": Maggie Scarf, "The Mind of the Unabomber," *The New Republic*, June 10, 1996.

88 "little of the attention": Grant Buckler, Newsbyte News Network, October 24, 1995.

88 "nobody actually read it": Wentz, "Unabomber May Be Crazy," *The Oregonian*, October 11, 1995.

89 *Rainforest*, a story for small children: Helen Cowcher, *Rainforest* (New York: Farrar, Straus & Giroux, 1988).

90 A junior high school geography text: Melvin Schwartz and John O'Connor, *Exploring a Changing World* (Englewood Cliffs, NJ: Globe Book Co., 1993), p. 490.

90 A college text: G. Tyler Miller, *Environmental Science: Sustaining the Earth* (Belmont, CA: Wadsworth Publishing Co., 1986), p.278.

90 "The chief reason for the environmental": Barry Commoner, *The Closing Circle* (New York: Knopf, 1971), p. 175.

90 "the modern world has been shaped": E. F. Schumacher, *Small Is Beautiful: Economics As If People Mattered* (New York: Harper & Row, 1973), p. 155.

90 "advertising on television": Fritjof Capra, *The Turning Point* (New York: Bantam Books, 1982), p. 218.

91 "technological society not only": Bill Devall and George Sessions, *Deep Ecology* (Salt Lake City: Gibbs M. Smith, 1985), p. 48.

91 "the scientific worldview": Kirkpatrick Sale, *Dwellers in the Land: The Bioregional Vision* (San Francisco: Sierra Club Books, 1985), pp. 20–21.

91 "a global culture": Arne Naess, *Ecology, Community and Lifestyle*, trans. and ed. David Rothenberg (New York: Cambridge University Press, 1989), p. 23.

91 "every family's owning": Bill McKibben, *The End of Nature* (New York: Random House, 1989), pp. 186, 190, 204.

92 Jacques Ellul: Jacques Ellul, *The Technological Society*, trans. John Wilkenson (New York: Knopf, 1964, French edn. publ. 1954).

92 "when I read the book": T. J. Kaczynski's comments on Johnson Report, unpublished.

92 "Despite its debt to Ellul": Scott Corey, "On the Unabomber," *Telos*, 118 (Winter 2000). See also Tim Luke, "Re-Reading the Unabomber Manifesto," *Telos*, 107 (Spring 1996).

92 Ellul's later works: Jacques Ellul, *Autopsy of Revolution* (New York: Knopf, 1965); Jacques Ellul, *Propaganda*, trans. Konrad Kellen and Jean Lerner (New York: Vintage Books, 1965); and Ellul, *The Ethics of Freedom*, trans. and ed. Geoffrey W. Bromiley (Grand Rapids, MI: William B. Eerdmans Publishing Company, 1976).

94 Its first discussion of "wild nature": Corey, "On the Unabomber," p. 169.

94 "An ideology, in order to gain": Manifesto, paragraph 183.

94 "I don't even believe": Sentencing Memorandum, Exhibit 10.

96 "is the discontent of": Arthur O. Lovejoy and George Boas, *Primitivism and Related Ideas in Antiquity* (Baltimore: Johns Hopkins University Press, 1935), pp. 1, 11.

97 Each kind of primitivism: *Ibid.*, pp. 1–7, 11ff.

97 "Since the beginning of the present": *Ibid.*, p. ix.

97 "doubts and apprehensions": *Ibid.*

98 Leopold Kohr, whose book: Leopold Kohr, *The Breakdown of Nations* (New York: Rinehart, 1957).

98 In Great Britain in the 1960s: Interviews with John Papworth, Leopold Kohr, and Edward Goldsmith, November 1989.

99 Restoring "pre-Columbian conditions": For a full discussion of federal policies on "recreating the primitive scene," "restoring late-successional conditions," and "restoring pre-Columbian conditions," see my books *Playing God in Yellowstone* (New York: Atlantic Monthly Press, 1986) and *In a Dark Wood*.

Chapter 6

101 "An American, insofar": Wallace Stegner, letter to Outdoor Recreation Resources Review Commission, December 3, 1960. Reprinted as "The Wilderness Idea," which appeared in *The Sound Of Mountain Water* (New York: Doubleday, 1969).

104 Special agents Don Sachtleben, "Mad Max": Sachtleben interview, April 30, 2001; Turchie interview, May 30, 2001. See also Candice DeLong, *Special Agent* (New York: Hyperion Books, 2001), pp. 252ff.

106 "would be utilized in the manufacture": Turchie Affidavit.

107 scientifically verifiable: Kaczynski, unpublished autobiography, "Truth vs. Lies." Author's copy.

107 David, by contrast: *Ibid.* See also FBI interview with David Kaczynski, February 24–25, 1996.

108 One weekend, the two drove: "Truth vs. Lies," Bill of sale for 1.4 acres more or less from Clifford D. Gehring, Sr., to Theodore J. Kaczynski and David R. Kaczynski, brothers, dated June 19, 1971.

108 David stayed: *Ibid.*

108 "We both worried": Richard Lacayo, "A Tale of Two Brothers," *Time* magazine, April 22, 1996.

108 "more disaffected than his older brother": Kaczynski, "Truth vs. Lies."

110 "You've got a screwy brother": David Johnston and Janny Scott, "The Tortured Genius of Theodore Kaczynski," Promise to the Unabom Suspect," *New York Times*, May 26, 1996; "How David Kaczynski Came to Realize Brother Might Be Unabomber," Scripps-Howard News Service, April 10, 1996.

110 But doubts surfaced again: FBI interview with David Kaczynski, February 18, 1996.

110 "my jaw literally dropped": "Blood Bond," *People* magazine, August 10, 1998.

111 David was badly shaken: Johnston and Scott, "The Tortured Genius of Theodore Kaczynski," *New York Times*, May 26, 1996.

111 One phrase in particular: "How David Kaczynski Came to Realize Brother Might Be Unabomber," Scripps-Howard.

111 The " 'feel' and tone": FBI interview with David Kaczynski, February 24–25, 1996.

111 He and Ted had long argued: *Ibid.*

111 the same curious word usage: Turchie Affidavit; Graysmith, *Unabomber*, p. 367.

111 The overlap was impossible to ignore: *Ibid.*

111 would "swing back and forth": David Kaczynski to Mike Wallace, CBS, *60 Minutes*, September 15, 1996.

112 "I get just choked with frustration": "Documents Portray Kaczynski's Troubled Relations With Family," Associated Press, November 3, 1997, taken from court documents. See also Graysmith, *Unabomber*, p. 365.

112 In late October, Linda Patrik turned": Interview with Anthony Bisceglie, October 10, 1997.

112 "Art forms that appeal": Cited in FBI interview with David Kaczynski, February 24–25, 1996.

113 "Either this is a historic": Bisceglie interview, October 10, 1997; "How David Kaczynski Came to Realize Brother Might Be Unabomber," Scripps-Howard.

113 "The Subject": Tony Bisceglie letter to Milly Flynn, FBI, February 12, 1996.

114 "He was walking back and forth": Wanda Kaczynski on *60 Minutes*, September 15, 1996.

114 "It was not David": Ellen Beckor and Tom McPheeters, "A Tale of Intuition and Trust," *Journal of Family Life*, vol. 4, no. 3, 1998, pp. 7–13.

115 Meanwhile, Gray and DeLong hid in a cabin: DeLong, *Secret Agent*, and Sachtleben and Turchie interviews.

116 Inside the tiny dwelling: Search Warrant, Attachment B, "Items to be Seized," April 15, 1996.

117 "chemicals and other materials": *Ibid.*

117 they found tableware: *Ibid.*

118 "Class 1. Hide carefully": Sentencing Memorandum, Exhibit 18.

119 for "knowingly possessing [an unregistered] firearm": Theodore John Kaczynski, Warrant for Arrest, April 4, 1996. (Note: Warrant was filed the day after Kaczynski was apprehended.)

119 After dark, Noel and Turchie: Len Iwanski, "Unabomber," *Independent Record* (Helena), April 4, 1996.

119 in a Chevy Blazer: Brett French, "University Students Snap Photos of a Lifetime," *Independent Record*, April 5, 1996. Interview with Todd Fisher, former owner of the *Blackfoot Valley Dispatch*, May 21, 1997.

Chapter 7

120 The hanging tree: "Hanging Tree," unsigned, *Independent Record*, October 24, 1996.

121 As soon as federal agents: Fisher interview, May 21, 1997; Sidney Godolphin interview, March 4, 1998.

121 "This is the biggest thing": Nicholas K. Geranios, "Helena's Most Famous Prisoner," *Independent Record*, April 6, 1996.

121 "We're lacking in nationally ranked": *Ibid.*

122 "This was big for Lincoln": Cynthia Hubert, "When Unabomb Probe Arrived, Few Asked Questions," *Sacramento Bee*, April 15, 1996.

123 "Any conversation you had with Ted": Parick Hoge, "Rural Acquaintances Say Kaczynski Attracted Little Notice," *Sacramento Bee* April 5, 1996.

123 "irresponsible logging practices": Kaczynski, "Truth vs. Lies."

124 "the hermit on the hill": *Time* magazine, April 15, 1996.

125 One was Teresa Garland: Interview with Teresa Garland, May 22, 1997.

125 He felt at ease: Interview with Irene Preston, May 22, 1997.

125 Even Chris Waits: See Chris Waits and Dave Shorts, *Unabomber: The Secret Life of Ted Kaczynski* (Missoula, MT: Independent Record, 1999).

126 The town library staff, too: Interviews with Mary Spurlin and Sherri Wood, May 22, 1997.

126 "There are women who are in love with him": Quentin Hardy, "Ted Kaczynski Sat Here, in the Library Sherri Wood Runs," *Wall Street Journal*, August 12, 1997.

126 "has many seasonal residents": Richard Perez Pena, "Unabomb Suspect: A Quiet Loner Whom Few Noticed," *New York Times*, April 4, 1996.

126 "attracted little attention": Patrick Hoge, "Rural Acquaintances Say Kaczynski Attracted Little Notice."

127 "occasionally retreated to his own": *Time* magazine, April 15, 1996.

127 "while his brother studied wiring diagrams": *Newsweek*, April 22, 1996.

Chapter 8

131 consortium run by: Rich Harris of Associated Press, chairman of the Unabom Committee of Media Organizations, from letter, "Dear Fellow Journalist," September 23, 1997.

131 only "bona fide" journalists: Unabom Trial Media Group, "General Guidelines for Credentials."

132 "Your honor, before these proceedings": Official Trial Transcript of proceedings, *United States* vs. *Kaczynski*, January 5, 1998, 8:02 A.M., *In Camera, ex Parte* contacts with Defendant.

132 What happened?: Cynthia Hubert and Denny Walsh, "Kaczynski Derails Start of Trial," *Sacramento Bee*, January 6, 1998; William Glaberson, "Disrupting Unabomber Trial—but to What End?" *New York Times*, January 11, 1998; Cynthia Hubert and Denny Walsh, "Is Kaczynski Manipulating Legal System? Experts Disagree," *Sacramento Bee*, January 11, 1998.

133 On June 18, 1996, a federal grand jury: Indictment by U.S. Attorney Robert Steven Lapham, June 18, 1996; Cynthia Hubert and Denny Walsh, "Kaczynski Accused of Four Blasts," *Sacramento Bee*, June 19, 1996.

133 On June 23, Kaczynski was flown: Cynthia Hubert, "Alleged Unabomber Arrives a Day Early," *Sacramento Bee*, June 24, 1996.

133 two days after Kaczynski's arrival: Howard Mintz, "'Complete Lawyer' in Kaczynski's Corner," *The Recorder*, June 18, 1996.

133 And the next month (July 18, 1996), Denvir added Judy Clarke: Howard Mintz, "NACDL President-Elect to Join Kaczynski Defense," *The Recorder*, July 16, 1996.

133 the search warrant had been legally flawed: Notice of Motion to Suppress Evidence and Memorandum of Points and Authorities in Support of Defendant's Motion to Suppress, *United States* vs. *Kaczynski*, CR-D-96-0259 GEB (E.E. filed March 3, 1997). See also Michael Mello, *The United States* vs. *Theodore John Kaczynski* (New York: Context Books, 1999).

134 "I categorically refuse": Quoted from Circuit Judge Stephen Reinhardt's dissenting opinion, Theodore J. Kaczynski appeal, filed February 12, 2001, p. 1887.

134 As he told the appeals court: *Ibid.*, p. 1889.

134 Meanwhile, beginning in early 1997: Serge F. Kovaleski, "Kaczynski Letters Reveal Tormented Mind," *Washington Post*, January 20, 1997.

135 "knows very well that": Kaczynski, "Truth vs. Lies."

135 Media and public opinion shifted: Stephen Chapman, "Needed by Needless Unabomber Trial," *Washington Times*, January 15, 1998; Michael J. Sniffen, "Opposition Grows to Death Penalty in Unabomber Trial," Associated Press, January 15, 1998.

135 But perhaps there was an alternative: Finnegan, "On the Unabomber," and Mello, *United States* vs. *Theodore John Kaczynski*, p. 52.

135 "always suspicious of conclusions": Scharlotte Holdman, e-mail to the author, October 9, 2000.

136 Kaczynski broke off the interview: Sally C. Johnson, psychiatric competency report.

136 invited Xavier F. Amador: Declaration of Xavier F. Amador, Ph.D., November 16, 1997. See also Finnegan, "On the Unabomber," p. 55.

136 Karen Bronk Froming: Declaration of Karen Bronk Froming, Ph.D., November 17, 1997.

136 David Vernon Foster: Declarations of David Vernon Foster, M.D., November 12 and 17, 1997.

137 Although tests alone suggested to Froming: Finnegan, "On the Unabomber," p. 54.

137 to enter his Montana cabin: Linda Deutsch, "Cabin Could Be Key in Kaczynski Defense," *Sacramento Bee*, November 10, 1997; Linda Deutsch, "Kaczynski Cabin to Be Trucked to Capital," *Sacramento Bee*, December 1, 1997; Linda Deutsch, "Kaczynski Cabin Arrives," *Sacramento Bee*, December 5, 1997.

138 "I intend to start killing people": Prosecution exhibit submitted into evidence, November 18, 1997.

138 the computer guru Esther Dyson: Leslie Bennetts, "Wired at Heart," *Vanity Fair* (November 1997).

138 "I find him to be": Trial transcript, January 7, 1998, Document 470.

139 Phillip J. Resnick: Interview with Phillip J. Resnick, April 16, 1998.

139 Ohio neuropsychologist John T. Kenny: Memorandum from John T. Kenny, Ph.D., ABPP, Neuropsychologist, to Ms. Kathleen Puckett, re. "Analysis of Neuropsychological Testing on Theodore J. Kaczynski," December 29, 1997.

139 a "pathological dread": Defense brief filed November 12, 1997, p. 9.

139 "We have no credible evidence": Declaration of Park Elliott Dietz, M.D., November 19, 1997.

140 "It is my opinion": Declaration of Phillip J. Resnick, M.D., November 19, 1997.

140 Kaczynski claims: Theodore J. Kaczynski to Judge Garland E. Burrell, Jr., December 1, 1997, postscript dated December 17, 1997.

141 his "bad experience at Harvard": Bisceglie interview, October 10, 1997.

141 "The assessment arrived at": Kaczynski, "Truth vs. Lies."

141 the Minnesota Multiphasic: Kenny to Puckett memorandum, December 29, 1997.

142 "No one knows why": ABC Television, "The Unabomber: An Unprecedented Look at the Serial Killer," *20/20*, May 4, 1998.

142 Bertram Karon: "Case of Lawful," TAT. Group IV< LAWFUL ('62). "Blind" scoring of Ted Kaczynski's TAT answers given during the Harvard Murray Study, with notation from T. J. Kaczynski attached: "according to

a note that Quin Denvir gave me on April 30, 1998, the blind scoring was done by Professor Bertram Karon of Michigan State University."

142 "neuropsychological testing": Linda Deutsch, "Kaczynski a No-Show as Jury Selection Continues," Associated Press, November 26, 1997; trial transcript for November 25, 1997.

143 "believed that his counsel": Theodore John Kaczynski Appeal, filed with the Ninth Circuit Court, December 22, 1999.

143 Kaczynski wrote Judge Burrell: Theodore J. Kaczynski to Judge Garland E. Burrell, Jr., December 1, 1997, postscript dated December 17, 1997.

143 "I had been tricked and humiliated": *Ibid.*

143 Kaczynski mistakenly thought: Kaczynski Appeal, December 22, 1999.

144 "may raise important": Robert Cleary letter to the court, December 24, 1997, Docket 446; Denny Walsh, "Kaczynski Cites Defense Concerns: Unhappy with Team's Actions," *Sacramento Bee*, December 27, 1997.

145 "that he be permitted": Court transcript, January 8, 1998.

145 "We look at this": *Ibid.*

145 a "provisional" diagnosis: Johnson, Psychiatric Competency Report.

147 "suffers from serious mental illness": William Glaberson, "Lawyers for Kaczynski Agree He Is Competant to Stand Trial," *New York Times*, January 21, 1998.

147 "paranoid schizophrenia": Cynthia Hubert and Denny Walsh, "Kaczynski Competent, Doctor Says," *Sacramento Bee*, January 21, 1998.

147 "a paranoid schizophrenic": "Kaczynski Diagnosed Fit to Stand Trial," Associated Press, January 21, 1998.

147 "suffers from the grandiose fantasies": William Booth, "Kaczynski Pleads in Bombings," *Washington Post*, January 23, 1998.

147 "found that he was a delusional": Tamela Edwards, "Crazy Is as Crazy Does," *Time* magazine, February 2, 1998.

147 "suffers from schizophrenia": Editorial, "Justice in the Unabomber Case," *New York Times*, January 23, 1998.

147 "something odd": Finnegan, "On the Unabomber," p. 62.

147 describes the decision as "bizarre": Mello, *United States* vs. *Theodore John Kaczynski*, p. 116.

148 "How do we justify this travesty?": Thomas Szasz, interview with the author. Quote from "The Unapatient Manifesto," *Liberty*, vol. 11, no. 4 (March 1998), p. 9.

148 "Burrell seemed to be scrambling": Mello, *United States* vs. *Theodore John Kaczynski*, p. 112.

148 Perhaps, as Finnegan speculates: Finnegan, "On the Unabomber," p. 60.

148 a "suicide forum": Trial transcript, January 22, 1998.

149 "put me in such a position": Ted Kaczynski, letter to the editor, *Live Wild or Die!* no. 7 (Spring 1998).

149 he pleaded guilty: "Kaczynski Pleads Guilty to Blasts," Associated Press, January 23, 1998; Cynthia Hubert and Denny Walsh, "Kaczynski Pleads Guilty to Blasts: Unabomber Will Spend Rest of His Life Behind Bars," *Sacramento Bee*, January 23, 1998.

149 "A few days ago": Sentencing Memorandum, May 4, 1998.

149 "While we are relieved": Associated Press, "Widow Wants Unabomber Proof Released," *Las Vegas Review Journal*, January 25, 1998.

150 "I must acknowledge that": David Kaczynski, letter to the author, August 25, 1997.

150 "challenges the basic assumptions": Mello, *United States* vs. *Theodore John Kaczynski*, p. 46.

151 "if libertarian individualism": Corey, "On the Unabomber," p. 179.

PART II
Chapter 9

156 a Polish working-class community: Interview with Howard Finkle, July 13, 1998. See also Robert D. McFadden, "From a Child of Promise to Unabomb Suspect," *New York Times*, May 26, 1996.

156 Neither he nor Wanda was religious: Interview with Paul Carlston, July 12, 1998.

156 overshadowed the quieter Wanda: Carlston interview, July 12, 1998; also interviews with Ralph Meister, March 19, 2000; Mike Conklin, July 15, 1998; and David Radl, March 25, 2001.

157 "Everywhere the machine holds the center": Lewis Mumford, *The Condition of Man* (New York: Harcourt, Brace, 1944), p. 394.

157 "the end of everything we call": H. G. Wells, *Mind at the End of its Tether* (London: Heinemann, 1945), p. 1.

158 Turk followed these world events: Interviews with Carlston, Meister, Radl, and Conklin.

158 "certain factors in the modern": Erich Fromm, *Escape from Freedom* (New York: Rinehart, 1941), p. 265.

158 "feelings about our family": CBS, *60 Minutes*, September 15, 1996.

159 "I would try to draw Ted out": Serge F. Kovaleski and Lorraine Adams, "A Stranger in the Family Picture," *Washington Post*, June 16, 1996.

159 like "a little rag doll": CBS, *60 Minutes*, September 15, 1996.

159 "I ponder endlessly over it": Kovaleski and Adams, "A Stranger in the Family Picture."

160 within three weeks: Kaczynski, "Truth vs. Lies."

161 "plays well with children": Ibid.
161 "he had a strong sense of security": Kovaleski and Adams, "A Stranger in the Family Picture."
161 Carpenter Street lay in a tough neighborhood: Kaczynski, "Truth vs. Lies."
162 "always regarded themselves as": Ibid.
162 Wanda tended to be fearful: Ibid.; also various interviews.
162 "there was an undercurrent": Kaczynski, "Truth vs. Lies."
162 Whenever Turk got angry: Ibid.
163 "crabby and irritable": Ibid.
163 an IQ test: Ibid.; and Kovaleski and Adams, "A Stranger in the Family Picture."
163 his parents would lecture him: Kaczynski, "Truth vs. Lies."
163 "with Turk there was no question": Carlston interview, July 12, 1998.

Chapter 10

165 the "Village of Churches": Finkle interview.
165 In 1952, when Ted was ten: Kaczynski, "Truth vs. Lies."
166 "Them niggers": Carlston interview, July 12, 1998.
167 "Never had American youth": William Manchester, *The Glory and the Dream* (Boston: Little, Brown, 1974), p. 576.
168 "Kids read stories about 'Tootle'": William Strauss and Neil Howe, *Generations* (New York: Morrow, 1991), p. 286.
168 the Silents "were so good": Gail Sheehy, *New Passages* (New York: Ballantine Books, 1995), p.29.
169 "became teenagers when": Quoted in Strauss and Howe, *Generations*, p. 286.
170 Evergreen Park's fragmented school system: Interviews with Eugene Howard, and Finkle, and with Spencer Gilmore, July 7, 1998. See also Evergreen Park Community High School *Student Handbook* (1958 and 1955), and dedication brochure (1955).
171 "The fact to keep in mind": Interview with Paul Jenkins, November 20, 1997. For a sense of the school's emphasis on scholarship, see Lois Skillen and Eugene Howard, "Community Support for a Scholarship Program," *The School Executive*, vol. 79, no. 4 (December 1959).
172 "The clique composition of a school": Eugene R. Howard, "There May Be No Fair Play in American Rigged Schools," *Changing Schools*, vol. 17, no. 1 (Winter 1989), p. 3.
172 the enemy was "the system": Goodman, *Growing Up Absurd*, pp. ix, 10, 24, 34, 241.
174 "You will act and dress": Evergreen Park Community High School, "What will High School be like?" *Student Handbook* (1958).

174 on the "caucus committee": Interview with Lois Skillen, April 5, 2000, and Jenkins interview, November 20, 1997.

174 When he woke to find: Kaczynski, "Truth vs. Lies."

174 calling him "sick": *Ibid.*

174 had been "painfully shy": Lisa Black and Steve Mills, "Kacyznski's Past," *Chicago Tribune*, April 14, 1996.

174 "a pocket protector and briefcase": Richard Cole, "Kaczynski's Spiral— Boy Genius to '60s Wallflower to Embittered Hermit," Associated Press, April 21, 1996.

174 "socially inept": Barry Witt, "Schoolmate's 'Funny Feeling,'" *San Jose Mercury News*, April 17, 1996.

175 "funereal portrait": Robert D. McFadden, "From a Child of Promise to the Unabomb Suspect."

175 "so powerful that it broke": Lisa Black and Steve Mills, *Chicago Tribune*, April 16, 1996.

175 "I probably knew Ted better": Interview with Russell Mosny, July 7, 1998.

176 "I know the stereotype of Ted": Jenkins interview, November 20, 1997.

177 "wasn't antisocial, just introverted": Interview with James Oberto, July 12, 1998.

177 "honest, ethical and sociable": Interview with Robert Rippey, July 7, 1998.

177 seemed to be their "ringleader": Interview with Philip Pemberton, July 7, 1998.

177 "Of all the youngsters": Quote from Kaczynski, "Truth vs. Lies," confirmed by Skillen interview, April 5, 2000.

178 "Ted's success meant too much": Oberto interview, July 12, 1998.

178 "There was a gradual increasing": Johnson, Psychiatric Competency Report.

179 Mosny recalls: Mosny interview, July 7, 1998.

180 "He's too young": Oberto interview, July 12, 1998.

Chapter 11

182 Von Stade's well-intentioned idea: Interview with Francis Murphy, September 2, 1998.

182 "I lived at Prescott Street": Interview with Michael Stucki, September 2, 1998.

182 "a serious, quiet bunch": Murphy interview, September 2, 1998.

183 He owned just two pairs: Kaczynski, "Truth vs. Lies."

183 a "tremendous thing for me": *Ibid.*

184 "was as normal as I am": Gerald Burns, letter to the editor, *Fifth Estate*, vol. 32, no. 2 (Fall 1997).

184 "Good impression created": Kaczynski, "Truth vs. Lies." School records of Theodore John Kaczynski, Harvard University, p. 45.

185 "general education": See Alston Chase, "The Rise and Fall of General Education," *Academic Questions*, vol. 6, no. 2 (Spring 1993); Frederick Rudolph, *Curriculum* (San Francisco: Jossey-Bass, 1977); Daniel Bell, *The Reforming of General Education* (New York: Columbia University Press, 1966); and Gerald Grant and David Riesman, *The Perpetual Dream* (Chicago: University of Chicago Press, 1978).

186 Between 1944 and 1947, curriculum committees: Dennison University *Bulletin* (1947–48); University of Minnesota Committee on General Education, Report to the Dean of the College of Science, Literature and the Arts; and Gail Kennedy, *Education at Amherst* (New York: Harper & Row, 1955).

186 These views found common expression: The President's Commission on Higher Education, *Higher Education for American Democracy: A Report of the President's Commission on Higher Education* (New York: Harper & Row, 1947), pp. 42–49.

187 the *locus classicus* of general education: Harvard Committee, *General Education in a Free Society* (Cambridge, MA: Harvard University Press, 1945), pp. viii–ix.

187 "a new impetus": Rudolph, *Curriculum*, pp. 259–61.

188 During the 1920s and 1930s, several colleges: See Bell, *The Reforming of General Education*, and Chase, "The Rise and Fall of General Education."

188 "Until President James B. Conant": Rudolph, *Curriculum*, p. 257.

Chapter 12

191 embrace terror: Stephane Courtois et al., eds., *Black Book of Communism: Crimes, Terror, Repression,*, trans. Jonathan Murphy and Mark Kramer (Cambridge, MA: Harvard University Press, 1999); Gerhard L. Weinberg, *A World at Arms: A Global History of World War II* (New York: Cambridge University Press, 1994). For the official account of the Dresden bombing, see USAF Historical Division, Air University, "Historical Analysis of the 14–15 February 1945 Bombings of Dresden," available at: www.airforcehistory.hq.af.mil/PopTopcis/dresden.htm.

192 "Disinterested intellectual curiosity": G. M. Trevelyan, *English Social History* (New York: Longmans, Green and Co., 1942), p. viii.

192 "beautiful, perfect and admirable": Cardinal John Henry Newman, *The Idea of a University*, (New Haven, CT: Yale University Press, 1996), discourse 7, section 5.

192 "The intellectual virtues": Robert Maynard Hutchins, *The Higher Learning in America* (New Haven: Yale University Press, 1936) p. 67.

194 "The highest object of knowledge": Plato, *The Republic*, trans. F. M. Cornford (Oxford: Oxford University Press, 1945), p. 215.

194 "The good of man": Aristotle, *The Nichomachean Ethics*, trans. H. Rackham (Cambridge, MA: Harvard University Press, 1947), p. 33.

195 "natural law": See Heinrich A. Rommen, *Natural Law* (St. Louis: Herder Books, 1947); A. P. d'Entreves, *Natural Law* (London: Hutchinson University Library, 1961); and Otto Gierke, *Natural Law and the Theory of Society, 1500 to 1800* (Boston: Beacon Press, 1960).

195 "permeated with the study": Rudolph, *Curriculum*, p. 30.

195 "very nearly equivalent": Samuel Eliot Morison, *The Founding of Harvard College* (Cambridge, MA: Harvard University Press, 1935, pp. 12–17.

196 "that knowledge is of those things": Francis Lord Bacon, "Of the Proficience and Advancement of Learning, Divine and Moral," in *The Works of Lord Bacon* (London: William Ball, 1837), p. 2.

197 "The desire for knowledge": Laurence Sterne, *Life and Opinions of Tristram Shandy, Gentleman* (New York: Knopf, 1991), book II, chap. 3.

197 refused to accept limits: See Johann Wolfgang von Goethe, *Faust*, parts One and Two, trans. George Madison Priest (New York: Knopf, 1959).

197 "if the opinions of the philosophers": Jan Morris, ed., *The Oxford Book of Oxford* (Oxford: Oxford University Press, 1978), p. 78, "Laud's Code: Divine Truth."

197 "every one shall consider": *The Laws Liberties and order of Harvard College Confirmed by the Overseers and President of the College in the Years 1642, 1643, 1644, 1645, and 1646. And Published to the Scholars for the Perpetual Preservation of their Welfare and Government*, in Samuel Eliot Morison, *The Founding of Harvard College*, pp. 333–37; See also Richard Hofstadter and Wilson Smith, eds., *American Higher Education: A Documentary History* (Chicago: University of Chicago Press, 1961).

198 "the Enlightenment Project": Alasdair MacIntyre, *After Virtue* (South Bend, IN: University of Notre Dame Press, 1981), p. 48.

198 the "Faustian" culture: Oswald Spengler, *The Decline of the West* (New York: Knopf, 1926).

199 "a god-devil who has power": Karl, *Readers Guide*, p. 138.

199 "All Europe contributed": Joseph Conrad, *Heart of Darkness*, in Dauwen Zabel Morton, ed., *The Portable Conrad* (New York: Viking, 1969), p. 561.

200 "the scientific spirit incarnate": Wilson, *The Outsider*, p. 19.

200 "A frightful queerness has come to life": Wells, *Mind at the End of its Tether*, p. 4–5.

201 a "naturalistic fallacy": G. E. Moore, *Principia Ethica* (Cambridge: Cambridge University Press, 1903), p. 9.

201 the so-called Vienna Circle: Rudolf Carnap, *Philosophy and Logical Syntax* (London: Kegan Paul, 1935). See also A. J. Ayer, ed. *Logical Positivism* (Glencoe, IL: Free Press, 1959), pp. 3–9.

204 "For long before I dallied": Thomas Mann, *Dr. Faustus*, trans. H. T. Lowe-Porter (New York: Knopf, 1948), p. 394.

204 "Ethical neutrality": Derek Bok, "The President's Report," Harvard University, 1976–77, reprinted in *Harvard Magazine* (May–June 1978).

204 "an expression of 'the establishment'": Rudolph, *Curriculum*, p. 262.

206 "Imagination does not breed": Chesterton, *Orthodoxy*, p. 21.

Chapter 13

208 "has long been called": Henry Rosovsky, Dean of the Faculty, Harvard University, "The Report of The Task Force on College Life," October 1976.

209 "unimaginative, conventional": Kaczynski, "Truth vs. Lies."

210 "man is a creature": Sigmund Freud, *The Future of an Illusion*, trans. W. D. Robson-Scott (New York: Liveright, 1953), p. 84.

210 "the intellectual desolation": Karl Marx, *Capital*, trans. from the 4th German edn. by Eden and Cedar Paul (New York: E. P. Dutton, 1957), vol. 1, p. 424.

210 "The absurd is the essential concept": Albert Camus, *The Myth of Sisyphus*, trans. Justin O'Brien, (New York: Vintage Books, 1961), p. 23.

210 "I carry the weight of the world": Jean-Paul Sartre, *Being and Nothingness*, trans. Hazel E. Barnes (New York: Philosophical Library, 1956), pp. 555–56.

210 "so long as the machine process": Thorstein Veblen, *The Place of Science in Modern Civilization* (New Brunswick, NJ: Transaction Publishers, 1990), p. 30. See also Veblen, *The Engineers and the Price System* (New York: August M. Kelly, 1965); Veblen, "Pecuniary Canons of Taste," from *The Theory of the Leisure Class* (London: Allen & Unwin, 1949), reprinted in Louis G. Locke, William M. Gibson, and George Arms, eds., *Toward Liberal Education* (New York: Rinehart, 1953), pp. 533–44.

210 "insignificance and powerlessness": Erich Fromm, "The Illusion of Individuality," a selection from Fromm's *Escape from Freedom* reprinted in *Toward Liberal Education*, p. 551.

210 the "new industrial revolution": Norbert Wiener, "The First and Second Industrial Revolution," a selection from Wiener's *The Human Use of Human Beings* (New York: Houghton Mifflin, 1950), reprinted in *Toward Liberal Education*, p. 640.

211 "the power of total destruction": Norman Cousins, "Modern Man Is Obsolete," originally published in the *Saturday Review of Literature*; reprinted in *Toward Liberal Education*, pp. 641–42.

211 "This machine-technics": Oswald Spengler, *Man and Technics* (New York, Knopf, 1932), p. 105.

211 "I am a sick man": Fyodor Dostoevsky, *Notes from Underground*, trans. C. J. Hogarth (New York: E. P. Dutton, 1953), pp. 1, 12.

211 "I did not kill a human being": Fyodor Dostoevsky, *Crime and Punishment*, trans. Constance Garnett (New York: Bantam Books, 1971), p. 238.

212 "we have created industrial order": Mumford, *The Conduct of Life*, p. 181.

212 "The achievements of modern technology": Mumford, "Looking Forward," a selection from Ruth Nana Anshen, ed., *Science and Man* (New York: Harcourt Brace, 1942), reprinted in *Toward Liberal Education*, pp. 480–88.

212 "The last thirty years": Lewis Mumford, *The Condition of Man* (New York: Harcourt, Brace, 1944), pp. 391, 395.

213 "I'm thinkin' he wouldn't": Eugene O'Neill, *Complete Plays, 1920–1931* (New York: Library of America, 1988), pp. 821–85.

Chapter 14

215 McIntosh had "roomed": Interview with Patrick McIntosh, April 11, 1997.

215 "I have chosen not to waste time": *Harvard Class of 1962 10th Anniversary Report*, and McIntosh interview.

215 "Ted would not volunteer": ABC Television, "The Unabomber: An Unprecedented Look at the Serial Killer." *20/20*, May 4, 1998.

215 "Ted was one of the strangest": Tom Morganthau, "Probing the Mind of a Killer," *Newsweek*, April 15, 1996.

215 "In three years": Johnston and Scott, "The Tortured Genius of Theodore Kaczynski," *New York Times*, May 26, 1996.

215 "would go to his room": Susan Sword and Kevin Fagan, "The Solitude and the Fury," *San Francisco Chronicle*, April 12, 1996.

216 "Ted and I were wonks": Interview with Keith Martin, May 6, 1997.

217 "Do you remember me?": Interview with Professor Andrew Gleason, June 29, 1998.

217 "My acquaintace with Kaczynski": Quoted in Kaczynski, "Truth vs. Lies," and confirmed by Gleason.

218 "he was a typical mathematician": Interviews with Napoleón Williams, October 10, 2000.

218 "Even a society depending": David Riesman, *The Lonely Crowd* (New Haven: Yale University Press, 1953), p. 280.

218 "Crosman can't remember": Interview with Robert Crosman, January 23, 2001.

218 "Harvard was using me up": Robert Crosman, "Innocent Bystander: An Autobiografiction," chap. 3, "Letters Home," unpublished MS.

220 a study of Harvard and Radcliffe undergraduates: William G. Perry, Jr., *Forms of Intellectual and Ethical Development in College Years* (Cambridge, MA: Bureau of Study Counsel, Harvard University, 1968) pp. 103, 244–46, 283, 289–90.

222 Calvin Trillin writes: Calvin Trillin, *Remembering Denny* (New York: Time Warner Books, 1993) pp. 7–8.

223 in Arby's restaurant: Jeff Baker, "Gerald F. Burns, Poet, Dies at Age 58," *The Oregonian*, July 24, 1997.

223 "I too have ended up": Gerald Burns, letter to the editor, *Fifth Estate*, vol. 32, no. 2 (Fall 1997).

225 King's business fortunes declined: Interviews with Carmel High School classmates at the school's class of 1953 forty-fifth reunion, October 2–4, 1998.

225 King disappeared: "Carmel Man Listed as Missing Person," *Monterey Herald*, October 15, 1991.

226 "Letter Bomb to Ted": Harvard College class of 1962, *Thirty-fifth Anniversary Report* (1997).

227 "It's possible to develop": Williams interview, October 10, 2000.

Chapter 15

228 "Would you be willing": Consent Form, H. A. Murray, "Multiform Assessments of Personality Development Among Gifted College Men, 1941–1962."

229 "at the extreme of avowed alienation": H. A. Murray, "Brief Summary of Baleen Researches, 1959–61," Harvard Archives. See also Murray, "Research Plan," Application for Research Grant, National Institute of Mental Health, Grant No. M-1287, September 1, 1959–August 31, 1960.

229 "Murray was very good": Alden E. Wessman interview, April 2, 2000.

230 "a strong sense of cosmic outcastness" and the quotes that follow: Kenneth Keniston, *The Uncommitted: Alienated Youth in American Society* (New York: Dell Publishing, 1965), pp. 69, 72, 79, 95, 101, 125, 185, 193, 213–14, 423.

232 "stressful disputation": Murray, "Progress Report," Grant No. 1287, October 1958, Harvard Archives; Murray, "Brief Summary of Baleen Researches, 1959–61"; Murray, "Research Plan," M-1287; Murray, "Studies of Stressful Interpersonal Disputations," *American Psychologist*, vol. 18, no. 1 (January 1963).

233 unpublished progress report: H. A. Murray, "Progress Report," Research Grant No. M-1287, October 1958, Harvard Archives.

233 "As instructed": Forrest Robinson, *Love's Story Told: A Life of Henry A. Murray* (Cambridge, MA: Harvard University Press, 1992), pp. 337–38.

235 "each student had spent": Keniston, *The Uncommitted*, p. 15.

236 "Later, I thought": Interview with Alden E. Wessman, April 2, 2000.

236 the Nuremberg Code: See Jonathan D. Moreno, *Undue Risk: Secret State Experiments on Humans* (New York: Routledge, 2001).

237 "many and perhaps even most": *Final Report of the President's Advisory Committee on Human Radiation Experiments* (New York: Oxford University Press, 1996), pp. 89–91.

237 In a particularly infamous experiment: See Arthur G. Miller, *The Obedience Experiments* (New York: Praeger, 1986).

238 "to finish writing a book": Murray, "Research Plan," M-1287.

238 "Murray was not the most systematic scientist": Interviews with Keniston, February 25, March 26, and April 14, 2000.

238 "develop a theory of dyadic systems": H. A. Murray, "Notes on Dyadic Research (Tertiary Spout No. 7)," March 16, 1959.

238 "Cui bono?": Murray, "Notes on Dyadic Research," March 16, 1959, Harvard Archives.

238 "Are the costs in man-hours": H. A. Murray, "Brief Summary of Baleen Research," January 18, 1960, Harvard Archives.

238 one person attacked another: Transcript of interview conducted by Forrest G. Robinson, Harvard Archives.

238 "degree of anxiety and disintegration": "Notes on Dyadic Research," March 16, 1959.

239 "elusive, exasperating": Forrest Robinson interview with Leopold Bellak, Harvard Archives.

239 "mysterious and ungraspable": Robinson, *Love's Story Told*, p. 245.

Chapter 16

241 "personology": Henry A. Murray et al., *Explorations in Personality* (New York: Oxford University Press, 1938). See also Edwin S. Shneidman, ed., *Endeavors in Psychology: Selections from the Personology of Henry A. Murray* (New York: Harper & Row, 1981); Eugene Taylor, "'What Is Man, Psychologist, That Thou Art Unmindful of Him?': Henry A. Murray and the Historical Relation Between Classical Personality Theory and Humanistic Psychology," *Journal of Humanistic Psychology*, vol. 40, no 3, (Summer 2000).

241 the Thematic Apperception Test: C. D. Morgan and H. A. Murray, "A Method of Investigating Fantasies: The Thematic Apperception Test," *Archives of Neurology and Psychiatry*, 34 (1935), pp. 289–306. See also

Christiana D. Morgan, "Thematic Apperception Test," in Murray et al., *Explorations in Personality*.

241 helped develop a system: H. A. Murray and Morris Stein, "Note on the Selection of Combat Officers," *Psychosomatic Medicine*, vol. V, no. 4, (October 1943).

241 "the most important book": Shneidman interview, October 1, 2001.

241 "a great initiator": Claire Douglas, *Translate This Darkness: The Life of Christiana Morgan, the Veiled Woman in Jung's Circle* (Princeton: Princeton University Press, 1933).

242 "The great Murray": Frank Barron, *No Rootless Flower* (Cresskill, NJ: Hampton Press, 1995), p. 19.

242 "hurt people by his consistent paranoia": Robinson interview with David McClelland, June 18, 1970, Murray Papers, Harvard Archives.

242 "is the logical & predictable": Robinson, *Love's Story Told*, p. 287.

243 "Murray was no scientist": Interview with Henry Riecken March 25, 2001.

243 "It became clear": Robinson, *Love's Story Told*, p. viii.

244 "Harry Ahab-Murray Melville": Barron, *No Rootless Flower*, p. 199.

244 "I wish that with Harry": Christiana Morgan, Notebook, Cambridge, England, February 1925, Harvard Archives, cited in Claire Douglas, *Translate This Darkness*, p. 133.

244 Murray's wife, Jo, discovered: Douglas, *Translate This Darkness*, p. 187.

245 "would wonder in coming years": *Ibid.*, pp. 138–39.

245 "a complete survey of human": *Ibid.*, pp. 193, 204.

245 "deeper layers of personality": Robinson, *Love's Story Told*, p. 176.

245 "Mansol returns from 1000 Islands": Christiana Morgan, Chronological and Topical File, Murray Papers, Harvard Archives.

245 "discovered that our life": Robinson, *Love's Story Told*, p. 253.

245 "They chronicled their sexual": Douglas, *Translate This Darkness*, p. 261.

245 the "Red and Gold Diary": Excerpted in Christiana Morgan, "Annuesta Notes," December 12, 1936, Murray Papers, Harvard Archives.

246 "Could you love anyone": Robinson, *Love's Story Told*, p. 258; Murray Papers, Harvard Archives.

246 a stone tower: See Robinson, *Love's Story Told*, pp. 256–58; and Douglas, *Translate This Darkness* pp. 222–27.

246 "The tower gave": Forrest Robinson interview with Ina May Greer, June 27, 1970, Murray Papers, Harvard Archives.

247 "Christiana got the short end": Forrest Robinson interview with Carl Binger, April 15 and 18, 1970, Murray Papers, Harvard Archives.

247 "an elegant but distant lady": Douglas, *Translate This Darkness*, p. 287.

248 he was introduced to LSD: Forrest Robinson interview with H. A. Murray, August 18, 1970. See also "Prospect for Psychology: A vision of the future, as reconstructed after one encounter with the hallucinogenic drug psilocybin," *Science* (May 1962), and Douglas, *Translate This Darkness*, p. 288.

248 "had at least eleven unfinished": Douglas, *Translate This Darkness*, pp. 287–88, 299.

248 He "took amphetamines": Robinson interviews, Murray Papers, Harvard Archives.

248 A former friend: Forrest Robinson interview with Conrad Aiken, July 28, 1971. See also Douglas, *Translate This Darkness*, pp. 314–15.

249 "perhaps as suspicious": Douglas, *Translate This Darnkess*, p. 315.

249 "I have been asked": Untitled document dated February 3, 1988, Murray Papers, Harvard Archives.

249 "To the very end of his life": Robinson, *Love's Story Told*, p. 5.

249 "Harry doesn't like the picture": Forrest Robinson interview with Alvin Barach, July 2, 1970, Murray Papers, Harvard Archives.

Chapter 17

252 "I said to myself": Interview with Ralph Blum, January 21, 2001.

252 Platt thinks it was the other way round: Interview with Charlie Platt, January 23, 2001.

252 a graduate student in social relations: Interview with Kiji Morimoto, January 24, 2001; Blum and Platt interviews.

252 none can remember doing it: Interviews with Morimoto, Platt, and Blum; interview with Sean Sweeney, January 29, 2001.

252 Robert Worth Bingham, Jr.: Robert Worth Bingham, Jr., personal communication with author, September 1955 and *passim*.

253 creating a new "democratic man": For a complete discussion of this effort to transform America's "national character," see Ellen Herman, *The Romance of American Psychology: Political Culture in the Age of Experts* (Berkeley: University of California Press, 1995); Christopher Simpson, *Science of Coercion: Communication Research and Psychological Warfare, 1945–1960* (New York: Oxford University Press, 1994); and Brett Gary, *The Nervous Liberals: Propaganda Anxieties from World War I to the Cold War* (New York: Columbia University Press, 1999).

253 In July 1940, a small group: See Herman, *Romance of American Psychology*, p. 49; Robinson, *Love's Story Told*, p. 276.

253 "often on request": Robinson, *Love's Story Told*, p. 176.

253 "We must see this war": Margaret Mead, *And Keep Your Powder Dry: An Anthropologist Looks at America* (New York: Morrow, 1942), p. 261.

254 "to prepare the profession": Quoted in Herman, *Romance of American Psychology*, p. 17.

255 "The fateful question for the human species": Sigmund Freud, *Civilization and its Discontents*, trans. James Strachey (New York: W. W. Norton, 1961), p. 111.

255 "mass opinion was dangerous": Herman, *Romance of American Psychology*, p. 55.

255 the "crisis of democratic theory": Edward A. Purcell, Jr., *The Crisis in Democratic Theory* (Lexington, KY: Univ. of Kentucky Press, 1973).

256 "Successful social and political management": Quoted in Simpson, *Science of Coercion*, p. 18.

256 "Representative government": Quoted in *ibid.*, p. 17

256 "Man is to-day's great problem": Murray et al., *Explorations in Personality*, pp. 1, 34–35.

257 "involves transformations of personality": Quoted in Robinson, *Love's Story Told*, p. 287. See also Henry A. Murray, "Time for a Positive Morality," *Survey Graphic* (March 1947); and Henry A. Murray, "America's Mission," *Survey Graphic* (October 1948).

257 "the formidable task assigned": Murray, "Prospect for Psychology," p. 487.

257 By war's end . . . and the details that follow: See Herman, *Romance of American Psychology*, p. 84.

258 "military personnel on the committee": Sigmund Diamond, *Compromised Campus* (New York: Oxford University Press, 1992), p. 52. See also Robin Winks, *Cloak and Gown: Scholars in the Secret War, 1939–1961* (New Haven: Yale University Press, 1987).

258 "began to contract out": Diamond, *Compromised Campus*, p. 52.

259 "tested a recruit's ability": John Marks, *The Search for the "Manchurian Candidate"* (New York: W. W. Norton, 1979), p. 19.

259 "The candidate immediately went downstairs": Henry A. Murray et al., *Selection of Personnel for Clandestine Operations* (Laguna Hills, CA: Aegean Park Press, 1948), pp. 134–35. See also Henry A. Murray, "Assessment of OSS Personnel," *Journal of Consulting Psychology*, vol. X, no. 2 (1946); and Henry A. Murray and Morris Stein, "Note on the Selection of Combat Officers," *Psychosomatic Medicine*, vol. V, no. 4 (October 1943).

259 "flourished as a leader": Robinson, *Love's Story Told*, p. 266.

260 In the spring of 1945, the OSS: *Ibid.*, p. 283; "H. A. Murray, Theatre Service Record, 31 July 1945" and "OSS Notice of Alert and Call to Report to Aerial Post of Embarkation, 16 May 1945," CIA classified documents, released April 2000. See also Robinson interviews with Murray, Harvard Archives.

260 the Assessment Center Method: See letter, January 8, 1982, from Doug Bray, inviting Murray to make a contribution to the tenth annual International Congress on the Assessment Center Method, Harvard Archives.

260 provided Murray with the idea: Murray did not begin to use the term "Dyad" until after his work with the OSS during World War II.

260 "What is required is a profound": Henry A. Murray, "Analysis of the Personality of Adolph [sic] Hitler with Predictions of His Future Behavior and Suggestions for Dealing with Him Now and After Germany's Surrender," October 1943, OSS Confidential (copy 24 of 30), National Archives.

261 "The classic psycho-political analysis": Memorandum to [redacted], Subject: Malenkov Test Case, from [redacted], dated March 26, 1953.

262 the National Science Foundation: See Simpson, Science of Coercion, p. 52.

262 "Between 1945 and the mid-1960s": Herman, Romance of American Psychology, p. 126.

262 "improved performance in counter-insurgency": Christopher Simpson, ed., Universities and Empire (New York: New Press, 1998), p. 83.

262 "consultant" for clandestine research: Letter to Henry A. Murray from Whitney Young, security officer, HumRRO, George Washington University Human Resources office, "Operating under Contract with the Department of the Army," March 26, 1953, Harvard Archives.

263 "under private, academic cover": Simpson (ed.) quotes Henry A. Murray, Mark A. May, and Hadley Cantril, "Some Glimpses of Soviet Psychology," American Psychologist, vol. 14, no. 6 (June 1959), in ibid., pp. 303–7. See also John M. Crewdson and Joseph Treaster, "Worldwide Propaganda Network Built by CIA," New York Times, December 26, 1977, and Hadley Cantril, The Human Dimension: Experiences in Policy Research (New Brunswick, NJ: Rutgers University Press, 1967).

263 conducted at Boston's Peter Bent Brigham: Rough Draft, Army Application, Renewal of Contract No. DA 49-007-MD-213, "Psychological and Pituitary-Adrenal Responses to Stress," March 23, 1956. See S. Richardson Hill et al., "Studies on Adrenocortical and Psychological Response to Stress in Men," Archives of Internal Medicine, 97 (1956); Henry M. Fox et al., "Adrenal Steroid Excretion Patterns in Eighteen Healthy Subjects," Psychosomatic Medicine, vol. 23, no. 1 (1960), and Henry M. Fox and Sanford Gifford, "Psychological Responses to ACTH and Cortisone," Psychosomatic Medicine, vol. 15, no. 6 (1953).

263 "A certain number of patients": "Psychological and Pituitary-Adrenal Responses to Stress."

263 "we were sometimes surprised": Fox et al., "Adrenal Steroid Excretion Patterns."

263 "ties to the academic world": Loch Johnson, *America's Secret Power: The CIA in a Democratic Society* (New York: Oxford University Press, 1989), pp. 157–59.

264 "asked his staff to find out": Victor Marchetti and John D. Marks, *The CIA and the Cult of Intelligence* (New York: Knopf, 1974), pp. 58–59, 232–33.

264 the "behavior science network": Quoted in Simpson, *Science of Coercion*, p. 60.

265 "twilight zone" research think tanks: Herman, *Romance of American Psychology*, p. 136.

265 "The CIA probably used": "CIA Secret Financing of Private Groups Disclosed," *Congressional Quarterly Almanac*, February 24, 1967.

265 "funding and nominal supervision": Internal memorandum, MKULTRA, July 9, 1958, John Marks Papers, National Security Archive, George Washington University.

265 "three-quarters of all university research": Richard Norton Smith, *The Harvard Century* (Cambridge, MA: Harvard University Press, 1986), p. 219.

266 "approved attaching universities": Diamond, *Compromised Campus*, p. 95.

266 Clyde Kluckhohn was the CIA's big man on: See *ibid.*, p. 109; and John Trumpbour, ed., *How Harvard Rules: Reason in the Service of Empire* (Boston: South End Press, 1989).

266 "one of the best kept of Harvard's": Diamond, *Compromised Campus*, p. 109.

266 Yet not until 1967: Interview with Humphrey Doermann, September 23, 2001. See also James Reston, "CIA Aid on Campus," *New York Times*, February 15, 1967; and Stanley K. Scheinbaum, "The University on the Make," *Ramparts* magazine, April 4, 1966, pp. 11–22.

266 between 1960 and 1966 the CIA: "Harvard Learns of CIA Help," *Boston Globe*, April 15, 1967.

Chapter 18

267 "blow minds and make people crazy": Martin A. Lee and Bruce Shlain, *Acid Dreams: The Complete Social History of LSD: The CIA, the Sixties, and Beyond* (New York: Grove Press, 1985), p. 21.

268 established a "truth drug" committee: See Marks, *The Search for the "Manchurian Candidate,"* p. 6.

268 an obscure Swiss chemist: *Ibid.*, pp. 3–5.

268 the world's first acid trip: *Ibid.*, p. 4. See also Lee and Shlain, *Acid Dreams*, pp. 12ff.

268 Nazi doctors were testing: Lee and Shlain, *Acid Dreams*, pp. 5–6.

269 "Operation Paperclip": *Ibid.*, p. 6. See also Linda Hunt, *Secret Agenda: The United States Government, Nazi Scientists, and Operation Paperclip, 1945 to 1990* (New York: St. Martin's Press, 1991); and Tom Bower, *The Paperclip Conspiracy: The Hunt for Nazi Scientists* (Boston: Little, Brown, 1987).

269 having conducted the ghoulish: Hunt, *Secret Agenda*, pp. 88ff.

269 At Edgewood and Fort Holabird: *Ibid.*, pp. 166ff.

269 Kauders gave a lecture on LSD: Marks, *The Search for the "Manchurian Candidate,"* pp. 56–57.

269 Hyde's ensuing trip: *Ibid.*, p. 58.

270 the CIA was in hot pursuit: *Ibid.*, p. 31.

270 "apply special methods": *Ibid.*, p. 23.

270 According to a later agency review: Central Intelligence Agency, "Affiliated Notifications," Artichoke-MKULTRA, undated, John Marks Papers, National Security Archive, George Washington University.

271 70 percent had either made confessions: Marks, *The Search For the "Manchurian Candidate,"* p. 134.

271 under the direction of Sidney Gottlieb: *Los Angeles Times*, Sidney Gottlieb obituary, April 4, 1999. See also Select Committee to Study Governmental Operations, with Respect to Intelligence Activities, U.S. Senate, *Intelligence Activities and the Rights of Americans* (Washington, DC: Government Printing Office, 1976).

271 "almost overnight a whole new market": Lee and Shlain, *Acid Dreams*, pp. 19–20.

271 Harold Abramson, an acquaintance of Gregory Bateson's: Marks, *The Search for the "Manchurian Candidate,"* pp. 66, 129.

271 "to investigate whether and how": Lee and Shlain, *Acid Dreams*, p. xxiii.

272 During the ten years of MKULTRA's existence: Memorandum for Director of Central Intelligence, "IG Report on Inspection of MKULTRA," July 26, 1963.

272 an eminently prestigious psychologist: See Lee and Shlain, *Acid Dreams*; Harvey Weinstein, *A Father, a Son and the CIA* (Toronto: James Lorimer & Co., 1988); and Gordon Thomas, *Journey into Madness* (New York: Bantam Books, 1989).

272 "depatterning": Lee and Shlain, *Acid Dreams*, pp. 123–24. See also Weinstein, *A Father, a Son and the CIA.*

272 "Nearly every drug that appeared": *Ibid.*, pp. xxiv–xxv.

272 "the Bureau of Narcotics and Dangerous Drugs": Marks, *The Search For the "Manchurian Candidate,"* p. 129.

273 "Fremont-Smith organized": *Ibid.*

273 "on the subjective effects of psycho-active": Barron, No Rootless Flower, p. 196.

274 "the wizard of personality assessment": Timothy Leary, Flashbacks (New York: Putnam, 1983), p. 37.

274 he had attended Fremont-Smith's Macy Foundation": Marks, The Search For the "Manchurian Candidate," p. 127.

274 "took a keen interest in Leary's work": Lee and Shlain, Acid Dreams, p. 74. Murray confirmed that Leary introduced Murray to psilocybin in his August 18, 1970, interview with Forrest Robinson.

274 By that time, Gregory Bateson: At a Macy Foundation conference on April 22–24, 1959, Bateson revealed how Abramson introduced him to LSD. See Harold A. Abramson, ed., "The Use of LSD in Psychotherapy: Transactions of a Conference on d-Lysergic Acid Diethylamide (LSD-25)," April 22, 23, and 24, 1959, Princeton, NJ.

274 At Leary's suggestion: Forrest Robinson interview with David McClelland, June 18, 1970.

274 featured "a highly literate rendering": Robinson, Love's Story Told, p. 336; and Henry A. Murray, "Prospect for Psychology."

274 conducted LSD research on unwitting subjects: Final Report of the President's Advisory Committee on Human Radiation Experiments, p. 79.

275 "CIA documents describing experiments": Lee and Shlain, Acid Dreams, pp. xxiv–xxv.

275 Harold Blauer: See Marks, The Search for the "Manchurian Candidate"; Lee and Shlain, Acid Dreams; and H. P. Albarelli, Jr., and John Kelly, "New Evidence in Army Scientist's Death," Worldnet Daily, July 6, 2001.

276 part of a larger cooperative venture: Albarelli and Kelly, "New Evidence in Army Scientist's Death"; interview with Eric Olson, May 3, 2001.

276 Fort Detrick biochemist fell: Interview with Eric Olson; Michael Ignatieff, "What Did the CIA Do to His Father?" New York Times Magazine, April 1, 2001.

276 In 1949 and 1950, he worked briefly: Olson interview, H. P. Albarelli, Jr., and John Kelly, "The Strange Story of Frank Olson," Tampa Weekly Planet, December 2, 2000; and Albarelli and Kelly, "New Evidence in Army Scientist's Death."

276 "the center for the development": Ignatieff, "What Did the CIA Do to His Father?"

277 On November 19, Gottlieb met with: Ibid.

277 nembutal and bourbon: Ibid.

277 "What's behind this?" Ibid.

277 Around 2:00 A.M.: Ibid.

278 The CIA hushed up Olson's death: Ibid. See also Marks, The Search for the "Manchurian Candidate," and Lee and Shlain, Acid Dreams.

278 an autopsy was performed: Ignatieff, "What Did the CIA Do to His Father?"

278 "a collapse of faith": Herman, *Romance of American Psychology*, p. 122.

279 "transformed into a militant pacifist": *Ibid.*, p. 46.

279 "there is a great need *now*": Murray, "Analysis of the Personality of Adolph [*sic*] Hitler. . . ."

279 Cord Meyer: See Nina Burleigh, *A Very Private Woman* (New York: Bantam Books, 1998); and various personal papers of Cord Meyer, Library of Congress.

279 and from the National Institute of Mental Health: See Marks, *The Search for the "Manchurian Candidate"*; and Lee and Shlain, *Acid Dreams*.

280 worked from HumRRO: Letter to Henry A. Murray from Whitney Young, security officer, HumRRO, George Washington University Human Resources office, "Operating under Contract with the Department of the Army," March 26, 1953, Harvard Archives.

280 Harvard's Social Relations Department: Diamond, *Compromised Campus*, p. 73.

280 Surgeon General's Clinical Psychology Advisory Board: Letter from Walter V. Bingham, chief psychologist for Personnel Research and Procedures, to H. A. Murray, dated November 19, 1946, confirming Murray's appointment to the Clinical Psychology Advisory Board; letter from George S. Stevenson, medical director of the National Committee For Mental Hygiene, to H. A. Murray, dated August 22, 1946, Murray Papers, Harvard Archives.

Chapter 19

281 "development of a system of procedures": Henry A. Murray, Proposal, "A. Theory and Practice of Assessment," from Henry A. Murray to the Rockefeller Foundation, February 20, 1948.

282 "over 1,000 variables": Forrest Robinson interview with Murray, July 27, 1970.

282 "Bulwer" admitted that: All material quoted here and below is taken from the data sets, "Multiform Assessments of Personality Development Among Gifted College Men, 1941–1962."

285 "the use of deceptive techniques": American Psychological Association Draft Ethical Guidelines, Draft 7, "Ethical Principles of Psychologists and Code of Conduct," April 15, 2002.

286 Some defenders of the practice: Arthur G. Miller, *The Obedience Experiments*; interview with Arthur Miller, February 27, 2002.

286 According to the most cited survey of this kind: See Steven S. Smith and Deborah Richardson, "Amelioration of Deception and Harm in Psychological Research: The Important Role of Debriefing," *Journal of Personality and Social Psychology*, vol. 4, no. 5 (1983).

286 "The harm the minority of subjects report": Diana Baumrind, "Research Using Intentional Deception," *American Psychologist*, vol. 40, no. 2 (February 1985), pp. 168–69.

286 "My own belief": Diana Baumrind, "Principles of Ethical Conduct in the Treatment of Subjects," *American Psychologist*, vol. 26, no. 10 (October 1971), p. 888.

287 According to a 1972 summary of such research: Quoted in Baumrind, "Research Using Intentional Deception," p. 169.

287 "I found the experience devastating": *Ibid.*, p. 168.

287 Robert Levine: Interview with Robert Levine, April 19, 2002.

288 "Could such experiments": Interview with Paul Applebaum, April 22, 2002.

288 "the squire": Forrest Robinson interview with Frederick Wyatt, August 27, 1970.

288 "a man of style": Forrest Robinson interview with Leopold Bellak, July 4, 1971.

289 "this man didn't want": Kaczynski, "Truth vs. Lies."

289 Murray had divided these essays: Miscellaneous note, "The philosophies," Murray Papers, Harvard Archives.

290 "The main contentions of the emotive theory": Paul Edwards, ed., *Enclyclopedia of Philosophy* (New York: Macmillan, 1967), p. 493.

290 "is purely 'emotive'": A. J. Ayer, *Language, Truth and Logic*, 2nd ed. (London: Gollancz, 1946), p. 108.

290 the author of the emotive theory itself: Charles L. Stevenson, "The Emotive Meaning of Ethical Terms," *Mind*, 46 (1937). See also Charles L. Stevenson, *Ethics and Language* (New Haven: Yale University Press, 1944).

290 "words implying moral judgments": Robert H. Thouless, "Emotional Meanings," in Toward Liberal Education, Locke, Gibson, and Arms, eds., *Toward Liberal Education*, p. 213.

291 "Lawful," the team found: Henry A. Murray, "Correlation of the Amount of Disagreement to the Dyad with that between Philosophies," Murray Papers, Harvard Archives.

291 "midyear performance of three A's": John Finley's evaluation of T. J. Kaczynski at the end of the latter's junior year at Harvard, quoted in "Truth vs. Lies."

291 "one of those machines": Friedrich Nietzsche, *Birth of Tragedy*, W. A. Hauseman (New York: Macmillan, 1909), p. 232.

291 "I never attempted to put any such fantasies": Johnson, psychiatric competency report.

292 would tell the *Green Anarchist*: "Ted Speaks," *Green Anarchist*, no. 57–58 (Autumn 1999), pp. 20–21.

292 is among those who believe: Skillen interview, April 5, 2000.

292 Ralph Meister: Interview with Ralph Meister, March 19, 2000.

293 In 1971 or 1972: "Ted Speaks," *Green Anarchist*.

294 "I had already developed": T. J. Kaczynski commentary on Johnson psychiatric competency report, Michael Mello copy.

PART III
Chapter 20

298 "I would build up": Johnson, psychiatric competency report.

299 He failed to graduate with honors: T. J. Kaczynski, "Truth vs. Lies."

299 a former member of the graduate admissions committee: Interview with Peter Duren, December 6, 1997.

299 "true mathematical genius": T. J. Kaczynski, letter to the author, September 26, 1998.

300 Kaczynski "was brilliant": Stephen Cain, "Kaczynski Brilliant but a Loner at U-M," *Ann Arbor News*, April 4, 1996.

300 "one of the best students": Duren interview, December 6, 1997. See also Cain, "Kaczynski Brilliant but a Loner at U-M."

300 "a lot of native power": Allen Shields, Memorandum to Doctoral Committee, "Re: Thesis of Theodore John Kaczynski," undated.

300 "first-rate": Interview with George Piranian, December 6, 1997.

300 "I remember Kaczynski": Interview with Joel Shapiro, July 8, 1998; and Shapiro e-mail to the author, July 9, 1998.

301 "I didn't appreciate": Shapiro e-mail to the author, July 9, 1998.

301 "Boundary Functions": Theodore John Kaczynski, *Boundary Functions* (Ann Arbor, MI: University Microfilms, 1967).

301 awarded the Sumner Myers Prize: Stephen Cain, "Career Abandonment Remains a Puzzle," *Ann Arbor News*, April 6, 1996.

301 A few weeks later: Piranian interview, December 6, 1997.

302 Kaczynski dropped by Shields's office: Shields Memorandum to Doctoral Committee.

302 "works almost entirely on his own": *Ibid.*

302 "a loner": Duren interview, December 6, 1997.

302 "He went very much his own way": Cain, "Kaczynski Brilliant but a Loner at U-M,"; and Duren interview, December 6, 1997.

303 "Anyone who becomes obsessed": Piranian interview, December 6, 1997.

303 "a sport coat and tie": Cain, "Kaczynski Brilliant But a Loner at U-M."

303 He began studying: Kaczynski, "Truth vs. Lies"; and the Johnson report.

304 "During my years at Michigan": Johnson, psychiatric competency report.

305 frequent and noisy sex: *Ibid.*, and Kaczynski's commentary on the Johnson report.

305 only by becoming a woman . . . and the text that follows: Johnson, psychiatric competency report.

Chapter 21

307 just another campus riot: "Berkeley Activism," from Berkeley Resource Web site maintained by New Student Services, University of California, Berkeley, available at: http://uga.berkeley.edu/resource/webfiles/r10_3.html.

308 His own University of Michigan thesis adviser: Duren interview, December 6, 1997. See also William J. Broad, "Did Antiwar Tumult in '60s Ignite Unabomber?" *New York Times News Service*, June 3, 1996.

309 "one of the three most radical": Cited in "Brilliant Misfit Caught in Changing Times," *Boston Globe*, April 6, 1996.

309 others rated his lectures "useless": *The Slate* (Berkeley's unofficial course guide): "MATH 135: Introduction to the theory of Sets. The six available questionnaires from the last year agreed that KACZYNSKI'S lectures were useless and right from the book. Three questionnaires from the Math 120A class last spring said he showed no concern for the students. 'He absolutely refuses to answer questions by completely ignoring the students.'"

311 Harvard's Gen Ed program: See my articles, "Rise and Fall of General Education," *Academic Questions* (Spring 1993); "Skipping Through College: Reflections on the Decline of Liberal Arts Education," *The Atlantic* (September 1978); and *Group Memory: A Guide to College and Student Survival in the 1990s* (Boston: Atlantic Monthly Press, 1980). Also Christopher Jencks and David Riesman, *The Academic Revolution* (Garden City, NY: Doubleday, 1968).

312 "Whatever the specifics of their ideologies": Norman Cantor, "The Real Crisis in the Humanities Today," *The New Criterion*, vol 3, no. 10 (June 1985), pp. 28–38.

313 Meeting in Fort Huron, Michigan: David Horowitz, *Radical Son: A Generational Odyssey* (New York: Simon & Schuster, 1997), pp. 105–6.

313 "The revolutionary idea": *Ibid*, p. 102.

313 "gray is the color of truth": McGeorge Bundy speech at the Cosmos Club, Washington, DC, May 1967. Quoted in Kai Bird, *The Color of Truth* (New York: Simon & Schuster, 1998), p. 7.

313 "knew the right path": David Halberstam, *The Best and the Brightest* (New York: Ballantine Books, 1969), p. 655.

314 "Drug-taking became classified as a political act": Richard Norton Smith, *The Harvard Century* (Cambridge, MA: Harvard University Press, 1986), p. 237.

315 around 150,000 people: See James Trager, ed. *The People's Chronology* (New York: Henry Holt, 1992), p. 1008.

315 "The United States unquestionably": Ted Robert Gurr, *Violence in America*, 2 vols. (Newbury Park, CA: Sage Publications, 1989), vol. 2, p. 121.

315 "more than six million Americans" *Ibid.*, pp. 105, 109.

316 Without warning, three hundred students: Roger Rosenblatt, *Coming Apart: A Memoir of the Harvard Wars of 1969* (Boston: Little, Brown, 1997), pp. 8ff.

316 "was pushed and dragged": *Ibid.*, pp. 10–11, 16.

317 "the most disruptive and wrenching": *Ibid.*, pp. 212–13.

Chapter 22

319 "Ahead for the country": Rosenblatt, *Coming Apart*, pp. 227–28.

319 "We poison the caddis flies": Rachel Carson, *Silent Spring* (Boston: Houghton Mifflin, 1962), pp. 169–70.

320 Cybernetics was an exciting idea: See Walter David Hellman, "Norbert Wiener and the Growth of Negative Feedback in Scientific Explanation, with a Proposed Research Program of 'Cybernetic Analysis,'" Ph.D. dissertation, Oregon State University, 1982; and Frank Benjamin Golley, *A History of the Ecosystem Concept in Ecology: More Than the Sum of the Parts* (New Haven: Yale University Press, 1993).

320 In 1946, the Josiah J. Macy Foundation: Peter J. Bowler, *The Norton History of the Environmental Sciences* (New York: W. W. Norton, 1992). See especially p. 539: "He [Hutchinson] was also aware of the possibility that the same concept [i.e., the ecosystem] could be extended to the social sciences, and participated in conferences on this theme organized by the Macy Foundation between 1946 and 1953."

320 "Ecosystems": G. Evelyn Hutchinson, *The Kindly Fruits of the Earth: Recollections of an Embryo Ecologist* (New Haven: Yale University Press, 1979); G. Evelyn Hutchinson, "Circular Causal Systems in Ecology," *Annals of the New York Academy of Sciences*, 50 (1948).

321 "ecological collapse": Barry Commoner first introduced this notion to lay readers in 1971. See Commoner, *The Closing Circle*.

321 "The new systems theory": Bowler, *Norton History of the Environmental Sciences*, p. 539.

321 government began backing ecology: See Golley, *History of the Ecosystem Concept in Ecology*.

321 sent the Odum brothers to Eniwetok: Odum quote from Joel Hagen, *An Entangled Bank: The Origins of Ecosystem Ecology* (New Brunswick, NJ: Rutgers University Press, 1992), p. 102.

322 the International Biological Programme: See Golley, *History of the Ecosystem Concept*; Bowler, *Norton History of the Environmental Sciences*.

322 There is no balance of nature: See Donald Worster, *The Wealth of Nature* (New York: Oxford University Press, 1993). For a popular account of this new awareness among biologists of the importance of disturbance, see William K. Stevens, "New Eye on Nature: The Real Constant Is Eternal Turmoil," *New York Times*, July 31, 1990. And, for a more scholarly presentation of the same idea, P. S. White and S. T. A. Pickett, eds., *The Ecology of Natural Disturbance and Patch Dynamics: An Introduction* (Orlando, FL: Academic Press, 1985).

322 However mistaken, the idea remained: Although scientists abandoned the idea of the balance of nature by the early 1980s, most environmentalists, including writers who popularized ecology, still cling to it. For a history of this issue, see Chase, *In a Dark Wood: The Fight Over Forests and the Myths of Nature*.

322 They failed to see the connection: For an excellent account of how the modern ecosystem idea was derived from a mechanical model, see Daniel B. Botkin, *Discordant Harmonies: A New Ecology for the 21st Century* (New York: Oxford University Press, 1990).

323 "through psychological means to draw from man": Ellul, *The Technological Society*, p. 324.

324 the "entry point": Marilyn Ferguson, *The Aquarian Conspiracy: Personal and Social Transformation in the 1980s* (Los Angeles: J. P. Tarcher, 1980), pp. 85–87.

325 at war with "the corporate state": Charles Reich, *The Greening of America* (New York: Bantam Books, 1970), pp. 277ff.

325 "grown up just as the world": Gail Sheehy, *New Passages* (New York: Ballantine Books, 1995), p. 31.

Chapter 23

328 One wintry night during the fall: Interview with Nancy Hepburn, March 18, 2002.

329 "I tended to feel that I was": Sentencing Memorandum, Exhibit 12.

329 Kaczynski's life plan was not: Kaczynski, "Truth vs. Lies." See also Johnston and Scott, "The Tortured Genius of Theodore Kaczynski."

330 the lot "was not nearly as isolated": Kaczynski, "Truth vs. Lies."

331 completing the untitled essay: Turchie Affidavit, Attachment 3.

331 inspired by a passage: Kaczynski, "Truth vs. Lies."

331 a "discussion and debate": FBI interview with David Kaczynski, February 24–25, 1996.

332 "concerned TED's belief that": *Ibid.*

332 "mentally alert, curious": Don Richard Riso with Russ Hudson, *Personality Types* (Boston: Houghton Mifflin, 1996). Interview with Dr. Ron Kirschner, March 18, 2002; interview with Dr. Hillel Zeitlin, April 2, 2002.

333 "increasingly detached": Riso with Hudson, *Personality Types*, pp. 173–74.

333 "in the 1970s and 1980s hundreds": Paul R. Ehrlich, *Population Bomb*, revised edn. (New York: Ballantine, 1971), p. xi.

333 an "environmental crisis": Commoner, *The Closing Circle*, p. 1.

334 the "psychology of science": Roszak, *Where the Wasteland Ends*, pp. xxi, xxvii, 3ff.

334 a "sudden and uncontrollable": Donella H. Meadows et al., *Limits to Growth* (New York: Signet, 1972), p. 29.

334 "If present trends continue": Gerald O. Barney, study director, Executive Office of the President, Council on Environmental Quality, *The Global 2000 Report to the President: Entering the 21st Century*, 1980.

334 "with each succeeding year": Arthur Levine, *When Dreams and Heroes Died: A Portrait of Today's College Student* (San Francisco: Jossey-Bass, 1980), p. 104.

334 "It is a crisis": President Jimmy Carter, Address to the Nation, July 15, 1979.

335 "the use of unexpected violence": Gurr, *Violence in America*, vol. 2, p. 201.

335 "other groups have continued": *Ibid.*, p. 216.

336 known as "monkeywrenching": Ed Abbey, *The Monkey Wrench Gang* (New York: Avon Books, 1975). See also Dave Foreman and Bill Haywood, *Ecodefense: A Field Guide to Monkeywrenching* (Tucson, AZ: New Ludd Books, 1987).

336 They staged picturesque protests: For a history of monkeywrenching, see Chase, *In a Dark Wood*.

336 "the Arizona Phantom": Chase, *In a Dark Wood*; interviews conducted with Marc Gaede between 1991 and 1995. Gaede admitted to the author that he was, indeed, the "Arizona Phantom."

337 "Few years ago": T. J. Kaczynski coded diary, deciphered by FBI.

338 They "love to take ideas": Riso with Hudson, *Personality Types*, pp. 191–92, 195–96.

339 "Last summer": Kaczynski coded diary, deciphered by FBI.

340 "DON'T SEND ME ANY MORE": Ted Kaczynski to Wanda, quoted in Kaczynski, "Truth vs. Lies."

342 "My motive for doing what I am": Sentencing Memorandum, Exhibit 8.

342 "I think that perhaps I could": Sentencing Memorandum, Exhibits 3 and 17.

343 "Before leaving Montana": Sentencing Memorandum, Exhibit 15.

343 "I am proud of what I did": Sentencing Memorandum, Exhibits 15–16.

343 In mid-July, he fell in love: Kaczynski, "Truth vs. Lies." See also McFadden, "From Child of Promise to the Unabom Suspect."

344 "has done strange things": Sentencing Memorandum, Exhibit 16.

344 "During the last few months": Sentencing Memorandum, Exhibit 6.

344 "The bomb . . . used match-heads": Sentencing Memorandum, Exhibit 23.

345 stayed at Prince Castle: As the second Northwestern University bomb was planted on May 9, 1979, Kaczynski must have made it while he was staying with his parents in Lombard, unless he returned for a time to Montana that spring. In any case, how and where he made this second bomb remains unexplained.

345 "Plan to blow up airline in flight": Government's Motion in Limine, Appendix B, p. 5.

345 "Late October mailed package": There's a puzzle here that has never been solved. Kaczynski's secret journal says the airline bomb was mailed in late October. But according to the FBI it was posted from Chicago on November 14th and it detonated on board the American Airlines flight 444 on November 15th. There is no clear explanation for this discrepancy. Apparently, Kaczynski just made one of his rare mistakes.

Chapter 24

347 On some of these trips: Turchie Affidavit.

347 On April 18, 1980: Kaczynski stayed the nights of April 14–18 in Room 104. Author's interview with the hotel proprietors, Jack and Barbara McCabe, May 22, 1997.

347 "I feel better": Sentencing Memorandum, Exhibit 27.

348 "Since acquiring the ability": Sentencing Memorandum, Exhibit 6.

348 "I want to use the pistol": Sentencing Memorandum, Exhibit 91.

348 "They become extremely isolated": Riso with Hudson, *Personality Types*, pp. 199–201.

349 Kaczynski picked up the pace: Turchie Affidavit.

349 he bought David's share: Kaczynski, "Truth vs. Lies." Quit Claim Deed 346016, May 12, 1982.

349 "the package got me very upset": Quoted in Kaczynski, "Truth vs. Lies."

350 "They have reduced their activities": Riso with Hudson, *Personality Types*, pp. 201–7.

350 He ate less, became increasingly unkempt: Spurlin and Wood, interviews; FBI interview with Carolyn Goren, M.D., March 6, 1996; and Waits, *Unabomber*.

350 "In the morning of October 3rd": Sentencing Memorandum, Exhibits 49–50.

352 "I recently wrote a letter to my brother": Kaczynski coded diary, deciphered by FBI.

352 "Guilty feelings?": Sentencing Memorandum, Exhibit 27.

352 "I must admit I feel badly": Government's Motion in Limine, Appendix B, p. 11.

353 "a white male": Turchie Affidavit.

353 "Description (several versions)": Ibid.

353 He reacted with fury: Kaczynski, "Truth vs. Lies"; McFadden, "From Child of Promise to the Unabom Suspect"; Turchie Affidavit.

353 to invite him to his July wedding: Kaczynski, "Truth vs. Lies"; McFadden, "From Child of Promise to the Unabom Suspect."

353 he hadn't "shed any tears": Letter quoted from Kaczynski, "Truth vs. Lies."

353 did not bring the familial bickering: Turchie Affidavit.

354 an accident and not intentional: Kaczynski, "Truth vs. Lies."

354 "I have got to know": Serge F. Kovaleski, "Kaczynski's Letters Reveal Tormented Mind," Washington Post, January 20, 1997. See also "Documents Portray Kaczynski's Troubled Relations with Family," Associated Press, November 3, 1997.

354 Even his library friends: Spurlin and Wood interviews.

354 "feel as though they had no space": Riso with Hudson, Personality Types, pp. 204–8.

355 In November he wrote to David: Turchie Affidavit.

355 Ted sold David's original half interest: Kaczynski, "Truth vs. Lies"; Warranty Deed, Lewis and Clark County, March 27, 1995, M 16, p. 7341.

356 "WARNING. The terrorist group FC": Cynthia Hubert and Laura Mecoy, "Unabom Letter: Threat's a 'Prank,'" Sacramento Bee, June 29, 1995.

356 slowing air traffic: Graysmith, Unabomber, pp. 323–31.

356 yet another missive: Hubert and Mecoy, "Unabom Letter."

356 When authorities arrested Kaczynski: Don Sachtleben and Tom Mohnal, interviews.

357 "My opposition to the technological society": Sentencing Memorandum, Exhibit 9.

Chapter 25

359 he filed the brief himself: T. J. Kaczynski letter to the author, January 11, 1999. Also, Michael Mello interview, July 9, 1999.

359 so unendurable: John Howard, "Kaczynski Asks Permission for Appeals Court to Review Case," Sacramento Bee, June 17, 1999; T. J. Kaczynski,

"Brief Supporting Claim That Guilty Plea Was Involuntary," filed for Theodore John Kaczynski, December 15, 1999.

359 Although the Ninth Circuit Court agreed: Claire Cooper, "Kaczynski Appeal Will Be Heard," *Sacramento Bee*, October 23, 1999; "Unabomber Appeal Denied," CBS Worldwide, March 18, 2002.

360 "For those who realize": "Ted Speaks," *Green Anarchist*, no. 57–8 (Autumn 1999), pp. 201. See also Brian McQuarrie, "Kaczynski Says Road Triggered 'Revenge,'" *Boston Globe*, September 30, 1999.

360 two thousand of Zerzan's comrades: Kim Murphy, "A Revolutionary Movement Hits Small-Town America," *Los Angeles Times*, August 4, 1999. See also Geov Parris, "The New Anarchists," *Seattle Weekly* (September 2–9, 1999).

360 "Battle of Seattle": David Postman, "Group Rejects Others' Pleas of 'No Violence,'" *Seattle Times*, December 1, 1999.

360 "I fully approve": Interview with Rick Sallinger, January 26, 2000, who provided me with a photocopy of the note. See also Mark Eddy and Steve Lipsher, "Officials Rule Vail Fires Arson," *Denver Post*, October 23, 1998.

360 an editorial: Theresa Kintz, "Fanning the Flames of Resistance," *Earth First!* (Yule 1999).

360 "Why are young people increasingly": Kenneth Keniston, "Alienation and the Decline of Utopia," *The American Scholar* (Spring 1960), pp. 162–63.

362 "Letting off steam:" Tom Wolfe, "The Boiler Room and the Computer," in *Mauve Gloves and Madmen, Clutter and Vine* (New York: Farrar, Straus & Giroux, 1976), pp. 188–93.

363 "is the enemy of thought": Joseph Conrad, *Nostromo* (New York: Doubleday, 1904), part I, chap. 6.

363 "You want deliberate belief": Conrad, *Heart of Darkness*, pp. 540, 560.

363 "still serves technology": Ellul, *Autopsy of Revolution*, p. 585.

364 to "prediction and control": Many of today's college courses in the humanities, transformed by their professors into vehicles for promoting favored political ideologies, no longer cover literature and the arts and have become merely social science under another name.

364 "an extremely popular methodological tool": Nicholas Epley and Chuck Huff, "Suspicion, Affective Response, and Educational Benefit as a Result of Deception in Psychology Research," *Personality and Social Psychology Bulletin*, vol. 24, no. 7 (July 1998), p. 759.

364 according to one survey of this practice: *Ibid.*

364 the administration of drugs: Peter R. Breggin, M.D., "Eric Harris Was Taking Luvox [a Prozac-like drug] at the Time of the Littleton Murders," *Talking Back to Ritalin: What Doctors Aren't Telling You About Stimulants and ADHD* (Cambridge, MA: Perseus, 2001); Jeff Jacoby, "The Class-

room Culture That Spawned Kip Kinkel," *Boston Globe*, May 28, 1998; and Richard DeGrandpre, *Ritalin Nation* (New York: W. W. Norton, 1999).

364 who in recent years have gone berserk: See "Facts About Violence Among Youth and Violence in Schools," Centers for Disease Control and Prevention, April 21, 1999.

365 the Columbine High School killers: Nick Gillespie, "Schools of Alienation," *Reason Online*, October 17, 1998; Deborah Mathis, "Nation Searches for Causes, Solutions to Youth Violence," Gannett News Service, May 11, 1999; and John Cloud, "The Legacy of Columbine," *Time* magazine, March 19, 2001. For information on what Klebold and Harris carried on their Web sites, see "Eric Harris and Dylan Klebold," www.disastercenter.com/killers.html.

365 "with their heads down": Quoted from Gillespie, "Schools of Alienation."

365 trendy philanthropies: Valerie Richardson, "Law Catches Up to Ecoterrorist, *Washington Times*, March 24, 2002. See also Natasha Clerihue, "The Philanthropy of the Celebrity Left: Entertainers Embrace New Legal Rights, Faddish Causes," *Foundation Watch* (January 2000).

365 "has many faces": John J. Fialka and Joe Davidson, "From Oklahoma to Atlanta, U. S. Struggles to Deal with Diversity and Randomness of Terrorism," *Wall Street Journal*, July 29, 1996.

365 "the level of acts committed": Statement for the Record, Louis J. Freeh, Director, Federal Bureau of Investigation, on the Threat of Terrorism to the United States, before the U.S. Senate Committees on Appropriations, Armed Services, and Select Committee on Intelligence, May 10, 2001.

365 "The most recognizable single-issue terrorists": Statement for the Record, Louis J. Freeh, Director, Federal Bureau of Investigation, on President's Fiscal Year 2000 Budget, before the U.S. Senate Committee on Appropriations, Subcommittee for the Departments of Commerce, Justice, and State, the Judiciary, and Related Agencies, February 4, 1999.

366 have "become the nation's most destructive": "Special Report: Law Catches Up to Eco-Terror," *Washington Times*, March 24, 2002; Statement of James F. Jarboe, Domestic Terrorism Section Chief, Counterterrorism Division, Federal Bureau of Investigation, before the House Resources Committee, Subcommittee on Forests and Forest Health, at a hearing on "Eco-terrorism and Lawlessness in the National Forests," February 12, 2002.

366 "Bands of Khaki-outfitted": Reuters Business Alert, "USA: International— Militant Ecologists Take Arms to Save Wilderness," April 18, 1996.

366 "Escalating sabotage to save the environment": Bryan Denson and James Long, "Eco-Terrorism Sweeps the West—Part I: Crimes in the Name of the Environment," *The Oregonian*, September 26, 1999.

367 are suspected in sixty-nine more major arson attacks: Bryan Denson, "Eco-Terror Acts Ease, but Reasons Are Unclear," *The Oregonian*, April 2, 2002; Sam Howe Verhovek and Carol Kaesuk Yoon, "Fires Believed Set as Protest Against Genetic Engineering," *New York Times*, May 23, 2001.

367 "I think we've come very close": Denson and Long, "Eco-Terrorism Sweeps the West."

367 "Carlos the Jackal": Clark Staten, "Carlos Captured; Revolutionary Terrorist," EmergencyNet News Service, October 10, 1994.

368 "Industrialism is a *system*": Mikal Jakubal, "Why I Did It, Why I'll Never Do It Again, . . ." *Live Wild or Die!*, "Industrial Civilization Collapse" First Pre-anniversary issue (February 16, 1998).

368 "I tell you, freedom and human rights": CNN News, "Bin Laden's Sole Post–September 11 TV Interview Aired," February 5, 2002.

368 there is no "differential between": John Miller, "Greetings America, My Name is Osama bin Laden . . . ," PBS Frontline Web site, pbs.org, excerpted from Miller's article published in *Esquire*, February 1, 1999.

369 to "treat humanity": Immanuel Kant, *Foundations of the Metaphysics of Morals*, trans. Lewis White Beck, ed. Robert Paul Wolf (Indianapolis, IN: Bobbs-Merrill, 1969), p. 54.

369 murdered an estimated 15 million: See Weinberg, *A World at Arms*, p. 894.

369 IQ tests given their leaders: See Florence R. Miale and Michael Selzer, *The Nuremberg Mind: The Psychology of the Nazi Leaders* (New York: Quadrangle/The New York Times Book Co., 1975); and Leonard Mosley, *The Reich Marshal: A Biography of Hermann Goering* (Garden City, NY: Doubleday, 1974).

369 collectively murdered 100 million souls: Stephane Courtois et al., eds., *Black Book of Communism: Crimes, Terror, Repression*, trans. Jonathan Murphy and Mark Kramer (Cambridge, MA: Harvard University Press, 1999), p. 4.

370 a degree at Patrice Lumumba University: Staten, "Carlos Captured."

370 Osama bin Laden has a degree: "Mujahid Usamah Bin Ladin Talks Exclusively to Nida'ul Islam About the New Powder Keg in the Middle East," *Nida'ul Islam Magazine* (October–November 1996).

370 Even Timothy McVeigh: See Lou Michel and Dan Herbeck, *American Terrorist* (New York: Regan Books, 2001).

371 "eliminate the entire": Ted Kaczynski, "Hit Where It Hurts," *Green Anarchy*, no. 8 (Spring 2002), pp. 1, 18–19.

372 In July 2001, in Genoa: Randy Carroll, "Italy to Study Genoa Violence," *The Guardian* (London), July 31, 2001.

372 protests against a meeting: Giles Tremlett, "Anti-Globalization Protesters Clash with Police," *The Guardian*, March 16, 2002.

372 May Day, 2001 was the occasion: Special Report, "The London May Day Protests at a Glance"; Sarah Left, Simon Jeffery, Jane Perrone, and agencies; and Mark Tran, "May Day Around the World," all in *The Guardian*, May 1, 2001.

372 "I suspect that you underestimate": T. K. Kaczynski, letter to the author, September 26, 1998.

Index

421